A Handbook of CONTEMPORARY FICTION for Public Libraries and School Libraries

by
MARY K. BIAGINI

with the assistance of
JUDITH HARTZLER

The Scarecrow Press, Inc.
Metuchen, N.J., & London
1989

British Library Cataloguing-in-Publication data available

Library of Congress Cataloging-in-Publication Data

Biagini, Mary K. (Mary Kathryn)
  A handbook of contemporary fiction for public libraries and
school libraries / by Mary K. Biagini with the assistance of Judith
Hartzler.
    p.   cm.
  ISBN 0-8108-2275-X (alk. paper)
  1. Fiction--20th century--Bibliography. 2. Bibliography--Best
books--Fiction. 3. Popular literature--Bibliography. 4. Public
libraries--Book lists. 5. School libraries--Book lists. I. Hartzler,
Judith. II. Title.
Z5916.B5   1989
[PN3353]
016.80883--dc20   89-27859

Copyright © 1989 by Mary K. Biagini
Manufactured in the United States of America

Printed on acid-free paper

ACKNOWLEDGMENTS

Many people helped in the preparation of this Handbook. Judith Hartzler, who was my Graduate Student Assistant at Kent State University and is now a children's librarian at the Public Library of Columbus and Franklin County, was of enormous assistance in the preparation of the Handbook.

Preparation of camera-ready copy makes great demands, and I was fortunate to have the guidance of Joyce Seifried of the University of Pittsburgh in this task. Word processing by Peg Domer, and earlier by Marilyn Hardesty, Marge Hayden, and Janet Locke, transformed bits of information into crisp pages. Mem Catania, my Graduate Student Assistant at the University of Pittsburgh, tracked down information until the very end.

The Dean of the School of Library and Information Science at the University of Pittsburgh, Toni Carbo Bearman, and the Chair of the Department of Library Science, Blanche Woolls, were most supportive of my efforts to complete this project.

With so much support and assistance from friends and family, it is only fair to say that any mistakes I claim for myself.

Mary K. Biagini
Associate Dean and Associate Professor
School of Library and Information Science
University of Pittsburgh
Pittsburgh, PA 15260

TABLE OF CONTENTS

INTRODUCTION vii

PART I. POPULAR FICTION GENRES

ONE:	Romances, Romantic Adventures, Historical Romances, Family Sagas, and Gothics:	1
	Overview	1
	Reference and Bibliographic Sources	3
	Authors and Titles	4
TWO:	Horror, the Supernatural, and Suspense:	26
	Overview	26
	Reference and Bibliographic Sources	27
	Authors and Titles	29
THREE:	"Behind the Headlines" Novels:	36
	Overview	36
	Reference and Bibliographic Sources	37
	Authors and Titles:	38
	A. Crisis in the U.S. Government	38
	B. International Incidents & Intrigue	40
	C. World War II Twists: What If ?	45
FOUR:	Spy Stories:	49
	Overview	49
	Reference and Bibliographic Sources	49
	Authors and Titles	51
FIVE:	Mystery and Detective Stories:	56
	Overview	56
	Reference and Bibliographic Sources	63
	Authors and Titles	66
SIX:	Science Fiction and Fantasy:	109
	Overview	109
	Reference and Bibliographic Sources	110
	Authors and Titles:	112
	A. Science Fiction	112
	B. Fantasy	131
SEVEN:	Westerns:	140
	Overview	140
	Reference and Bibliographic Sources	140
	Authors and Titles	142
EIGHT:	Historical Fiction:	150
	Overview	150
	Reference and Bibliographic Sources	151
	Authors and Titles	153

		A. American Historical Fiction	153
		B. World Historical Fiction:	158
		1. General	158
		2. World War, 1939-1945	165
NINE:	The Trash Masters:		171
	Overview		171
	Reference and Bibliographic Sources		171
	Authors and Titles		172

PART II. CONTEMPORARY FICTION

TEN:	American Authors:		176
	Overview		176
	Reference and Bibliographic Sources		177
	Authors and Titles		178
ELEVEN:	Authors of the British Isles:		199
	Overview		199
	Reference and Bibliographic Sources		200
	Authors and Titles		201
TWELVE:	World Authors:		210
	Overview		210
	Reference and Bibliographic Sources		210
	Authors and Titles:		212
	A. Africa:		212
		1. Nigeria	212
		2. South Africa	212
	B. Asia:		212
		1. India	212
		2. Israel	213
		3. Japan	213
		4. Union of Soviet Socialist Republics	214
	C. Australia		214
	D. Europe:		215
		1. Czechoslovakia	215
		2. Denmark	215
		3. France	216
		4. Germany	219
		5. Greece	220
		6. Italy	220
		7. Spain	221
	E. North America--Canada		221
	F. South & Central America:		222
		1. Antigua	222
		2. Argentina	222
		3. Brazil	223
		4. Chile	223
		5. Colombia	223
		6. Mexico	223
		7. Peru	223
AUTHOR INDEX			224

INTRODUCTION

This Handbook is intended for librarians in public and school libraries who are involved in the selection of contemporary fiction and who are involved in any type of reader guidance. There are obviously many current sources to use in the selection of contemporary fiction, some designed for librarians, e.g., *Library Journal* and *Booklist*, and some designed for librarians and bookstores, e.g., *Publishers Weekly*, and some designed primarily for the literate public, e.g., *The New York Times Book Review*. Retrospective selection sources such as *Fiction Catalog* and cumulative sources such as *Book Review Digest* can also be very helpful with excerpts of reviews and subject indexes. Specialized bibliographies of specific topics or genres of fiction can be quite helpful in collection development and reader guidance; many smaller libraries, however, find it impossible to purchase such narrowly focused works because of budget limitations. Both current and retrospective sources are very important and much used in the selection process; they are not, however, of much use in reader guidance, primarily because of arrangement and lack of cumulations. There is a need to provide a single-volume ready reference source.

The idea for the development of this handbook grew out of a class I taught called "Materials and Services for Adults." Students often had very little reading background, and so I began to develop short reading lists of various types of books to help them build a reading background. Over the years these lists grew, and graduates would call me for updates once they were working. Based on my own experiences as a librarian and those of my students, I knew there was a need for a guide to contemporary fiction. There were always questions of other titles by a newly discovered author or what were the titles that featured a particular detective or the name of an Australian author. This Handbook evolved based on these needs and interests.

Guidelines For Inclusion:

The term "contemporary" is used in the broad sense of authors who achieved some prominence since the second world war. Some have just begun to earn their reputations in the 1980s, often on the strength of just one title. Some authors are included whose works were completed in the early part of the twentieth century, but owing to new translations or paperback editions have achieved a new or renewed reputation. In a few instances, classic authors of the nineteenth century, e.g., Edgar Allan Poe and Mary Shelley, have been included because of the continued appeal of their titles.

The Handbook is divided into two parts: Part I, Popular Genres (romances, mysteries, science fiction, westerns, etc.), and Part II, Contemporary Fiction. I included in the sections of popular genres, authors whose works are representative of that genre. The authors are not recommended in the sense that inclusion in this Handbook constitutes a recommendation for purchase. Some authors have written work included in several sections of the handbook.

The authors included in Part II, Contemporary Fiction, are more difficult to categorize, and so have been included in sections according to their countries. These authors have achieved some degree of critical acclaim by reviewers and literary critics in the United States. Each of the twelve sections concentrates on a specific genre or the critically acclaimed literature of a specific country.

Each section begins with an overview of the genre/country's literature, including definitions, identification of its most important and/or well known authors and their best known works. This introduction also includes a list of selected specialized bibliographic, selection and/or reference sources.

The overview is followed by an alphabetical listing of authors. The fiction and collected short stories of each author are listed chronologically by copyright date or date of publication in the United States.

For some genres additional information is included; e.g., in the chapters on mysteries and spy stories, the names of the detectives and spies created by the authors are listed. Nobel Prize winning authors are identified.

Standard bibliographies such as *Fiction Catalog*, specialized bibliographies for the genres and authors of specific countries, as well as standard works of criticism such as *Contemporary Literary Criticism* have been consulted in deciding which authors to include and in which categories. New titles as well as new authors have been identified through citations in *American Book Publishing Record* and reviews published in standard reviewing sources such as *Kirkus Reviews, The New York Times Book Review, Publishers Weekly* and *Library Journal*.

Limitations and Arrangement:

1. Only novels and collections of short stories by individual authors are included. If an author is well known for another kind of writing (e.g., poetry, nonfiction), that is noted at the end of the author's entry.

2. Titles published exclusively for a juvenile or young adult audience are not included.

3. Individual authors and titles are not annotated.

4. Not every work of fiction by every author is included, especially in cases in which the author is exceptionally prolific; e.g., Barbara Cartland, John Creasey, George Simenon. In these cases a sampling of the more recent or well known titles is included.

5. Authors and titles are placed in the category which seems most appropriate. Categories, however, are not always easy to determine because characteristics may overlap. Some authors and titles are listed in several categories.

6. Entries for each author are listed chronologically by copyright or publication date in the United States.

7. Titles in a series or sequence (a group of related books so designated by the publisher) are listed together under the series/sequence title.

8. Titles published through 1988 are included for each author.

Decisions:

1. Name Authority:

    a. Pseudonyms:

    If an author publishes a work under a pseudonym, the work is listed under that pseudonym. The author's real name is listed under the pseudonym if known, and there are cross references to other names used by the author if works written under that name are included in the book. E.g., the entry for Jack Higgins states:

    HIGGINS, JACK   1929-
    Real name: Harry Patterson; also writes as Harry Patterson & Hugh Marlow
    (Title Entries)
    See also as PATTERSON, HARRY, P.

    If works are not included under a specific pseudonym, that pseudonym is listed after the author's real name. No titles are listed for Hugh Marlow and so there is no "See also" for this name.

    b. Joint Authors:

    Titles are listed under the first name given on the title page. A "See" reference to this entry is listed under the second or joint author.

    c. Authors in Several Sections:

    Authors whose works fall into multiple chapters have "See also" references to all sections in which works by that author are included. Entry numbers are indicated. The Author Index may also be checked.

    d. Information about Authors:

    Birth and death dates and nationality are noted for authors when available. If no country is listed, the author is American.

    e. Disputed Copyright Dates:

    When copyright information differs in several sources and in an examination of the title, the copyright date listed in CBI *(Cumulative Book Index)* is used.

f. Foreign Language Translations:

   For titles of authors listed in Section Twelve, World Authors, who write in a language other than English, the date of the first English translation published in the United States is used. When known, the date of the publication of the work in its original country is given in parentheses after the title. E.g., Alberto Moravia 1963 More Roman Tales (1959).

2. Title Changes and Revisions:

   a. Revised Editions:

   Revisions are noted with publication date when known. E.g., John Fowles 1966 The Magus (Rev. ed., 1978).

   b. Title Changes:

   Title changes are noted when known and new dates given. In Section Five, Mysteries & Detective Stories, English titles are indicated in parentheses when known. These are worth noting because often U.S. paperback reprint editions of older British titles use the original British title, not the U.S. hardback title.

Abbreviation Used:

In order to save space, the following abbreviations have been used, and the sections in which they are used are noted in parentheses.

FS	Family Saga	(Section One)
G	Gothic	(Section One)
H	Horror	(Section Two)
HR	Historical Romance	(Section One)
Jt.	Joint Author	(Throughout)
NF	Nonfiction	(Throughout)
R	Romance	(Section One)
RA	Romantic Adventure	(Section One)
SN	Supernatural & the Occult	(Section Two)
S	Suspense	(Section Two)
SS	Short Stories	(Throughout)

SECTION ONE

ROMANCES, ROMANTIC ADVENTURES, HISTORICAL ROMANCES, FAMILY SAGAS, AND GOTHICS

OVERVIEW

Family Sagas (FS):

A family saga is a story of several generations (usually at least three) of a large family or several interrelated families. An early example is *The Forsyte Saga* (1922) by the English writer John Galsworthy.

Most family sagas currently being written take place in nineteenth and twentieth century America or the British Isles.

Representative Authors and Their Specialties:

Belva Plain and Cynthia Freeman--Jewish families.
Howard Fast--immigrant families.
R. D. Delderfield--English country families.
Susan Howatch--family stories; some based on famous historical figures of earlier centuries.

Gothics (G):

A gothic is a story of romance, suspense and mystery that usually involves a rather stock set of characters and situations: a large and unique house in a remote or unusual setting; a young woman, poor, spunky and an outsider, who comes to the house as a quasi governess/companion/secretary; a handsome, lonely and mysterious master of the house; several young, incorrigible children; sinister servants; and a missing or dead wife.

These novels are derived from the Gothic novels of the eighteenth century, especially those dealing with terror; e.g., *Mysteries of Udolpho* (1794) by Ann Radcliffe. A prototype is *Jane Eyre* (1847) by Charlotte Bronte, and a more contemporary prototype is *Rebecca* (1938) by Daphne Du Maurier. These novels often contain unrequited love and some romance but seldom any explicit sexual activity. Most are written by women or men using female pseudonyms.

Representative Authors include Victoria Holt, the most consistently successful author; Phyllis Whitney, who often uses tropical settings; Dorothy Daniels; and Anne Maybury.

Historical Romances (HR):

An historical romance is a story of love and romance set in a specific historical period and often deals with reversals of social and financial circumstances. Among the most popular periods are Regency England, Elizabethan England and nineteenth century America. Romance and social details such as costuming and social customs are emphasized much more than the historical events of the period. Sexual explicitness may vary from none to a great deal.

Subcategories include:

1. *Pure Romance:*
   Fluffy stories with no sexual activity, only the most discreet romantic encounters between young and beautiful women and dashing, but well mannered men. Representative authors include Barbara Cartland, Clare Darcy, and Georgette Heyer.

2. *Bodice Rippers:*
   Many scenes of explicit sexual activity (often described in very flowery romantic language) sometimes bordering on rape and violence. These love stories are very tempestuous and reveal a love-hate relationship between the man, who is extremely masculine, virile and dominating and the woman, who is headstrong and ravishingly beautiful. It is often not until the end of the book that the two finally realize their love for one another.

   Representative authors include Kathleen Woodiwiss, Rosemary Rogers, Jude Deveraux, Patricia Matthews, Laurie McBain, Bertrice Small, Joyce Verrette, and Jennifer Wilde.

Romances (R):

A romance is a contemporary story of love, usually among upper-middle and upper-class men and women. The settings are most often glamorous (New York, Rome) and the characters are independently wealthy or in interesting careers (doctors, lawyers, business tycoons, designers). After several adversities, the ending is happy. The sexual content varies.

Representative authors include Danielle Steel, Janet Dailey, Faith Baldwin, Catherine Cookson, Grace Livingston Hill (religious themes), and Helen Van Slyke.

Publishers series, paperback originals almost exclusively, are most important: e.g., Harlequin, Silhouette, Candlelight. These series are modified or discontinued depending upon sales.

Romantic Adventures (RA):

Romantic adventure is a story that combines the elements of romance and adventure, with romance emphasized more than adventure. The settings are always colorful and exotic. In many the protagonist is female and there tends to be very little violence. The most popular author is Mary Stewart.

REFERENCE AND BIBLIOGRAPHIC SOURCES

Cawelti, John G. *Adventure, Mystery, and Romance: Formula Stories as Art and Popular Culture.* Chicago, University of Chicago Press, 1976.

Falk, Kathryn. *Love's Leading Ladies.* New York: Pinnacle Books, 1982.

Fallon, Eileen. *Words of Love, a Complete Guide to Romance Fiction.* New York: Garland, 1984.

Frenier, Mariam Darce. *Good-bye Heathcliff: Changing Heroes, Heroines, Roles, and Values in Women's Category Romances.* New York: Greenwood Press, 1988.

Lowery, Marilyn M. *How to Write Romance Novels That Sell.* New York: Rawson, Wade, 1983.

Radway, Janice A. *Reading the Romance: Women, Patriarchy, and Popular Literature.* Chapel Hill: University of North Carolina Press, 1984.

Ramsdell, Kristin. *Happily Ever After: A Guide to Reading Interests in Romance Fiction.* Littleton, Co: Libraries Unlimited, 1987.

AUTHORS AND TITLES

0001
ADAMS, DORIS G
1966 The Price of Blood
1968 Power of Darkness
1969 No Man's Son

0002
AIKEN, JOAN 1924- G
England
1970 The Embroidered Sunset
1972 A Cluster of Separate Sparks
1974 Midnight Is a Place
1976 Castle Barebane
1978 The Five-Minute Marriage
1978 The Smile of the Stranger
1980 The Weeping Ash
1982 The Girl from Paris
1985 Mansfield Revisited
1987 If I Were You
Also writes novels for juveniles
See also MYSTERIES, 0389

0003
ALLARDYCE, PAULA
England
Real name: Ursula Torday; also writes as Charity Blackstock, Lee Blackstock, & Charlotte Keppel
1954 After the Lady
1955 The Doctor's Daughter
1955 A Game of Hazard
1956 Adam & Evelina
1956 The Man of Wrath
1957 The Lady & the Pirate
1957 Southern Folly
1958 Beloved Enemy
1958 My Dear Miss Emma
1959 Death My Lover
1959 A Marriage Has Been Arranged
1961 The Gentle Highwayman
1961 Witches' Sabbath
1965 Octavia
1967 Six Passengers for the "Sweet Bird"
1975 Eliza (1972)
1975 Gentleman Rogue (1966)
1975 Legacy of Pride (1963)
1976 The Carradine Affair (1974)
1976 Emily (1968)
1976 Paradise Row (1964)
1977 Miss Philadelphia Smith
1977 Shadowed Love (1970)
1978 Haunting Me
1979 The Rebel Lover (1960)
1979 The Rogue's Lady
1980 The Vixen's Revenge

0004
ARCHER, JEFFREY 1940- FS
England
1980 Kane & Abel
1982 The Prodigal Daughter (Sequel to Kane)
See also HEADLINES, 0230 & 0260

0005
BALDWIN, FAITH 1893-1978 R
1926 Three Women
1927 Departing Wings
1928 Alimony
1930 The Office Wife
1932 Week-End Marriage
1934 Wife Versus Secretary
1937 The Heart Has Wings
1941 Temporary Address: Reno
1944 Change of Heart
1944 He Married a Doctor
1947 Give Love the Air
1948 Marry for Money
1952 The Juniper Tree
1957 Three Faces of Love
1964 The Lonely Man
1966 There Is a Season
1969 The Velvet Hammer
1970 Take What You Want

"Little Oxford":
1939 Station Wagon Set
1971 Any Village
1973 No Bed of Roses
1974 Time & the Hour
1975 New Girl in Town
1976 Thursday's Child
1977 Adam's Eden
Selected titles; has been writing since the 1930s; Warners paperback series

0006
BANIS, V. J. 1937-
1978 This Splendid Earth
1978 The Sword & the Rose
1980 The Earth & All It Holds
1985 San Antone

Section 1 - Romances

0007
BARBER, NOEL   FS
1981 Tanamera
1983 A Farewell to France
1984 Säkkärä
1987 The Other Side of Paradise
1988 The Weeping & the Laughter

0008
BARRON, ANN FORMAN
1960 Murder Is a Gentle Kiss
1961 Spin a Dark Web
1969 Strange Legacy
1972 Dark Vengeance
1973 Bride of Menace
1973 Serpent in the Shadows
1975 Banner Bold & Beautiful
1977 Firebrand
See also as ERWIN, ANNABEL, 0047

0009
BEAUMAN, SALLY
England
1987 Destiny

0010
BERMANT, CHAIM   1929-   FS
1963 Jericho Sleep Alone
1964 Berl Make Tea
1964 Ben Preserve Us
1966 Diary of an Old Man
1967 Swinging in the Rain
1969 Here Endeth the Lesson
1971 Now Dowager
1972 Roses Are Blooming in Picardy
1973 The Last Supper
1976 The Second Mrs. Whitberg
1977 The Squire of Bor Shachor
1981 The Patriach
1983 The House of Women

"Titch Trilogy":
1987 Titch

0011
BINCHY, MAEVE
Ireland
1980 Central Line: Stories of Big City Life (SS)
1980 Victoria Line
1983 Light a Penny Candle
1984 The Lilac Bus
1986 Echoes
1986 London Transports
1988 Firefly Summer

0012
BLACK, LAURA   HR
1977 Glendraco
1978 Ravenburn
1979 Wild Cat
1971 Strathgallant
1986 Fall of Gard

0013
BLAKE, JENNIFER   1942-   HR
Also writes as Patricia Maxwell, Maxine Patrick, Patricia Ponder & Elizabeth Trehearne
1970 The Secret of Mirror House
1971 Stranger at Plantation Inn
1974 Dark Masquerade
1974 Bride of a Stranger
1974 The Bewitching Grace
1974 The Court of the Thorn Tree
1977 Love's Wild Assault
1977 Notorious Angel
1977 Love's Wild Desire
1979 Tender Betrayal
1979 The Storm & The Splendor
1980 Golden Fancy
1986 Prisoner of Desire
1988 Perfume of Paradise

0014
BLOOM, URSULA   1893-1984   HR
England
Also writes as Sheila Burns, Mary Essex, Rachel Harvey, Deborah Mann, Sara Sloane & Lozania Prole
1977 The Fire & the Rose
1978 Mirage of Love
1978 Born for Love
1979 Tomorrow Never Comes
1979 The Magnificent Courtesan
Began writing in 1920s; 520 titles in print in England; new to U.S.

0015
BRADFORD, BARBARA TAYLOR   1933-
1979 A Woman of Substance
1983 Voice of the Heart
1985 Hold the Dream (Sequel to Woman)
1986 Act of Will
1988 To Be the Best (Sequel to Hold)

0016
BRAMBLE, FORBES   1939-   FS
1977 Regent Square
1981 The Iron Roads

0017
BRENT, MADELEINE   G
1973 Moonraker's Bride
1975 Stranger at Wildings
1977 Merlin's Keep
1979 Tregaron's Daughter
1980 The Capricorn Stone
1984 Storm Swift
1986 Golden Urchin

0018
BRISCO, PATTY   1927-
1969 Merry's Treasure
1970 The Other People
1973 House of Candles
1976 Mist of Evil
See also as MATTHEWS, PATRICIA, 0098

0019
BRISKIN, JACQUELINE   1927-   FS
1973 Afterlove
1976 Rich Friends
1978 Paloverde
1982 The Onyx
See also TRASH, 1115

0020
BRISTOW, GWEN   1903-1980   HR, FS
Wrote mysteries with husband, Bruce Manning
1943 Tomorrow Is Forever
1950 Jubilee Trail
1959 Celia Garth
1970 Calico Palace
1980 Golden Dreams

"Plantation" Trilogy:
1937 Deep Summer
1938 The Handsome Road
1940 This Side of Glory
See also HISTORICAL FICTION, 0894

0021
BROMIGE, IRIS   R
1947 A Chance for Love
1973 The Golden Cage
1975 The Conway Touch
1975 Family Group
1975 Laurian Vale
1980 A Distant Song
1981 Rough Weather
1985 A Slender Thread

0022
BUCK, PEARL S. 1892-1973   FS, R
Also wrote as John Sedges
Nobel Prize, 1938
1930 East Wind: West Wind
1941 Other Gods
1942 Dragon Seed
1943 The Promise
1946 Pavilion of Women
1948 Peony
1951 God's Men
1952 The Hidden Flower
1953 Come, My Beloved
1956 Imperial Woman
1957 Letter from Peking
1959 Command the Morning
1963 The Living Reed
1965 Death in the Castle
1967 The Time Is Noon
1968 The New Year
1969 The Good Deed (SS)
1969 The Three Daughters of Madame Liang
1970 Mandala
1972 The Goddess Abides
1973 All Under Heaven
1974 The Rainbow
1975 East & West (SS)
1976 Secrets of the Heart
1978 Mrs. Stoner & the Sea
1979 The Woman Who Was Changed

"House of Earth" Trilogy:
1931 The Good Earth
1932 Sons
1935 A House Divided
Also wrote nonfiction & novels for juveniles

0023
BUTLER, GWENDOLINE   1922-
1975 The Vesey Inheritance
1977 Meadowsweet
1979 The Red Staircase
1982 Albion Walk
See also MYSTERIES, 0409; ROMANCES, 0100 & MYSTERIES, 0518 as MELVILLE, JENNIE

0024
CADELL, ELIZABETH   1903-
1947 Last Straw for Harriet
1949 Iris in Winter
1950 Brimstone in the Garden
1950 Sun in the Morning
1951 Enter Mrs. Belchamber
1953 Crystal Clear

Section 1 - Romances

1954 Around the Rugged Rock
1954 The Cuckoo in Spring
1955 The Lark Shall Sing
1955 Money to Burn
1956 I Love a Lass
1958 Shadows on the Water
1960 The Yellow Brick Road
1961 Six Impossible Things
1962 Honey for Tea
1962 The Toy Sword
1963 Come Be My Guest
1965 Canary Yellow
1966 The Corner Shop
1966 The Fox from His Lair
1968 Mrs. Westerby Changes Course
1969 The Golden Collar
1970 The Past Tense of Love
1971 The Friendly Air
1972 Home for the Wedding
1973 Royal Summons
1974 Deck with Flowers
1975 The Fledgling
1976 Game in Diamonds
1977 Parson's House
1978 The Round Dozen
1979 Return Match
1980 The Marrying Kind
1981 Any Two Can Play
1982 A Lion in the Way
1983 Remains to Be Seen
1985 The Waiting Game
1986 The Empty Nest

0025
CALDWELL, TAYLOR   1900-1985
Real name: Janet Miriam Taylor Holland Caldwell
1938 Dynasty of Death
1940 The Eagles Gather
1941 The Earth Is the Lord's
1942 The Strong City
1943 The Arm & the Darkness
1943 The Turnbulls
1944 The Final Hour
1945 The Wide House
1947 There Was a Time
1948 Melissa
1949 Let Love Come Last
1951 The Balance Wheel
1952 The Devil's Advocate
1953 Maggie, Her Marriage
1954 Never Victorious, Never Defeated
1956 Tender Victory
1957 The Sound of Thunder
1960 The Listener
1961 A Prologue to Love
1963 Grandmother & the Priests
1965 Pillar of Iron

1966 No One Hears But Him
1967 Dialogue with the Devil
1968 Testimony of Two Men
1972 Captains & the Kings
1975 The Romance of Atlantis
1976 Ceremony of the Innocent
1978 Bright Flows the River
1981 Answer as a Man
See also HISTORICAL FICTION, 0896 & 0957; ROMANCES, 0113 as REINER, MAX

0026
CARR, PHILIPPA   1906-   R, HR
Real name: Eleanor Hibbert; also writes as Eleanor Burford, Elbur Ford, Kathleen Kellow & Ellalice Tate
1972 The Miracle at St. Bruno's
1973 The Lion Triumphant
1975 The Witch from the Sea
1976 Saraband for Two Sisters
1977 Lament for a Lost Lover
1978 The Love Child
1979 The Song of the Siren
1981 Will You Love Me in September?
1982 The Adulteress (Sequel to Will)
1983 Knave of Hearts
1984 Voices in a Haunted Room
1985 The Return of the Gypsy
1986 Midsummer's Eve
1987 The Pool of St. Branck (Sequel to Midsummer)
See also HISTORICAL FICTION, 0958; ROMANCES, 0071 as HOLT, VICTORIA; HISTORICAL FICTION, 1008 as PLAIDY, JEAN

0027
CARTLAND, BARBARA   1902-   HR, R
England
Also writes as Barbara McCorquodale. Wrote her first book in 1925; many titles republished in 1970s. See Barbara Cartland Library of Love Series --approximately 300 titles published by Bantam Books; others published in "Camfield Novel of Love" series & by Jove, Pyramid & Duron.
1925 Jigsaw
1945 Armour against Love
1947 The Dream Within
1970 Duel of Hearts
1970 Love Is Mine
1970 The Royal Pledge
1974 Against the Storm
1974 Castle of Fear
1974 The Lessons in Love
1974 The Penniless Peer

1977 Dance on My Heart
1977 Love Locked In
1977 The Marquis Who Hated Women
1978 Loves, Lord, & Lady Birds
1979 Journey to Paradise
1979 Imperial Splendor
1979 Love in the Clouds
1980 Desire of the Heart
1980 Punished with Love
1980 A Song of Love
1980 Women Have Hearts
1981 Love at the Helm
1981 The Unknown Heart
1981 The Heart of the Clan
1981 Pure & Untouched
1981 Touch a Star
1982 A King in Love
1982 Riding to the Moon
1985 Royal Punishment
1986 A Dream in Spain
1986 The Devil Defeated
1987 Forced to Marry
1987 Love Joins the Clan
1988 Little Tongues of Fire
1988 Lovers in Lisbon

0028
CHESTER, DEBORAH 1957- R, HR
1980 A Love So Wild
1981 French Slippers
1982 Royal Intrigue

0029
CLARK, NORMA LEE HR
1978 Mallory
1978 Hester
1979 Emily
1979 Megan
1979 Sophia & Augustan
1980 Fanny
1980 Zandra
1981 The Tynedale Daughters
1982 Lady Jane

0030
COFFMAN, VIRGINIA 1914- G
Also writes as Victor Cross
1965 Curse of the Island Pool
1966 A Haunted Place
1966 High Terrace
1966 Castle at Witches Coven
1968 The Candidate's Wife
1968 The Mist at Darkness
1969 The Dark Gondola
1969 The Devil's Mistress
1970 Isle of the Undead
1970 Devil's Virgin
1971 Masque of Satan
1971 Chalet Diabolique
1972 From Satan, with Love
1972 Mistress Devon
1972 The House on the Moat
1972 Night at Sea Abbey
1973 The Dark Palazzo
1974 The House of Sandalwood
1974 Hyde Place
1975 Veronique
1976 Marsanne
1976 The Rest Is Silence
1978 The Gaynor Women
1978 Fire Dawn
1979 Dinah Faire
1979 Legacy of Fear
1980 Of Love & Intrigue
1984 The Orchid Tree
1985 Dark Winds

"Lombard Family":
1981 Pacific Cavalcade
1982 The Lombard Cavalcade
1983 The Lombard Heiress

"Moura":
1959 Moura
1965 Beckoning from Moura
1970 The Vampyre of Moura
1971 Vicar of Moura (1966 Devila Vicar)
1977 The Dark beyond Moura
See also as DUVAUL, VIRGINIA, 0042

0031
COLEMAN, LONNIE 1920-1982 FS
Real name: William Laurence Coleman
1944 Escape the Thunder
1947 Time Moving West
1951 The Sound of Spanish Voices
1952 Clara
1953 Adam's Way
1958 The Southern Lady
1959 Sam
1962 The Golden Vanity
1967 King
1975 Orphan Jim
1981 Mark

"Beulah":
1973 Beulah Land
1977 Look Away, Beulah Land
1980 The Legacy of Beulah Land

0032
COOKSON, CATHERINE 1906- R

Section 1 - Romances

England
Also writes as Fanny McBride
1950 Kate Hannigan
1952 The Fifteen Streets
1953 Color Blind
1954 Maggie Rowan
1957 Rooney
1958 Menagerie
1959 Slinky Jane
1960 Fenwick Houses
1962 The Garment
1963 The Blind Miller
1964 Hannah Massey
1965 The Tide of Life
1965 Matty Doolin
1966 The Unbaited Trap
1967 Katie Mulholland
1967 House on the Fens
1968 Joe & the Gladiator
1968 The Round Tower
1969 The Nice Bloke
1970 The Glass Virgin
1970 The Invitation
1970 The Nipper
1971 The Dwelling Place
1972 Blue Baccy
1972 Feathers in the Fire
1973 Pure as the Lily
1974 The Garment
1974 Our John Willie
1975 The Gambling Man
1975 The Invisible Cord
1976 The Slow Awakening
1976 The Long Corridor
1977 Color Blind
1977 The Girl
1978 The Cinder Path
1979 The Man Who Cried
1980 Go Tell It to Mrs. Golightly
1982 The Whip
1983 Hamilton
1984 The Black Velvet Gown
1985 The Bannaman Legacy
1987 The Parson's Daughter
1988 The Harrogate Secret

"Mallen":
1973 The Mallen Streak
1974 The Mallen Girl
1974 The Mallen Lot

"Mary Ann":
1955 A Grand Man!
1956 The Lord & Mary Ann
1958 The Devil & Mary Ann
1961 Love & Mary Ann
1964 Life & Mary Ann
1964 Marriage & Mary Ann
1965 Mary Ann's Angels
1966 Mary Ann & Bill

"Tilly":
1980 Tilly
1981 Tilly Wed
1982 Tilly Alone
See also as MARCHANT, CATHERINE, 0093

0033
COURTER, GAY   1944-   FS
1981 The Midwife
1984 River of Dreams
1986 Code Ezra

0034
CROMWELL, ELSIE   1912-
1969 The Governess
1970 Iverstone Manor

0035
DAILEY, JANET   1944-   R
1976 Dangerous Masquerade
1977 Bluegrass King
1977 Fiesta San Antonio
1977 The Indi Man
1979 The Bride of the Delta Queen
1979 Sweet Promise
1979 Touch the Wind
1980 Difficult Decision
1980 Heart of Stone
1980 Lord of the High Lonesome
1980 The Mating Season
1980 One of the Boys
1980 Ride the Thunder
1980 The Rogue
1980 The Thawing of Man
1981 Dakota Dreamin'
1981 Night Way
1981 A Tradition of Pride
1981 The Traveling Kind
1981 Wild & Wonderful
1982 Northern Magic
1983 The Best Way to Lose
1983 Separate Cabins
1983 Western Man
1984 Silver Wings, Santiago Blue
1985 The Glory Game
1985 The Price of Hannah Wade
1986 The Great Alone
1987 Heiress

"Calder Saga":
1981 This Calder Sky
1982 This Calder Range
1983 Stand a Calder Man

1984 Calder Born, Calder Bred
Wrote many titles for Harlequin

0036
DANIELS, DOROTHY   1915-   G
Also writes as Danielle Dorset, Angela Gray, Cynthia Kavanaugh, Helaine Ross, Suzanne Somers, Geraldine Thayer & Helen Gray Weston
1965 Dockhaven
1970 Lady of the Shadows
1971 Conover's Folly
1971 Diablo Manor
1971 House of Many Doors
1972 House of Broken Dolls
1972 The Lanier Riddle
1972 Mystic Manor
1972 Larrabee Heiress
1973 The Caldwell Shadow
1973 The Duncan Dynasty
1974 Dark Haven
1974 Child of Darkness
1974 The Two Worlds of Peggy Scott
1974 The Dark Stage
1975 Emerald Hill
1975 Illusion at Haven's Edge
1975 Marble Hills
1975 The Possessed
1975 The Unlamented
1976 Dark Island
1976 Juniper Hill
1976 Portrait of a Witch
1976 Summer House
1976 Vineyard Chapel
1976 Whistle in the Wind
1977 A Mirror of Shadows
1977 Nightfall
1977 Poison Flower
1977 The Spanish Chapel
1978 Perrine
1978 The Magic Ring
1979 The Cormac Legend
1979 Night Shadow
1979 Yesterday's Evil
1980 Bridal Black
1980 House of Silence
1980 The Purple & the Gold
1980 Valley of the Shadows
1980 Veil of Treachery
1981 Monte Carlo
1981 The Sisters of Valcour

0037
DARCY, CLARE   HR
England
1971 Georgina
1972 Cecily
1973 Lydia or Love in Town
1974 Victoire
1974 Allegra
1975 Lady Pamela
1976 Elyza
1977 Cressida
1977 Eugenia
1977 Regina
1978 Gwendolen
1978 Rolande
1980 Darcy
1980 Letty
1982 Caroline & Julia

0038
DELDERFIELD, R. F.   1912-1972   FS
England
1947 All Over the Town
1949 Seven Men of Gascony
1950 Farewell the Tranquil
1958 The Avenue
1960 Diana
1963 Mr. Sermon
1967 Return Journey
1972 To Serve Them All My Days
1976 Charlie, Come Home
1978 Stop at a Winner

"The Horseman Riding":
1966 Post of Honor
1967 A Horseman Riding By
1968 The Green Gauntlet
1973 Long Summer Day

"Swann Family":
1970 God Is an Englishman
1971 Theirs Was the Kingdom
1973 Give Us This Day

0039
DENYS, THERESA   1947-   HR
1981 The Flesh & the Devil

0040
DEVERAUX, JUDE   1947-   HR
Real name: Jude Gilliam White
1978 The Enchanted Land
1980 The Black Lyon
1981 The Velvet Promise
1982 Casa Grande
1982 Highland Velvet
1983 Sweetbriar
1983 Velvet Angel
1983 Velvet Song
1984 Counterfeit Lady
1985 Lost Lady

Section 1 - Romances

1985 River Lady
1985 Twin of Fire
1985 Twin of Ice
1986 The Temptress

0041
DU MAURIER, DAPHNE   1907-1989 G
England
1931 The Loving Spirit
1938 Rebecca
1949 The Parasites
1951 My Cousin Rachel
1962 Castle d'Or
1963 The Glass Blowers
1965 The Flight of the Falcon
1977 The Winding Stair
See also HORROR, 0171; HISTORICAL FICTION, 0969; BRITISH AUTHORS, 1357

0042
DUVAUL, VIRGINIA   1914-
1967 The Chinese Door
1970 Priestess of the Damned
1973 The Cliffs of Dread
1973 Evil at Queen's Priory
See also as COFFMAN, VIRGINIA, 0030

0043
EDEN, DOROTHY   1912-1982 G, R, FS
New Zealand
Also wrote as Mary Paradise
1940 Singing Shadows
1948 Daughters of Ardmore Hall
1950 The Voice of the Dolls
1950 Crow Hollow
1952 Cat's Prey
1953 Lamb to the Slaughter
1954 Bride By Candlelight
1957 The Pretty Ones
1958 Listen to Danger
1959 The Sleeping Bride
1959 Deadly Travellers
1962 Lady of Mallow
1964 Darkwater
1965 The Marriage Chest
1965 Ravenscroft
1966 Never Call It Loving
1968 The Shadow Wife
1969 The Vines of Yarrabee
1970 Melbury Square
1970 Waiting for Willa
1971 An Afternoon Walk
1972 Speak to Me of Love
1974 The Millionaire's Daughter
1975 Bridge of Fear
1975 The Time of the Dragon

1976 The House on Hay Hill
1977 The Slalmanca Drum
1977 Whistle for the Crows
1977 Siege in the Sun
1978 Winterwood
1978 The Storrington Papers
1980 The American Heiress
1981 Sleep in the Woods
1982 An Important Family

0044
EDGAR, JOSEPHINE   1907-   R
Real name: Mary Mussi; also writes as Mary Howard
1941 Unchartered Romance
1948 Strange Paths
1956 A Lady Fell In Love
1964 My Sister Sophie
1968 Bachelor Girls
1972 The Devil's Innocents
1973 Soldiers & Lovers
1973 The Stranger at the Gate
1976 Duchess
1976 Countess
1983 Margaret Normanby
1986 Bright Young Things

0045
ELEGANT, ROBERT   1928-   FS
1976 Dynasty
See also HISTORICAL FICTION, 0970

0046
ELWARD, JAMES   1928-
1974 Storm's End
1976 The House Is Dark
1979 Tomorrow Is Mine
1984 Ask for Nothing More
See also as Jt. author with VAN SLYKE, HELEN, 0142

0047
ERWIN, ANNABEL
1976 Liliane
1980 Aurielle
See also as BARRON, ANN FORMAN, 0008

0048
FAST, HOWARD   1914-   FS
Also writes as Walter Ericson & E. V. Cunningham
1962 Power
1982 Max

1985 The Outsider
1987 The Dinner Party

"Lavelle Family Saga":
1977 The Immigrants
1978 Second Generation
1979 The Establishment
1981 The Legacy
1985 The Immigrant's Daughter
See also HISTORICAL FICTION, 0906, 0971 & 1054; MYSTERIES, 0431 as CUNNINGHAM, E. V.

0049
FLEMING, THOMAS 1927- FS
Also writes as Cristopher Cain, T. F. James & J. R. Thomas
1961 All Good Men
1966 King of the Hill
1967 A Cry of Whiteness
1969 Romans, Countrymen, Lovers
1970 The Sandbox Tree
1974 The Good Shepherd
1977 Rulers of the City
1978 Promises to Keep
1979 A Passionate Girl
1981 The Officers' Wives
1985 The Spoils of War
1987 Time & Tide

0050
FREEMAN, CYNTHIA 1920-1988 FS
Real name: Bea Feinberg
1975 A World Full of Strangers
1977 Fairytales
1978 The Days of Winter
1979 Portraits
1980 Come Pour the Wine
1981 No Time for Tears
1982 Catch the Gentle Dawn
1985 Illusions of Love
1986 Seasons of the Heart
1988 The Last Princess

0051
GALLAGHER, PATRICIA R
1961 The Sons & the Daughters
1964 Answer to Heaven
1966 The Fires of Brimstone
1967 Shannon
1971 Shadows of Passion
1971 Summer of Sighs
1974 The Thicket
1976 Castles in the Air
1977 Mystic Rose
1985 On Wings of Dreams

0052
GASKIN, CATHERINE 1929- R, HR
Ireland
1947 This Other Eden
1949 With Every Tear
1950 Dust in the Sunlight
1951 All Else Is Folly
1952 Daughter of the House
1955 Sara Dane
1958 Blake's Reach
1960 Corporation Wife
1962 I Know My Love
1963 The Tilsit Inheritance
1965 The File on Devlin
1967 Edge of Glass
1970 Fiona
1972 A Falcon for a Queen
1974 The Property of a Gentleman
1976 The Lynmara Legacy
1977 The Summer of the Spanish Woman
1980 Family Affairs
1982 Promises
1986 The Ambassador's Women

0053
GEESLIN, CAMPBELL 1925- FS
1981 The Bonner Boys

0054
GELLIS, ROBERTA 1927- HR
Also writes as Leah Jacobs
1964 Knight's Honor
1965 Bond of Blood
1977 The Dragon & the Rose
1977 The Sword & the Swan
1980 English Heiress
1981 The Cornish Heiress
1981 Siren Song
1982 Winter Song
1982 Kentish Heiress
1984 Fire Song
1984 A Woman's Estate
1985 A Tapestry of Dreams

"Roselynde Chronicles":
1978 Roselynde
1978 Alinor
1978 Joanna
1979 Gilliane
1982 Rhiannon

0055
GIDLEY, CHARLES 1938- FS
1981 The River Running By
1985 The Raging of the Sea

Section 1 - Romances

1987 Armada

0056
GOLON, SERGEANNE   1903-1972   HR
Real name: Anne Golon
1958 Angelique
1960 Angelique & the King
1961 Angelique & the Sultan
1961 Angelique in Barbary
1962 Angelique in Revolt
1963 Angelique in Love
1967 The Countess Angelique
1969 The Temptation of Angelique
1973 Angelique & the Demon
1977 Angelique & the Ghosts

0057
GOUDGE, ELIZABETH   1900-1984
1934 Island Magic
1936 A City of Bells
1938 Towers in the Mist
1939 The Middle Window
1940 Smoky House
1942 The Castle on the Hill
1944 Green Dolphin Street
1949 Gentian Hill
1951 God So Loved the World
1956 The Rosemary Tree
1958 The White Witch
1960 The Dean's Watch
1963 The Scent of Water

"Eliot Family":
1940 The Bird in the Tree
1948 Pilgrim's Inn
1953 The Heart of the Family
See also HISTORICAL FICTION, 0980

0058
GRANT, MAXWELL   1897-   FS
1981 Inherit the Sun
1986 Blood Red Rose

0059
GROSS, JOEL   1951-   FS
1970 Bubble's Shadow
1975 The Young Man Who Wrote Soap Operas
1979 The Books of Rachel
1981 Maura's Dream
1982 Home of the Brave
1983 This Year in Jerusalem
1984 The Lives of Rachel
1986 Spirit in the Flesh
1987 Sarah

0060
HAGER, JEAN   1915-
1970 The Secret of Riverside Farm
1970 The Whispering House
1980 Portrait of Love
1981 Captured by Love
1981 Web of Desire
1981 Yellow-Flower Moon
1984 Terror in the Sunlight
See also as McALLISTER, AMANDA, 0088; KYLE, MARLAINE, 0080; NORTH, SARA, 0104; STEPHENS, JEANNE, 0133

0061
HAINES, PAMELA   1929-   FS
1981 The Kissing Game
1984 The Diamond Waterfall
1986 The Golden Lion

0062
HARRIS, MARILYN   1931-
Real name: Marilyn Harris Springer
1967 King's Ex
1969 In the Midst of Earth
1970 The Peppersalt Land
1976 Bledding Sorrow
1981 The Last Great Love
1985 Warrick

"Eden Family":
1977 This Other Eden
1978 The Prince of Eden
1979 The Eden Passion
1980 The Women of Eden
1982 Eden Rising
See also HORROR, 0183

0063
HEAVEN, CONSTANCE   1911-   HR
Real name: Constance Fecher
1966 The Queen's Delight
1972 The House of Kuragin
1973 The Astrov Legacy
1975 Castle of Eagles
1975 Fires of Glenlochy
1975 The Place of Stones
1977 The Queen & the Gypsy
1978 Heir to Kuragin
1978 Lord of Ravensley
1981 The Wildcliffe Bird
1982 The Ravensly Touch
1983 Daughter of Marignee
1984 Castle of Doves
1986 The Craven Legacy

0064
HEYER, GEORGETTE 1902-1974 HR
England
Also wrote as Stella Martin
1921 The Black Moth
1922 The Great Roxhythe
1923 Instead of the Thorn
1928 The Masqueraders
1929 Beauvallet
1930 Barren Corn
1930 Powder & Patch: The Transformation of Philip Manners
1931 The Conqueror
1934 Devil's Cub
1934 The Convenient Marriage
1935 Regency Buck
1935 Death in the Stocks
1936 The Talisman Ring
1937 An Infamous Army
1938 Royal Escape
1940 The Corinthian
1940 The Spanish Bride
1941 Beau Wyndham
1941 Faro's Daughter
1946 Friday's Child
1946 The Reluctant Widow
1948 The Foundling
1949 Arabella
1950 The Grand Sophy
1951 The Quiet Gentleman
1953 Cotillion
1954 The Toll-Gate
1955 Bath Tangle
1956 Sprig Muslin
1957 April Lady
1957 Sylvester, or, The Wicked Uncle
1957 These Old Shades
1958 Venetia
1959 The Unknown Ajax
1961 A Civil Contract
1962 The Nonesuch
1964 False Colours
1965 Fredrica
1966 Black Sheep
1968 Cousin Kate
1970 Charity Girl
1972 Lady of Quality
Author of more than 60 Regency romances & mysteries
See also MYSTERIES, 0471 & HISTORICAL FICTION, 0987

0065
HIGH, MONIQUE (RAPHEL) 1949- FS
1980 The Four Winds of Heaven
1981 Encore
1983 The Eleventh Year

0066
HILL, FIONA 1952- G, HR
Real name: Ellen Jane Pall
1975 The Practical Heart
1975 The Trellised Lane
1975 The Wedding Portrait
1976 Love in a Major Key
1977 The Love Child
1977 Sweet's Folly
1978 The Autumn Rose
1981 The Stanbroke Girls
1987 The Country Gentleman

0067
HILL, GRACE LIVINGSTON 1865-1947 R
Representative titles:
1903 The Story of a Whim
1911 Aunt Crete's Emancipation
1913 Lo, Michael
1914 The Best Man
1914 The Man of the Desert
1916 The Finding of Jasper Holt
1916 The Voice in the Wilderness
1920 Exit Betty
1928 Crimson Roses
1932 Happiness Hill
1932 The Patch of Blue
1934 Amorelle
1935 Beauty for Ashes
1936 April Gold
1936 Mystery Flowers
1937 Brentwood
1940 Partners
1942 Crimson Mountain
1943 Sound of the Trumpet
1943 Spice Box
1945 All through the Night
1946 Bright Arrows
1949 Morning Is for Joy
1957 Duskin
Has been writing since 1930s; published by Spire Books & Revell & by Bantam in an original paperback series

0068
HILL, PAMELA 1920- G, HR
England
Also writes as Sharon Fiske
1954 The King's Vixen
1955 The Crown & the Shadow
1956 Marjorie of Scotland
1957 Here Lies Margot
1963 Maddalena
1965 Forget Not Ariadne
1967 Julia
1973 The Devil of Aske
1973 The Malvie Inheritance

Section 1 - Romances

1974 The Incumbent
1975 Whitton's Folly
1976 The Heatherton Heritage
1977 Norah
1977 The Green Salamander
1977 Tsar's Woman
1978 Daneclere
1978 Stranger's Forest
1979 Homage to a Rose
1980 Daughter of Midnight
1980 Fire Opal
1980 A Place of Ravens
1981 The House of Cray
1982 Dutchess Cain
1982 The Fairest One of All
1983 The Copper-Haired Marshall
1984 The Bride of Ae
1984 Children of Lucifer
1984 Still Blooms the Rose
1985 The Governess
1985 Sable for the Count
1987 My Lady Glamis

0069
HODGE, JOAN AIKEN 1917- HR
1964 Maulever Hall
1965 The Adventurers
1966 Watch the Wall My Darling
1967 Here Comes a Candle
1968 The Winding Stair
1968 Master of Penrose
1969 Marry in Haste
1970 Greek Wedding
1971 Savannah Purchase
1973 Shadow of a Lady
1973 Strangers in Company
1975 One Way to Venice
1975 Rebel Heiress
1975 Runaway Bride
1976 Judas Flowering
1977 Red Sky at Night, Lover's Delight
1979 Last Act
1981 Wide Is the Water (Sequel to Judas)
1982 The Lost Garden
1985 Secret Island
1987 Polonaise

0070
HOLLAND, ISABELLE 1920- G, HR
1967 Cecily
1974 Kilgaren
1974 Trelawny
1975 Moncrieff
1976 Darcourt
1976 Grenelle
1977 The deMaury Papers
1978 Tower Abbey
1979 The Marchington Inheritance
1980 Counter Point
1981 The Lost Madonna
Also writes novels for young adults
See also MYSTERIES, 0476

0071
HOLT, VICTORIA 1906- G, HR
England
Real name: Eleanor Hibbert; also writes as Eleanor Burford, Elbor Ford, Kathleen Kellow & Elalice Tate
1960 Mistress of Mellyn
1962 Kirkland Revels
1963 Bride of Pendorric
1965 The Legend of the Seventh Virgin
1966 Menfreya in the Morning
1967 The King of the Castle
1968 The Queen's Confession
1969 The Shivering Sands
1970 The Secret Woman
1971 The Shadow of the Lynx
1972 On the Night of the Seventh Moon
1973 The Curse of the Kings
1974 The House of a Thousand Lanterns
1975 Lord of the Far Island
1976 The Pride of the Peacock
1977 The Devil on Horseback
1978 My Enemy the Queen
1979 The Spring of the Tiger
1980 The Mask of the Enchantress
1981 The Judas Kiss
1982 The Demon Lover
1983 The Time of the Hunter's Moon
1984 The Landower Legacy
1985 The Road to Paradise Island
1986 Secret for a Nightingale
1987 The Silk Vendetta
1988 The India Fan
See also as CARR, PHILIPPA, 0026; HISTORICAL FICTION, 0958 as CARR, PHILIPPA & 1008 as PLAIDY, JEAN

0072
HOWATCH, SUSAN G, HR, FS
1940-
England
1965 The Dark Shore
1966 The Waiting Sands
1967 Call in the Night
1968 The Shrouded Walls
1969 April's Grave
1970 The Devil on Lammas Night
1971 Penmarric

1974 Cashelmara
1977 The Rich Are Different
1980 Sins of the Father (Sequel to Rich)
1984 The Wheel of Fortune
1987 Glittering Images

0073
HUFF, TOM   1938?-
1973 Nine Bucks Row
1974 Meet a Dark Stranger
1976 Susannah, Beware
1977 Whisper in the Darkness
1979 Marabelle
See also as MARLOW, EDWINA, 0094; PARKER, BEATRICE, 0107; ST. CLAIR, KATHERINE, 0119; WILDE, JENNIFER, 0146

0074
JOHNSON, BARBARA   1923-   HR
1975 Lionors
1977 Delta Blood
1978 Tara's Song
1980 Homeward Winds the River
1980 The Heirs of Love

0075
JOHNSTON, VELDA   G
1967 Along a Dark Path
1968 House above Hollywood
1968 A Howling in the Woods
1969 I Came to a Castle
1970 The Light in the Swamp
1970 The Phantom Cottage
1971 The Face in the Shadows
1971 The People on the Hill
1972 The Late Mrs. Fanselt
1972 The Mourning Trees
1973 Masquerade in Venice
1973 The White Pavilion
1975 The House on the Left Bank
1976 A Room with Dark Mirrors
1976 The Frenchman
1976 Deveron Hall
1977 The Etruscan Smile
1978 I Came to the Highlands
1978 The Hour before Midnight
1979 The People from the Sea
1980 A Presence in an Empty Room
1980 The Silver Dolphin
1981 The Fateful Summer
1981 The Stone Maiden
1983 The Other Karen
1984 Voice in the Night
1985 The Crystal Cat
1985 Shadow behind the Curtain

1986 Fatal Affair
1987 The Girl on the Beach
1987 The House on Bostwick Square
1988 The Man at Windmere

0076
KAYE, M. M. (Mary Margaret)   HR, FS
1911-
Also writes children's books as Mollie Hamilton & Mollie Kaye
1959 House of Shade
1978 The Far Pavilions
1979 Shadow of the Moon
1981 Trade Wind
See also MYSTERIES, 0485

0077
KELLEY, WILLIAM   1929-
1979 The Tyree Legend

0078
KEYES, FRANCES PARKINSON   R
1885-1970
1919 The Old Gray Homestead
1933 Senator Marlowe's Daughter
1936 Honor Bright
1938 Parts Unknown
1939 The Great Tradition
1940 Fielding's Folly
1941 All That Glitters
1942 Crescent Carnival
1945 The River Road
1947 Came a Cavalier
1948 Dinner at Antoine's
1950 Joy Street
1952 Steamboat Gothic
1954 The Royal Box
1957 Blue Camellia
1958 Victorine
1959 Station Wagon in Spain
1960 The Chess Players
1962 Madame Castel's Lodger
1963 Three Ways of Love
1964 The Explorer
1966 I, the King
1966 Tongues of Fire
1968 The Heritage

0079
KOEN, KARLEEN
1986 Through a Glass Darkly

0080
KYLE, MARLAINE   1915-

Section 1 - Romances

Real name: Jean Hager
1982 A Suitable Marriage
See also as HAGER, JEAN, 0060;
MCALLISTER, AMANDA, 0088; NORTH,
SARA, 0104; STEPHENS, JEANNE, 0133

0081
LAKER, ROSALIND   HR
Also writes as Barbara Ovestedal &
Barbara Paul
1975 The Smuggler's Bride
1977 Ride the Blue Riband
1979 Claudine's Daughter
1979 Warwyck's Woman
1980 Warwyck's Choice
1981 Banners of Silk
1982 Gilded Splendor
1983 Jewelled Path
1984 What the Heart Keeps
1985 This Shining Land
1986 Tree of Gold
1987 The Silver Touch

0082
LA TOURETTE, JACQUELINE   1926-
1971 The Joseph Stone
1972 A Matter of Sixpence
1974 The Previous Lady
1975 The Pompeii Scroll
1979 Shadows in Umbria
1981 The Wild Harp
1983 Patarran
1984 The House on Octavia Street
1986 The Incense Tree

0083
LINDLEY, ERICA   1930-
1975 The Brackenrayd Inheritance
1977 Devil in Crystal
1978 Belladona
1979 Harvest of Destiny

0084
LOFTS, NORAH   1904-1983   HR
England
Also wrote mysteries as Peter Curtis
1935 I Met a Gypsy
1937 White Hell of Pity
1940 Hester Roon
1944 The Golden Fleece
1946 To See a Fine Lady
1947 Silver Nutmeg
1951 The Lute Player
1954 Bless This House
1958 Heaven in Your Hand (SS)

1969 Madselin
1970 Lovers All Untrue
1970 A Rose for Virtue
1972 Out of the Dark
1972 The Maude Reed Tale
1973 Nethergate
1974 Crown of Aloes
1976 Here Was a Man
1976 Blossom Like the Rose
1977 The Lonely Furrow
1978 Emma Hamilton
1978 Checkmate
1979 Jassy
1980 The Day of the Butterfly
1980 A Wayside Tavern
1981 Requiem for Idols
1981 You're Best Alone
1982 The Old Priory
1983 Saving Face (SS)

"Reed House"
1959 The Town House
1961 The House at Old Vine
1962 The House at Sunset
See also HORROR, 0198 & HISTORICAL
FICTION, 0994

0085
LORD, BETTE BAO   1938-   FS
1981 Spring Moon

0086
LORING, EMILIE BAKER   R
1922 The Trail of Conflict
1924 Here Comes the Sun!
1925 A Certain Crossroad
1927 The Solitary Horseman
1928 Gay Courage
1929 Swift Water
1930 Lighted Windows
1931 Fair Tomorrow
1932 Uncharted Seas
1933 Hilltops Clear
1934 We Ride the Gale!
1934 With Banners
1935 It's a Great World
1936 Give Me One Summer
1937 As Long as I Live
1938 Today Is Yours
1938 High of Heart
1939 Across the Years
1940 There Is Always Love
1941 Stars in Your Eyes
1941 Where Beauty Dwells
1942 Rainbow at Dusk
1943 When Hearts Are Light Again
1944 Keepers of the Faith

1945 Beyond the Sound of Guns
1946 Bright Skies
1947 Beckoning Trails
1948 I Hear Adventure Calling
1949 Love Came Laughing By
1950 To Love & to Honor
1952 For All Your Life
1954 My Dearest Love
1954 I Take This Man
1955 The Shadow of Suspicion
1956 What Then Is Love
1957 Look to the Stars
1958 Behind the Cloud
1959 With This Ring
1960 How Can the Heart Forget
1961 Throw Wide the Door
1963 Follow Your Heart
1964 A Candle in Her Heart
1965 Forever & a Day
1966 Spring Always Comes
1968 In Times Like These
1969 Love with Honor
1970 No Time for Love
1971 Forsaking All Others
1972 The Shining Years

"Emilie Loring Series," original paperbacks published by Bantam

0087
LYLE, ELIZABETH   HR
1981 Cassy
1983 Claire

0088
MCALLISTER, AMANDA   1915-   R
Real name: Jean Hager
1976 Pretty Enough to Kill
1976 No Need for Fear
1976 Waiting for Caroline
1977 Terror in the Sunlight
See also as HAGER, JEAN, 0060; KYLE, MARLAINE, 0080; NORTH, SARA, 0104; STEPHENS, JEANNE, 0133

0089
MCBAIN, LAURIE   1949-   HR
1975 Devil's Desire
1977 Moonstruck Madness
1979 Tears of Gold
1980 Chance the Winds of Fortune
1982 Dark before the Rising Sun
1983 Wild Bells to the Wild Sky
1985 When the Splendor Falls

0090
MCCULLOUGH, COLLEEN   1938?-   FS
Australia
1974 Tim
1977 The Thorn Birds
1981 An Indecent Obsession
1985 A Creed for the Third Millennium
1987 The Ladies of Missalonghi
See also WORLD AUTHORS, 1421

MCDONALD, MALCOLM
See ROSS-MACDONALD, MALCOLM, 0117

0091
MACINTYRE, LORN   FS
1979 Cruel in the Shadow
1981 The Blind Bend

0092
MALPASS, ERIC   1910-   FS
1978 The Wind Brings Up the Rain

0093
MARCHANT, CATHERINE   1908-   R
1963 Heritage of Folly
1963 The Fen Tiger
1964 House of Men
1965 Evil at Roger's Cross
1976 Miss Martha Mary Crawford
1976 The Slow Awakening
1980 The Iron Facade
See also as COOKSON, CATHERINE, 0032

0094
MARLOW, EDWINA   1938?-
Real name: Tom Huff
1975 Danger at Dahlkari
1975 Midnight at Mallyncourt
1976 When Emmalyn Remembers
See also as HUFF, TOM, 0073; PARKER, BEATRICE, 0107; ST. CLAIR, KATHERINE, 0119; WILDE, JENNIFER, 0146

0095
MARSHALL, CATHERINE   1914-1983   FS
1967 Christy
1984 Julie

0096
MARTIN, WILLIAM   FS

Section 1 - Romances

1979 Back Bay
1984 Nerve Endings

0097
MATTHEWS, CLAYTON
See as Jt. author with MATTHEWS, PATRICIA, 0098

0098
MATTHEWS, PATRICIA 1927- HR
1977 Love Forever More
1977 Love's Avenging Heart
1977 Love's Wildest Promise
1978 Love's Daring Dream
1978 Love's Pagan Heart
1979 Love's Golden Destiny
1979 Love's Magic Moment
1980 Love's Bold Journey
1980 Love's Raging Tide
1980 Love's Sweet Agony
1981 Tides of Love
1982 Embers of Dawn
1982 Flames of Glory
1983 Dancer of Dreams
1985 Gambler in Love
1985 Tame the Restless Heart
1987 Enchanted
See also as BRISCO, PATTY, 0018

With MATTHEWS, CLAYTON 1918- R
1981 Midnight Whispers
1982 Empire

0099
MAYBURY, ANNE G
1961 Someone Waiting
1961 Stay until Tomorrow
1962 I Am Gabriella!
1962 The Night My Enemy
1964 The Brides of Bellenmore
1965 The Pavilion at Monkshood
1966 The House of Fand
1967 The Moonlit Door
1968 The Minerva Stone
1970 The Terracotta Palace
1971 Ride a White Dolphin
1972 Walk in the Paradise Garden
1972 The Winds of Night
1973 The Midnight Dancers
1976 Jessamy Court
1976 The Jeweled Daughter
1977 Dark Star
1977 Falcon's Shadow
1977 Whisper in the Dark
1979 Radiance

0100
MELVILLE, JENNIE 1922- G
Real name: Gwendoline Butler
1972 Iron Wood
1973 Nun's Castle
1975 Raven's Forge
1976 Dragon's Eye
1978 Tarot's Tower
See also MYSTERIES, 0518; ROMANCES, 0023 & MYSTERIES, 0409 as BUTLER, GWENDOLINE

0101
MERCER, CHARLES 1917-
1975 Enough Good Men
1980 Murray Hill

0102
MICHAELS, BARBARA 1927-
Real name: Barbara Gross Mertz
1966 The Master of Blacktower
1967 Sons of the Wolf
1972 Grey Gallows
1975 The Sea King's Daughter
1976 Legend in Green Velvet
1976 Patriot's Dream
1977 Wings of the Falcon
1978 Wait for What Will Come
1982 Black Rainbow
1987 Search the Shadows
See also HORROR, 0206 & MYSTERIES, 0531 as PETERS, ELIZABETH

0103
NORTH, JESSICA G
1973 The High Valley
1975 River Rising
1979 The Legend of the Thirteenth Pilgrim
1981 Mask of the Jaguar

0104
NORTH, SARA 1915-
Real name: Jean Hager
1978 Evil Side of Eden
1989 Shadow of the Tamaracks
See also as HAGER, JEAN, 0060; KYLE, MARLAINE, 0080; MCALLISTER, AMANDA, 0088; STEPHENS, JEANNE, 0133

0105
OGILVIE, ELISABETH 1917-
1949 Rowan Head
1950 My World is an Island

1954 The Dawning of the Day
1956 No Evil Angel
1959 How Wide the Heart
1959 The Witch Door
1962 Call Home the Heart
1964 There May Be Heaven
1966 The Seasons Hereafter
1968 Waters on a Starry Night
1969 Bellwood
1970 The Face of Innocence
1970 A Theme for Reason
1972 Weep & Know Why
1973 Strawberries in the Sea
1974 Image of a Lover
1975 Where the Lost Aprils Are
1976 The Dreaming Swimmer
1979 A Dancer in Yellow
1980 The Devil in Tartan
1981 The Silent Ones
1981 Until the End of Summer
1983 The Road to Nowhere
1984 Jennie About to Be
1987 The Summer of the Osprey

"Tide":
1944 High Tide at Noon
1945 Storm Tide
1947 The Ebbing Tide
1978 An Answer in the Tide
Also writes for juveniles

0106
PARKER, BEATRICE 1938?-
Real name: Tom Huff
1975 Jamintha
1975 Wherever Lynn Goes
See also as HUFF, TOM, 0073; MARLOW, EDWINA, 0094; ST. CLAIR, KATHERINE, 0119; WILDE, JENNIFER, 0146

0107
PEARCE, MARY EMILY 1932- FS
1975 Jack Mercybright
1975 The Sorrowing Wind
1976 Apple Tree Lean Down
1977 Cast a Long Shadow
1980 Seedtime & Harvest
1981 The Land Endures (Sequel to Apple)
1983 Polsinney Harbour
1985 The Two Farms

0108
PEARSON, DIANE 1931- FS
1967 Bride of Tancred
1975 Csardas

1984 The Summer of the Barshinskeys
See also HISTORICAL FICTION, 1006

0109
PILCHER, ROSAMUNDE FS
England
1972 Snow in April
1973 The Empty House
1974 Another View
1974 Sleeping Tiger
1975 The Day of the Storm
1975 The End of Summer
1976 Under Gemini
1978 Wild Mountain Thyme
1987 The Shell Seekers

0110
PLAIN, BELVA 1919- FS
1978 Evergreen
1980 Random Winds
1982 Eden Burning
1984 Crescent City
1986 The Golden Cup
1988 Tapestry (Sequel to Golden)

0111
PRICE, REYNOLDS 1933- FS
1962 A Long & Happy Life
1963 The Names & Faces of Heroes (SS)
1966 A Generous Man
1968 Love & Work
1970 Permanent Errors (SS)
1975 The Surface of Earth
1981 The Source of Light
1986 Kate Vaiden
1988 Good Hearts

0112
RANDALL, RONA HR
1969 Broken Tapestry
1972 The Arrogant Duke
1974 Dragonmede
1974 The Witching Hour
1975 Watchman's Stone
1975 Mountain of Fear
1976 The Willow Herb
1977 God of Mars
1977 Lyonhorst
1978 The Eagle at the Gate
1979 The Mating Dance
1981 The Ladies of Hanover Square

Section 1 - Romances

0113
REINER, MAX 1900-1985
Real name: Janet Miriam Taylor Holland Caldwell
1941 Time No Longer
See also as CALDWELL, TAYLOR, 0025, 0896 & 0957

0114
ROCK, PHILLIP 1927- FS
1967 The Extraordinary Seaman

"Passing Bells" Trilogy:
1979 The Passing Bells
1981 Circles of Time
1985 A Future Arrived

0115
ROGERS, ROSEMARY 1932 HR
1974 Sweet Savage Love
1974 The Wildest Heart
1975 Dark Fires
1975 Dangerfield Devils
1976 Wicked Loving Lies
1982 Surrender to Love
1985 The Wanton
See also TRASH, 1146

0116
ROSS, MARILYN 1912- G
Canada
Real name: William Edward Daniel Ross
1977 Cauldron of Evil
1977 Phantom of the Snow
1977 This Evil Village
1977 This Frightened Lady
1978 Awake to Terror
1978 Dead of Winter!
1978 Horror of Fog Island
1978 Pleasure's Daughter
1978 The Twice Dead
1979 Passion Cargo

"Marilyn Ross Gothic Series"; original paperbacks published by Warner

0117
ROSS-MACDONALD, MALCOLM FS
1932-
Also writes as Malcolm Ross & Malcolm Macdonald
1962 Birds in the Sun
1975 The World from Rough Stones
1976 The Rich Are with You Always
1978 Sons of Fortune
1979 Abigail
1981 Goldeneye
1984 For They Shall Inherit
1987 The Silver Highways

0118
ROWAN, HESTER
1978 Death & the Maiden
1978 Snowfall
1979 Alpine Encounter
1980 Lunatic Fringe
1982 A Talent for Destruction
See also MYSTERIES, 0540 as RADLEY, SHEILA

0119
ST. CLAIR, KATHERINE 1938?-
Real name: Tom Huff
1975 Room beneath the Stairs
See also as HUFF, TOM, 0073; MARLOW, EDWINA, 0094; PARKER, BEATRICE, 0107; WILDE, JENNIFER, 0146

0120
SEGAL, ERICH 1937-
1970 Love Story
1976 Oliver's Story (Sequel to Love)
1980 Man, Woman & Child
1985 The Class
1988 Doctors

0121
SELLERS, CON 1922-
Also writes as Robert Crane, Lee Raintree & 42 other pseudonyms
1978 Marlee
1979 Sweet Caroline
1979 Last Flower
1979 Feed among the Lilies

0122
SETON, ANYA HR
1954 Katherine
1968 Dragonwyck
1973 Green Darkness
1975 Smouldering Fires
See also HORROR, 0214 & HISTORICAL FICTION, 0935 & 1016

0123
SHERIDAN, JANE R
1979 Damaris

1981 My Lady Hoyden
1982 Love at Sunset

0124
SIMMONS, MARY KAY   1933-   G
1970 The Hermitage
1970 The Captain's House
1971 The Year of the Rooster
1971 Megan
1972 The Diamonds of Alcazar
1972 Cameron Hill
1972 The Willow Pond
1974 The Gypsy Grove
1974 The Girl with the Key
1974 Saracen Gardens
1975 Flight from Rivers Edge
1975 Haggard's Cove
1975 The Kill Cross
1976 Smuggler's Gate
1976 The Clock Face
1976 Dark Holiday
1977 Fire in the Blood
1978 Domino
1978 With Rapture Bound

0125
SLAUGHTER, FRANK   1908-   R
Also writes as C. V. Terry
1941 That None Should Die
1943 Air Surgeon
1944 Battle Surgeon
1945 A Touch of Glory
1947 Spencer Brade, M.D.
1949 Divine Mistress
1952 East Side General
1953 Storm Haven
1955 Flight from Natchez
1955 The Healer
1957 Sword & Scalpel
1958 Daybreak
1959 Lorena
1960 Pilgrims in Paradise
1961 Epidemic!
1963 Devil's Harvest
1964 A Savage Place
1966 Surgeon, U.S.A.
1967 Doctors' Wives
1969 Surgeon's Choice
1971 Code Five
1972 Convention, M.D.
1974 Women in White
1975 The Stonewall Brigade
1976 Plague Ship
1978 Devil's Gamble
1979 The Passionate Rebel
1981 Doctor's Daughters
1983 Doctors at Risk

1984 Gospel Fever
1985 No Greater Love
1987 Transplant
Also writes religious novels
See also HISTORICAL FICTION, 1020

0126
SMALL, BERTRICE   1937-   HR
1978 The Kadin
1978 Love Wild & Fair
1980 Adora
1982 Unconquered
1983 Beloved

"O'Malley Family Saga":
1980 Skye O'Malley
1984 All The Sweet Tomorrows
1985 This Heart of Mine
1986 A Love for All Time

0127
SMITH, JOAN   1935-   HR
1977 An Affair of the Heart
1977 Aunt Sophie's Diamonds
1978 Dame Durden's Daughter
1979 Flowers of Eden
1979 Imprudent Lady
1979 Talk of the Town
1980 Aurora
1980 Babe
1980 Endure My Heart
1980 Lace for Milady
1981 The Blue Diamond
1981 Lover's Vows
1981 Perdita
1982 Love's Way
1982 The Reluctant Bride
1982 Wiles of a Stranger
1985 The Devious Duchess

0128
SMITH, WILBUR A.   1933-
1979 A Sparrow Falls

"Ballantyne Saga":
1982 Flight of the Falcon
1983 The Angels Weep
1983 Men of Men

"South Africa"
1985 The Burning Shore
1986 Power of the Sword
1987 Rage
See also HEADLINES, 0308

Section 1 - Romances

0129
SOLOMON, RUTH FREEMAN   1908-
1967 The Candlestick & the Cross
1971 The Eagle & the Dove
1974 The Ultimate Triumph
1975 Two Lives, Two Lands
1976 The Wolf & the Leopard

0130
SONDHEIM, VICTOR   FS
1981 Inheritors of the Storm

0131
STATHAM, FRANCES PATTON   1931-
1978 Flame of New Orleans
1986 To Face the Sun

0132
STEEL, DANIELLE   R
1973 Going Home
1977 Passion's Promise
1978 Now & Forever
1978 The Promise
1979 Season of Passion
1980 The Ring
1980 Summer's End
1981 Loving
1981 To Love Again
1981 Palamino
1981 Remembrance
1982 Crossings
1982 Once in a Lifetime
1982 A Perfect Stranger
1983 Changes
1983 Thurston House
1984 Full Circle
1985 Family Album
1985 Secrets
1986 Wanderlust
1987 Fine Things
1987 Kaleidoscope
1988 Star
1988 Zoya

0133
STEPHENS, JEANNE   1915-
Real name: Jean Hager
1980 Mexican Nights
1981 Wonder & Wild Desire
See also as HAGER, JEAN, 0060; KYLE, MARLAINE, 0080; MCALLISTER, AMANDA, 0088; NORTH, SARA, 0104

0134
STEWART, EDWARD   FS
1981 For Richer, for Poorer
See also HORROR, 0220 & TRASH, 1149

0135
STEWART, FRED MUSTARD   1936-   FS
1971 Lady Darlington
1973 The Mannings
1976 Six Weeks
1978 A Rage against Heaven
1981 Century
1983 Ellis Island
1985 The Titan
See also HORROR, 0221

0136
STEWART, MARY   1916-   RA
England
1956 Madam, Will You Talk?
1956 Wildfire at Midnight
1957 Thunder on the Right
1958 Nine Coaches Waiting
1960 My Brother Michael
1961 The Ivy Tree
1962 The Moonspinners
1964 This Rough Magic
1965 Airs above the Ground
1967 The Gabriel Hounds
1976 Touch Not the Cat
See also HEADLINES, 0309 & SCIENCE FICTION, 0805

0137
STUBBS, JEAN   1926-   FS
1962 The Rose Grower
1963 The Travelers
1964 Hanrahan's Colony
1966 The Straw Crown
1967 My Grand Enemy
1970 The Case of Kitty Ogilvie
1970 Eleanora Duse
1972 An Unknown Welshman
1973 Dear Laura
1974 The Painted Face
1976 The Golden Crucible
1987 A Lasting Spring

"The Howarth Family":
1979 By Our Beginnings
1981 An Imperfect Joy
1982 The Vivian Inheritance
1984 The Northern Correspondent

0138
TATTERSALL, JILL   1931-   HR
England
1965 A Summer's Cloud
1966 Enchanter's Castle
1967 The Midnight Oak
1968 Lyonesse Abbey
1969 A Time at Tarragon
1970 Lady Ingram's Room
1972 Midsummer Masque
1973 The Wild Hunt
1974 The Witches of All Saints
1976 The Shadow of Castle Fosse
1978 Dark at Noon
1978 Chanters Chase
1979 Damnation Reef

0139
TENNENBAUM, SILVIA   1928-   FS
1978 Rachel the Rabbi's Wife
1981 Yesterday's Streets

0140
THORPE, SYLVIA   R
1957 Sword of Vengeance
1964 Fair Shine the Day
1974 The Silver Nightingale
1975 The Scarlet Domino
1976 The Sword & the Shadow
1976 Golden Panther
1977 Beggar on Horseback
1977 The Reluctant Adventuress
1977 Romantic Lady
1977 The Scapegrace
1977 Tarrington Chase
1978 Beloved Rebel
1978 The Changing Tide
1978 A Flash of Scarlet
1979 The House at Bell Orchard
1980 Captain Gallant
1980 Dark Enchantress
1980 Devil's Bondman
1980 The Highwayman
1980 Varleigh Medallion

0141
TURNBULL, AGNES SLIGH   HR
1888-1982
1936 The Rolling Years
1938 Remember the End
1942 The Day Must Dawn
1947 The Bishop's Mantle
1952 The Gown of Glory
1955 The Golden Journey
1960 The Nightingale
1963 The King's Orchard

1966 The Wedding Bargain
1968 Many a Green Isle
1970 Whistle & I'll Come to You
1972 The Flowering
1974 The Richlands
1977 The Winds of Love
1980 The Two Bishops

0142
VAN SLYKE, HELEN   1919-1979   R
1971 The Rich & the Righteous
1972 All Visitors Must Be Announced
1975 The Heart Listens
1975 The Mixed Blessing
1976 The Best Place to Be
1977 Always Is Not Forever
1978 Sisters & Strangers
1979 A Necessary Woman
1980 No Love Lost
1981 The Santa Ana Wind

With ELWARD, JAMES   1928-
1982 Public Smile, Private Tears:
       The Last Novel

0143
VERRETTE, JOYCE   1939-   HR
1976 Dawn of Desire
1978 Desert Fires
1980 Sunrise of Splendor
1980 Winged Priestess
1981 Fountain of Fire
1982 Sweet Wild Wind
1984 To Love & to Conquer

0144
WALLER, LESLIE   1923-   FS
1968 The Family
1974 The Coast of Fear
1976 The Swiss Account
1977 Trocadero
1980 Blood & Dreams
1980 The Brave & the Free
1980 Hide in Plain Sight

0145
WHITNEY, PHYLLIS   1903-   G, RA
1943 Red Is for Murder
1956 The Trembling Hills
1958 The Moonflower
1960 Thunder Heights
1961 Blue Fire
1962 Window on the Square
1963 Seven Tears for Apollo
1964 Black Amber

Section 1 - Romances

1965 Sea Jade
1966 Columbella
1967 Silverhill
1968 Hunter's Green
1969 The Winter People
1970 Lost Island
1972 Listen for the Whisperer
1973 Snowfire
1974 The Turquoise Mask
1975 Spindrift
1976 The Golden Unicorn
1977 The Stone Bull
1978 The Glass Flame
1979 Domino
1980 Poinciana
1981 Vermilion
1983 Emerald
1984 Rainsong
1985 Dream of Orchids
1985 Flaming Tree
1987 Silversword
1988 Feather on the Moon

0146
WILDE, JENNIFER   1938?-   G, HR
Real name: Tom Huff
1975 Midnight at Mallyn Count
1976 Love's Tender Fury
1978 Dare to Love (Sequel to Love's)
1981 Love Me, Marietta (Sequel to Dare)
1984 When Love Commends
See also as HUFF, TOM, 0073; MARLOW, EDWINA, 0094; PARKER, BEATRICE, 0107; ST. CLAIR, KATHERINE, 0119

0147
WOODIWISS, KATHLEEN E.   HR
1972 The Flame & The Flower
1974 The Wolf & The Dove
1977 Shanna
1979 Ashes in the Wind
1984 A Rose in Winter
1985 Come Love a Stranger

0148
WRIGHT, PATRICIA   1932-
England
Also writes as Mary Napier
1976 A Space of the Heart
1977 Journey into Fire
1979 Shadow of the Rock
1980 Heart of the Storm
1981 The Storms of Fate
1982 While Paris Danced
1987 I Am England

0149
YERBY, FRANK   1916-   HR
1946 The Foxes of Harrow
1947 The Vixens
1949 Pride's Castle
1950 Floodtide
1951 A Woman Called Fancy
1952 The Saracen Blade
1953 The Devil's Laughter
1954 Bride of Liberty
1954 Benton's Row
1957 Fairoaks
1960 Gillian
1964 Old God's Laugh
1965 An Odor of Sanctity
1970 A Darkness at Ingraham's Crest: A Tale of the Slaveholding South
1972 The Girl from Storyville
1985 McKenzie's Hundred

SECTION TWO

HORROR, THE SUPERNATURAL, AND SUSPENSE

OVERVIEW

Suspense (S):

A novel or short story with elements of mystery and emphasis on twists of plot involving great danger (physical/psychological) to the protagonist and/or the protagonist's family. Plot is the most important element, and there is usually a surprise or twist in the plot at the end. In a good suspense story, the reader should not be able to predict the plot or the ending.

Horror (H):

A story whose purpose is to terrify the reader. There are several popular types of horror stories:

1. *Nature Gone Mad:*
    Natural forces rage out of control: *Blizzard* by George Stone. Animals revolt or go mad: *Cujo* by Stephen King and *Feral* by Berton Roueche.

2. *Mental Aberrations:*
    Individuals who are psychotic and dangerous rage out of control: A classic--*Dr. Jekyll & Mr. Hyde* by Robert Louis Stevenson; a contemporary--*Red Dragon* by Thomas Harris. The "Dollenganger Children" and "Casteel Family" series by V. C. Andrews are Hansel-and-Gretel tales of parents and grandparents inflicting psychological and sometimes physical abuse on their children.

Supernatural and the Occult (SN):

A story whose purpose is to terrify the reader through the use of some unexplainable element. There are many varieties:

1. *Vampires, Werewolves & Zombies:*
    Based on the traditional legends of the living dead and creatures that cannot be killed: *Salem's Lot* by Stephen King; *The Vampire Tapestry* by Suzy McKee Charnas.

2. *Paranormal Abilities:*
    Persons who have physical and mental abilities which are beyond the normal, such as ESP (extrasensory perception) and telekinesis: *Carrie* and *Firestarter* by Stephen King and the novels of John Saul.

3. *Immortality with the Help of the Devil:*
    Variations on the Faust legend, in which an individual trades his or her soul to the devil for some gift in return. A classic, *The Picture of*

Section 2 - Horror, the Supernatural, and Suspense

Dorian Grey by Oscar Wilde; a contemporary, *The Mephisto Waltz* by Fred Mustard Stewart.

4. *The Forces of Evil*:
   Variations on the power of the devil and the theme of possession by evil forces: *The Exorcist* by William Blatty; *Rosemary's Baby* by Ira Levin.

5. *Supernatural Beings*:
   Ghosts, hauntings, haunted houses: Classics, *The Turn of the Screw* by Henry James and *The Haunting of Hill House* by Shirley Jackson and the contemporary *Ghost Story* by Peter Straub.

6. *The Occult*:
   Esoteric secret rituals by secret cults; witchcraft and black magic: *Harvest Home* by Tom Tryon.

7. *Reincarnation*:
   A soul takes possession of another's body to continue to live: *The Reincarnation of Peter Proud* by Max Erhlich.

REFERENCE AND BIBLIOGRAPHIC SOURCES

Ashley, Michael. *Who's Who in Horror and Fantasy Fiction.* New York: Taplinger, 1978.

Barzon, Jacques, and Wendell H. Taylor. *A Catalog of Crime.* New York: Harper, 1971.

Bleiler, Everett Franklin, ed. *Guide to Supernatural Fiction: A Full Description of 1,775 Books from 1750-1960, Including Ghost Stories, Weird Fiction, Stories of Supernatural Horror, Fantasy, Gothic Novels, Occult Fiction, and Similar Literature.* Kent, OH: Kent State University Press, 1983.

_____. Supernatural Fiction Writers: Fantasy and Horror. New York: Scribner, 1985.

Collings, Michael R. *The Annotated Guide to Stephen King, A Primary and Secondary Bibliography of the Works of America's Premier Horror Writer.* Mercer Island, WA: Starmont House, 1986.

Fisher, Benjamin Franklin. *The Gothic's Gothic, Study Aids to the Tradition of the Tale of Terror.* New York: Garland, 1988.

Heller, Terry. *The Delights of Terror, An Aesthetics of the Tale of Terror.* Urbana: University of Illinois Press, 1987.

Schweitzer, Darrell, ed. *Discovering Modern Horror Fiction.* San Bernadino, CA: Borgo Press, 1985.

Science Fiction, Fantasy, and Horror. Oakland, CA: Locus Press, 1987. (Annual).

Tynn, Marshall B., ed. *Critical Studies in Horror Literature; A Selected Annotated Bibliography.* Mercer Island, WA: Starmont House, 1985.

_____. Horror Literature: A Core Collection and Reference Guide. New York: Bowker, 1981.

Winter, Douglas E., ed. *Shadowings, The Reader's Guide to Horror Fiction.* Mercer Island, WA: Starmont House, 1983.

Section 2 - Horror, the Supernatural, and Suspense

AUTHORS AND TITLES

0150
ADAMS, RICHARD 1920- SN
England
1980 The Girl in a Swing
See also SCIENCE FICTION, 0740 &
BRITISH AUTHORS, 1344

0151
ANDREWS, V. C. (Virginia Cleo) H
1924?-1986
1982 My Sweet Audrina

"Dollanganger Children":
1979 Flowers in the Attic
1980 Petals on the Wind
1981 If There Be Thorns
1984 Seeds of Yesterday
1987 Garden of Shadows (Prequel)

"Casteel Family":
1985 Heaven
1986 Dark Angel

0152
ANSON, JAY 1921-1980 SN
1977 The Amityville Horror (NF)
1981 666

0153
BACHMAN, RICHARD 1947-
Real name: Stephen King
1977 Rage
1979 The Long Walk
1981 Roadwork
1982 The Running Man
1984 Thinner
See also as KING, STEPHEN, 0191

0154
BAINBRIDGE, BERYL 1933-
England
1973 Harriet Said . . .
See also BRITISH AUTHORS, 1346

0155
BARKER, CLIVE 1952-
1986 The Inhuman Condition (SS)
1987 Damnation Game
1987 Weaveworld
1988 Cabal

0156
BENCHLEY, PETER 1940-
1974 Jaws
1976 The Deep
1978 Jaws 2
1979 The Island
1986 Q Clearance

0157
BLATTY, WILLIAM PETER 1928- SN
1967 Twinkle, Twinkle, Killer Kane
1971 The Exorcist
1983 The Legion

0158
BRADBURY, RAY 1920- SN
1955 The October Country (SS)
1957 Dandelion Wine
1959 A Medicine for Melancholy (SS)
1962 Something Wicked This Way
       Comes
See also SCIENCE FICTION, 0609

0159
BUCHANAN, MARIE SN
1972 Anima
1973 Unofficial Breath
1975 The Dark Backward
1977 Morgana

0160
CAMERON, JOHN SN
1972 The Astrologer

0161
CAMPBELL, RAMSEY 1946- H
1976 The Doll Who Ate His Mother
1980 The Parasite
1981 The Nameless
1982 Dark Companions (SS)
1983 The Face That Must Die
1983 Incarnate
1985 Obsession
1986 The Hungry Moon
1987 The Influence
1987 Scared Stiff

0162
CAVE, EMMA
1977 Little Angie
1979 The Blood Bond

0163
CHARNAS, SUZY McKEE   1939-   SN
1980 The Vampire Tapestry
1986 Dorthea Dreams
See also SCIENCE FICTION, 0617

0164
CLINE, C. TERRY, JR.   1935-
1975 Damon
1979 Cross Current
1979 Death Knell
1979 Mindreader
1981 Missing Persons
1985 Prey
1987 Quarry

0165
COOK, ROBIN   1931-   S
1977 Coma
1979 Sphinx
1981 Brain
1982 Fever
1984 Godplayer
1985 Mindbind
1987 Outbreak
1988 Mortal Fear
1988 Mutation

0166
COYNE, JOHN   1940-   SN
1979 The Piercing
1979 The Legacy
1980 The Searing
1981 Hobgoblin

0167
DAHL, ROALD   1916-   H
England
1953 Someone Like You
1960 Kiss, Kiss (SS)
1974 Switch Bitch (SS)
1980 My Uncle Oswald
1986 Two Fables
Also writes for juveniles

0168
DAVIES, L. P.   1914-   H, SN
England
1964 The Paper Dolls
1965 The Artificial Man
1966 Psychogeist
1966 The Lampton Dreamers
1967 The Reluctant Medium
1968 A Grave Matter
1968 Twilight Journey
1969 The White Room
1970 The Shadow Before
1973 What Did I Do Tomorrow?
1976 Possession
1979 The Land of Leys

0169
DE FELITTA, FRANK   1921-   SN
1972 For Love of Audrey Rose
1973 Oktoberfest
1976 Audrey Rose
1978 The Entity
1980 Sea Trial
1984 Golgotha Falls, an Assault on the Fourth Dimension

0170
DERLUTH, AUGUST
See as author with LOVECRAFT, H. P., 0199

0171
DU MAURIER, DAPHNE   1907-1989 SN
England
1953 Kiss Me Again, Stranger (SS)
1959 The Breaking Point (SS)
1969 The House on the Strand
1971 Don't Look Now (SS)
1977 Echoes from the Macabre (SS)
See also ROMANCES, 0041; HISTORICAL FICTION, 0969; BRITISH AUTHORS, 1357

0172
EHRLICH, MAX   1909-1983   SN
1964 Deep Is the Blue
1971 The Edict
1974 The Reincarnation of Peter Proud
1978 The Cult
1979 Reincarnation in Venice
1981 Shaitan

0173
ERICSON, ERIC
1980 The Woman Who Slept with Demons

Section 2 - Horror, the Supernatural, and Suspense

0174
FARRIS, JOHN   H
1962 The Long Light of Dawn
1967 When Michael Calls
1969 The Captors
1974 Sharp Practice
1976 The Fury
1978 All Heads Turn When the Hunt Goes By
1981 Catacombs
1982 Shatter
1982 The Uninvited
1985 Son of the Endless Night
1986 Wildwood

0175
FEELEY, PAT   1941-
1977 Best Friend

0176
FLEETWOOD, HUGH   1944-   H
England
1972 A Painter of Flowers
1973 Foreign Affairs
1973 The Girl Who Passed for Normal
1976 The Order of Death
1978 Roman Magic
1979 The Beast (SS)
1982 The Redeemer
1986 Paradise
1987 The Past

0177
FLETCHER, DAVID   1940-
1975 A Lovable Man
1975 A Respectable Woman
1985 On Suspicion

0178
GALLICO, PAUL   1897-1976
1964 The Hand of Mary Constable
Also wrote fables, humor & novels for juveniles
See also HISTORICAL FICTION, 1061

0179
GLOAG, JULIAN   1896-1981   H
England
1963 Our Mother's House
1981 Lost & Found
1985 Blood for Blood
1986 Only Yesterday

0180
GOLDMAN, WILLIAM 1931-
1976 Magic
See also SPY STORIES, 0365; SCIENCE FICTION, 0774; TRASH, 1127

0181
GORDON, RICHARD   1921-   H
1980 Jack the Ripper
Also writes the "Doctor" series

0182
GREER, BEN   1948-   H
1978 Halloween

0183
HARRIS, MARILYN   1931-   SN
1974 The Conjurers
1980 The Portent
1982 The Diviner
1987 Night Games
See also ROMANCES, 0062

0184
HARRIS, THOMAS   H
1981 Red Dragon
1988 The Silence of the Lambs (Sequel to Red)
See also HEADLINES, 0282

0185
HERZOG, ARTHUR   1927-   S
1974 The Swarm
1975 Earthsound
1976 Heat
1977 IQ 83
1977 Orca
1980 Aries Rising
1982 The Craving

0186
HINTZE, NAOMI   1909-   SN
1969 You'll Like My Mother
1971 The Stone Carnation
1972 Aloha Means Goodbye
1974 Listen, Please Listen
1975 Cry Witch

0187
HOUSEHOLD, GEOFFREY   1900-   SN
1968 Dance of the Dwarfs
1980 The Sending

1981 Summon the Bright Water
See also SPY STORIES, 0372 & SCIENCE
FICTION, 0780

0188
JACKSON, SHIRLEY   1919-1965   SN
1949 The Lottery (SS)
1959 The Haunting of Hill House
1962 We Have Always Lived in the
      Castle
See also AMERICAN AUTHORS, 1235

0189
JAMES, HENRY   1843-1916   SN
1898 The Turn of the Screw (SS)
1970 Stories of the Supernatural

0190
JOHNSON, MENDAL   1928-1976   H
1974 Let's Go Play at the Adams'

0191
KING, STEPHEN   1947-   H, SN
Also writes as Richard Bachman
1974 Carrie
1975 Salem's Lot
1977 The Shining
1978 Night Shift
1979 The Dead Zone
1980 Firestarter
1981 Cujo
1981 Danse Macabre (NF)
1982 Different Seasons (SS)
1983 Christine
1983 Pet Sematary
1984 Cycle of the Werewolf
1985 Skeleton Crew (SS)
1986 It
1987 Misery
1987 The Tommyknockers

"Dark Tower":
1988 The Gunslinger
See also as BACHMAN, RICHARD, 0153
& SCIENCE FICTION, 0783

With STRAUB, PETER
1984 The Talisman
See also STRAUB, PETER, 0225

0192
KING, TABITHA   1949-   H
1981 Small World

1983 Caretakers
1985 The Trap

0193
KONVITZ, JEFFREY   1944-   H
1974 The Sentinel

0194
KOONTZ, DEAN R.   1945-   H
Also writes as K. R. Dwyer
1970 Antiman
1970 Beastchild
1973 Demon Seed
1975 Nightmare Journey
1976 Night Chills
1977 The Vision
1980 Whispers
1983 Phantoms
1983 Shattered
1984 Darkfall
1985 The Face of Fear
1986 Strangers
1987 Watchers
1988 Lightning
Also writes science fiction

0195
KYLE, DUNCAN   1930-
Real name: John Franklin Broxholme
1976 Whiteout
See also HEADLINES, 0341

0196
LEVIN, IRA   1929-   H, SN
1967 Rosemary's Baby
1972 The Stepford Wives
See also HEADLINES, 0342 & SCIENCE
FICTION, 0674

0197
LIEBERMAN, HERBERT   1933-   H
1971 Crawlspace
1979 The Climate of Hell
1984 Nightbloom

0198
LOFTS, NORAH   1904-1983   SN
1970 The Little Wax Doll
1975 Hauntings: Is There Anybody
      There? (SS)
1978 Gad's Hall
1979 The Haunting of Gad's Hall
      (Sequel to Gad's)

Section 2 - Horror, the Supernatural, and Suspense

1982 The Claw
See also ROMANCES, 0084 & HISTORICAL FICTION, 0994

0199
LOVECRAFT, H. P. (Howard Phillips)   H
1890-1937
1927 The Case of Charles Dexter Ward
1955 The Dream-Quest of Unknown Kadath (SS)
1965 Dagon & Other Macabre Tales
1971 The Doom That Came to Sarnath

With DERLETH, AUGUST:
1926 The Lurking Fear
1945 The Lurker at the Threshold
1959 The Shuttered Room & Other
1963 The Dunwich Horror
1964 Colour Out of Space
1964 At the Mountains of Madness (SS) (ed. by Derleth)
1968 Shadow Out of Time (SS)
1969 The Tomb

"The Cthulhu Mythos":
1943 Fungi from Yuggoth & Other Poems
1969 Tales of the Cthulhu Mythos, Vols. I & II
1972 The Spawn of Cthulhu

0200
McEWAN, IAN   1948-
1975 First Love, Last Rites (SS)
1978 The Cement Garden
1978 In Between the Sheets (SS)
1981 The Comfort of Strangers
1987 The Child in Time

0201
McGIVERN, WILLIAM   1922-1982
1973 Reprisal
1974 Night of the Juggler
1982 Summitt
Also writes mysteries

0202
MARASCO, ROBERT   SN
1973 Burnt Offerings
1979 Parlor Games

0203
MARLOWE, DEREK   1938-
England

1976 Nightshade
See also SPY STORIES, 0379

0204
MARLOWE, STEPHEN   1928-
Real name: Milton Lesser
1976 Translation
See also HEADLINES, 0295 & 0344

0205
MATHESON, RICHARD   1926-   H
1954 Fury on Sunday
1954 I Am Legend
1971 Hell House

0206
MICHAELS, BARBARA   1927-   SN
Real name: Barbara Gross Mertz
1968 Ammie, Come Home
1969 Prince of Darkness
1970 The Dark on the Other Side
1971 The Crying Child
1973 Witch
1974 House of Many Shadows
1979 The Walker in the Shadows
1980 The Wizard's Daughter
1981 Someone in the House
1983 Here I Stay
1984 The Grey Beginning
1985 Be Buried in the Rain
1986 Shattered Silk
See also ROMANCES, 0102 & MYSTERIES, 0531 as PETERS, ELIZABETH

0207
RACINA, THOM   1946-
1977 The Great Los Angeles Blizzard

0208
RICE, ANNE   1941-   H
Also writes as Anne Rampling
"Chronicles of the Vampires":
1976 Interviews with the Vampire
1985 The Vampire Lestat
1988 The Queen of the Damned
See also AMERICAN AUTHORS, 1298

0209
RICE, JEFF   H
1973 The Night Stalker
1974 The Night Strangler

0210
ROUECHE, BERTON 1911- H
1974 Feral
1977 Fago

0211
SAMSON, JOAN 1937-1976 H
1975 The Auctioneer

0212
SAUL, JOHN 1942- H
1977 Suffer the Children
1978 Punish the Sinners
1978 The Birds of Prey
1980 Comes the Blind Fury
1981 When the Wind Blows
1985 Brainchild

0213
SELTZER, DAVID 1920?- SN
1976 The Omen
1979 Prophecy

0214
SETON, ANYA SN
1973 Green Darkness
See also ROMANCES, 0122 &
HISTORICAL FICTION, 0935 & 1016

0215
SHELLEY, MARY 1797-1851 H
Wollstonecroft, England
1818 Frankenstein

0216
SMITH, MARTIN CRUZ 1942- H
1977 Nightwing
See also MYSTERIES, 0558 & HISTORICAL FICTION, 1099

0217
STANWOOD, BROOKS 1937-
1979 The Glow
1982 The Seventh Child

0218
STEIN, SOL 1926- H
1975 The Childkeeper
1979 Other People
1980 The Resort

0219
STEVENSON, ROBERT LOUIS 1850-1894
1886 Dr. Jekyll & Mr. Hyde
1895 The Body Snatcher

0220
STEWART, EDWARD
1980 The Great Los Angeles Fire
See also ROMANCES, 0134 & TRASH, 1149

0221
STEWART, FRED MUSTARD 1936- SN
1969 The Mephisto Waltz
1970 The Methuselah Enzyme
1974 Star Child
See also ROMANCES, 0135

0222
STEWART, RAMONA 1922- SN
1970 The Possession of Joel Delaney
1979 Sixth Sense

0223
STOKER, BRAM 1847-1912 SN
Ireland
1897 Dracula

0224
STONE, GEORGE
1977 Blizzard

0225
STRAUB, PETER 1943- SN
1975 Julia
1979 Ghost Story
1980 Shadowland
1983 Floating Dragon
1984 Wild Animals (includes Julia)
1988 Koko

With KING, STEPHEN
1984 The Talisman
See also KING, STEPHEN, 0191

0226
TRYON, TOM 1926- SN
1971 The Other
1973 Harvest Home
See also TRASH, 1153

0227
WILDE, OSCAR   1854-1900
Ireland/England
1891 The Picture of Dorian Gray

0228
WOOD, BARI   1936-   SN
1975 The Killing Gift
1981 The Tribe
1984 Lightsource
1987 Amy Girl
See also TRASH, 1158

SECTION THREE

"BEHIND THE HEADLINES" NOVELS

OVERVIEW

"Behind the headlines" novels are often called thrillers, because they contain elements of adventure, are based on a "what if?" premise, and contain plots which could be based on the headlines of the day. This genre is not as popular as it once was because it has become difficult for writers to match the reality of the news. Often the plot involves a government, and most involve the governments of several countries. The plots are the most important element of these novels and often are quite ingenious with a constant buildup of suspense.

There are several types:

Crisis in the U.S. Government:

These started in the late 1950s with plots of political infighting between President and legislature (the novels of Allen Drury), Americans interfering in foreign governments (*The Ugly American* by William Lederer and Eugene Burdick), plots by the military to take over the U. S. government (*Seven Days in May* by Fletcher Knebel and C. Bailey), and possible nuclear mistakes (*Fail Safe* by Eugene Burdick). These kinds of stories are not written as much today.

International Incidents & Intrigue:

In these adventure stories, the protagonist is almost always a male with no governmental connection, who by chance becomes involved in an international intrigue. These works always take place in an exotic location, primarily in Europe, and the plots often involve Communist governments. Terrorism has become a major plot. An early example is *The Day of the Jackel* by Frederick Forsyth.

Best known authors: Robert Ludlum, Helen MacInnes.

World War II Twists: What If ?:

These stories are based on the premise, "what if?": What if Churchill was assassinated? (*The Eagle Has Landed* by Jack Higgins.) What if England lost the war? (*SS-GB* by Len Deighton.) Very popular plots deal with the Nazis and Nazis still alive and functioning (*The Boys from Brazil* by Ira Levin and *The Odessa File* by Frederick Forsyth).

Adventure in Nature:

Primarily oriented to male readers, these stories pit a group of men against overwhelming odds of nature; e.g., a ship wreck in a storm, Arctic exploration.

Section 3 - "Behind The Headlines" Novels

Best known authors: Hammond Innes, Alistair MacLean.

High Finance:

These stories are based on the manipulation of the money supply, the stock market and/or on the manipulation of a commodity.

Best known author: Paul Erdman (*The Panic of '89*).

REFERENCE AND BIBLIOGRAPHIC SOURCES

Cawelti, John G. *Adventure, Mystery, and Romance: Formula Stories as Art and Popular Culture.* Chicago: University of Chicago Press, 1976.

Hagen, Ordian A. *Who Done It?: A Guide to Detective, Mystery and Suspense Fiction.* New York: Bowker, 1969.

McCormick, Donald, *Who's Who in Spy Fiction.* New York: Taplinger, 1977.

Palmer, Jerry. *Thrillers: Genesis and Structure of a Popular Genre.* New York: St. Martin's Press, 1979.

Rully, John M., ed. *Twentieth Century Crime and Mystery Writers.* New York: St. Martin's Press, 1980.

Skene-Melvin, David, and Ann Skene-Melvin, comps. *Crime, Detective, Espionage, Mystery, and Thriller Fiction and Film: A Comprehensive Bibliography of Critical Writing through 1979.* Westport, CT: Greenwood Press, 1980.

AUTHORS AND TITLES

A. CRISIS IN THE U.S. GOVERNMENT

0229
ANDERSON, PATRICK   1936-
1970 The Approach to Kings
1974 Actions & Passions
1976 The President's Mistress
1978 First Family
1986 Sinister Forces
Also writes nonfiction

0230
ARCHER, JEFFREY   1940-
England
1977 Shall We Tell the President?
1982 The Prodigal Daughter
See also INTERNATIONAL INCIDENTS, 0260 & ROMANCES, 0004

0231
BAILEY, C.
See as Jt. author with KNEBEL, FLETCHER, 0242

0232
BURDICK, EUGENE   1918-1965
1964 The 480
See also LEDERER, WILLIAM & BURDICK, EUGENE, 0244

With WHEELER, HARVEY 1918-
1962 Fail Safe

0233
COHEN, WILLIAM S.
See as Jt. author with HART, GARY, 0238

0234
CONDON, RICHARD   1915-
1959 The Manchurian Candidate
1974 Winter Kills
1976 The Whisper of the Axe

1978 Death of a Politician
See also AMERICAN AUTHORS, 1188

0235
DE BORCHGRAVE, ARNAUD   1926- & MOSS, ROBERT   1942-
1980 The Spike
1983 Monimbo
See also MOSS, ROBERT, 0297

0236
DRURY, ALLEN   1918-
1959 Advise & Consent
1962 A Shade of Difference
1966 Capable of Honor
1968 Preserve & Protect
1971 The Throne of Saturn
1973 Come Ninevah, Come Tyre
1975 The Promise of Joy
1977 Anna Hastings
1979 Mark Coffin, U.S.S.
1981 The Hill of Summer
1983 Decision
1984 The Roads of Earth
1986 Pentagon
See also HISTORICAL FICTION, 0968

0237
EHRLICHMAN, JOHN   1925-
1976 The Company
1979 The Whole Truth
1986 The China Card

0238
HART, GARY   1936-
1987 The Strategies of Zeus

With COHEN, WILLIAM S.
1985 The Double Man

0239
HIGGINS, GEORGE V.   1939-
1975 A City on a Hill
1982 The Patriot Game
See also MYSTERIES, 0472 & AMERICAN AUTHORS, 1228

0240
HOWAR, BARBARA   1934-
1973 Laughing All the Way
1976 Making Ends Meet

Section 3 - "Behind The Headlines" Novels

0241
KALB, MARVIN 1930- & KOPPEL, TED 1940-
1977 In the National Interest
See also INTERNATIONAL INCIDENTS, 0287

0242
KNEBEL, FLETCHER 1911-
1965 Night of Camp David
1966 The Zinzin Road
1968 Vanished . . .
1969 Trespass
1972 Dark Horse
1978 Dave Sulkin Cares
See also INTERNATIONAL INCIDENTS, 0288

With BAILEY, C.
1962 Seven Days in May
1964 Convention

0243
KOPPEL, TED 1940-
See as Jt. author with KALB, MARVIN, 0241

0244
LEDERER, WILLIAM 1912- & BURDICK, EUGENE 1918-1965
1958 The Ugly American
See also BURDICK, EUGENE, 0232

0245
LUDLUM, ROBERT 1927-
1972 The Chancellor Manuscript
See also INTERNATIONAL INCIDENTS, 0291 & WW II TWISTS, 0343

0246
MCCARRY, CHARLES 1930-
1975 The Tears of Autumn
See also SPY STORIES, 0378

0247
MOSS, ROBERT 1942-
See as Jt. author with DE BORCHGRAVE, ARNAUD, 0235
See also INTERNATIONAL INCIDENTS, 0297

0248
NESSEN, RON 1934-
1979 The First Lady

0249
PEARSON, DREW 1897-1969
1968 The Senator
1970 The President

0250
SAFIRE, WILLIAM 1929-
1977 Full Disclosure
Best known for nonfiction, e.g., On Language, 1980.

0251
SANDERS, LAWRENCE 1920-
1984 The Passion of Molly T.
See also INTERNATIONAL INCIDENTS, 0303 & MYSTERIES, 0549

0252
SERLING, ROBERT 1918-
1967 The President's Plane Is Missing
1978 Wings

0253
STOVALL, WALTER
1978 Presidential Emergency
1980 The Minus Pool

0254
WALLACE, IRVING 1916-
1964 The Man
1976 The R Document
1980 The Second Lady
1982 The Almighty
See also WW II TWISTS, 0350 & TRASH, 1155

0255
WHEELER, HARVEY 1918-
See as Jt. author with BURDICK, EUGENE, 0232

0256
WHITTEN, LES 1928-
1976 Conflict of Interest
1979 Washington Cycle
1985 A Day without Sunshine

B. INTERNATIONAL INCIDENTS & INTRIGUE

0257
ALBERT, MARVIN H.
1961 Clayburn
1975 The Gargoyle Conspiracy
1978 The Dark Goddess
1981 Hidden Lives
1982 The Medusa Complex
See also WW II TWISTS, 0318

0258
ALDRIDGE, JAMES   1918-
1962 A Captive in the Land
1974 Mockery in Arms

0259
ANTHONY, EVELYN   1928-
England
Real name: Evelyn Bridget Patricia Ward-Thomas; also writes as Anthony Evelyn
1968 The Rendezvous
1969 The Legend
1970 The Assassin
1971 The Tamarind Seed
1972 The Pollenberg Inheritance
1973 Stranger at the Gates
1974 Mission to Malaspiga
1975 The Persian Price
1977 The Silver Falcon
1978 The Return
1979 The Grave of Truth
1980 The Janus Imperative
1985 Voices on the Wind
1987 A Place to Hide
See also SPY STORIES, 0353 & HISTORICAL FICTION, 0950

0260
England
ARCHER, JEFFRY
1976 Not a Penny More, Not a Penny Less
1984 First among Equals
1986 A Matter of Honor
See also CRISIS IN THE U.S. GOVERNMENT, 0230 & ROMANCES, 0004

0261
BULLIET, RICHARD   1940-
1975 The Camel & the Wheel
1979 The Tomb of the Twelfth Iman

1984 The Gulf Scenario

0262
CANNING, VICTOR   1911-1986
England
Also writes as Alan Gould
1947 The Chasm
1948 Panther's Moon
1949 The Golden Salamander
1950 Bird of Prey
1950 Forest of Eyes
1952 The House of the Seven Flies
1954 A Handful of Silver
1954 The Man from the "Turkish Slave"
1955 Twist of the Knife
1956 Burden of Proof
1957 The Manasco Road
1958 The Dragon Tree
1960 The Burning Eye
1961 A Delivery of Furies
1963 Black Flamingo
1963 The Limbo Line
1964 The Scorpio Letters
1970 Queen's Pawn
1971 The Great Affair
1972 Firecrest
1973 The Rainbird Pattern
1974 The Finger of Saturn
1975 The Mask of Memory
1976 The Doomsday Carrier
1979 Birdcage
1979 The Satan Sampler
1981 Memory Boy
1983 Vanishing Point
1985 Birds of a Feather
See also WW II TWISTS, 0323; MYSTERIES, 0411; SCIENCE FICTION, 0752

0263
CARROLL, JAMES   1943?-
1976 Madonna Red
See also AMERICAN AUTHORS, 1185

0264
CLANCY, TOM   1923-
1984 The Hunt for Red October
1986 Red Storm Rising
1987 Patriot Games
1988 The Cardinal of the Kremlin

0265
CLAVELL, JAMES   1924-
1981 Noble House
1986 Whirlwind

Section 3 - "Behind The Headlines" Novels

See also HISTORICAL FICTION, 0959 & 1041

0266
COLLINS, LARRY 1929- &
LAPIERRE, DOMINIQUE 1931-
1980 The Fifth Horseman
Also write nonfiction, e.g., Is Paris Burning?
See also WW II TWISTS, 0327 & HISTORICAL FICTION, 1043

0267
COPPEL, ALFRED 1921-
Also writes as Robert Cham Gilman & A. C. Marin
1977 The Dragon
1980 The Hastings Conspiracy
1981 The Apocalypse Brigade
1983 The Burning Mountain
1987 Show Me a Hero
1988 A Land of Mirrors

0268
CORLEY, EDWIN 1931-1981
1970 The Jesus Factor
1977 Sargasso
1978 Air Force One
1980 The Genesis Rock

0269
CRICHTON, MICHAEL 1942-
1976 Eaters of the Dead
1980 Congo
See also SCIENCE FICTION, 0622 & HISTORICAL FICTION, 0902

0270
CUSSLER, CLIVE 1931-
1973 The Mediterranean Caper
1975 Iceberg
1978 Vixen 03
1981 Night Probe!
1982 Pacific Vortex!
1984 Deep Six

"Dirk Pitt":
1976 Raise the Titanic!
1986 Cyclops
1988 Treasure

0271
DAVIDSON, LIONEL 1922-
1961 The Night of Wenceslas
1962 The Rose of Tibet
1967 The Menorah Men
1971 Smith's Gazelle
1976 The Sun Chemist

0272
DEMILLE, NELSON 1943-
Real name: Leonard Jordan
1978 By the Rivers of Babylon
1981 Cathedral
1988 The Charm School

0273
EGLETON, CLIVE 1927-
England
1970 A Piece of Resistance
1971 Last Post for a Partisan (Sequel to Piece)
1972 The Judas Mandate
1973 Seven Days to a Killing
1974 The October Plot
1975 Skirmish
1978 The Mills Bomb
1979 Backfire
1981 The Eisenhower Deception
1982 The Russian Enigma
1983 A Conflict of Interest
1984 Troika
1985 A Different Drummer
1988 Missing from the Record
See also WW II TWISTS, 0329

0274
ERDMAN, PAUL E. 1932-
1973 The Billion Dollar Sure Thing
1974 The Silver Bears
1976 The Crash of 79
1981 The Last Days of America
1986 The Panic of '89

0275
FOLLETT, KEN 1949-
England
1979 Triple
1982 The Man from St. Petersburg (WW I)
1986 Lie Down with Lions
See also WW II TWISTS, 0330

0276
FORBES, COLIN 1923-
Real name: Raymond H. Sawkins
1973 Target Five

1974 Year of the Golden Ape
1975 The Stone Leopard
1977 Avalanche Express
1982 The Stockholm Syndicate
1984 Terminal
1986 Cover Story
1988 The Janus Man
See also HISTORICAL FICTION, 0972 & 1056

0277
FORSYTH, FREDERICK 1938-
1971 The Day of the Jackal
1974 The Dogs of War
1980 The Devil's Alternative
1984 The Fourth Protocol
See also WW II TWISTS, 0331

0278
FRANK, PAT 1907-1964
1946 Mr. Adam
1948 An Affair of State
1952 Hold Back the Night
1956 Forbidden Area
1959 Alas, Babylon

0279
FREEMANTLE, BRIAN 1936-
1976 The Man Who Wanted Tomorrow
1986 Dirty White
See also SPY STORIES, 0362

0280
GERSON, NOEL B. 1914-
1976 Neptune
1976 Special Agent
1977 The Smugglers
See also HISTORICAL FICTION, 0910 & 0978

0281
HACKETT, JOHN (SIR) 1910-
England
1979 The Third World War: August 1985

0282
HARRIS, THOMAS 1940?-
1975 Black Sunday
See also HORROR, 0184

0283
HIGGINS, JACK 1929-
Real name: Henry Patterson;
also writes as Hugh Marlowe
1971 Night Judgment at Sinos
1972 The Savage Day
1973 A Prayer for the Dying
1981 Solo
1982 Touch the Devil
1984 Exocet
1985 Confessional
See also WW II TWISTS, 0335; WW II TWISTS, 0346 as PATTERSON, HARRY

0284
HUNTER, STEPHEN 1946-
1982 The Second Saladin
See also WW II TWISTS, 0337

0285
HYDE, ANTHONY
1985 The Red Fox

0286
INNES, RALPH HAMMOND 1913-
Also writes as Ralph Hammond & Hammond Innes
1947 Fire in the Snow
1948 The Blue Ice
1949 The Survivors
1954 The Naked Land
1958 The Land God Gave to Cain
1960 The Doomed Oasis
1962 Atlantic Fury
1965 The Strode Venturer
1971 Levkas Man
1973 The Golden Soak
1975 North Star
1977 The Big Footprints
1980 Solomon's Seal
1983 The Black Tide
1985 High Stand
Also writes pure adventure, e.g.
The Wreck of the Mary Deare, 1956

0287
KALB, BERNARD 1932- &
KALB, MARVIN 1930-
1981 The Last Ambassador
See also KALB, MARVIN, 0241

0288
KNEBEL, FLETCHER 1911-
1974 The Bottom Line
1981 Crossing in Berlin
1983 Poker Game

Section 3 - "Behind The Headlines" Novels   43

1986 Sabotage
See also CRISIS IN U.S. GOVERNMENT,
0242

0289
LAPIERRE, DOMINIQUE
See as Jt. author with COLLINS, LARRY,
0266

0290
LOURIE, RICHARD   1937-
1985 First Loyalty
1987 Zero Gravity

0291
LUDLUM, ROBERT   1927-
1973 The Matlock Paper
1976 The Gemini Contenders
1978 The Holcroft Covenant
1979 The Matarese Circle
1982 The Parsifal Mosaic
1984 The Aquitaine Progression
1988 The Icarus Agenda

"Jason Bourne":
1980 The Bourne Identity
1986 The Bourne Supremacy
See also CRISIS IN U.S. GOVERNMENT,
0245 & WW II TWISTS, 0343

0292
MACINNES, HELEN   1907-1985
1941 Above Suspicion
1942 Assignment in Brittany
1944 While Still We Live
1945 Horizon
1949 Rest & Be Thankful
1951 Neither Five Nor Three
1953 I & My True Love
1955 Pray for a Brave Heart
1958 North from Rome
1960 Decision at Delphi
1963 The Venetian Affair
1964 Home Is the Hunter
1966 The Double Image
1968 The Salzburg Connection
1971 Message from Malaga
1974 The Snare of the Hunter
1976 Agent in Place
1978 Prelude to Terror
1980 The Hidden Target
1982 Cloak of Darkness
1984 Ride a Pale Horse

0293
MACLEAN, ALISTAIR   1922-1987
Scotland
Also wrote mysteries as Ian Stuart
1958 South by Java Head
1959 The Secret Ways
1960 Night without End
1961 Fear Is the Key
1962 The Golden Rendezvous
1963 Ice Station Zebra
1966 When Eight Bells Toll
1969 Puppet on a Chain
1970 Caravan to Vaccares
1971 Bear Island
1973 The Way to Dusty Death
1974 Breakheart Pass
1975 Circus
1976 The Golden Gate
1977 Seawitch
1978 Goodbye California
1980 Athabasca
1981 River of Death
1984 Floodgate
1985 San Andreas
1986 The Lonely Sea (SS)
1987 Santorini
See also HISTORICAL FICTION, 1085

0294
MALING, ARTHUR   1923-
1969 Decoy
1970 Go-Between
1971 Loophole
1973 The Snowman
1974 Dingdong
1975 Bent Man
1976 Ripoff
1977 Schroeder's Game
1978 Lucky Devil
1979 The Koberg Link
1979 The Rheingold Route
1981 From Thunder Bay
1983 A Taste of Treason
See also MYSTERIES, 0511

0295
MARLOWE, STEPHEN
Real name: Milton Lesser
1968 Come Over, Red Rover
1970 The Summit
1974 The Man with No Shadow
1981 1956
See also WW II TWISTS, 0344 &
HORROR, 0204

0296
MORRELL, DAVID   1943-
1972 First Blood
1984 The Brotherhood of the Rose
1985 Fraternity of the Stone
1985 Rambo
1987 The League of Night & Fog

0297
MOSS, ROBERT   1942-
1981 Death Beam
1985 Moscow Rules
1987 Carnival of Spies
See also as Jt. author with DE
BORCHGRAVE, ARNAUD, 0235

0298
PATTERSON, JAMES   1935-
1976 The Thomas Berryman Number
1978 The Season of the Machete
1979 The Jericho Commandment
1980 Virgin

0299
PILHES, RENE VICTOR
1975 Ultimatum
1978 The Provacateur

0300
RATHBONE, JULIAN   1935-
England
1986 Lying in State
See also MYSTERIES, 0541

0301
ROHMER, RICHARD   1924-
Canada
1980 Periscope Red

0302
ROYCE, KENNETH   1920-
England
Real name: Kenneth Royce Gandley;
also writes as Oliver Jacks
1974 The Woodcutter Operation
1976 Bustillo
1980 The Third Arm
1981 10,000 Days
1988 Patriots
See also WW II TWISTS, 0347 &
MYSTERIES, 0547

0303
SANDERS, LAWRENCE   1920-
1970 The Anderson Tapes
1971 The Pleasures of Helen
1975 The Tomorrow File
1976 The Tangent Objective
1977 The Marlow Chronicles
1978 The Tangent Factor
1986 The Loves of Harry Dancer
See also CRISIS IN THE U.S.
GOVERNMENT, 0251 & MYSTERIES, 0549

0304
SEYMOUR, GERALD   1941-
1976 Harry's Game
1976 The Glory Boys
1978 Kingfisher
1980 The Harrison Affair
1981 The Contract
1982 Archangel
1984 In Honor Bound
1986 A Song in the Morning
1988 An Eye for an Eye

0305
SHELDON, SIDNEY   1917-
1987 Windmills of the Gods
See also TRASH, 1147

0306
SHUTE, NEVIL   1899-1960
1957 On the Beach

0307
SLOAN, JAMES P.
1972 The Case History of Comrade V
1987 The Last Cold-War Cowboy

0308
SMITH, WILBUR A.   1933-
South Africa
1964 When the Lion Feeds
1965 The Train from Katanga
1966 The Roar of Thunder
1968 Shout at the Devil
1970 Gold Mine
1972 The Diamond Hunters
1973 The Sunbird
1974 Eagle in the Sky
1976 The Eye of the Tiger
1977 Cry Wolf
1978 Hungry as the Sea
1981 The Delta Decision
1984 The Leopard Hunts in Darkness

Section 3 - "Behind The Headlines" Novels   45

See also ROMANCES, 0128

0309
STEWART, MARY   1916-
England
Also writes as Florence Elinor
1956 Madam, Will You Talk?
1956 Wildfire at Midnight
1958 Thunder on the Right
1959 Nine Coaches Waiting
1960 My Brother Michael
1963 The Moonspinners
1964 This Rough Magic
1965 Airs above the Ground
1967 The Gabriel Hounds
See also ROMANCES, 0136 & SCIENCE FICTION, 0805

0310
THOMAS, CRAIG   1942-
Also writes as David Grant
1978 Wolfsbane
1980 Snow Falcon
1981 Sea Leopard
1982 Jade Tiger
1985 Lion's Run
See also SPY STORIES, 0385

0311
THOMAS, MICHAEL M.   1936?-
1980 Green Monday
1982 Someone Else's Money
1985 Hard Money
1987 The Ropespinner Conspiracy

0312
THOMPSON, ANNE ARMSTRONG   1939-
1974 The Swiss Legacy
1975 Message from Absalom
1978 The Romanov Ransom

0313
URIS, LEON   1924-
1967 Topaz
1984 The Haj
See also HISTORICAL FICTION, 1026 & 1102

0314
VAN GREENAWAY, PETER   1929-
1972 The Judas Gospel
1973 The Medusa Touch
1988 The Killing Cup

0315
WAGER, WALTER   1924-
1971 Viper Three
1972 Swap
1975 Telefon
1977 Time of Reckoning
1987 58 Minutes
See also MYSTERIES, 0574

0316
WEST, MORRIS   1916-
1959 The Devil's Advocate
1961 Daughter of Silence
1963 The Shoes of the Fisherman
1965 The Ambassador
1967 The Tower of Babel
1974 Harlequin
1975 The Salamander
1976 The Navigator
1979 Proteus
1981 The Clowns of God
1987 Cassidy

0317
WILLIAMS, ALAN   1933-
1973 The Beria Papers
1976 A Bullet for the Shah (Shah-mak)
1979 The Widow's War

C. WORLD WAR II TWISTS: WHAT IF?

0318
ALBERT, MARVIN H.
1983 Operation Lila
See also INTERNATIONAL INCIDENTS, 0257

0319
BARAK, MICHAEL   1938-
Israel
Real name: Michael Bar-Zohar
1976 The Secret List of Heinrich Roehm
1978 The Enigma
1980 The Phantom Conspiracy
See also WORLD AUTHORS, 1405

0320
BARWICK, JAMES
1978 Shadow of the Wolf
1981 The Hangman's Crusade
1986 The Devil at the Crossroads

0321
BUCHHEIM, LOTHAR-GUENTHER 1918-
Germany
1975 The Boat
1978 The U-Boat War
See also WORLD AUTHORS, 1450

0322
BURGER, NEAL
See as Jt. author with SIMPSON, GEORGE, 0349

0323
CANNING, VICTOR 1911-
England
Also writes as Alan Gould
1965 The Whip Hand
See also INTERNATIONAL INCIDENTS, 0262; MYSTERIES, 0411; SCIENCE FICTION, 0752

0324
CHALKER, JACK L. 1944-
1976 A Jungle of Stars
1978 Dancers in the Afterglow
1979 And the Devil Will Drag You Under
1981 The Devil's Voyage

0325
CHEVALIER, PAUL 1925-
1980 The Grudge

0326
CLIVE, JOHN
1980 The Last Liberator
See also as Jt. author with CLIVE, JOHN, 0334

0327
COLLINS, LARRY 1929-
1985 Fall from Grace
See also INTERNATIONAL INCIDENTS, 0266 & HISTORICAL FICTION, 1043

0328
DEIGHTON, LEN 1929-
England
1970 Bomber
1979 SS-GB: Nazi-Occupied Britain 1941
1981 XPD

1982 Goodbye Mickey Mouse
See also SPY STORIES, 0359 & HISTORICAL FICTION, 1047

0329
EGLETON, CLIVE 1927-
England
1974 The Bormann Brief

See also INTERNATIONAL INCIDENTS, 0273

0330
FOLLETT, KEN 1949-
1978 The Eye of the Needle
1979 Triple
1980 The Key to Rebecca
See also INTERNATIONAL INCIDENTS, 0275

0331
FORSYTH, FREDERICK 1938-
1972 The Odessa File
1976 The Shepherd
1980 The Devil's Alternative
1982 No Comebacks (SS)
See also INTERNATIONAL INCIDENTS, 0277

0332
GARFIELD, BRIAN 1939-
Also writes as Frank Wynne & Frank O'Brian
1969 Thousand Mile War
1970 Sliphammer
1970 The Hit
1971 Sweeny's Honor
1972 Line of Succession
1974 Kolchak's Gold
1974 The Romanov Succession
1980 The Paladin
See also MYSTERIES, 0452 & WESTERNS, 0844

0333
GIFFORD, THOMAS 1937-
1974 Benchwarmer Bob
1975 The Wind-Chill Factor
1977 The Man from Lisbon
1978 The Glendower Legacy
1979 Hollywood Gothic

Section 3 - "Behind The Headlines" Novels   47

0334
GILMAN, J. D.   1920-   &
CLIVE, JOHN   1933-
1977   KG 200
See also CLIVE, JOHN, 0326

0335
HIGGINS, JACK   1929-
Real name: Henry Patterson
1975   The Eagle Has Landed
1976   Storm Warning
1981   Luciano's Luck
1987   Night of the Fox
See also INTERNATIONAL INCIDENTS, 0283 & in WW II TWISTS, 0346 as PATTERSON, HARRY,

0336
HITCHCOCK, RAYMOND   1922-
1979   Attack the Lusitania!
1980   The Canaris Legacy

0337
HUNTER, STEPHEN   1946-
1980   The Master Sniper
See also INTERNATIONAL INCIDENTS, 0284

0338
KANFER, STEFAN   1933-
1981   Fear Itself
1978   The Eighth Sin

0339
KELLY, JOHN
1976   The Wooden Wolf

0340
KLEIN, EDWARD   1936-
1981   The Parachutists

0341
KYLE, DUNCAN   1930-
Real name: John Franklin Broxholme
1978   Black Camelot
1981   Stalking Point
See also HORROR, 0195

0342
LEVIN, IRA   1929-
1976   The Boys from Brazil

See also HORROR, 0196 & SCIENCE FICTION, 0674

0343
LUDLUM, ROBERT   1927-
1971   The Scarlatti Inheritance
1974   The Rhinemann Exchange
1978   The Holcroft Covenant
See also CRISIS IN U.S. GOVERNMENT, 0245 & INTERNATIONAL INCIDENTS, 0291

0344
MARLOWE, STEPHEN   1928-
Real name: Milton Lesser
1978   The Valkyrie Encounter

See also INTERNATIONAL INCIDENTS, 0295 & HORROR, 0204

0345
MORGULAS, JERROLD   1934-
1980   The Torquemada Principle
1981   Scorpion East

0346
PATTERSON, HARRY   1929-
Real Name: Henry Patterson; also writes as Jack Higgins & Hugh Marlowe
1978   The Valhalla Exchange
1979   To Catch a King
See also in INTERNATIONAL INCIDENTS, 0283; WW II TWISTS, 0335 as HIGGINS, JACK

0347
ROYCE, KENNETH   1920-
England
Real name: Kenneth Royce Gandley; also writes as Oliver Jacks
1982   Channel Assault
See also INTERNATIONAL INCIDENTS, 0302 & MYSTERIES, 0547

0348
SHAGAN, STEVE   1927-
1980   The Formula
1984   The Discovery

0349
SIMPSON, GEORGE   1944-   &
BURGER, NEAL
1975   Ghostboat

0350
WALLACE, IRVING   1916-
1986 The Seventh Secret
See also CRISIS IN U.S. GOVERNMENT,
0254 & TRASH, 1155

0351
WESTHEIMER, DAVID   1917-
1971 Lighter than a Feather
See also HISTORICAL FICTION, 1104

SECTION FOUR

SPY STORIES

OVERVIEW

In spy stories, adventure combined with intellectual puzzle is the focus. These are the stories of men and women who work as professional spies for governmental intelligence agencies, especially British Intelligence (M15, M16) and the C.I.A. Often the plot turns on finding a "mole" (a double agent hidden in the intelligence of one country by the intelligence of another country) or helping agents defect.

Best known authors: The classic author is Graham Greene, especially in such novels as *The Confidential Agent* and *The Third Man*. Among the best known of the contemporary authors of spy stories is John LeCarre, whose most famous agent is George Smiley of British Intelligence.

Well-known British Agents:

Author:	Agent:
Ambler, Eric	Arthur Abdel Simpson
Anthony, Evelyn	Davina Graham
Coles, Manning	Tommy Hambledon
Creasy, John	Dr. Palfrey, Z5
Deighton, Len	Harry Palmer
	Bernard Samson
Fleming, Ian/Gardner, John	James Bond, 007
Hall, Adam	Quiller
Le Carré, John	George Smiley
Perry, Ritche	Philis, SR (2)
Trevanian	Dr. Jonathan Hemlock

Well-known American Agents:

Buckley, William F.	Blackford Oakes, C.I.A.
Freemantle, Brian	Charlie Muffin
Gilman, Dorothy	Mrs. Pollifax
Granger, Bill	Devereaux, Code Name-November
Thomas, Craig	Gant--Firefox

REFERENCE AND BIBLIOGRAPHIC SOURCES

Atkins, John Alfred. *The British Spy Novel, Styles in Treachery*. New York: Riverrun Press, 1984.

Cawelti, John G. *The Spy Story*. Chicago: University of Chicago Press, 1987.

Dover, J. Kenneth. *Murder in the Millions: Erle Stanley Gardner, Mickey Spillane, Ian Fleming.* New York: Ungar, 1984.

East, Andy. *The Cold War File.* Metuchen, NJ: Scarecrow Press, 1983.

Keating, H.R.F. *Whodunit? A Guide to Crime, Suspense, and Spy Fiction.* New York: Van Nostrand Reinhold, 1982.

McCormick, Donald. *Who's Who in Spy Fiction.* New York: Taplinger, 1977.

Monaghan, David. *Smiley's Circus: A Guide to the Secret World of John Le Carre.* London: Orbis, 1986.

Palmer, Jerry. *Thrillers, Genesis and Structure of a Popular Genre.* New York: St. Martin's Press, 1979.

Panek, Leroy. *The Special Branch: The British Spy Novel, 1890-1980.* Bowling Green, OH: Bowling Green State University Popular Press, 1981.

Sauerberg, Lars Ole. *Secret Agents in Fiction: Ian Fleming, John le Carré, Len Deighton.* New York: St. Martin's Press, 1984.

Skene-Melvin, David, and Ann Skene-Melvin, Comps. *Crime, Detective, Espionage, Mystery, and Thriller Fiction and Film: A Comprehensive Bibliography of Critical Writing through 1979.* Westport, CT: Greenwood Press, 1980.

Smith, Myron J. *Cloak and Dagger: An Annotated Guide to Spy Thrillers.* Santa Barbara, CA: ABC-CLIO, 1982.

AUTHORS AND TITLES

0352
AMBLER, ERIC   1909-
England
1936 The Dark Frontier
1937 Background to Danger
1938 Cause for Alarm
1938 Epitaph for a Spy
1939 A Coffin for Dimitrios
1940 Journey into Fear
1951 Judgment on Deltchev
1953 The Schirmer Inheritance
1956 State of Siege
1960 Passage of Arms
1964 A Kind of Anger
1969 The Intercom Conspiracy
1972 The Levanter
1974 Doctor Frigo
1977 The Siege of the Villa Lipp
1981 The Care of Time

"Arthur Abdel Simpson"
1962 The Light of Day
1967 Dirty Story

0353
ANTHONY, EVELYN   1928-
England
Real name: Evelyn Bridget Patricia Ward-Thomas; also writes as Anthony Evelyn
"Davina Graham"
1981 The Avenue of the Dead
1981 The Defector
1983 Albatross
1983 The Company of Saints
See also HEADLINES, 0259 & HISTORICAL FICTION, 0950

0354
BARLAY, STEPHEN   1930-
Hungary
1981 In the Company of Spies

0355
BUCKLEY, WILLIAM F.   1925-
"C.I.A. Agent Blackford Oakes"
1976 Saving the Queen
1978 Stained Glass
1980 Who's on First
1982 Marco Polo If You Can
1984 The Story of Henri Tod
1985 See You Later Alligator
1986 High Jinx
1987 Mongoose, R.I.P.

0356
COLES, MANNING   1899-1965
Real name: Cyril Henry Coles; Manning Coles is a joint pseudonym with Adelaide Frances Oke Manning
"Tommy Hambledon, British Intelligence"
1940 Drink to Yesterday
1941 A Toast to Tomorrow
1946 The Fifth Man
1952 Alias Uncle Hugo
1957 Death of an Ambassador
1958 No Entry
1960 Concrete Crime

0357
COX, RICHARD   1931-
England
1977 Sam 7
1978 The Botticelli Madonna
1981 The KGB Directive

0358
CREASEY, JOHN   1908-1973
England
"Dr. Palfrey, Z5 International Protective Organization"
1966 The Depths (1963)
1966 The Inferno
1966 The Terror: The Return of Dr. Palfrey (1962)
1967 The Drought (1959)
1968 The Blight
1968 The Famine
1968 The Plague of Silence (1958)
1968 The Sleep! (1964)
1969 The Flood (1956)
1969 The Touch of Death (1954)
1970 The Oasis
1970 Traitors' Doom (1942)
1971 The Killers of Innocence, rev. (1952)
1971 The Smog
1972 The Unbegotten
1973 The Insulators
1973 The Perilous Country (1943; 1966)
1974 Dangerous Quest (1965)
1974 The Legion of the Lost (1943; 1965)

1974 The Voiceless Ones
1975 The House of the Bear (1945; 1962)
1976 Death in the Rising Sun (1945; 1970)
1976 The Thunder Maker
1977 Dark Harvest (1947; 1962)
1977 The Mists of Fear (1955)
1978 The Prophet of Fire (1951)
1978 The Wings of Peace (1948)
See also MYSTERIES, 0428 & HISTORICAL FICTION, 1044; MYSTERIES as ASHE, GORDON, 0394; HUNT, KYLE, 0477; MARRIC, J.J., 0514; MORTON, ANTHONY, 0522; YORK, JEREMY, 0588

0359
DEIGHTON, LEN   1929-
England
1976 Catch a Falling Spy

"Harry Palmer"
1962 The Ipcress File
1963 Horse under Water
1964 Funeral in Berlin
1966 The Billion Dollar Brain
1967 An Expensive Place to Die
1974 Spy Story
1975 Eleven Declarations of War (SS)
1975 Yesterday's Spy

"Bernard Samson, British Intelligence"
1984 Berlin Game
1985 Mexico Set
1986 London Match
See also HEADLINES, 0328 & HISTORICAL FICTION, 1047

0360
DOLINER, ROY   1932-
1961 The Orange Air
1966 Sandra Rifkin's Jewels
1967 The Antagonists
1978 On the Edge
1980 The Thin Line
1985 The Twelfth of April

0361
FLEMING, IAN   1908-1964
England
"James Bond, Agent 007"
1953 Casino Royale
1954 Live & Let Die
1955 Moonraker
1956 Diamonds Are Forever
1957 From Russia with Love
1958 Doctor No
1959 Goldfinger
1960 For Your Eyes Only (SS)
1961 Thunderball
1962 The Spy Who Loved Me
1963 On Her Majesty's Secret Service
1964 You Only Live Twice
1965 The Man with the Golden Gun
1966 Octopussy (& The Living Daylights)
Series continued by GARDNER, JOHN, 0363

0362
FREEMANTLE, BRIAN   1936-
1973 Goodbye to an Old Friend
1975 Face Me When You Walk Away
1984 The Lost American

"Charlie Muffin"
1977 Charlie M
1978 Here Comes Charlie M
1979 The Inscrutable Charlie Muffin
1980 Charlie Muffin, U.S.A.
1986 Blind Run
1987 See Charlie Run
See also HEADLINES, 0279

0363
GARDNER, JOHN (EDMUND)   1926-
England
1985 The Secret Generations
1987 The Secret Houses (Sequel to Generations)

"James Bond, Agent 007" series continued
1981 License Renewed
1982 For Special Services
1983 Icebreaker
1984 Role of Honor
1986 Nobody Lives Forever
1987 No Deals, Mr. Bond
1988 Scorpius
Also writes other spy novels & novels

0364
GILMAN, DOROTHY   1923-
Real name: Dorothy Gilman Butters
"Mrs. Pollifax"
1966 The Unexpected Mrs. Pollifax
1970 The Amazing Mrs. Pollifax
1971 The Elusive Mrs. Pollifax
1973 A Palm for Mrs. Pollifax
1977 Mrs. Pollifax on Safari
1983 Mrs. Pollifax on the China Station

Section 4 - Spy Stories

1985 Mrs. Pollifax & the Hong Kong Buddha
1988 Mrs. Pollifax and the Golden Triangle
See also MYSTERIES, 0457

0365
GOLDMAN, WILLIAM   1931-
1974 Marathon Man
1982 Control
1985 Heat
1987 Brothers (Sequel to Marathon)
See also HORROR, 0180; SCIENCE FICTION, 0774; TRASH, 1127

0366
GRANGER, BILL
Also writes mysteries as Bill Griffith
"Devereaux, Code name November, R Section, rival of CIA"
1979 The November Man
1981 Schism
1982 The Shattered Eye
1983 The British Cross
1984 The Zurich Numbers
1985 Hemingway's Notebook
1986 There Are No Spies
1987 The Infant of Prague

0367
GREENE, GRAHAM   1904-
England
1932 The Orient Express
1939 The Confidential Agent
1943 The Ministry of Fear
1950 The Third Man
1958 Our Man in Havanna
1978 The Human Factor
1988 The Captain & the Enemy
See also BRITISH AUTHORS, 1365

0368
GRIFFITHS, JOHN
"CIA"
1980 A Loyal & Dedicated Servant
1981 Memory Man

0369
HALL, ADAM   1920-
England
Real name: Trevor Elleston; also writes as Elleston Trevor
"Quiller, British Intelligence"
1965 The Quiller Memorandum
1966 The 9th Directive
1971 The Warsaw Document
1973 The Tango Briefing
1975 The Mandarin Cypher
1969 The Striker Portfolio
1976 The Kobra Manifesto
1978 Sinking Executive
1980 The Scorpion Signal

0370
HILL, REGINALD   1936-
England
Also writes as Dick Morland, Patrick Ruell, & Charles Underhill
1980 The Spy's Wife
1982 Who Guards the Prince?
1986 Traitor's Blood (1983)
See also MYSTERIES, 0474

0371
HONE, JOSEPH   1937-
"Peter Marlow"
1971 The Private Sector
1975 The Sixth Directorate
1980 The Oxford Gambit

0372
HOUSEHOLD, GEOFFREY   1900-
England
1939 Rogue Male
1951 A Time to Kill
1955 Fellow Passenger
1960 Watcher in the Shadows
1971 Doom's Caravan
1972 The Three Sentinels
1975 Red Anger
1977 Hostage: London
1978 The Last Two Weeks of Georges Rivac
1982 Rogue Justice (Sequel to Male)
See also HORROR, 0187 & SCIENCE FICTION, 0780

0373
HUNT, E. HOWARD   1918-
Also writes as John Baxter, Gordon Davis, Robert Dietrich, David St. John
1980 The Hargrave Deception
1981 The Gaza Intercept
1985 The Kremlin Conspiracy
1986 Guadalajara

0374
LE CARRÉ, JOHN   1931-

England
Real name: David Cornwell
1965 The Looking Glass War
1968 A Small Town in Germany
1983 The Little Drummer Girl
1986 A Perfect Spy

"George Smiley, British Intelligence"
1963 The Spy Who Came in from the Cold
1974 Tinker, Tailor, Soldier, Spy
1977 The Honourable Schoolboy
1980 Smiley's People
See also MYSTERIES, 0493

0375
LIDDY, G. GORDON   1930-
1979 Out of Control

0376
LITTELL, ROBERT   1896-1963
1973 The Defection of A. J. Lewinter
1976 The October Circle
1978 Mother Russia
1979 The Debriefing
1981 The Amateur
1986 The Sisters

0377
MACBETH, GEORGE   1932-
Scotland
1975 The Samuri
1979 The Seven Witches
1981 The Katana

0378
MCCARRY, CHARLES
1973 The Miernik Dossier
1975 The Tears of Autumn
1977 The Secret Lovers
1983 The Last Supper
See also HEADLINES, 0246

0379
MARLOWE, DEREK   1938-
England
1966 A Dandy in Aspic
1979 The Rich Boy from Chicago
See also HORROR, 0203

0380
MARQUAND, JOHN P.   1893-1960
Real name: John Phillips

"Mr. Moto, Japan"
1936 Mr. Moto Is So Sorry
1936 Thank You, Mr. Moto
1937 Think Fast, Mr. Moto
1942 Last Laugh, Mr. Moto
1977 Your Turn, Mr. Moto
1985 Right You Are, Mr. Moto (1957, Stopover Tokyo)

0381
MAUGHAM, SOMERSET   1874-1965
England
1926 The Casuarina Tree (SS)
1928 Ashenden; or, The British Agent (SS)
1933 Ah King (SS)

0382
MITGANG, HERBERT   1920-
1981 The Montauk Fault
1983 Kings in the Counting House

0383
PERRY, RITCHIE   1942-
England
Real name: John Allen
"Frank MacAllister, Private Investigator"
1984 MacAllister
1987 Presumed Dead

"Philis, SR (2), British Intelligence"
1972 The Fall Guy
1973 A Hard Man to Kill
1974 Ticket to Ride
1975 Holiday with a Vengeance
1976 Your Money & Your Wife
1977 One Good Death Deserves Another
1979 Bishop's Pawn
1980 Fool's Mate
1980 Grand Slam
1982 Foul Up
1985 Kolwezi

0384
PORTER, JOYCE
"Edmund Brown, Reluctant Spy"
1966 Sour Cream with Everything
1967 The Chinks in the Curtain
1970 Neither a Candle Nor a Pitchfork
1971 Only with a Barge Pole
See also MYSTERIES, 0535

Section 4 - Spy Stories

0385
THOMAS, CRAIG   1942-
"Gant--Firefox"
1977 Firefox!
1983 Firefox Down!
1987 Winter Hawk
See also HEADLINES, 0310

0386
THOMAS, ROSS   1926-
Also writes as Oliver Bleeck
1967 The Seersucker Whipsaw
1969 The Singapore Wink
1971 The Fools in Town Are on Our Side
1978 Chinaman's Chance
1979 The Eighth Dwarf
1981 The Mordida Man
1983 Missionary Stew
1987 Out on the Rim

"Mac McCorkle & Mike Padillo"
1966 The Cold War Swap
1967 Cast a Yellow Shadow
1971 The Backup Man

0387
TREVANIAN   1930-
England
"Dr. Jonathan Hemlock"
1972 The Eiger Sanction
1973 The Loo Sanction
1979 Shibumi

0388
WISEMAN, THOMAS   1931-
Austria
1980 A Game of Secrets

SECTION FIVE

MYSTERY AND DETECTIVE STORIES

OVERVIEW

Most writers of mysteries create a "detective" or "solver of the crime" and continue to develop cases for that person to solve. Most mysteries involve at least one murder and often other crimes as well. In a good mystery series, there is growth of character although it is difficult for an author to be in top form on plot and character development in each book.

Readers often enjoy mysteries of specific types. One way to categorize mysteries is by the "solver of the crime". Several broad categories: police procedurals (a police department is responsible for investigating the crime), private investigators (an independent investigator is hired by someone to solve the crime), amateur detectives (persons of independent means solve the crime simply for the fun and challenge of it). A new trend is the "solver" who is not a professional detective either with the police or in private practice but is employed in another profession and happens to become involved in a mystery as part of his or her job.

Most writers are either British or American and readers often prefer only British mysteries or only American mysteries. There are not many mysteries which are popular in translation; some obvious exceptions are George Simenon's detective stories about Inspector Maigret, which are translated from the French, and the Stockholm police novels of Maj Sjöwall and Per Wahlöö, which are translated from the Swedish.

A list of representative authors in these categories include:

POLICE PROCEDURALS

1. *Police Procedurals--American:*

Author:	Detective:
Ball, John	Chief Jack Talon, Whitewater, WA, Police Dept.
Biggers, Earl Derr	Det. Sgt. Charlie Chan Honolulu Police Dept.
Chastain, Thomas	Deputy Chief Inspt. Max Kaufmann, New York Police Dept.
Constantine, K. C.	Mario Balzic, Chief of Police, Rocksburg, PA
Cunningham, E. V.	Det. Masao Masuto, Beverly Hills Police Dept.
Daley, Robert	New York Police Dept.

Section 5 - Mysteries   57

Author	Detective
Hillerman, Tony	Lt. Joe Leaphorn & Sgt. Jim Chee, Navaho Tribal Police
Lewin, Michael Z.	Lt. Leroy Powder, Indianapolis Police Dept.
Lockridge, Frances & Richard	Cpt./Inspt. Merton Heimrich, State Police, New York
McBain, Ed	5th Precinct, New York Police Dept. 87th Precinct, New York Police Dept. Det. Steve Carella
McDonald, Gregory	Inspt. Francis Xavier Flynn, Boston Police Dept.
O'Donnell, Lillian	Lt. Norah Mulcahaney, New York Police Dept.
Oliver, Anthony	Det. Inspt. John Webber & Elizabeth Thomas
Pronzini, Bill	The Nameless Detective, San Francisco
Shannon, Dell	Lt. Luis Mendoza, Los Angeles, Police Dept.
Uhnak, Dorothy	Det. Christie Opara, New York Police Dept.
Wambaugh, Joseph	Los Angeles Police Dept.
Wilcox, Collin	Lt. Frank Hastings, San Francisco Police Dept. Marshall McCloud, New York

2. Police Procedurals--British:

Author:	Detective:
Aird, Catherine	Det. Inspt. C. D. Sloan, C.I.D., Calleshire
Ashe, Gordon	Deputy Commissioner Patrick Dawlish, Scotland Yard
Barnard, Robert	Supt. Perry Trethowan, Scotland Yard
Bellairs, George	Chief Supt. Littlejohn, Scotland Yard
Butler, Gwendoline	Divisional Det. John Coffin, South London District
Creasy, John	Inspt. Roger West, Scotland Yard
Dickinson, Peter	Inspt. Supt. Jimmy Pibble, Scotland Yard
Dickson, Carter	Sir Henry Merrivale, Scotland Yard
Erskine, Margaret	Inspt. Septimus Finch, Scotland Yard
Fraser, James	Supt. Aveyard, Birton Police Force
Gilbert, Michael	Inspt. Hazelrigg, Scotland Yard
Grimes, Martha	Supt. Richard Jury, Scotland Yard
Hare, Cyril	Inspt. Mallett, C.I.D., Scotland Yard;
Haymon, S. T.	Det. Inspt. Ben Jurnet, Scotland Yard
Heyer, Georgette	Supt. Hannasyde Inspt. Hemingway
Hill, Reginald	Supt. Andrew Dalziel & Inspt. Peter Pascoe; mid-Yorkshire C.I.D.
Hunter, Alan	Chief Supt. Gently, Scotland Yard
Innes, Michael	Inspt. Appleby, Scotland Yard
James, P. D.	Supt. Adam Dalgliesh, Scotland Yard

Author	Detective
Jeffreys, J. G.	Jeremy Sturrock, Bow Street Runners
Knox, Bill	Supt. Colin Thane & Phil Moss, Glasglow C.I.D.
Lemarchand, Elizabeth	Det. Chief Inspt. Tom Pollard & Sgt. Gregory Toye, Scotland Yard
Lovesey, Peter	Sgt. Cribb & Constable Thackeray, Scotland Yard, Victorian Period
Marric, J. J.	Commander George Gideon, C.I.D., Scotland Yard
Marsh, Ngaio	Roderick Alleyn, C.I.D., Scotland Yard
Melville, Jennie	Det. Charmian Daniels, Deerham Police
Moyes, Patricia	Chief Supt. Henry Tibbett, Scotland Yard
Perry, Anne	Inspt. Pitt, Scotland Yard, Victorian period
Peters, Ellis	Det. Inspt. George Felse
Porter, Joyce	Inspt. Wilfred Dover, Scotland Yard
Radley, Sheila	Chief Inspt. Quantrill & Det. Sgt. Tait, Breckham Market, East Anglia
Rendell, Ruth	Chief Inspt. Reg Wexford & Inspt. Michael Burden, Kingsmarkham C.I.D., Scotland Yard
Scott, Jack S.	Inspt. Peter Parsons
	Det. Inspt. Alfred Stanley Rosher, C.I.D., Scotland Yard
Selwyn, Francis	Sgt. Verity, Scotland Yard, Victorian period
Tey, Josephine	Inspt. Alan Grant, Scotland Yard
Thomson, June	Det. Inspt. Jack Rudd, Chelmsford C.I.D., Scotland Yard
Watson, Colin	Inspt. Purbright, Flaxborough Village
Wentworth, Patricia	Inspt. Lamb, Scotland Yard
Winslow, Pauline Glen	Det. Supt. Merle Capricorn, C.I.D., Scotland Yard
York, Jeremy	Supt. Folly, Scotland Yard

3. *Police Procedurals--International:*

Author:	Detective:
Cleary, Jon	Det. Sgt. Scobie Malone, Sydney, Australia, Police Dept.
Craig, Alisa	Det. Inspt. Madoc Rhys, Royal Canadian Mounted Police
Ebersohn, Wessel	Yudel Gordon, Police Psychiatrist, Dept. of Prisons, Pretoria, South Africa
Freeling, Nicholas	Commissaris Piet Van der Valk, Amsterdam Central Research
	Officer Henri Castang, Regional Service of the P.J., France
Gill, Bartholomew	Chief Supt. Peter McGarr, Garda Siochana, Ireland
Grayson, Richard	Inspt. Gautier, Sureté, Paris
Keating, H. R. F.	Inspt. Ganesh Ghote, Bombay Police

Section 5 - Mysteries

McClure, James	Lt. Tromp Kramer & Det. Sgt. Mickey Zondi, Murder Squad, Trekkersburg, South Africa
Mantell, Laurie	Det. Sgt. Steven Arrow & Chief Inspt. Jonas Peacock, Police Dept., Petone, New Zealand
Marshall, William	Det. Chief Inspt. Harry Feiffer, Yellowthread St. Station, Hong Kong Lt. Felix Elizalde, Manila Police Dept.
Melville, James	Supt. Otani, Prefectural Police, Kobe, Japan
Poe, Edgar Allan	C. Auguste Dupin, Sureté, Paris
Rathbone, Julian	Commissioner Jan Argand, Brabt Police (fictional Low Country) Col. Nur Arslan, National Police, Turkey
Simenon, Georges	Maigret, Sureté, Paris
Sjöwall, Maj & Wahlöö, Per	Martin Beck, Stockholm Police
Van de Wetering, Janwillem	Adjutant Griipstra & Sgt. de Gier, Amsterdam Police Dept.
Wright, Eric	Inspt. Charlie Salter, Toronto Police Dept.

PRIVATE INVESTIGATORS

1. *Private Investigators--American:*

Author:	Detectives:
Ball, John	Virgil Tibbs, Black PI, Pasadena, CA
Barnes, Linda	Carlotta Carlyle, PI, Ex-cop
Chandler, Raymond	Philip Marlowe, PI, Los Angeles
Collins, Michael	Dan Fortune, One-armed PI, New York
Estleman, Loren D.	Amos Walker, PI, Detroit
Fair, A. A.	Donald Lam & Bertha Cool, the Cool-Lam Detective Agency
Grafton, Sue	Kinsey Millhone, PI, California
Hammett, Dashiell	Sam Spade, PI; The Continental Op
Latimer, Jonathan	Bill Crane, PI
Lewin, Michael Z.	Albert Sampson, PI, Indianapolis
Lyons, Arthur	Jacob Asch, PI, West Coast
McDonald, Gregory	Fletch, PI, Boston
McDonald, John D.	Travis McGee, PI, Ft. Lauderdale, FL
McDonald, Ross	Lew Archer, PI, Southern California
Paretsky, Sara	V.I. Warshawski, Female PI, Chicago
Parker, Robert	Spenser, PI, Boston
Pentecost, Hugh	David Cotter, PI
Prather, Richard Scott	Shell Scott, PI, Los Angeles
Rosten, Leo	Silky Pincus, PI, New York
Simon, Roger L.	Moses Wine, PI, California
Smith, J. C. S.	Quentin Jacoby, Retired Subway Police Officer, New York
Spillane, Mickey	Mike Hammer, PI
Stout, Rex	Nero Wolfe, PI, New York

Tidyman, Ernest — John Shaft, Black PI
Valin, Jonathan — Henry Stoner, PI, Cincinnati
Wager, Walter — Alison B. Gordon, Female PI, Los Angeles

2. *Private Investigators--British:*

Author: Detective:

Canning, Victor — Rex Carver, PI
Christie, Agatha — Hercule Poirot, PI
Doyle, Sir Arthur Conan — Sherlock Holmes
Francis, Dick — Sid Halley, Ex-jockey PI
James, P. D. — Cordelia Grey, Female PI
MacKenzie, Donald — John Raven, Ex-cop, Scotland Yard
Royce, Kenneth — Spider Scott, the XYZ Man
Wentworth, Patricia — Miss Maud Silver, PI, London

AMATEUR SLEUTHS

These sleuths have independent means, don't have to work and enjoy solving mysteries and crimes.

1. *Amateur Sleuths--American:*

Author: Detective:

Asimov, Isaac — The Black Widowers
Barth, Richard — Margaret Binton, Elderly Widow, Manhattan
Hammett, Dashiell — Nick & Nora Charles
Lockridge, Frances & Richard — Mr. & Mrs. North
Queen, Ellery — Ellery Queen, New York
Sanders, Lawrence — Edward X. Delaney, retired Chief of Detectives, New York Police Dept.
Van Dine, S. S. — Philo Vance, New York

2. *Amateur Sleuths--British:*

Author: Detective:

Allingham, Margery — Albert Campion
Bentley, E.C. — Trent
Blake, Nicholas — Nigel Strangeways & Clare Massinger, Sculptor
Brett, Simon — Mrs. Pargeter, Widow of gentleman-crook
Carr, John Dickson — Dr. Gideon Fell
Carter, Youngman — Albert Campion
Charteris, Leslie — Simon Templer, the Saint
Christie, Agatha — Tommy & Tuppence Beresford
Miss Jane Marple, Saint Mary Mead
Creasey, John — The Toff, the Honorable Richard Rollison
Ferrars, E. X. — Virginia Freer & Ex-husband Felix

Section 5 - Mysteries   61

 Grimes, Martha   Melrose Plant, Aristocrat & helper of Supt. Jury of Scotland Yard
 McDonald, Philip   Colonel Anthony Ruthven Gethryn, London
 Morton, Anthony   The Baron, John Mannering, Ex-jewel thief
 Sayers, Dorothy   Lord Peter Wimsey & Harriet Vane, Writer

3. Amateur Sleuths—International:

 Author: Detective:

 Freeling, Nicholas   Arlette Van der Valk, Widow of police officer

SLEUTHS WITH OTHER PROFESSIONS

1. American:

 Author: Detective:

 Barnes, Linda   Michael Spraggue, Wealthy Actor, Boston
 Box, Edgar   Peter Cutler Sargeant, III Public relations firm
 Cross, Amanda   Dr. Kate Fansler, Professor of English, University in New York City
 Dominic, R. B.   Ben Safford, Democrat, U.S. House of Representatives, Ohio
 Estleman, Loren D.   Peter Macklin, Mob connections, Detroit
 Gardner, Erle Stanley   Perry Mason, Criminal lawyer
 Greeley, Andrew   Father Blackie Ryan, Catholic priest
 Hansen, Joseph   David Brandstetter, Gay insurance investigator
 Kallen, Lucille   C. B. Greenfield, Newspaper editor, New York
 Kellerman, Jonathan   Alex Delaware, Child psychologist, Los Angeles
 Kemelman, Harry   Rabbi David Small, New England
 Kienzle, William X.   Father Robert Koesler, Catholic priest, Detroit
 Lathen, Emma   John Putnam Thatcher, Investment banker, New York
 McBain, Ed   Andrew Broom, Lawyer, Midwest Matthew Hope, Lawyer, Florida
 McInerny, Ralph   Father Roger Dowling, Catholic priest, Chicago
 MacKay, Amanda   Dr. Hanna Land, Professor of political science, Duke University, North Carolina
 Maling, Arthur   Brock Potter, Brokerage firm, New York
 Muller, Marcia   Sharon McCone, Investigator for legal cooperative, San Francisco

Author:	Detective:
	Elena Oliverez, Museum curator
	Joanna Stark, Art-security expert
Pentecost, Hugh	Pierre Chambrun, Hotel manager, New York
	John Jericho, Artist, New York
	Julian Quist, Partner in public relations firm, New York
Peters, Elizabeth	Dr. Vicki Bliss, Museum curator & art historian
	Jacqueline Kirby, College librarian
Westlake, Donald E.	John Archibald Dortmunder, Master burglar
Wilcox, Collin	Stephen Drake, Crime reporter

2. *British:*

Author:	Detective:
Brett, Simon	Charles Paris, English actor
Canning, Victor	Samuel Miles Smiler, Young animal lover
Chesterton, G. K.	Father Brown
Crispin, Edmund	Gervase Fen, Professor of Language & Literature, Oxford
Ferrars, E. X.	Professor Andrew Basnett
Francis, Dick	Kit Fielding, Steeplechase jockey
Fraser, Antonia	Jemima Shore, TV personality, London
Gash, Jonathan	Lovejoy, Antiques dealer, London
Hare, Cyril	Francis Pettigrew, Barrister
Heald, Tim	Simon Bognor, British Board of Trade
Higgins, George	Jerry Kennedy, Sleazy lawyer, Boston
Hunt, Kyle	Dr. Emmanuel Cellini, Psychiatrist
Knox, Bill	Chief Officer Webb Carrick, Scottish Fishery Protection Service
Le Carré, John	George Smiley, British Intelligence
Marsh, Ngaio	Troy Alleyn, Artist & wife of Roderick Alleyn, Scotland Yard
Moffat, Gwen	Miss Melinda Pink, Mountain Climber & Writer, London
Morice, Anne	Tessa Crichton Price, Actress, London
Peters, Elizabeth	Amelia Peabody, Archeologist, Victorian period
Peters, Ellis	Brother Cadfael, Monk, Wales, 12th century
Warner, Mignon	Mrs. Edwina Charles, Clairvoyante
Williams, David	Mark Treasure, Banker, London
Woods, Sara	Anthony Maitland, Lawyer, London
Yorke, Margaret	Dr. Patrick Grant, Professor of Literature, Oxford

3. *International:*

Author:	Detective:

Section 5 - Mysteries

Gulik, Robert Hans Van	Judge Dee, Magistrate, China, Tang Dynasty
Kallen, Lucille	C. B. Greenfield, Newspaper editor, New York
Philips, Judson	Peter Styles, Newsmagazine reporter, New York
Quill, Monica	Sister Mary Teresa, Chicago
Watson, Clarissa	Persis Willum, Artist & Gallery Director

BY TIME PERIOD:

"Classic" or "golden age": The period between the two world wars; such authors as Dorothy Sayers, Agatha Cristie, S.S. Van Dine, Ellery Queen, Philip MacDonald, Margarey Allingham, and John Dickinson Carr were at the height of their careers then.

BY PLOT DEVICE:

Some examples are:

1. *The Locked Room:*
   A crime is committed in a room for which there could have been no escape. Some of the early books by Ellery Queen and S.S. Van Dine use this device that was originated by Edgar Allan Poe in Murders in the Rue Morgue.

2. *The Country House Week-End:*
   A favorite of English writers. A group of wealthy people spend the weekend at a country house and someone is murdered. Ngaio Marsh's Death and the Dancing Footman is a classic; many authors have used this including Agatha Christie.

3. *The Sins of the Fathers*
   A crime committed in one generation continues to fester through the next generation or two. The Ross MacDonald novels with Lew Archer, Los Angeles private investigator, use this device; and it is a popular theme in stories of private investigators.

4. *Suspense:*
   A novel or short story with elements of a mystery and emphasis on twists of plot involving great danger (physical/ psychological) to the protagonist and/or the protagonists family. Plot is the most important element, and there is usually a surprise or twist in the plot at the end. In a good suspense story, the reader should not be able to predict the plot or the ending.

REFERENCE AND BIBLIOGRAPHIC SOURCES

Allen, Dick & David Chacko, eds. Detective Fiction: Crime and Compromise. New York: Harcourt, Brace, 1974.

Barzun, Jacques & Wendell H. Taylor. *A Catalog of Crime.* New York: Harper, 1971.

Breen, Jon L. *Novel Verdicts: A Guide to Courtroom Fiction.* Metuchen, NJ: Scarecrow Press, 1984.

_____. *What about Murder? A Guide to Books about Mystery and Detective Fiction.* Metuchen, NJ: Scarecrow Press, 1981.

Cawelti, John G. *Adventure, Mystery and Romance: Formula Stories as Art and Popular Culture.* University of Chicago Press, 1976.

Geherin, David. *The American Private Eye: The Image in Fiction.* New York: Ungar, 1985.

Goulart, Ron, ed. *The Great British Detective.* New York: New American Library, 1982.

Gribbin, Lenore S. *Who's Whodunit: A List of 3218 Detective Story Writers and Their 1100 Pseudonyms.* Chapel Hill: University of North Carolina Library, 1968.

Hagen, Ordean A. *Who Done It? A Guide to Detective, Mystery and Suspense Fiction.* New York: Bowker, 1969.

Hubin, Allen J. *Crime Fiction, 1749-1980, A Comprehensive Bibliography.* New York: Garland, 1984. *1981-1985 Supplement.* New York: Garland, 1988.

Mandel, Ernest. *Delightful Murder: A Social History of the Crime Story.* University of Minnesota Press, 1985.

Menendez, Albert J. *The Subject Is Murder: A Selective Subject Guide to Mystery Fiction.* New York: Garland, 1986.

Olderr, Steven. *Mystery Index, Subjects, Settings, and Sleuths of 10,000 Titles.* Chicago: American Library Association, 1987.

Queen, Ellery. *Queen's Quorum: A History of the Detective Crime Short Story as Revealed by the 106 Most Important Books Published in this Field since 1845.* New York: Biblo and Tannon, 1969.

Reilly, John M., ed. *Twentieth Century Crime and Mystery Writers.* New York: St. Martin's Press, 1980.

Skene-Melvin, David, and Ann Skene-Melvin. *Crime, Detective, Espionage, and Thriller Fiction and Film: A Comprehensive Bibliography of Critical Writing through 1979.* Westport, CT: Greenwood Press, 1980.

Steinbrunner, Chris, and Otto Penzler, eds. *Encyclopedia of Mystery and Detection.* New York: McGraw-Hill, 1976.

Symons, Julian. *Mortal Consequences.* New York: Harper, 1972.

Section 5 - Mysteries

Van Dover, J. Kenneth. *Murder in the Millions; Erle Stanley Gardner, Mickey Spillane, Ian Fleming.* New York: Ungar, 1984.

Winn, Dilys, ed. *Murder Ink: The Mystery Reader's Companion.* New York: Workman, 1977.

_____. *Murderess Ink: The Better Half of the Mystery.* New York: Workman, 1979.

Periodicals and Columns in Periodicals:

The Armchair Detective. The Mysterious Press. Quarterly.
   (129 W. 56th Street, New York, N.Y. 10019)

"Murder in Print" *Wilson Library Bulletin.* Various issues.

AUTHORS AND TITLES

If an author is noted for a detective, the detective's name & position are listed in quotation marks above the books about that detective.

0389
AIKEN, JOAN   1924-
England
1964 The Silence of Herondale
1965 The Fortune Hunters
1966 Beware of the Bouquet
1967 Dark Interval
1968 The Crystal Crow
1969 Night Fall
1970 The Embroidered Sunset
1971 Green Flash (SS)
1971 Nightly Deadshade
1972 A Cluster of Separate Sparks
1972 Died on a Rainy Sunday
1975 Voices in an Empty House
1977 Last Movement
1980 A Touch of Chill (SS)
1983 Foul Matter
Also writes for juveniles
See also ROMANCES, 0002

0390
AIRD, CATHERINE   1930-
England
Real name: Kinn Hamilton McIntosh
1967 A Most Contagious Game

"Det. Inspt. C. D. Sloan, C.I.D., Calleshire"
1966 The Religious Body
1968 Henrietta Who?
1970 The Stately Home Murder
1971 A Late Phoenix
1973 His Burial Too
1976 Slight Mourning
1978 A Parting Breath
1979 Some Die Eloquent
1980 Passing Strange
1982 Last Respects
1984 Harm's Way
1987 A Dead Liberty

0391
ALLAN, STELLA
1978 An Inside Job
1979 A Mortal Affair
1981 A Dead Giveaway

0392
ALLINGHAM, MARGERY   1904-1966
England
"Albert Campion, Amateur Sleuth"
1930 The Black Dudley Murder
1930 Mystery Mile
1931 The Gyrth Chalice Mystery
1932 Police at the Funeral
1933 Kingdom of Death (The Fear Sign)
1934 Death of a Ghost
1936 Flowers for the Judge
1937 The Case of the Late Pig
1938 The Fashion in Shrouds
1939 Mr. Campion & Others (SS)
1941 Traitor's Purse
1943 Who Killed Chloe? (Dancers in Mourning, 1937)
1945 Pearls before Swine
1949 Deadly Duo
1949 More Work for the Undertaker
1952 The Tiger in the Smoke
1954 No Love Lost
1954 The Patient at Peacock's Hall
1954 Safer than Love
1955 The Estate of the Beckoning Lady
1958 Tether's End
1962 The China Governess
1965 The Mind Readers
1968 Cargo of Eagles (Completed by Youngman Carter)
1971 The Allingham Casebook (SS)
1971 Mr. Campion's Quarry (Completed by Youngman Carter)
See also CARTER, YOUNGMAN, 0413

0393
ARMSTRONG, CHARLOTTE   1905-1969
Also wrote as Jo Valentine
1946 The Unsuspected
1948 The Chocolate Cobweb
1950 Mischief
1951 The Black-Eyed Stranger
1952 Catch-as-Catch-Can
1954 The Better to Eat You
1955 The Dream Walker
1956 A Dram of Poison

Section 5 - Mysteries

1957 The Albatross (SS)
1959 The Seventeen Widows of Sans Souci
1962 Something Blue
1962 Then Came Two Women
1962 Who's Been Sitting in My Chair?
1963 A Little Less Than Kind
1963 The Mark of the Hand
1963 The One-Faced Girl
1963 The Witch's House
1965 The Turret Room
1966 Dream of Fair Woman
1966 The Gift Shop
1966 I See You (SS)
1967 Lemon in the Basket
1968 The Balloon Man
1969 Seven Seats to the Moon
1970 The Protege

"MacDougal Duff"
1942 Lay On, Mac Duff!
1943 The Case of the Weird Sisters
1945 The Innocent Flower

0394
ASHE, GORDON   1908-1973
England
Real name: John Creasey
"Deputy Commissioner Patrick Dawlish, Scotland Yard, Crime-Haters"
1959 The Pack of Lies
1960 The Crime-Haters
1960 The Man Who Laughed at Murder
1961 Rogues' Ransom
1964 A Promise of Diamonds
1966 A Taste of Treasure
1968 Death from Below (1963)
1969 A Clutch of Coppers
1969 Double for Death (1954)
1970 A Scream of Murder
1971 The Kidnaped Child (1955)
1971 A Nest of Traitors
1972 A Rabble of Rebels
1972 Wait for Death (1957)
1973 The Croaker (1939)
1973 A Life for a Death
1974 Murder with Mushrooms (1950; rev., 1971)
1975 The Big Call (1964)
1975 A Blast of Trumpets
1975 A Herald of Doom
1976 A Shadow of Death (1968)
1977 Elope to Death (1959)
1977 A Plague of Demons
1978 Day of Fear (1956)
See also as CREASEY, JOHN, 0428; HUNT, KYLE, 0477; MARRIC, J. J., 0514; MORTON, ANTHONY, 0522; YORK, JEREMY, 0588; SPY STORIES, 0358 & HISTORICAL FICTION, 1044 as CREASY, JOHN

0395
ASIMOV, ISAAC   1920-
1968 A Whiff of Death (The Death Dealers, 1958)
1976 Murder at the ABA
1977 The Key Word (SS)
1983 The Union Club Mysteries
1985 The Disappearing Man (SS)
"Elijah Baley, Robot Detective"
1954 The Caves of Steel
1957 The Naked Sun
1983 The Robots of Dawn
1985 Robots & Empire (Descendents of Baley)

"Black Widowers"
1974 Tales of the Black Widowers
1976 More Tales of the Black Widowers
1980 Casebook of the Black Widowers
1984 Banquets of the Black Widowers
See also SCIENCE FICTION, 0595

0396
BALL, JOHN   1911-1988
1978 A Killing in the Market
1979 The Murder Children

"Virgil Tibbs, Black Private Investigator, Pasadena, CA"
1965 In the Heat of the Night
1966 The Cool Cottontail
1969 Johnny Get Your Gun
1972 Five Pieces of Jade
1976 The Eyes of Buddha
1980 Then Came Violence
1986 Singapore

"Chief Jack Talon, Whitewater, WA, Police Dept."
1977 Police Chief
1981 Trouble for Tallon
1984 Chief Tallon & the S.O.R.
Also writes adventure novels

0397
BARNARD, ROBERT   1936-
England
1976 A Little Local Murder
1977 Blood Brotherhood
1977 Death of an Old Goat
1977 Death on the High C's

1978 Death of a Mystery Writer
1979 Death of a Literary Widow
1980 Death in a Cold Climate
1981 Death of a Perfect Mother
1983 School for Murder
1984 Corpse in a Gilded Cage
1985 Fete Fatale (Disposal of Living)
1985 Out of the Blackout
1986 Political Suicide
1988 The Skeleton in the Grass
1988 At Death's Door

Supt. Perry Trethowan, Scotland Yard
1981 Death by Sheer Torture
1982 Death & the Princess
1983 The Case of the Missing Bronte
1986 Bodies
1987 The Cherry Blossom Corpse

0398
BARNES, LINDA
Carlotta Carlyle, Private Investigator/Ex-cop
1987 A Trouble of Fools

Michael Spraggue, Wealthy Actor/Sleuth, Boston
1982 Blood Will Have Blood
1983 Bitter Finish
1984 Dead Heat
1986 Cities of the Dead

0399
BARTH, RICHARD
Margaret Binton, elderly widow, Manhattan
1978 The Rag Bag Clan
1981 A Ragged Plot
1982 One Dollar Death
1985 The Condo Kill
1988 Deadly Climate

0400
BELLAIRS, GEORGE   1902-
England
Real name: Harold Blundell
Chief Supt. Littlejohn, Scotland Yard
1943 Death of a Busybody
1943 Murder Will Speak
1944 The Murder of a Quack
1945 Calamity at Harwood
1946 Death in the Night Watches
1948 The Case of the Seven Whistlers
1949 The Case of the Famished Parson
1949 Death on the Last Train
1950 The Case of the Demented Spiv

1951 Dead March for Penelope Blow
1951 Death Brings in the New Year
1952 Death in Dark Glasses
1962 Death before Breakfast
1964 Death in the Wasteland
1975 Fear Round About
1976 All Roads to Sospel
1980 Devious Murder (1973)

0401
BENTLEY, E. C.   1895-1956
England
Trent
1913 Trent's Last Case
1936 Trent's Own Case
1938 Trent Intervenes (SS)

0402
BERCOVICI, ERIC
1979 Wolftrap
1981 So Little Cause for Caroline

0403
BERKELEY, ANTHONY   1893-1971
England
Real name: Anthony Berkeley Cox
1930 The Piccadilly Murder
1937 Trial & Error
1938 A Puzzle in Poison
1939 Death in the House

Roger Sheringham, Amateur Detective, London
1927 The Mystery at Lovers' Cave
1928 The Silk Stocking Murders
1929 The Layton Court Mystery
1929 The Poisoned Chocolates Case
1930 The Wychford Poisoning Case
1931 The Second Shot
1931 Top Story Murder
1932 Murder in the Basement
1933 Dead Mrs. Stratton
1934 Mr. Pidgeon's Island
See also as ILES, FRANCIS, 0479

0404
BIGGERS, EARL DERR   1884-1933
Det. Sgt. Charlie Chan, Honolulu Police Dept.
1925 The House without a Key
1926 The Chinese Parrot
1928 Behind That Curtain
1929 The Black Camel
1930 Charlie Chan Carries On
1932 The Keeper of the Keys

Section 5 - Mysteries

0405
BLAKE, NICHOLAS   1904-1972
England
Real name: Cecil Day Lewis
1958 A Penknife in My Heart
1960 Death & Daisy Bland (A Tangled Web, 1956)
1968 The Private Wound

Nigel Strangeways, Sleuth, & Clare Massinger, Sculptor
1935 A Question of Proof
1936 Thou Shell of Death
1937 There's Trouble Brewing
1938 The Beast Must Die
1939 The Smiler with the Knife
1941 The Corpse in the Snowman
1947 Minute for Murder
1949 Head of a Traveler
1953 The Dreadful Hollow
1954 The Whisper in the Gloom
1955 Catch & Kill
1957 End of Chapter
1959 The Widow's Cruise
1961 The Worm of Death
1964 Malice with Murder (1940)
1964 The Sad Variety
1966 The Morning after Death

0406
BOUCHER, ANTHONY   1911-1968
Real name: William Anthony Parker White; also wrote as H. H. Holmes & Herman W. Mudgett; edited many mystery anthologies.
1937 The Case of the Seven of Calvary
1983 Exeunt Murderers (SS)

Fergus O'Breen, Irish Private Investigator in Los Angeles, & Det. Lieut. Jackson, LAPD
1939 The Case of the Crumpled Knave
1940 The Case of the Baker Street Irregulars
1940 Nine Times Nine
1941 The Case of the Solid Key
1942 The Case of the Seven Sneezes

0407
BOX, EDGAR
Real name: Gore Vidal
Peter Cutler Sargeant III, Public Relations Firm
1952 Death in the Fifth Position
1953 Death before Bedtime
1954 Death Likes It Hot

See as SCIENCE FICTION, 0729; HISTORICAL FICTION, 0941; AMERICAN AUTHORS, 1331 as VIDAL, GORE

0408
BRETT, SIMON   1945-
England
1984 A Shock to the System
1985 Dead Romantic
1985 Tickled to Death (SS)

Melita Pargeter, Widow of a Crook
1987 A Nice Class of Corpse

Charles Paris, Actor/Sleuth
1975 Cast, in Order of Disappearance
1976 So Much Blood
1977 Star Trap
1978 An Amateur Corpse
1979 A Comedian Dies
1980 The Dead Side of the Mike
1981 Situation Tragedy
1982 Murder Unprompted
1983 Murder in the Title
1984 Not Dead, Only Resting
1985 Dead Giveaway
1987 What Bloody Man is That?

0409
BUTLER, GWENDOLINE   1922-
England
1974 Sarsen Place

Divisional Det. John Coffin, South London District
1960 Dine & Be Dead
1963 Coffin for Baby
1965 Coffin in Malta
1965 Coffin Waiting
1967 A Nameless Coffin
1970 A Coffin from the Past
1974 Olivia

See also ROMANCES, 0023; MYSTERIES, 0518 & ROMANCES, 0100 as MELVILLE, JENNIE

0410
CAIN, JAMES M.   1892-1977
1934 The Postman Always Rings Twice
1937 Serenade
1941 Mildred Pierce
1942 Love's Lovely Counterfeit
1943 Three of a Kind: Career in C Major, The Embezzler, Double Indemnity
1946 Past All Dishonor

1947 The Butterfly
1947 Sinful Woman
1948 Jealous Woman
1948 The Moth
1951 The Root of His Evil
1953 Galatea
1962 Mignon
1965 The Magician's Wife
1975 Rainbow's End
1976 The Institute
1984 Cloud Nine
1985 The Enchanted Isle

0411
CANNING, VICTOR 1911- England
Also writes as Alan Gould
1974 The Finger of Saturn
1976 The Kingsford Mark
1981 Fall from Grace

"Rex Carver, Private Investigator"
1965 The Whip Hand
1967 Doubled in Diamonds
1968 The Melting Man
1968 The Python Project

"Samuel Miles Smiler, Animal Lover"
1972 The Runaways
1973 Flight of the Grey Goose
1974 The Painted Tent
See also HEADLINES, 0262 & 0323 & SCIENCE FICTION, 0752

0412
CARR, JOHN DICKSON 1906-1977
England
1932 Poison in Jest
1937 The Burning Court
1942 The Emperor's Snuff Box
1950 The Bride of Newgate
1951 The Devil in Velvet
1955 Captain Cut-Throat
1956 Patrick Butler for the Defence
1957 Fire, Burn
1959 Scandal at High Chimneys
1961 The Witch of the Lowtide
1962 The Demoniacs
1968 Papa La-bas
1969 The Ghosts' High Noon
1971 Deadly Hall
1972 The Hungry Goblin
1978 Notes for the Curious (1952, Nine Wrong Answers)

"Bencolin, French Detective"
1930 It Walks by Night
1937 The Four False Weapons

1959 Castle Skull (1931)
1960 The Corpse in the Waxworks (1932)
1986 Lost Gallows

"Dr. Gideon Fell"
1933 Hag's Nook
1933 The Mad Hatter Mystery
1934 The Blind Barber
1934 The Eight of Swords
1935 Death-Watch
1935 The Three Coffins
1936 The Arabian Nights Murder
1938 The Crooked Hinge
1938 To Wake the Dead
1939 The Problem of the Green Capsule
1939 The Problem of the Wire Cage
1940 The Man Who Could Not Shudder
1941 The Case of the Constant Suicides
1941 Death Turns the Tables
1944 Till Death Do Us Part
1946 He Who Whispers
1947 The Sleeping Sphinx
1948 The Dead Man's Knock
1949 Below Suspicion
1954 The Third Bullet (SS)
1960 In Spite of Thunder
1965 The House at Satan's Elbow
1966 Panic in Box C
1967 Dark of the Moon
See also as DICKSON, CARTER, 0434

0413
CARTER, YOUNGMAN
Continues Albert Campion series begun by his wife. See ALLINGHAM, MARGERY, 0392
"Albert Campion, Amateur Sleuth"
1968 Cargo of Eagles
1969 Mr. Campion's Farthing
1971 Mr. Campion's Quarry

0414
CASPARY, VERA 1904-1987
1943 Laura
1945 Bedelia
1946 The Murder in the Stork Club
1946 Stranger Than Truth
1950 The Weeping & the Laughter
1952 Thelma
1954 False Face
1957 The Husband
1960 Evvie
1964 A Chosen Sparrow

Section 5 - Mysteries

1966 The Man Who Loved His Wife
1967 The Rosecrest Cell
1971 Final Portrait
1972 Ruth
1975 The Dreamers
1978 Elizabeth X
1979 The Secret of Elizabeth

0415
CHANDLER, RAYMOND   1885-1959
"Philip Marlowe, Private Investigator, Los Angeles"
1939 The Big Sleep
1940 Farewell, My Lovely
1942 The High Window
1943 The Lady in the Lake
1949 The Little Sister
1950 Trouble Is My Business (SS)
1954 The Long Goodbye
1958 Playback
1958 The Simple Art of Murder (SS)
1964 Killer in the Rain (SS)

0416
CHARTERIS, LESLIE   1907-
England
"Simon Templer, the Saint"
1929 Meet the Tiger!
1931 Alias the Saint
1931 The Avenging Saint
1931 Enter the Saint
1931 Featuring the Saint
1932 The Saint Versus Scotland Yard
1933 The Brighter Buccaneer
1933 The Saint & Mr. Teal
1933 The Saint's Getaway
1934 The Saint Intervenes
1935 The Saint Goes On
1935 The Saint in New York
1936 The Saint Overboard
1937 Ace of Knaves
1938 Follow the Saint
1939 The Happy Highwayman
1940 The Saint in Miami
1941 The Saint Closes the Case
1941 The Saint in London
1941 The Saint Meets His Match
1942 The Saint Bids Diamonds
1942 The Saint Goes West
1942 The Saint Plays with Fire
1944 The Saint Steps In
1946 The Saint on Guard
1946 The Saint Sees It Through
1948 Call for the Saint
1948 Saint Errant
1953 The Saint in Europe
1955 The Saint on the Spanish Main
1956 The Saint around the World
1957 Thanks to the Saint
1958 Senor Saint
1959 The Saint to the Rescue
1962 Trust the Saint
1963 The Saint in the Sun
1964 Vendetta for the Saint
1968 The Saint & the Fiction Makers
1968 The Saint on TV
1969 The Saint Abroad
1970 The Saint in Pursuit
1972 The Saint & the People Importers
1975 Catch the Saint
1976 The Saint & the Hapsburg Necklace
1977 Send for the Saint
1979 The Saint & the Templar Treasure
1980 Count on the Saint
1983 Salvage for the Saint
Also writes short stories & novelettes about the Saint

0417
CHASTAIN, THOMAS
1962 Judgment Day
1977 Vital Statistics
1982 Nightscape
1987 The Picture-Perfect Murders

"Deputy Chief Inspt. Max Kaufmann, New York Police Dept."
1974 Pandora's Box
1976 911
1979 High Voltage
1981 The Diamond Exchange

"The Robins Family"
1983 Who Killed the Robins Family?
1984 The Revenge of the Robins Family

0418
CHESTERTON, G. K.   1874-1936
(Gilbert Keith)
England
1908 The Man Who Was Thursday
1937 The Paradoxes of Mr. Pond (SS)

"Father Brown"
1911 The Innocence of Father Brown (SS)
1914 The Wisdom of Father Brown (SS)
1926 The Incredulity of Father Brown (SS)
1927 The Secret of Father Brown (SS)
1935 The Scandal of Father Brown (SS)

0419
CHRISTIE, AGATHA   1890-1976
England
Also wrote as Mary Westmacott
1924 The Man in the Brown Suit
1925 The Secret of Chimneys
1929 The Seven Dials Mystery
1930 The Mysterious Mr. Quin (The Passing of Mr. Quin)
1931 Murder at Hazelmoor (The Sittaford Mystery)
1932 The Tuesday Club Murders (The 13 Problems)
1933 The Hound of Death
1934 The Boomerang Clue (Why Didn't They Ask Evans?)
1934 The Listerdale Mystery
1934 Mr. Parker Pyne, Detective (Parker Pyne Investigates)
1939 Easy to Kill (Murder Is Easy)
1940 And Then There Were None
1941 The Mystery of the Crime in Cabin 66
1943 The Mystery of the Baghdad Chest
1944 Towards Zero (SS) (Come & Be Hanged)
1944 Death Comes as the End
1945 Remembered Death (Sparkling Cyanide)
1948 Three Blind Mice (The Mousetrap) (SS)
1948 The Witness for the Prosecution
1949 Crooked House
1951 They Came to Baghdad
1951 Underdog (SS)
1955 Destination Unknown (So Many Steps to Death)
1958 Ordeal by Innocence
1961 Double Sin (SS)
1961 13 for Luck
1962 The Pale Horse
1965 Surprise! Surprise!
1968 Endless Night
1970 Passenger to Frankfurt

"Tommy & Tuppence Beresford"
1922 The Secret Adversary
1929 Partners in Crime
1941 N or M?
1968 By the Pricking of My Thumbs
1973 Postern of Fate

"Miss Jane Marple, St. Mary Mead"
1930 Murder at the Vicarage
1942 The Body in the Library
1942 The Moving Finger
1950 A Murder is Announced
1952 Murder with Mirrors (They Do It with Mirrors)
1953 A Pocket Full of Rye
1957 What Mrs. McGillicuddy Saw! (4:50 from Paddington; Murder She Said; Eyewitness to Murder)
1963 The Mirror Crack'd (The Mirror Crack'd from Side to Side)
1965 At Bertram's Hotel
1965 A Caribbean Mystery
1967 Murder in Our Midst
1967 13 Clues for Miss Marple
1971 Nemesis
1976 Sleeping Murder

"Hercule Poirot, Private Investigator"
1920 The Mysterious Affair at Styles
1923 The Murder on the Links
1925 Poirot Investigates (SS)
1926 The Murder of Roger Ackroyd
1927 The Big Four
1928 The Mystery of the Blue Train
1932 Peril at End House
1933 Thirteen at Dinner (Lord Edgeware Dies)
1934 Murder in the Calais Coach (Murder on the Orient Express)
1935 Death in the Air (Death in the Clouds)
1935 Murder in Three Acts (Three Act Tragedy)
1936 The A. B. C. Murders
1936 Murder in Mesopotamia
1937 Cards on the Table
1937 Dead Man's Mirror
1937 Poirot Loses a Client (The Dumb Witness)
1938 Appointment with Death
1938 Death on the Nile
1939 The Regatta Mystery
1940 Sad Cypress
1941 Evil under the Sun
1941 The Patriotic Murders (One, Two, Buckle My Shoe)
1942 Murder in Retrospect (Five Little Pigs)
1943 Triple Threat
1946 Murder after Hours (The Hollow)
1946 Poirot Knows the Murderer
1946 Poirot Lends a Hand
1947 A Holiday for Murder (Hercule Poirot's Christmas)
1947 The Labours of Hercules (SS)
1948 There Is a Tide (Taken at the Flood)
1952 Mrs. McGinty's Dead (Blood Will Tell)
1953 Funerals Are Fatal (After the Funeral)

Section 5 - Mysteries

1955 Hickory Dickory Death
1956 Dead Man's Folly
1959 Cat Among the Pigeons
1963 The Adventure of the Christmas Pudding
1963 The Clocks
1966 Third Girl
1969 Hallowe'en Party
1970 Poirot's Early Cases
1972 Elephants Can Remember
1975 Curtain

0420
CLARK, MARY HIGGINS   1931-
1975 Where Are the Children?
1977 A Stranger Is Watching
1980 The Cradle Will Fall
1982 A Cry in the Night
1984 Stillwatch
1987 Weep No More, My Lady

0421
CLEARY, JON   1917-
Australia
1978 Vortex

"Det. Sgt. Scoble Malone, Sydney, Australia, Police Dept."
1966 The High Commissioner
1970 Helga's Web
1973 Ransom
1988 Dragons at the Party
See also HISTORICAL FICTION, 1042 & WORLD AUTHORS, 1418

0422
COE, TUCKER   1933-
Real name: Donald Westlake; also writes as Richard Stark
"Mitch Tobin, Ex-cop, NYPD"
1966 Kinds of Love, Kinds of Death
1968 Murder among Children
1970 Wax Apple
1971 A Jade in Aries
1972 Don't Lie to Me
See also as WESTLAKE, DONALD E., 0581

0423
COLLINS, MAX ALLAN   1948-
"Nolan, Aging thief"
1973 Bait Money
1981 Blood Money
1981 Fly Paper
1981 Hush Money
1981 Hard Cash

1982 Scratch Fever

"Quarry, Hired killer & Viet vet"
1976 The Broker
1976 The Broker's Wife
1976 The Dealer
1977 The Slasher

"Nathan Heller, Private Investigator"
1983 True Detective
1984 True Crime

"Mallory, Mystery writer"
1983 The Baby Blue Rip-Off
1983 No Cure for Death
1984 Kill Your Darlings
1985 A Shroud for Aquarius
1986 Nice Weekend for a Murder

0424
COLLINS, MICHAEL   1924-
Real name: Dennis Lynds; also writes as William Arden, Nick Carter, John Crowe, Carl Dekker, Maxwell Grant, Dennis Lynds & Mark Sadler
"Dan Fortune, One-armed Private Investigator, New York"
1967 Act of Fear
1969 The Brass Rainbow
1970 Night of the Toads
1971 Walk a Black Wind
1972 Shadow of a Tiger
1973 The Silent Scream
1975 Blue Death
1976 The Blood-Red Dream
1978 The Nightrunners
1980 The Slasher
1983 Freak
1987 Minnesota Strip
1988 Red Rosa

0425
COLLINS, WILKIE   1824-1889
England
1860 The Woman in White
1868 The Moonstone

0426
CONSTANTINE, K. C.
"Mario Balzic, Chief of Police, Rocksburg, PA"
1972 The Rocksburg Railroad Murders
1973 The Man Who Liked to Look at Himself
1974 The Blank Page
1975 A Fix Like This

1982 The Man Who Liked Slow Tomatoes
1983 Always a Body to Trade
1985 Upon Some Midnight Clear
1988 Joey's Case

0427
CRAIG, ALISA   1922-
1983 The Terrible Tide

"The Grub-&-Stakers"
1981 The Grub-&-Stakers Move a Mountain
1985 The Grub-&-Stakers Quilt a Bee

"Det. Inspt. Madoc Rhys, Royal Canadian Mounted Police"
1981 Murder Goes Mumming
1982 A Pint of Murder
1986 A Dismal Thing to Do
See also as MACLEOD, CHARLOTTE, 0510

0428
CREASEY, JOHN   1908-1973
England
Published more than 600 books
1972 Man on the Run (1953)

"The Toff, The Honorable Richard Rollison"
1938 Introducing the Toff
1941 Salute the Toff
1964 A Knife for the Toff (1951)
1964 A Rocket for the Toff (1960)
1964 The Toff & the Runaway Bride (1959)
1964 The Toff in New York (1956)
1964 The Toff on the Farm (1958)
1965 A Doll for the Toff
1965 Double for the Toff (1959)
1965 Leave It to the Toff (1963)
1965 Model for the Toff (1957)
1965 Poison for the Toff (1946)
1965 The Toff & the Kidnapped Child (1960)
1965 The Toff & the Stolen Tresses (1958)
1966 Fool the Toff (1950)
1966 Kill the Toff (1950)
1966 A Mask for the Toff (1951)
1966 The Toff & the Spider (1965)
1966 The Toff in Wax
1966 The Toff on Fire (1957)
1967 Here Comes the Toff
1967 Follow the Toff (1961)
1967 Make-Up for the Toff (1956)
1967 The Toff & the Deep Blue Sea (1955)
1967 The Toff & the Great Illusion (1944)
1967 The Toff Goes to Market (1942)
1968 A Bundle for the Toff
1968 Stars for the Toff
1968 The Toff & the Toughs (1961)
1968 The Toff at the Fair (1954)
1968 The Toff Proceeds (1941)
1969 Call the Toff (1953)
1969 Hunt the Toff (1952)
1969 A Six for the Toff (1955)
1969 The Toff & the Curate (1944)
1969 The Toff & the Golden Boy
1969 The Toff Down Under (1953)
1970 Feathers for the Toff (1945; Rev., (1964)
1970 The Toff & Old Harry (1948)
1970 The Toff & the Fallen Angels
1971 Vote for the Toff
1972 The Toff Takes Shares (1948)
1972 The Toff & the Trip-Trip-Triplets
1973 The Toff & the Terrified Taxman
1973 The Toff on Board (1949)
1974 The Toff Is Back (1942)
1975 Accuse the Toff (Rev., 1943)
1975 The Toff & the Lady (1946)
1975 The Toff & the Sleepy Cowboy (1974)
1976 The Toff among the Millions (1943, Rev., 1964)
1976 The Toff at Butlin's (1954)
1977 The Toff & the Crooked Copper
1977 The Toff in Town (Rev., 1948)

"Inspt. Roger West, Scotland Yard"
1943 Inspector West Leaves Town
1948 A Battle for Inspector West
1952 The Creepers (1950)
1952 The Figure in the Dusk
1954 The Blind Spot
1954 Give a Man a Gun
1956 The Beauty Queen Killer
1956 Gelignite Gang
1957 Death of a Postman
1957 Hit & Run
1958 The Case against Paul Raeburn
1959 The Trouble at Saxby's
1960 Death of an Assassin
1960 Murder: One, Two, Three
1961 The Killing Strike (1958)
1961 Murder, London-New York
1962 Death in Cold Print
1962 Death of a Race Horse
1963 Hang the Little Man
1963 Murder on the Line (1960)
1963 The Scene of the Crime
1964 Policeman's Dread

Section 5 - Mysteries

1965 Look Three Ways at Murder
1965 Murder, London-Australia
1966 The Case of the Innocent Victims
1966 Murder, London-South Africa
1967 The Dissemblers
1967 The Executioners
1968 So Young to Burn
1969 Murder, London-Miami
1970 A Part for a Policeman
1971 Alibi
1972 Inspector West Takes Charge
1972 A Splinter of Glass
1973 Inspector West at Home (1944)
1973 The Theft of Magna Carta
1974 The Extortioners
1975 Inspector West Alone (1950)
1976 Send Superintendent West
1978 A Sharp Rise in Crime
See also as ASHE, GORDON, 0394; HUNT, KYLE, 0477; MARRIC, J. J., 0514; MORTON, ANTHONY, 0522; YORK, JEREMY, 0588; SPY STORIES, 0358 & HISTORICAL FICTION, 1044 as CREASY, JOHN

0429
CRISPIN, EDMUND   1921-1978
England
Real name: Robert Bruce Montgomery; also writes under this name
"Gervase Fen, Professor of Language & Literature, Oxford University"
1944 The Case of the Gilded Fly (Obsequies at Oxford)
1945 Holy Disorders
1946 The Moving Toyshop
1947 Dead & Dumb (Swan Song)
1948 Love Lies Bleeding
1949 Buried for Pleasure
1950 Sudden Vengeance
1951 The Long Divorce
1953 Beware of the Trains
1977 The Glimpses of the Moon
1980 Fen Country (SS)

0430
CROSS, AMANDA   1926-
Real name: Carolyn Heilbrun
"Dr. Kate Fansler, Professor of English, university in New York City"
1964 In the Last Analysis
1967 The James Joyce Murder
1970 Poetic Justice
1971 The Theban Mysteries
1976 The Question of Max
1981 Death in a Tenured Position
1984 Sweet Death, Kind Death

1986 No Word from Winifred

0431
CUNNINGHAM, E. V.   1914-
Real name: Howard Fast
1960 Sylvia
1962 Phyllis
1963 Alice
1964 Lydia
1964 Shirley
1965 Penelope
1966 Helen
1966 Margie
1967 Sally
1969 The Assassin Who Gave Up His Gun
1973 Millie
1986 The Wabash Factor

"Det. Masao Masuto, Beverly Hills Police Dept."
1967 Samantha
1977 The Case of the One-Penny Orange
1978 The Case of the Russian Diplomat
1979 The Case of the Poisoned Eclairs
1981 The Case of the Sliding Pool
1982 The Case of the Kidnapped Angel
1984 The Case of the Murdered MacKenzie
See also ROMANCES, 0048; HISTORICAL FICTION, 0906, 0971 & 1054 as FAST, HOWARD

0432
DALEY, ROBERT   1930-
1983 The Dangerous Edge

"New York Police Dept."
1973 Target Blue
1976 To Kill a Cop
1979 Prince of the City
1981 Year of the Dragon
1985 Hands of a Stranger
1988 Man with a Gun

0433
DICKINSON, PETER   1927-
England
Real name: Malcolm De Brissac
1973 The Green Gene
1974 The Poison Oracle
1975 The Lively Dead
1976 King & Joker
1977 Walking Dead

1981 A Summer in the Twenties
1982 The Last House Party
1983 Hindsight
1985 Death of a Unicorn
1986 Tefuga
1988 Perfect Gallows

"Inspt. Supt. Jimmy Pibble, Scotland Yard"
1968 The Glass Sided Ants' Nest (Skin Deep)
1969 The Old English Peep Show (A Pride of Heroes)
1970 The Sinful Stones (The Seals)
1971 Sleep & His Brother
1972 The Lizard in the Cup
1979 One Foot in the Grave

0434
DICKSON, CARTER   1906-1977
England
Real Name: John Dickson Carr
1940 The Department of Queer Complaints (SS)
1956 Fear is the Same

"Sir Henry Merrivale, Scotland Yard"
1934 The Plague Court Murders
1934 The White Priory Murders
1935 The Red Widow Murders
1935 The Unicorn Murders
1937 The Peacock Feather Murders
1937 The Punch & Judy Murders
1938 Death in Five Boxes
1938 The Judas Window
1939 Fatal Descent
1939 The Reader is Warned
1940 And So to Murder
1942 The Gilded Man
1943 She Died a Lady
1944 He Wouldn't Kill Patience
1945 The Curse of the Bronze Lamp
1946 My Late Wives
1948 The Skeleton in the Clock
1949 A Graveyard to Let
1950 Night at the Mocking Widow
1952 Behind the Crimson Blind
1953 The Cavalier's Cup
1959 Cross of Murder (1940 Seeing is Believing)
1959 Murder in the Atlantic (1940 Nine & Death Makes Ten)
See also as CARR, JOHN DICKSON, 0412

0435
DILLON, EILÍS   1920-

Ireland
1963 Death at Crane's Court
1986 Death in the Quadrangle (1956)
1986 Sent to His Account (1954)
See also HISTORICAL FICTION, 0966

0436
DISNEY, DORIS MILES
"Jeff Dimarco, Insurance Claims Investigator"
1946 Dark Road
1949 Family Skeleton
1951 Straw Man
1955 Trick or Treat
1957 Method in Madness
1959 Did She Fall or Was She Pushed?
1962 Find the Woman
1971 The Chandler Policy

"David Madden, Postal Inspector"
1956 Unappointed Rounds
1958 Black Mail
1961 Mrs. Meeker's Money
"Jim O'Neil, CT City Police"
1943 Compound for Death
1945 Murder on a Tangent
1947 Appointment at Nine
1950 Fire at Will
1954 The Last Straw

0437
DOMINIC, R. B.
Real names: Martha Hennisart & Mary J. Latsis
"Ben Safford, Member of the U.S. House of Representatives; Democrat, Ohio"
1968 Murder, Sunny Side Up
1970 Murder in High Places
1971 There is No Justice
1974 Epitaph for a Lobbyist
1976 Murder Out of Commission
1980 The Attending Physician
1984 Unexpected Developments
See also as LATHAM, EMMA, 0491

0438
DOYLE, SIR ARTHUR CONAN
1859-1930
England
"Sherlock Holmes"
1890 A Study in Scarlet
1892 The Adventures of Sherlock Holmes (SS)
1893 The Sign of Four
1894 The Memoirs of Sherlock Holmes (SS)

Section 5 - Mysteries

1902 The Hound of the Baskervilles
1914 The Valley of Fear
See homage paid to Holmes by
NICHOLAS MEYER, 0519

0439
EBERHART, MIGNON GOOD   1899-
1933 The Dark Garden
1933 The White Cockatoo
1935 The House on the Roof
1936 Fair Warning
1937 Danger in the Dark
1937 The Pattern
1938 The Glass Slipper
1938 Hasty Wedding
1939 The Chiffon Scarf
1940 The Hangman's Whip
1941 Speak No Evil
1941 Strangers in Flight
1941 With This Ring
1943 The Man Next Door
1943 Unidentified Woman
1944 Escape the Night
1945 Wings of Fear
1946 The White Dress
1947 Another Woman's House
1949 House of Storm
1950 Hunt with the Hounds
1951 Never Look Back
1952 Dead Men's Plans
1953 The Unknown Quantity
1956 Postmark Murder
1957 Another Man's Murder
1960 Jury of One
1961 The Cup, the Blade or the Gun
1961 The Promise of Murder (1959, Melora)
1962 Enemy in the House
1963 Run Scared
1964 Call after Midnight
1965 R.S.V.P. Murder
1966 Witness at Large
1967 Woman on the Roof
1968 Message from Hong Kong
1971 Two Little Rich Girls
1972 The House by the Sea
1973 Murder in Waiting
1974 Danger Money
1976 Enemy in the House
1976 The Man Next Door
1977 Five Passengers from Lisbon (1946)
1977 Nine O'Clock Tide
1980 Casa Madrone
1981 Family Affair
1982 Next of Kin
1983 The Patient in Cabin C
1984 Alpine Condo Crossfire
1986 A Fighting Chance
1988 Three Days for Emeralds

"Sarah Keate, Nurse, & Lance O'Leary, Detective"
1929 The Patient in Room 18
1930 The Mystery of Hunting's End
1930 While the Patient Slept
1931 From This Dark Stairway
1932 Murder by an Aristocrat
1942 Wolf in Man's Clothing
1954 Man Missing
Has been writing since the 1930s; also writes romances; Aeonian Press & Popular Library reprints.

0440
EBERSOHN, WESSEL
South Africa
"Yudel Gordon, Police Psychiatrist, Dept. of Prisons, Pretoria, South Africa"
1979 A Lonely Place to Die
1981 Divide the Night

0441
ERSKINE, MARGARET
England
Real name: Margaret Wetherby Williams
"Inspt. Septimus Finch, Scotland Yard"
1947 The Whispering House
1949 Give Up the Ghost
1951 The Silver Ladies
1954 Dead by Now
1955 The Dead Don't Speak
1956 The Voice of Murder
1959 A Graveyard Plot
1961 The Woman at Belguardo
1963 No 9 Belmont Square
1966 The Family at Tammerton
1967 Case with Three Husbands
1968 The Ewe Lamb
1969 Sleep No More (1958)
1970 The Case of Mary Fielding
1971 The Brood of Folly
1972 Caravan of Night
1972 Don't Look Behind You
1972 The Painted Mask
1973 Besides the Wench Is Dead
1975 Harriet, Farewell
1977 The House in Hook Street

0442
ESTLEMAN, LOREN D.
"Amos Walker, Private Investigator, Detroit"

1980 Motor City Blue
1981 Angel Eyes
1982 The Midnight Man
1983 The Glass Highway
1984 Sugartown
1985 Every Brilliant Eye
1987 Lady Yesterday
1988 Downriver
1988 General Murders (SS)

"Peter Macklin, Mob Connections, Detroit"
1984 Kill Zone
1985 Roses Are Dead (Sequel to Kill Zone)
1986 Any Man's Death
See also WESTERNS, 0839

0443
FAIR, A. A.   1889-1970
Real name: Erle Stanley Gardner
"Donald Lam & Bertha Cool, the Cool-Lam Detective Agency"
1939 The Bigger They Come
1940 Gold Comes in Bricks
1940 Turn On the Heat
1941 Double or Quits
1941 Spill the Jackpot
1942 Bats Fly at Dusk
1942 Owls Don't Blink
1943 Cats Prowl at Night
1944 Give 'em the Ax
1946 Crows Can't Count
1947 Fools Die on Friday
1949 Bedrooms Have Windows
1952 Top of the Heap
1953 Some Women Won't Wait
1956 Beware the Curves
1957 Some Slips Don't Show
1957 You Can Die Laughing
1958 The Count of Nine
1959 Pass the Gravy
1960 Kept Women Can't Quit
1961 Bachelors Get Lonely
1961 Shills Can't Cash Chips
1962 Try Anything Once
1963 Fish or Cut Bait
1964 Up for Grabs
1965 Cut Thin to Win
1966 Widows Wear Weeds
1967 Traps Need Fresh Bait
1970 All Grass Isn't Green
See also as GARDNER, ERLE STANLEY, 0451

0444
FERRARS, E. X. (Elizabeth X.)   1907-
England
Real Name: Morna Doris Brown
1945 I, Said the Fly
1946 Cheat the Hangman (Murder among Friends)
1949 The March Hare Murders
1950 Hunt the Tortoise
1952 Alibi for a Witch
1952 The Clock That Wouldn't Stop
1955 Enough to Kill a Horse
1956 Kill or Cure
1956 We Haven't Seen Her Lately
1957 Count the Cost
1958 Depart This Life
1960 Fear the Light
1960 Sleeping Dogs
1962 Seeing Double
1962 The Wandering Widows
1963 The Decayed Gentlewoman
1963 The Doubly Dead
1966 No Peace for the Wicked
1967 Zero at the Bone
1968 The Swaying Pillars
1969 Skeleton Staff
1970 Seven Sleepers
1971 A Stranger & Afraid
1972 Breath of Suspicion
1972 Foot in the Grave
1973 The Small World of Murder
1974 Hanged Man's House
1975 Alive & Dead
1975 The Cup & the Lip
1975 Drowned Rat
1976 Blood Flies Upwards
1977 The Pretty Pink Shroud
1978 Murders Anonymous
1979 Witness before the Fact
1980 Designs on Life (SS)
1981 Experiment with Death
1982 Skeleton in Search of a Closet
1987 Come to Be Killed

"Professor Andrew Basnett"
1983 Something Wicked
1984 Root of All Evil
1985 The Crime & the Crystal
1987 The Other Devil's Name

"Toby Dyke"
1941 Murder of a Suicide
1941 Rehearsals for a Murder
1942 The Shape of a Stain
1943 Neck in a Noose

"Virginia Freer & Ex-husband Felix"
1978 In at the Kill
1978 Last Will & Testament
1980 Frog in the Throat
1982 Thinner than Water

Section 5 - Mysteries

1983 Death of a Minor Character
1986 I Met Murder

0445
FINNEY, JACK   1911-
1954 Five Against the House
1957 The House of Numbers
1959 Assault on a Queen
1970 Time & Again
1977 The Night People
See also SCIENCE FICTION, 0770

0446
FRANCIS, DICK   1920-
England
1962 Dead Cert
1964 Nerve
1965 For Kicks
1967 Flying Finish
1968 Blood Sport
1969 Enquiry
1969 Forfeit
1969 Three to Show
1971 Rat Race
1972 Bonecrack
1972 Smokescreen
1974 Slayride
1975 Knockdown
1976 High Stakes
1977 In the Frame
1978 Risk
1979 Trial Run
1981 Reflex
1982 Twice Shy
1983 Banker
1984 The Danger
1985 Proof
1988 Hot Money

"Kit Fielding, Steeplechase Jockey"
1986 Break In
1987 Bolt
"Sid Halley, Ex-jockey/Private Investigator"
1966 Odds Against
1980 Whip Hand

0447
FRASER, ANTONIA   1932-
England
"Jemima Shore, TV Personality, London"
1977 Quiet as a Nun
1978 The Wild Island
1982 Cool Repentance
1983 A Splash of Red
1985 Oxford Blood

1987 Jemina Shore's First Case (SS)
1988 Your Royal Hostage

0448
FRASER, JAMES
Real name: Alan White; also writes as Alec Whitney
"Supt. Bill Aveyard, Birton Police Force, England"
1969 The Cock-Pit of Roses
1969 The Evergreen Death
1970 Deadly Nightshade
1971 Death in a Pheasant's Eye
1972 Blood on a Widow's Cross
1973 The Five-Leafed Clover
1975 A Wreath of Lords & Ladies
1976 Who Steals My Name?
1977 Heart's Ease in Death

0449
FREELING, NICHOLAS   1927-
England
1965 Valparaiso
1968 This Is the Castle
1977 Gadget
1983 The Back of the North Wind
1985 A City Solitary

"Commissaris Piet Van der Valk, Amsterdam Central Research"
1962 Love in Amsterdam (Death in Amsterdam)
1963 Gun before Butter
1963 Question of Loyalty
1964 Because of the Cats
1965 Double-Barrel
1966 Criminal Conversation
1966 The King of the Rainy Country
1967 The Dresden Green
1967 Strike Out Where Not Applicable
1969 Tsing-Boom!
1971 The Lovely Ladies
1972 Apres De Ma Blonde
1975 Over the High Side

"Van der Valk's Widow, Arlette"
1979 The Widow
1981 Arlette

"Officer Henri Castang, Regional Service of the P.J., France"
1974 A Dressing of Diamond
1976 The Bugles Blowing
1977 Sabine
1978 The Night Lords
1980 Castang's City
1982 Wolfnight

1984 No Part in Your Death
1986 Cold Iron

0450
FREMLIN, CELIA   1914-
England
1958 The Hours before Dawn
1960 Uncle Paul
1961 Seven Lean Years
1961 Wait for the Wedding
1963 The Trouble Makers
1965 The Jealous One
1967 Prisoner's Base
1969 Possession
1970 Don't Go to Sleep in the Dark (SS)
1972 Appointment with Yesterday
1974 By Horror Haunted (SS)
1976 The Long Shadow
1978 The Spider-Orchid
1980 With No Crying
1982 The Parasite Person
1984 A Lovely Day to Die (SS)

0451
GARDNER, ERLE STANLEY   1889-1970
"Perry Mason, Criminal lawyer"
1933 The Case of the Velvet Claws
1933 The Case of the Sulky Girl
1934 The Case of the Curious Bride
1934 The Case of the Howling Dog
1934 The Case of the Lucky Legs
1935 The Case of the Counterfeit Eye
1936 The Case of the Caretaker's Cat
1936 The Case of the Sleepwalker's Niece
1937 The Case of the Dangerous Dowager
1937 The Case of the Lame Canary
1937 The Case of the Stuttering Bishop
1938 The Case of the Shoplifter's Shoe
1938 The Case of the Substitute Face
1939 The Case of the Perjured Parrot
1939 The Case of the Rolling Bones
1940 The Case of the Baited Hook
1940 The Case of the Silent Partner
1941 The Case of the Empty Tin
1941 The Case of the Haunted Husband
1942 The Case of the Careless Kitten
1942 The Case of the Drowning Duck
1943 The Case of the Buried Clock
1943 The Case of the Drowsy Mosquito
1944 The Case of the Black-Eyed Blond
1944 The Case of the Crooked Candle
1945 The Case of the Golddigger's Purse
1945 The Case of the Half-Wakened Wife
1946 The Case of the Borrowed Brunette
1947 The Case of the Fan Dancer's Horse
1947 The Case of the Lazy Lover
1948 The Case of the Lonely Heiress
1948 The Case of the Vagabond Virgin
1949 The Case of the Cautious Coquette
1949 The Case of the Dubious Bridegroom
1950 The Case of the Negligent Nymph
1950 The Case of the One-Eyed Witness
1951 The Case of the Angry Mourner
1951 The Case of the Fiery Fingers
1952 The Case of the Grinning Gorilla
1952 The Case of the Moth-Eaten Mink
1953 The Case of the Green-Eyed Sister
1953 The Case of the Hesitant Hostess
1954 The Case of the Fugitive Nurse
1954 The Case of the Restless Redhead
1954 The Case of the Runaway Corpse
1955 The Case of the Glamorous Ghost
1955 The Case of the Nervous Accomplice
1955 The Case of the Sun Bather's Diary
1956 The Case of the Demure Defendant
1956 The Case of the Gilded Lily
1956 The Case of the Terrified Typist
1957 The Case of the Daring Decoy
1957 The Case of the Lucky Loser
1957 The Case of the Screaming Woman
1958 The Case of the Calendar Girl
1958 The Case of the Foot-Loose Doll
1958 The Case of the Long-Legged Models
1959 The Case of the Deadly Toy
1959 The Case of the Mythical Monkeys
1959 The Case of the Singing Skirt
1960 The Case of the Duplicate Daughter
1960 The Case of the Shapely Shadow
1960 The Case of the Waylaid Wolf

Section 5 - Mysteries

1961 The Case of the Bigamous Spouse
1961 The Case of the Spurious Spinster
1962 The Case of the Blonde Bonanza
1962 The Case of the Ice-Cold Hands
1962 The Case of the Reluctant Model
1963 The Case of the Amorous Aunt
1963 The Case of the Mischievous Doll
1963 The Case of the Stepdaughter's Secret
1964 The Case of the Daring Divorcee
1964 The Case of the Horrified Heirs
1964 The Case of the Phantom Fortune
1965 The Case of the Beautiful Beggar
1965 The Case of the Troubled Trustee
1966 The Case of the Worried Waitress
1967 The Case of the Queenly Contestant
1968 The Case of the Careless Cupid
1969 The Case of the Fabulous Fake
1972 The Case of the Fenced-In Woman
1973 The Case of the Postponed Murder
See also as FAIR, A. A., 0443

0452
GARFIELD, BRIAN   1939-
Also writes as Frank Wynne & Frank O'Brian
1972 Death Wish
1972 Relentless
1974 The Threepersons Hunt
1975 Death Sentence
1976 Hopscotch
1977 Recoil
1984 Necessity
See also HEADLINES, 0332 & WESTERNS, 0844

0453
GARVE, ANDREW   1908-
England
Real name: Paul Winterton; also writes as Roger Bax & as Paul Somers
1950 Fontego's Folly
1950 No Tears for Hilda
1951 By-Line for Murder
1952 A Hole in the Ground
1952 Murder through the Looking Glass
1953 The Cuckoo Line Affair
1954 Death & the Sky Above
1955 The Riddle of Sampson
1956 The End of the Track
1957 The Megstone Plot
1958 The Galloway Case

1958 The Narrow Search
1959 A Hero For Leanda
1960 The Far Sands
1960 The Golden Deed
1961 The House of Soldiers
1962 Prisoner's Friend
1963 The Sea Monks
1964 Frame-Up
1965 The Ashes of Loda
1966 Hide & Go Seek
1967 A Very Quiet Place
1968 The Long Short Cut
1969 The Ascent of D-13
1970 Boomerang
1971 The Late Bill Smith
1972 The Case of Robert Quarry
1974 The Lester Affair
1976 Home to Roost
1978 Counterstroke

0454
GASH, JONATHAN   1933-
England
"Lovejoy, Antiques Dealer, London"
1977 The Judas Pair
1978 Gold by Gemini
1980 The Grail Tree
1981 Spend Game
1981 The Vatican Rip
1983 The Sleepers of Erin
1984 Firefly Gadroon
1984 The Gondola Scam
1985 Pearlhanger
1986 The Tartan Sell
1987 Moonspender

0455
GILBERT, MICHAEL   1912-
England
1955 The Country-House Burglar
1956 Be Shot for Sixpence
1959 Blood & Judgment
1963 After the Fine Weather
1967 The Crack in the Teapot
1967 Game without Rules
1967 Overdrive
1969 The Family Tomb
1972 The Body of a Girl
1973 The 92nd Tiger
1974 Flash Point
1976 The Night of the Twelfth
1977 Petrella at Q
1978 The Empty House
1980 The Killing of Katie Steelstock
1982 End-Game
1984 The Black Seraphim
1985 The Long Journey Home

1987 Trouble

"Inspt. Hazelrigg, Scotland Yard"
1949 He Didn't Mind Danger
1950 Smallbone Deceased
1952 The Danger Within
1952 Death Has Deep Roots
1953 Fear to Tread
1962 The Doors Open (1949)
1963 Close Quarters (1947)

0456
GILL, BARTHOLOMEW 1943-
"Chief Supt. Peter McGarr, Garda Siochana, Ireland"
1977 McGarr & The Sienese Conspiracy
1978 McGarr & the Politician's Wife
1978 McGarr on the Cliffs of Moher
1980 McGarr at the Dublin Horse Show
1984 McGarr & the Method of Descartes
1984 McGarr & the P.M. of Belgrave Square
1986 McGarr & the Legacy of a Woman Scorned

0457
GILMAN, DOROTHY 1923-
Real name: Dorothy Gilman Butters
1975 The Clairvoyant Countess
1975 A Nun in the Closet
1979 The Tightrope Walker
See also SPY STORIES, 0364

0458
GOLDTHWAITE, EATON K. 1907-
1942 Don't Mention My Name
1943 You Did It
1945 Scarecrow
1946 Date with Death
1948 Root of Evil
1951 Cut for Partners
1953 Sixpenny Dame
1968 Once You Stop, You're Dead
1971 The Marble Forest
1981 First You Have to Find Him

0459
GRAFTON, SUE
"Kinsey Millhone, California Private Investigator"
1984 A Is for Alibi
1985 B Is for Burglar
1986 C Is for Corpse

1987 D Is for Deadbeat
1988 E Is for Evidence

0460
GRAYSON, RICHARD 1951-
"Inspt. Gautier, Paris Sureté, Early 1900s"
1978 The Murders at Impasse Louvain
1980 The Monterant Affair
1981 The Death of Abbe Didier
1982 The Montmartre Murders
1984 Crime without Passion
1986 Death en Voyage
1988 Death on the Cards
See also as GRINDAL, RICHARD, 0463

0461
GREELEY, ANDREW 1928-
"Father Blackie Ryan, Catholic Priest"
1985 Happy Are the Meek
1986 Happy Are the Clean of Heart
1987 Happy Are Those Who Thirst for Justice
1987 Rite of Spring

"Time between the Stars"
1985 Virgin & Martyr
1986 Angels of September
1987 Patience of a Saint
See also SCIENCE FICTION, 0641 & TRASH, 1128

0462
GRIMES, MARTHA
"Supt. Richard Jury, Scotland Yard, & Melrose Plant, Aristocrat Sleuth"
1981 The Man with a Load of Mischief
1982 The Old Fox Deceiv'd
1983 The Anodyne Necklace
1984 The Dirty Duck
1984 Jerusalem Inn
1985 Help the Poor Struggler
1985 The Deer Leap
1986 I Am the Only Running Footman
1987 The Five Bells & Bladebone

0463
GRINDAL, RICHARD 1951-
1982 Death Stalk
1987 The Whiskey Murders
See also as GRAYSON, RICHARD, 0460

0464
GULIK, ROBERT HANS VAN 1910-1967

Section 5 - Mysteries

"Judge Dee, Bearded Detective & Magistrate, Pooyang District, 7th & 8th Century China, Tang Dynasty"
1957 The Chinese Maze Murders
1958 The Chinses Bell Murders
1959 The Chinese Gold Murders
1960 The Chinese Lake Murders
1961 The Chinese Nail Murders
1963 The Emperor's Pearl
1963 The Lacquer Screen
1965 The Monkey & the Tiger
1965 The Willow Pattern
1966 Murder in Canton
1966 The Phantom of the Temple
1967 Judge Dee at Work (SS)
1967 Necklace & Calabash
1968 Poets & Murder
1968 The Red Pavilion
1969 The Haunted Monastery

0465
GUTCHEON, BETH   1945-
1981 Still Missing

0466
HAMMETT, DASHIELL   1894-1961
1931 The Glass Key

"Sam Spade, Private Investigator"
1930 The Maltese Falcon

"The Continental Op"
1929 The Dain Curse
1929 Red Harvest
1948 The Big Knock-Over (SS)
1974 The Continental Op (SS)

"Nick & Nora Charles"
1934 The Thin Man

0467
HANSEN, JOSEPH   1923-
1982 Backtrack
1988 Bohannon's Books (SS)

"Dave Brandstetter, Gay Insurance Investigator"
1970 Fadeout
1973 Death Claims
1975 Troublemaker
1978 The Man Everybody Was Afraid Of
1979 Skinflick
1982 Gravedigger
1984 Brandstetter & Others (SS)
1984 Nightwork

1986 The Little Dog Laughed
1986 Steps Going Down
1987 Early Graves

0468
HARE, CYRIL   1900-1958
England
Real name: Alfred Alexander Gordon Clark
1951 An English Murder

"Francis Pettigrew, Barrister, & Inspt. Mallett, C.I.D., Scotland Yard"
1937 Tenant for Death
1938 Death Is No Sportsman
1943 Tragedy at Law
1946 With a Bare Bodkin
1950 The Wind Blows Death
1954 Death Walks the Woods
1954 Suicide Excepted
1958 Untimely Death
1959 Death among Friends (SS)

0469
HAYMON, S. T.
England
"Det. Inspt. Ben Jurnet, Scotland Yard"
1981 Death & the Pregnant Virgin
1982 Ritual Murder
1984 Stately Homicide
1987 Death of a God

0470
HEALD, TIM   1944-
England
"Simon Bognor, British Board of Trade"
1973 Unbecoming Habits
1974 Blue Blood Will Out
1975 Deadline
1976 Let Sleeping Dogs Lie
1979 Just Desserts
1981 Murder at Moose Jaw
1982 A Small Masterpiece
1986 Red Herrings
1988 Brought to Book

0471
HEYER, GEORGETTE   1902-1974
England
Also wrote as Stella Martin
1932 Footsteps in the Dark
1936 Why Shoot a Butler?
1937 The Unfinished Clue
1943 Penhallow

"Supt. Hannasyde"
1935 Merely Murder
1936 Behold, Here's Poison
1937 They Found Him Dead
1938 A Blunt Instrument
1970 Death in the Stocks (1935)

"Inspt. Hemingway"
1939 No Wind of Blame
1941 Envious Casca
1961 Detection Unlimited
1969 Duplicate Death
See also ROMANCES, 0064 &
HISTORICAL FICTION, 0987

0472
HIGGINS, GEORGE V.   1939-
1972 The Friends of Eddie Coyle
1973 The Digger's Game (Sequel to Friends)
1974 Cogan's Trade
1976 The Judgment of Deke Hunter
1977 Dreamland
1981 The Rat on Fire
1983 A Choice of Enemies
1985 Imposters

"Jerry Kennedy, Sleazy Lawyer, Boston"
1980 Kennedy for the Defense
1985 Penance for Jerry Kennedy
See also HEADLINES, 0239 &
AMERICAN AUTHORS, 1228

0473
HIGHSMITH, PATRICIA   1921-
Also writes as Claire Morgan
1950 Strangers on a Train
1954 The Blunderer
1957 Deep Water
1958 A Game for the Living
1960 This Sweet Sickness
1962 The Cry of the Owl
1964 The Glass Cell
1964 The Two Faces of January
1965 The Storyteller
1965 A Suspension of Mercy
1967 Those Who Walk Away
1969 The Tremor of Forgery
1970 The Snail-Watcher (SS)
1972 A Dog's Ransom
1975 The Animal Lover's Book of Beastly Murder (SS)
1977 Edith's Diary
1980 Little Tales of Misogyny (SS)
1987 Found in the Street
1988 The Black House (SS)

"Tom Ripley"
1955 The Talented Mr. Ripley (Published first under Claire Morgan)
1970 Ripley under Ground
1974 Ripley's Game
1980 The Boy Who Followed Ripley

0474
HILL, REGINALD   1936-
England
Also writes as Dick Morland, Patrick Ruell & Charles Underhill
1971 Fell of Dark
1972 A Fairly Dangerous Thing
1976 Another Death in Venice
1982 A Very Good Hater (1974)
1988 There Are No Ghosts in the Soviet Union (SS)

"Supt. Andrew Dalziel & Inspt. Peter Pascoe, Mid-Yorkshire C.I.D."
1970 A Clubbable Woman
1971 An Advancement of Learning
1975 An April Shroud
1977 Ruling Passion
1978 A Pinch of Snuff
1981 A Killing Kindness
1984 Deadheads
1984 Exit Lines
1987 Child's Play
1988 Underworld
See also SPY STORIES, 0370

0475
HILLERMAN, TONY   1925-
1971 The Fly on the Wall

"Lt. Joe Leaphorn, Sgt. Jim Chee, Navaho Tribal Police"
1970 The Blessing Way
1973 Dance Hall of the Dead
1978 Listening Woman
1980 People of Darkness
1982 The Dark Wind
1984 The Ghostway
1986 Skinwalkers
1988 A Thief of Time

0476
HOLLAND, ISABELLE   1920-
1984 A Death at St. Anselm's
1985 Flight of the Archangel
1986 A Lover Scorned
See also ROMANCES, 0070

Section 5 - Mysteries

0477
HUNT, KYLE   1908-1973
England
Real name: John Creasey
1958   Kill My Love

"Dr. Emmanuel Cellini, Psychiatrist & Detective"
1965   Cunning as a Fox
1966   Wicked as the Devil
1967   Sly as a Serpent
1968   Cruel as the Cat
1969   Too Good to Be True
1971   A Period of Evil
1972   As Empty as Hate
1972   As Lonely as the Damned
1973   As Merry as Hell
1976   The Man Who Was Not Himself
1985   This Man Did I Kill (1974)
See also as ASHE, GORDON, 0394; CREASEY, JOHN, 0428; MARRIC, J. J., 0514; MORTON, ANTHONY, 0522; YORK, JEREMY, 0588; SPY STORIES, 0358 & HISTORICAL FICTION, 1044 as CREASY, JOHN

0478
HUNTER, ALAN   1922-
England
"Chief Supt. Gently, Scotland Yard"
1955   Gently Does It
1956   Gently by the Shore
1957   Landed Gently
1960   Gently down the Stream
1964   Gently Floating
1964   Gently Go Man
1964   Gently in the Sun
1964   Gently to the Summit
1974   Gently with the Innocents
1974   Gently with the Ladies
1975   Gently in the Highlands
1975   Gently through the Woods
1976   Gently with the Painters
1980   The Honfleur Decision
1981   Death on the Heath
1981   The Scottish Decision
1982   Gently between Tides

0479
ILES, FRANCIS   1893-1970
Real name: Anthony Cox
1931   Malice Aforethought
1932   Before the Fact
1939   As for the Woman
See also as BERKELEY, ANTHONY, 0403

0480
INNES, MICHAEL   1906-
England
Real name: J. I. M. Stewart
1946   The Unsuspected Chasm
1946   What Happened at Hazelwood?
1949   The Case of the Journeying Boy
1953   Christmas at Candleshoe
1955   The Man from the Sea
1956   A Question of Queens
1962   The Case of Sonia Wayward
1965   Money from Holme
1966   A Change of Heir
1980   Going It Alone

"Inspt. Appleby, Scotland Yard"
1937   Seven Suspects
1937   Hamlet, Revenge!
1938   Lament for a Maker
1939   The Spider Strikes
1940   A Comedy of Terrors
1941   Appleby on Ararat
1941   The Secret Vanguard
1942   The Daffodil Affair
1943   The Weight of the Evidence
1945   Appleby's End
1947   A Night of Errors
1951   The Paper Thunderbolt
1952   One-Man Show
1954   Dead Man's Shows
1956   Appleby Talks Again (SS)
1957   Death on a Quiet Day
1958   The Long Farewell
1959   Hare Sitting Up
1961   Silence Observed
1962   The Crabtree Affair
1966   The Bloody Wood
1968   Death by Water
1969   Picture of Guilt
1970   Death at the Chase
1971   An Awkward Lie
1972   The Open House
1973   Appleby's Answer
1974   Appleby's Other Story
1975   The Appleby File
1977   The Gay Phoenix
1981   The Ampersand Papers
1982   Sheiks & Adders
1983   Appleby & Honeybath
1984   Carson's Conspiracy
1987   Appleby & the Ospreys

"Charles Honeybath, Royal Academy"
1975   The Mysterious Commission
1978   Honeybath's Haven
1981   Lord Mullion's Secret
1983   Appleby & Honeybath

0481
JAFFE, RONA 1932-
1981 Mazes & Monsters
See also TRASH, 1133

0482
JAMES, P. D. 1920-
England
1980 Innocent Blood

"Supt. Adam Dalgliesh, Scotland Yard"
1962 Cover Her Face
1963 A Mind to Murder
1967 Unnatural Causes
1971 Shroud for a Nightingale
1975 The Black Tower
1977 The Death of an Expert Witness
1986 A Taste for Death

"Cordelia Grey, Female Private Investigator"
1973 An Unsuitable Job for a Woman
1982 The Skull beneath the Skin

0483
JEFFREYS, J. G. 1908-
Real name: Benjamin James Healey; published as Jeremy Sturrock in England
"Jeremy Sturrock, Bow Street Runners"
1972 The Thieftaker
1973 A Wicked Way to Die
1975 The Wilful Lady
1977 A Conspiracy of Poisons
1981 Suicide Most Foul
1982 Captain Bolton's Corpse
1983 The Pangersbourne Murders
1987 The Thistlewood Plot

0484
KALLEN, LUCILLE
"C. B. Greenfield, Newpaper Editor & Maggie Rome, Employee, Sloan's Ford, NY"
1978 Introducing C. B. Greenfield
1980 C.B. Greenfield: The Tanglewood Murder
1982 C.B. Greenfield: No Lady in the House
1984 C.B. Greenfield: The Piano Bird
1985 C.B. Greenfield: A Little Madness

0485
KAYE, M. M. (Mary Margaret) 1911-
1953 Death Walked In Kashmir
1956 Death Walked In Cyprus
1983 Death In Berlin (1955 Death Walked in Berlin)
1983 Death In Kenya
1983 Death In Zanzibar
1985 Death In the Andamans (1960 Night on the Island)
See also ROMANCES, 0076

0486
KEATING, H. R. F. (Henry Raymond Fitzwalter) 1926-
1961 A Rush on the Ultimate
1962 The Dog It Was That Died
1963 Zen There Was a Murder
1965 Is Skin-Deep, Is Fatal
1966 Death of a Fat God
1973 Death & the Visiting Fireman
1976 A Remarkable Case of Burglary
1980 The Murder of the Maharajah
1985 Mrs. Craggs: Crimes Cleaned Up (SS)

"Inspt. Ganesh Ghote, Bombay Police"
1964 The Perfect Murder
1966 Inspector Ghote's Good Crusade
1967 Inspector Ghote Caught in Meshes
1968 Inspector Ghote Hunts the Peacock
1969 Inspector Ghote Plays a Joker
1971 Inspector Ghote Breaks an Egg
1972 Inspector Ghote Goes by Train
1973 Inspector Ghote Trusts the Heart
1974 Bats Fly Up for Inspector Ghote
1977 Filmi, Filmi, Inspector Ghote
1979 Inspector Ghote Draws a Line
1981 Go West, Inspector Ghote
1984 The Sheriff of Bombay
1986 Under a Monsoon Cloud
1987 The Body in the Billiard Room

0487
KELLERMAN, JONATHAN
"Alex Delaware, Child Psychologist, Los Angeles"
1985 When the Bough Breaks
1986 Blood Test
1987 Over the Edge
1988 The Butcher's Theater

0488
KEMELMAN, HARRY 1908-
1967 The Nine-Mile Walk: The Nicky Welt Stories

Section 5 - Mysteries

"Rabbi David Small, New England"
1964 Friday the Rabbi Slept Late
1966 Saturday the Rabbi Went Hungry
1969 Sunday the Rabbi Stayed Home
1972 Monday the Rabbi Took Off
1974 Tuesday the Rabbi Saw Red
1976 Wednesday the Rabbi Got Wet
1978 Thursday the Rabbi Walked Out
1985 Someday the Rabbi Will Leave
1987 One Fine Day the Rabbi Bought a Cross

0489
KIENZLE, WILLIAM X.
"Father Robert Koesler, Catholic Priest, Detroit"
1979 The Rosary Murders
1980 Death Wears a Red Hat
1981 Mind over Murder
1982 Assault with Intent
1983 Shadow of Death
1984 Kill & Tell
1985 Sudden Death
1986 Deathbed
1987 Deadline for a Critic

0490
KNOX, BILL   1928-
England
Also writes as Robert McLeod, Michael Kirk & Noah Webster
1963 The Drum of Ungara

"Chief Officer Webb Carrick, Scottish Fishery Protection Service"
1964 The Scavengers
1966 Devilweed
1967 Backlight
1968 Figurehead
1969 Blueback
1971 Seafire
1973 Stormtide
1974 Whitewater
1975 Dead Run
1976 Hellspout
1978 Witchrock
1980 Bombship
1983 Bloodtide
1985 Wavecrest
1988 Dead Man's Mooring

"Supt. Colin Thane & Phil Moss, Glasgow C.I.D., Scotland"
1960 Leave It to the Hangman
1961 In at the Kill
1962 The Grey Sentinels
1962 Little Drops of Blood

1963 The Killing Game
1965 The Taste of Proof
1966 The Ghost Car
1967 Justice on the Rocks
1969 The Tallyman
1970 Who Shot the Bull?
1972 To Kill a Witch
1973 Draw Batons!
1975 Rally to Kill
1977 Pilot Error
1978 Live Bait
1981 A Killing in Antiques
1984 The Hanging Tree
1986 The Crossfire Killings

0491
LATHEN, EMMA
Real names: Martha Hennissart & Mary J. Lattis
"John Putnam Thatcher, Investment Banker, New York City"
1961 Banking on Death
1963 A Place for Murder
1964 Accounting for Murder
1966 Death Shall Overcome
1966 Murder Makes the Wheels Go 'Round
1967 Murder against the Grain
1968 Come to Dust
1968 A Stitch in Time
1969 Murder to Go
1969 When in Greece
1970 Pick Up Sticks
1971 Ashes to Ashes
1971 The Longer the Thread
1972 Murder without Icing
1974 Sweet & Low
1975 By Hook or by Crook
1978 Double Double, Oil & Trouble
1981 Going for the Gold
1982 Green Grow the Dollars
1988 Something in the Air
See also as DOMINIC, R. B., 0437

0492
LATIMER, JONATHAN   1906-
1950 The Fifth Grave
1955 Sinners & Shrouds
1959 Black Is the Fashion for Dying

"Bill Crane, Private Investigator"
1934 Murder in the Madhouse
1935 Headed for a Hearse
1936 The Lady in the Morgue
1938 The Dead Don't Care
1955 Some Dames are Deadly (1939, Red Gardenias)

0493
LE CARRÉ, JOHN   1931-
England
Real name: David Cornwell
"George Smiley, British Intelligence"
1962 Call for the Dead
1963 A Murder of Quality
See also SPY STORIES, 0374

0494
LEMARCHAND, ELIZABETH   1906-
England
"Det. Chief Inspt. Tom Pollard & Sgt. Gregory Toye, Scotland Yard"
1967 Death of an Old Girl
1968 The Affacombe Affair
1973 Cyanide with Compliments
1974 No Vacation from Murder
1975 Buried in the Past
1975 Death on Doomsday
1977 Step in the Dark
1978 Unhappy Returns
1979 Suddenly while Gardening
1980 Change for the Worse
1981 Nothing to Do with the Case
1982 Troubled Waters
1983 The Wheel Turns
1984 Light through Glass
1986 Alibi for a Corpse
1986 Who Goes Home?

0495
LEONARD, ELMORE   1925-
1969 The Big Bounce
1969 The Moonshine War
1974 Fifty-Two Pickup
1974 Mr. Majestyk
1976 Swag
1977 The Hunted (Unknown Man #89)
1978 Ryan's Rules
1978 The Switch
1980 City Primeval: High Noon in Detroit
1980 Gold Coast
1981 Split Images
1982 Cat Chaser
1983 LaBrava
1983 Stick
1985 Glitz
1987 Bandits
1987 Touch
1988 Freaky Deaky
See also WESTERNS, 0859

0496
LEWIN, MICHAEL Z.   1942-

1980 Outside In

"Adele Buffington, Quasi-sleuth, Social Worker, Samson's Girlfriend"
1988 And Baby Will Fall

"Lt. Leroy Powder, Indianapolis Police Dept."
1976 Night Cover
1982 Hard Line
1986 Late Payments

"Albert Samson, Private Investigator, Indianapolis"
1971 Ask the Right Question
1973 The Way We Die Now
1974 The Enemies Within
1978 The Silent Salesman
1981 Missing Woman
1984 Out of Season

0497
LOCKRIDGE, FRANCES   1896-1963 &
LOCKRIDGE, RICHARD   1898-1982
1956 The Faceless Adversary
1957 The Tangled Cord
1958 Catch as Catch Can
1959 The Innocent House
1959 Murder & Blueberry Pie
1960 The Golden Man
1961 The Drill Is Death
1962 And Left for Dead
1962 Night of Shadows
1962 The Ticking Clock
1964 The Devious Ones
1964 Quest of the Bogeyman

"Cpt./Inspt. Merton Heimrich, State Police, New York"
1947 Think of Death
1948 I Want to Come Home
1949 Spin Your Web, Lady
1950 Foggy, Foggy Death
1951 A Client Is Canceled
1952 Death by Association
1953 Stand Up & Die
1954 Death & the Gentle Bull
1955 Burnt Offering
1955 Practice to Deceive
1956 Let Dead Enough Alone
1958 Accent on Murder
1960 Show Red for Danger
1961 With One Stone
1962 First Come, First Kill
1963 The Distant Clue

"Mr. & Mrs. North"
1936 Mr. & Mrs. North (R. Lockridge)

Section 5 - Mysteries

1940 The Norths Meet Murder
1941 Murder Out of Turn
1941 A Pinch of Poison
1942 Death on the Aisle
1942 Hanged for a Sheep
1943 Death Takes a Bow
1944 Killing the Goose
1945 Payoff for the Banker
1946 Death of a Tall Man
1946 Murder within Murder
1947 Untidy Murder
1948 Murder Is Served
1949 The Dishonest Murderer
1950 Murder in a Hurry
1951 Murder Comes First
1952 Dead as a Dinosaur
1953 Curtain for a Jester
1953 Death Has a Small Voice
1954 A Key to Death
1955 Death of an Angel
1956 Voyage Into Violence
1958 The Long Skeleton
1959 Murder Is Suggested
1960 The Judge Is Reversed
1961 Murder Has Its Points
1963 Murder by the Book
See also LOCKRIDGE, RICHARD, 0498

0498
LOCKRIDGE, RICHARD 1898-1982
1949 A Matter of Taste
1965 Squire of Death
1968 Murder in False Face
1968 A Plate of Red Herrings
1970 Troubled Journey
1970 Twice Retired
1972 Death in a Sunny Place
1972 Something Up a Sleeve
1974 Death on the Hour

"Cpt./Inspt. Merton Heimrich, State Police, New York"
1964 Murder Can't Wait
1966 Murder Roundabout
1967 With Option to Die
1969 A Risky Way to Kill
1971 Inspector's Holiday
1973 Not I, Said the Sparrow
1976 Dead Run
1977 The Tenth Life

"Lt. Nathan Shapiro, New York Police Dept."
1967 Murder for Art's Sake
1969 Die Laughing
1970 Preach No More
1972 Write Murder Down
1975 Or Was He Pushed?

1976 A Streak of Light
1980 The Old Die Young
See also LOCKRIDGE, FRANCES & LOCKRIDGE, RICHARD, 0497

0499
LOVESEY, PETER 1936-
England
1982 The False Inspector Dew
1983 Keystone
1986 Rough Cider
1988 Bertie & the Tinman

"Sgt. Cribb & Constable Thackeray, Scotland Yard, Victorian Period"
1970 Wobble to Death
1971 The Detective Wore Silk Drawers
1972 Abracadaver
1973 Mad Hatter's Holiday
1974 The Tick of Death
1975 A Case of Spirits
1976 Swing, Swing Together
1978 Waxwork

0500
LYONS, ARTHUR 1946-
"Jacob Asch, Private Investigator, West Coast"
1974 At the Hands of Another
1974 The Dead Are Discreet
1976 All God's Children
1977 Dead Ringer
1980 Castles Burning
1981 Hard Trade
1982 The Killing Floor
1984 Three with a Bullet

0501
MCBAIN, ED 1926-
Real name: Evan Hunter; also writes as Evan Hunter & Richard Marsten
1965 The Sentries
1975 Where There's Smoke
1976 Guns
1982 The McBain Brief (SS)

"Matthew Hope, Lawyer, Florida"
1978 Goldilocks
1982 Rumplestiltskin
1982 Beauty & the Beast
1984 Jack & the Beanstalk
1985 Snow White & Rose Red
1986 Cinderella
1987 Puss in Boots

"New York Police Dept., 5th Precinct, Chinatown, Little Italy"
1985 Another Part of the City

"New York Police Dept., 87th Precinct, Det. Steve Carella & Others"
1956 Cop Hater
1956 The Mugger
1956 The Pusher
1957 The Con Man
1958 Killer's Choice
1958 Killer's Payoff
1958 Lady Killer
1959 Killer's Wedge
1959 King's Ransom
1959 'Til Death
1960 Give the Boys a Great Big Hand
1960 The Heckler
1960 See Them Die
1961 Lady, Lady, I Did It!
1962 The Empty Hours
1962 Like Love
1963 Ten Plus One
1964 Ax
1965 Doll
1965 He Who Hesitates
1966 Eighty Million Eyes
1968 Fuzz
1969 Shotgun
1970 Jigsaw
1971 Hail, Hail, The Gang's All Here!
1972 Sadie When She Died
1973 Hail to the Chief
1973 Let's Hear It for the Deaf Man
1974 Bread
1975 Blood Relatives
1976 So Long as You Both Shall Live
1977 Long Time No See
1979 Calypso
1980 Ghosts
1981 Heat
1983 Ice
1984 Lightning
1986 Eight Black Horses
1986 Poison
1987 Tricks

0502
MCCLURE, JAMES   1939-
South Africa
1976 Rogue Eagle

"Lt. Tromp Kramer & Det. Sgt. Mickey Zondi, Murder Squad, Trekkersburg, South Africa"
1972 The Steam Pig
1973 The Caterpillar Cop
1974 The Gooseberry Fool

1976 Snake
1977 The Sunday Hangman
1981 The Blood of an Englishman
1984 The Artful Egg
Also writes nonfiction, Cop World, 1985

0503
MCDONALD, GREGORY   1937-
1980 Who Took Toby Rinaldi?

"Fletch, Private Investigator, Boston"
1974 Fletch
1976 Confess, Fletch
1978 Fletch's Fortune
1981 Fletch & the Widow Bradley
1982 Fletch's Moxie
1983 Fletch & the Man Who
1984 Carioca Fletch
1985 Fletch Won
1986 Fletch, Too

"Inspt. Francis Xavier Flynn, Boston Police Dept."
1977 Flynn
1982 The Buck Passes Flynn
1984 Flynn's In

0504
MACDONALD, JOHN D.   1916-1986
Real name: John Dann
"Travis McGee, Private Investigator, Ft. Lauderdale, FL"
1964 The Deep Blue Good-by
1964 Nightmare in Pink
1964 The Quick Red Fox
1964 A Purple Place for Dying
1965 Bright Orange for the Shroud
1965 A Deadly Shade of Gold
1966 Darker Than Amber
1966 One Fearful Yellow Eye
1968 Pale Gray For Guilt
1968 The Girl in the Plain Brown Wrapper
1969 Dress Her in Indigo
1970 The Long Lavender Look
1972 A Tan & Sandy Silence
1973 The Scarlet Ruse
1973 The Turquoise Lament
1975 The Dreadful Lemon Sky
1978 The Empty Copper Sea
1979 The Green Ripper
1981 Free Fall in Crimson
1982 Cinnamon Skin
1984 The Lonely Silver Rain
Also wrote mystery/adventure stories

Section 5 - Mysteries

0505
MACDONALD, PHILIP   1899-
England
Also wrote as Arthur Lawless, Martin Porlock, & W. J. Stuart.
1932   Escape
1959   The List of Adrian Messenger
1962   Death & Chicanery (SS)

"Colonel Anthony Ruthven Gethryn, London"
1925   The Rasp
1928   The White Crow
1930   The Link
1930   The Noose
1931   Crime Conductor
1931   Persons Unknown
1931   The Polferry Riddle
1931   The Rynox Murder
1931   The Wraith
1932   Rope to Spare
1938   Warrant for X

0506
MACDONALD, ROSS   1915-1983
Real name: Kenneth Millar; also wrote as John Macdonald & John Ross Macdonald
1948   The Three Roads
1953   Meet Me at the Morgue
1960   The Ferguson Affair
1980   The Dark Tunnel

"Lew Archer, Private Investigator, Southern California"
1949   The Moving Target
1950   The Drowning Pool
1951   The Way Some People Die
1952   The Ivory Grin
1954   Find a Victim
1955   The Name Is Archer (SS)
1956   The Barbarous Coast
1958   The Doomsters
1959   The Galton Case
1962   The Zebra-Striped Hearse
1964   The Chill
1965   The Far Side of the Dollar
1966   Black Money
1968   The Instant Enemy
1969   The Goodbye Look
1971   The Underground Man
1973   Sleeping Beauty
1976   The Blue Hammer
1977   Lew Archer, Private Investigator (SS)

0507
MCINERNY, RALPH M.   1929-
Also writes as Harry Austin, Ernan Mackey, & Monica Quill
1985   The Noonday Devil

"Andrew Broom, Midwestern Lawyer"
1987   Cause & Effect

"Father Roger Dowling, Catholic Priest, Chicago"
1977   Her Death of Cold
1977   The Seventh Station
1978   Bishop as Pawn
1979   Lying Three
1980   Second Vespers
1981   Thicker Than Water
1982   A Loss of Patients
1983   The Grass Widow
1984   Getting a Way with Murder
1985   Rest in Pieces
1987   The Basket Case
See also as QUILL, MONICA, 0539

0508
MACKAY, AMANDA
"Dr. Hannah Land, Professor of Political Science, Duke University, NC"
1976   Death Is Academic
1981   Death on the Eno

0509
MACKENZIE, DONALD   1918-
Canada
1955   Occupation Thief
1956   Manhunt
1958   Scent of Danger
1960   Dangerous Silence
1961   Knife Edge
1962   The Genial Stranger
1963   Double Exposure
1964   Cool Sleeps Balaban
1965   The Lonely Side of the River
1966   Salute from a Dead Man
1967   Death Is a Friend
1968   The Quiet Killer
1969   Dead Straight
1969   Night Boat from Puerto Vedra
1970   The Kyle Contract
1971   Sleep Is for the Rich
1973   Postscript to a Dead Letter
1975   The Spreewald Collection

"John Raven, Ex-cop, Scotland Yard"
1974   Zaleski's Percentage
1976   Raven in Flight
1977   Raven & the Kamikaze

1977 Raven & the Ratcatcher
1978 Raven Settles a Score
1979 Raven after Dark
1980 Raven & the Paperhangers
1982 Raven's Revenge
1984 Raven's Longest Night
1985 Raven's Shadow
1986 Nobody Here by That Name
1988 A Savage State of Grace

0510
MACLEOD, CHARLOTTE   1922-
Also writes as Alisa Craig & as Matilda Hughes
1980 We Dare Not Go A-Hunting
1987 Grab Bag

"Widow Sarah Kelling & Det. Max Bittersohn"
1979 The Family Vault
1980 The Withdrawing Room
1981 The Palace Guard
1983 The Bilbao Looking Glass
1984 The Convivial Codfish
1985 The Plain Old Man
1987 The Recycled Citizen
1988 The Silver Ghost

"Professor Peter Shandy, Balaclava Agricultural College"
1978 Rest You Merry
1979 The Luck Runs Out
1982 Wrack & Rune
1983 Something the Cat Dragged In
1985 The Curse of the Giant Hogweed
1987 The Corpse in Oozak's Pond
See also as CRAIG, ALISA, 0427

0511
MALING, ARTHUR   1923-
1988 Lover & Thief

"Brock Potter, Price, Potter & Petacque Brokerage, New York"
1976 Ripoff
1977 Schroeder's Game
1978 Lucky Devil
1979 The Koberg Link
1983 A Taste of Treason
See also HEADLINES, 0294

0512
MALZBERG, BARRY N.
See as Jt. author with PRONZINI, BILL, 0537. See also SCIENCE FICTION, 0681

0513
MANTELL, LAURIE
New Zealand
"Det. Sgt. Steven Arrow & Chief Inspt. Jonas Peacock, Police Dept., Petone, New Zealand"
1978 Murder in Fancy Dress
1980 Murder & Chips
1980 A Murder or Three
1985 Murder in Vain

0514
MARRIC, J. J.   1908-1973
England
Real name: John Creasey
"Commander George Gideon, C.I.D., Scotland Yard"
1955 Gideon's Day
1956 Gideon's Week
1957 Gideon's Night
1958 Gideon's Month
1961 Gideon's Fire
1962 Gideon's March
1963 Gideon's Ride
1964 Gideon's Lot
1964 Gideon's Vote
1965 Gideon's Badge
1967 Gideon's Wrath
1968 Gideon's River
1969 Gideon's Power
1970 Gideon's Sport
1971 Gideon's Art
1971 Gideon's Risk (1960)
1972 Gideon's Men
1973 Gideon's Press
1974 Gideon's Fog
1975 Gideon's Buy
1976 Gideon's Drive
1985 Gideon's Force (1978)
1986 Gideon's Law (1981)
1986 Gideon's Staff (1959)
1986 Gideon's Way
See also as ASHE, GORDON, 0394; CREASEY, JOHN, 0428; HUNT, KYLE, 0477; MORTON, ANTHONY, 0522; YORK, JEREMY, 0588; SPY STORIES, 0358 & HISTORICAL FICTION, 1044 as CREASEY, JOHN

0515
MARSH, NGAIO   1899-1982
New Zealand; England
"Roderick Alleyn, C.I.D., Scotland Yard & Troy Alleyn, Artist & Alleyn's Wife"
1938 Death in a White Tie
1938 Artists in Crime
1939 Overture to Death

Section 5 - Mysteries

1940 Death at the Bar
1940 Death of a Peer
1940 Vintage Murder
1941 Enter a Murderer
1941 Death in Ecstasy
1941 Death & The Dancing Footman
1941 The Nursing-Home Murder
1942 A Man Lay Dead
1943 Colour Scheme
1945 Died in the Wool
1947 Final Curtain
1949 A Wreath for Rivera
1951 Night at the Vulcan
1953 Spinsters in Jeopardy
1955 Scales of Justice
1956 Death of a Fool
1958 Singing in the Shrouds
1960 False Scent
1962 Hand in Glove
1963 Dead Water
1966 Killer Dolphin
1969 Clutch of Constables
1971 When in Rome
1972 Tied Up in Tinsel
1975 Black as He's Painted
1977 Last Ditch
1978 Grave Mistake
1980 Photo Finish
1982 Light Thickens

0516
MARSHALL, WILLIAM
1979 Shanghai

"Det. Chief Inspt. Harry Feiffer, Yellowthread St. Station, Hong Kong"
1975 Yellowthread Street
1977 Gelignite
1977 The Hatchet Man
1980 Skulduggery
1981 Sci-fi
1982 Thin Air
1983 Perfect End (1981)
1984 The Far Away Man
1985 Roadshow
1986 Head First
1987 Frogmouth
1988 War Machine

"Lt. Felix Elizalde, Manila Police Dept."
1986 Manila Bay
1988 Whisper

0517
MELVILLE, JAMES
England

"Supt. Otani, Prefectural Police, Kobe, Japan"
1981 A Sort of Samurai
1982 The Chrysanthemum Chain
1982 The Ninth Netsuke
1983 Sayonara, Sweet Amaryllis
1984 Death of a Daimyo
1985 The Death Ceremony
1986 Go Gently, Gaijin
1988 Kimono for a Corpse
1988 The Reluctant Ronin

0518
MELVILLE, JENNIE   1922-
England
Real name: Gwendoline Butler
1970 Hunter in the Shadows
1972 Ironwood
1976 Tarot's Tower

"Det. Charmian Daniels, Deerham Police"
1964 Burning Is a Substitute for Loving
1964 Come Home & Be Killed
1964 Murderers' Houses
1965 There Lies Your Love
1970 A New Kind of Killer
1988 Windsor Red
See also ROMANCES, 0100; MYSTERIES, 0409 & ROMANCES, 0023 as BUTLER, GWENDOLINE

0519
MEYER, NICHOLAS   1945-
1974 The Seven Per Cent Solution
1974 Target Practice
1976 The West End Horror
See also DOYLE, SIR ARTHUR CONAN, 0438

0520
MOFFAT, GWEN   1924-
England
"Miss Melinda Pink, Mountain Climber & Writer, London"
1975 Miss Pink at the Edge of the World
1976 Over the Sea to Death
1984 Grizzly Trail
1984 Last Chance Country
1988 Snare

0521
MORICE, ANNE   1918
England

Real name: Felicity Shaw
1988 Design for Dying

"Tessa Crichton Price, Actress, London"
1974 Death & the Dutiful Daughter
1974 Death of a Heavenly Twin
1975 Killing with Kindness
1975 Nursery Tea & Poison
1976 Death of a Wedding Guest
1977 Murder in Mimicry
1978 Scared to Death
1978 Murder by Proxy
1979 Murder in Outline
1980 Death in the Round
1981 The Men in Her Death
1982 Hollow Vengence
1982 Sleep of Death
1984 Getting Away with Murder
1984 Murder Post-dated
1985 Dead on Cue
1986 Publish & Be Killed
1987 Treble Exposure

0522
MORTON, ANTHONY   1908-1973
England
Real name: John Creasey
"The Baron, John Mannering, Ex-jewel Thief"
1937 The Man in the Blue Mask
1937 The Return of the Blue Mask
1938 Blue Mask at Bay
1938 Salute Blue Mask!
1939 Alias Blue Mask
1949 A Case for the Baron (1945)
1949 A Rope for the Baron
1950 The Baron & the Beggar (1947)
1950 Career for the Baron (1946)
1951 Blame the Baron (1948)
1952 Books for the Baron (1949)
1960 Blood Red (1958)
1961 Deaf, Dumb, & Blond (1954)
1961 The Double Frame (1957)
1962 If Anything Happens to Hester (1959)
1966 The Baron & the Chinese Puzzle (1965)
1966 The Baron & the Mogul Swords (1963)
1967 The Baron Branches Out (1961)
1967 The Baron & the Stolen Legacy (1962)
1968 Affair for the Baron (1967)
1968 Baron on Board (1964)
1968 Stars for the Baron
1969 The Baron & the Missing Old Masters (1968)
1969 Sport for the Baron (1966)
1970 The Baron & the Unfinished Portrait
1970 Cry for the Baron (1950)
1971 Last Laugh for the Baron
1971 Trap the Baron (1950)
1972 The Baron Goes A-Buying
1972 The Baron Goes Fast (1954)
1973 The Baron & the Arrogant Artist
1973 Call for the Baron (1940; Blue Mask Strikes Again, Blue Mask Victorious)
1973 Salute for the Baron (1960)
1974 Burgle the Baron (1973)
1974 Danger for the Baron (1953)
1975 The Baron at Large (1939, Challenge Blue Mask)
1975 The Baron, King-Maker
1976 The Baron in France (1953)
1977 Help from the Baron (1955)
1978 Hide the Baron (1956)
1979 Love for the Baron
See also as ASHE, GORDON, 0394; CREASEY, JOHN, 0428; HUNT, KYLE, 0477; MARRIC, J. J., 0514; YORK, JEREMY, 0588; SPY STORIES, 0358 & HISTORICAL FICTION, 1044 as CREASEY, JOHN

0523
MOYES, PATRICIA   1923-
England
"Chief Supt. Henry Tibbett & Emmy Tibbett, Tibbett's Wife"
1960 Dead Men Don't Ski
1961 Down among the Dead Men
1962 Death on the Agenda
1963 Murder A La Mode
1964 Falling Star
1966 Johnny Under Ground
1967 Murder Fantastical
1968 Death & the Dutch Uncle
1970 Many Deadly Returns
1971 Season of Snows & Sins
1973 The Curious Affair of the Third Dog
1975 Black Widower
1977 The Coconut Killings
1979 Who Is Simon Warwick?
1980 Angel Death
1983 A Six-Letter Word for Death
1985 Night Ferry to Death

0524
MULLER, MARCIA
"Elena Oliverez, Museum Curator"
1983 The Tree of Death
1985 The Legend of the Slain Soldiers

Section 5 - Mysteries

"Sharon McCone, Investigator for
Legal Cooperative, San Francisco"
1977 Edwin of the Iron Shoes
1982 Ask the Cards a Question
1983 The Cheshire Cat's Eye
1984 Games to Keep the Dark Away
1984 Leave a Message for Willie
1985 There's Nothing to Be Afraid Of
1988 Eye of the Storm

"Joanna Stark, Art-security Expert"
1986 The Cavalier in White
1988 There Hangs the Knife
See also as Jt. author with PRONZINI, BILL, 0537

0525
O'DONNELL, LILLIAN   1926-
1960 Death on the Grass
1961 Death Blanks the Screen
1963 Death Schuss
1964 Death of a Player
1964 Murder under the Sun
1965 The Babes in the Woods
1967 The Sleeping Beauty Murders
1968 The Face of the Crime
1968 The Tachi Tree
1971 Dive into Darkness

"Mici Anhalt, Sleuth"
1977 Aftershock
1979 Falling Star
1980 Wicked Designs

"Lt. Norah Mulcahaney, New York Police Dept."
1972 The Phone Calls
1973 Don't Wear Your Wedding Ring
1974 Dial 577 R-A-P-E
1975 The Baby Merchants
1976 Leisure Dying
1979 No Business Being A Cop
1981 Children's Zoo
1983 Cop without a Shield
1984 Ladykiller
1985 Casual Affairs
1988 The Other Side of the Door

0526
OLIVER, ANTHONY
"Det. Inspt. John Webber & Elizabeth Thomas"
1981 The Pew Group
1983 The Property of a Lady
1985 The Elberg Collection

0527
PARETSKY, SARA
"V. I. Warshawski, Female Private Investigator, Chicago"
1982 Indemnity Only
1984 Deadlock
1985 Killing Orders
1987 Bitter Medicine
1988 Blood Shot

0528
PARKER, ROBERT B.   1932-
1979 Wilderness

"Spenser, Private Investigator, Boston"
1973 The Godwulf Manuscript
1974 God Save the Child
1975 Mortal Stakes
1976 Promised Land
1978 The Judas Goat
1980 Looking for Rachel Wallace
1981 Early Autumn
1981 A Savage Place
1982 Ceremony
1983 The Widening Gyre
1984 Valediction
1985 A Catskill Eagle
1986 Taming a Seahorse
1987 Pale Kings & Princes
1988 Crimson Joy

0529
PENTECOST, HUGH   1903-
Real name: Judson Pentecost Philips
1946 Death Wears a Copper Tie (SS)
1947 Memory of Murder
1954 Lieutenant Pascal's Tastes in Homicides
1955 The Assassins
1960 The Kingdom of Death
1961 The Deadly Friend
1963 The Tarnished Angel
1964 Only the Rich Die Young

"Luke Bradley"
1939 Cancelled in Red
1940 The 24th Horse
1942 I'll Sing at Your Funeral
1943 The Brass Chills

"Pierre Chambrun, Hotel Manager, NY"
1962 The Cannibal Who Overate
1964 The Shape of Fear
1966 The Evil Men Do
1967 The Golden Trap
1968 The Gilded Nightmare
1969 Girl Watcher's Funeral

1971 The Deadly Joke
1972 Birthday, Deathday
1973 Walking Dead Man
1974 Bargain with Death
1975 Time of Terror
1976 The Fourteen Dilemna
1978 Death after Breakfast
1979 Random Killer
1980 Beware Young Lovers
1981 Murder in Luxury
1982 With Intent to Kill
1983 Murder in High Places
1984 Remember to Kill Me
1985 Murder Round the Clock (SS)
1986 Nightmare Time
1988 Murder Goes Round & Round

"David Cotter, Private Investigator"
1977 Murder as Usual

"John Jericho, Artist, NY"
1965 Sniper
1966 The Creeping Hours
1966 Hide Her from Every Eye
1967 Dead Woman of the Year
1969 The Girl with Six Fingers
1970 A Plague of Violence

"Julian Quist, Partner, Public Relations Firm, New York"
1971 Don't Drop Dead Tomorrow
1972 The Champagne Killer
1973 The Beautiful Dead
1974 The Judas Freak
1975 Honeymoon with Death
1976 Die after Dark
1977 The Steel Palace
1978 Deadly Trap
1979 The Homicidal Horse
1980 Death Mask
1981 Sow Death, Reap Death
1982 Past, Present, & Murder
1983 Murder Out of Wedlock
1984 The Substitute Victim
1985 The Party Killer
1987 Kill & Kill Again

"Grant Simon, Columnist, New York"
1958 The Obituary Club
1959 The Lonely Target

"Dr. John Smith, Psychiatrist"
1949 Where the Snow Was Red
1950 Shadow of Madness

"Uncle George, Retired County Attorney, New England"
1961 Choice of Violence
1970 Around Dark Corners (SS)

1983 The Copycat Killers
1984 The Price of Silence
1985 Murder Sweet & Sour
1986 Death by Fire
See also as PHILIPS, JUDSON, 0533

0530
PERRY, ANNE   1938-
"Inspt. Pitt & Charlotte Pitt, Pitt's Wife, Victorian England"
1979 The Cater Street Hangman
1980 Callander Square
1981 Paragon Walk
1981 Resurrection Row
1983 Rutland Place
1984 Bluegate Fields
1985 Death in Devil's Acre
1987 Cardington Crescent
1988 Silence in Hanover Close

0531
PETERS, ELIZABETH   1927-
Real name: Barbara Gross Mertz
1968 The Jackal's Head
1969 The Camelot Caper
1970 Dead Sea Cipher
1971 The Night of 400 Rabbits
1976 Legend in Green Velvet
1977 Devil May Care
1980 The Love Talker
1980 Summer of the Dragon
1982 The Copenhagen Connection

"Dr. Vicki Bliss, Museum Curator & Art Historian"
1973 Borrower of the Night
1978 Street of the Five Moons
1983 Silhouette in Scarlet
1987 Trojan Gold

"Jacqueline Kirby, College Librarian"
1972 The Seventh Sinner
1974 The Murders of Richard III
1984 Die for Love

"Amelia Peabody, Archeologist, Victorian England"
1975 Crocodile on the Sandbank
1981 The Curse of the Pharaohs
1985 The Mummy Case
1986 Lion in the Valley
1988 The Deeds of the Disturber
See also ROMANCES, 0102 & HORROR, 0206 as MICHAELS, BARBARA

Section 5 - Mysteries

0532
PETERS, ELLIS   1913-
England
Real name: Edith Mary Pargeter
1960 Death Mask
1964 Funeral of Figaro
1966 The Will & the Deed (1960, Where There's a Will)
1974 The Horn of Roland
1976 Never Pick Up Hitch-Hikers!

"Det. Inspt. George Felse"
1951 Fallen Into the Pit (as Pargeter)
1962 Death & the Joyful Woman
1964 Flight of a Witch
1965 Who Lies Here?
1966 The Piper on the Mountain
1967 Black Is the Color of My True Love's Heart
1968 The Grass Widow's Tale
1969 The House of Green Turf
1970 Mourning Raga
1971 The Knocker on Death's Door
1972 Death to the Landlords
1974 City of Gold & Shadows
1979 Rainbow's End

"Brother Cadfael, Monk, Wales, 12th Century"
1978 A Morbid Taste for Bones
1979 One Corpse Too Many
1980 Monk's Hood
1981 Saint Peter's Fair
1982 Leper of St. Giles
1983 The Sanctuary Sparrow
1983 The Virgin in the Ice
1984 The Devil's Novice
1984 The Pilgrim of Hate
1985 Dead Man's Ransom
1985 An Excellent Mystery
1986 The Raven in the Foregate
1987 The Rose Rent
1988 The Hermit of Eyton Forest

0533
PHILIPS, JUDSON   1903-
Real name: Judson Pentecost Philips
"Coyle & Donovan"
1941 Odds on the Hot Seat
1942 The Fourteenth Trump

"Peter Styles, Reporter, Newsview, NY"
1964 The Laughter Trap
1965 The Black Glass City
1965 The Twisted People
1966 The Wings of Madness
1967 Thursday's Folly
1968 Hot Summer Killing
1970 Nightmare at Dawn
1971 Escape a Killer
1972 The Vanishing Senator
1973 The Larkspur Conspiracy
1974 The Power Killers
1975 Five Roads to Death
1975 Walk a Crooked Mile
1976 Backlash
1978 A Murder Arranged
1979 Why Murder?
1980 Death Is a Dirty Trick
1982 Death as the Curtain Rises
1982 Target for Tragedy

"Carole Trevor & Max Blythe"
1938 Death Syndicate
1939 Death Delivers a Postcard
See also as PENTECOST, HUGH, 0529

0534
POE, EDGAR ALLAN   1809-1849
"C. Auguste Dupin"
1842 The Mystery of Marie Roget
1843 The Murders in the Rue Morgue
1844 The Purloined Letter

0535
PORTER, JOYCE   1924-
England
"Inspt. Wilfred Dover, Scotland Yard"
1964 Dover One
1965 Dover Two
1966 Dover Three
1967 Dover & the Unkindest Cut of All
1968 Dover Goes to Pott
1973 Dover Strikes Again
1973 It's Murder with Dover
1977 Dover & the Claret Tappers
1979 Dead Easy for Dover

"Honorable Constance Morrison-Burke"
1970 Rather a Common Sort of Crime
1972 A Meddler & Her Murder
See also SPY STORIES, 0384

0536
PRATHER, RICHARD SCOTT   1921-
Also writes as David Knight & Douglas Ring
1952 Dagger of Flesh
1952 Lie Down, Killer
1958 The Scrambled Yeggs

"Shell Scott, Private Investigator, Los Angeles"

1950 The Case of the Vanishing Beauty
1951 Bodies in Bedlam
1951 Everybody Had a Gun
1951 Find This Woman
1952 Darling, It's Death
1952 Way of a Wanton
1956 Too Many Crooks (1953, Ride a High Horse)
1954 Always Leave 'Em Dying
1955 Strip for Murder
1956 Dragnet: Case No. 561
1956 The Wailing Frail
1957 Have Gat, Will Travel (SS)
1957 Three's a Shroud (SS)
1958 Pattern for Murder
1958 Slab Happy
1958 Take a Murder, Darling
1959 Double in Trouble
1959 Over Her Dear Body
1960 The Comfortable Coffin
1960 Dance With the Dead
1961 Dig That Crazy Grave
1961 Pattern for Panic (1954)
1961 Shell Scott's Seven Slaughters
1962 Kill the Clown
1963 Dead Heat
1964 The Cockeyed Corpse
1964 Joker in the Deck
1964 The Trojan Hearse
1965 Dead Man's Walk
1965 Kill Him Twice
1965 The Meandering Corpse
1966 The Kubla Khan Caper
1967 Gat Heat
1969 The Cheim Manuscript
1969 Kill Me Tomorrow
1971 Dead-Bang
1972 The Sweet Ride
1975 The Sure Thing
1986 The Amber Effect
1987 Shellshock

0537
PRONZINI, BILL   1943-
Also writes as Jack Foxx & Alex Saxon
1971 The Stalker
1972 Panic!
1974 Snowbound
1976 Games
1981 Masques
1985 Graveyard Plots (SS)

"The Nameless Detective, San Francisco"
1971 The Snatch
1973 The Vanished
1973 Undercurrent
1977 Blowback
1980 Labyrinth
1981 Hoodwink
1982 Dragonfire
1982 Scattershot
1983 Bindlestiff
1983 Casefile (SS)
1984 Nightshades
1984 Quicksilver
1985 Bones
1986 Deadfall
1988 Shakles
See also WESTERNS, 0874

With MALZBERG, BARRY N.
1977 Acts of Mercy
1979 Night Screams
1976 The Running of Beasts
See also MALZBERG, BARRY N., in SCIENCE FICTION, 0681

With MULLER, MARCIA
1984 Double (McCone & The Nameless Det.)
1986 Beyond the Grave (Oliverez & Quincannon)
1987 The Lighthouse
See also MULLER, MARCIA, 0524

With WILCOX, COLLIN
1978 Twospot (The Nameless Det.)
See also WILCOX, COLLIN, 0582

0538
QUEEN, ELLERY
Joint pseudonym of Frederic Dannay, 1905- & Manfred B. Lee, 1905-1971; also wrote as Barnaby Ross. James Holding also writes as Ellery Queen.
"Ellery Queen, Amateur Sleuth, New York
1929 The Roman Hat Mystery
1930 The French Powder Mystery
1931 The Dutch Shoe Mystery
1932 The Egyptian Cross Mystery
1932 The Greek Coffin Mystery
1933 The American Gun Mystery
1933 The Siamese Twin Mystery
1934 The Chinese Orange Mystery
1935 The Spanish Cape Mystery
1936 Halfway House
1937 The Door Between
1938 The Devil to Pay
1938 The Four of Hearts
1939 The Dragon's Teeth
1942 Calamity Town
1943 There Was an Old Woman
1945 The Murderer Is a Fox

Section 5 - Mysteries

1948 Ten Days' Wonder
1949 Cat of Many Tails
1950 Double, Double
1951 The Origin of Evil
1952 The King Is Dead
1953 The Scarlet Letters
1954 The Glass Village
1956 Inspt. Queen's Own Case
1958 The Finishing Stroke
1963 The Player on the Other Side
1964 And on the Eighth Day
1965 The Fourth Side of the Triangle
1965 Queens Full (SS)
1966 A Study in Terror
1967 Face to Face
1968 The House of Brass
1969 Cop Out
1970 The Last Woman in His Life
1971 A Fine & Private Place

0539
QUILL, MONICA   1929-
"Sister Mary Teresa, Order of Martha & Mary, Chicago"
1981 Not a Blessed Thing
1982 Let Us Prey
1984 And Then There Was Nun
1985 Nun of the Above
1986 Sine Qua Nun
See also as MCINERNY, RALPH M., 0507

0540
RADLEY, SHEILA
"Chief Inspt. Quantrill & Det. Sgt. Tait, Breckham Market, East Anglia"
1979 Death in the Morning
1980 The Chief Inspector's Daughter
1982 A Talent for Destruction
1984 The Quiet Road to Death
1986 Fate Worse Than Death
See also ROMANCES as ROWAN, HESTER, 0118

0541
RATHBONE, JULIAN   1935-
England
1975 Bloody Marvellous
1976 Carnival!
1976 King Fisher Lives
1977 A Raving Monarchist
1983 A Spy of the Old School
1986 Lying in State
1987 Greenfinger

"Commissioner Jan Argand, Brabt (a fictional Low country) Police"

1981 Base Case
1981 The Euro-Killers
1983 Watching the Detectives

"Col. Nur Arslan, National Police, Turkey"
1967 Diamonds Bid
1968 Hand Out
1970 With My Knives I Know I'm Good
1972 Trip Trap
1975 Kill Cure
See also HEADLINES, 0300

0542
RENDELL, RUTH   1930-
England
Also writes as Barbara Vine
1965 To Fear a Painted Devil
1969 The Secret House of Death
1970 Vanity Dies Hard
1971 One Across, Two Down
1974 The Face of Trespass
1976 The Fallen Curtain (SS)
1977 A Demon in My View
1978 A Judgment in Stone
1979 Make Death Love Me
1980 The Lake of Darkness
1982 Master of the Moor
1983 The Fever Tree (SS)
1984 The Killing Doll
1985 The Tree of Hands
1985 The New Girlfriend (SS)
1986 Live Flesh
1987 Heartstones
1987 Talking to Strange Men

"Chief Inspt. Reg Wexford & Inspt. Michael Burden, Kingsmarkham, C.I.D., Scotland Yard"
1965 From Doon with Death
1967 Wolf to the Slaughter
1969 The Best Man to Die
1970 A Guilty Thing Surprised
1970 Sins of the Father (1967, A New Lease of Death)
1972 Murder Being Once Done
1972 No More Dying Then
1973 Some Lie & Some Die
1975 Shake Hands Forever
1978 A Sleeping Life
1980 Means of Evil (SS)
1981 Death Notes
1983 The Speaker of Mandarin
1985 An Unkindness of Ravens
1988 The Veiled One
See also as VINE, BARBARA, 0573

0543
RICH, VIRGINIA
"Mrs. Potter, Culinary Expert"
1982 The Cooking School Murders
1983 The Baked Bean Supper Murders
1985 The Nantucket Diet Murders

0544
RINEHART, MARY ROBERTS   1876-1958
1908 The Circular Staircase
1909 The Man in Lower Ten
1910 The Window at the White Cat
1913 The Case of Jennie Brice
1914 The After House
1926 The Bat
1926 The Red Lamp
1930 The Door
1932 Miss Pinkerton
1933 The Album
1938 The Wall
1940 The Great Mistake
1942 The Haunted Lady
1945 The Yellow Room
1952 The Swimming Pool
1953 The Frightened Wife (SS)
Also wrote "Hilda Adams, Nurse-Detective" series

0545
ROHMER, SAX   1883-1959
England
1919 Dope
1932 Yu'an Hee See Laughs

"Dr. Fu Manchu, Tibetan Sorcerer & Master Criminal & Nayland Smith, Western Intelligence & Crime Stopper"
1913 The Insidious Dr. Fu Manchu
1913 The Mystery of Fu Manchu
1916 The Return of Fu Manchu
1917 The Hand of Fu Manchu
1931 The Daughter of Fu Manchu
1932 The Mask of Fu Manchu
1933 Fu Manchu's Bride
1934 The Trail of Fu Manchu
1936 President Fu Manchu
1939 The Drums of Fu Manchu
1941 The Island of Fu Manchu
1948 Shadow of Fu Manchu
1957 Re-Enter Fu Manchu
1959 Emperor Fu Manchu

0546
ROSTEN, LEO   1908-
"Sidney 'Silky' Pincus, Private Investigator, New York"
1979 Silky! A Detective Story
1981 King Silky

0547
ROYCE, KENNETH   1920-
England
Real name: Kenneth Royce Gandley; also writes as Oliver Jacks
"Spider Scott, the XYZ Man"
1970 The XYZ Man
1971 The Concrete Boot
1972 The Miniatures Frame
1973 The Masterpiece Affair
1984 The Crypto Man
1985 The Mosley Receipt
See also HEADLINES, 0302 & 0347

0548
RUTHERFORD, DOUGLAS   1915-
Real name: James Douglas Rutherford McConnell
1959 On the Track of Death
1965 The Creeping Flesh
1966 The Black Leather Murders
1968 Skin for Skin
1971 The Gilt-Edged Cockpit
1972 Clear the Fast Lane
1972 The Gunshot Grand Prix
1974 Kick Start
1974 Killer on the Track
1974 Rally to the Death
1975 Mystery Tour
1977 Return Load
1980 Turbo
1983 Stop at Nothing

0549
SANDERS, LAWRENCE   1920-
"The Commandments":
1979 The Sixth Commandment
1980 The Tenth Commandment
1986 The Eighth Commandment

"Retired Chief of Detectives Edward X. Delaney, New York Police Dept."
1973 The First Deadly Sin
1977 The Second Deadly Sin
1981 The Third Deadly Sin
1985 The Fourth Deadly Sin

"Timothy"
1987 The Timothy Files
1988 Timothy's Game
See also HEADLINES, 0251 & 0303

Section 5 - Mysteries

0550
SAYERS, DOROTHY 1893-1957
England
"Lord Peter Wimsey; Harriet Vane, Writer"
1923 Whose Body?
1927 Unnatural Death
1927 Clouds of Witness
1928 Lord Peter Views the Body (SS)
1928 The Unpleasantness at the Bellona Club
1930 The Documents in the Case
1930 Strong Poison
1931 Five Red Herrings
1932 Have His Carcase
1933 Murder Must Advertise
1933 Hangman's Holiday (SS)
1934 The Nine Tailors
1936 Gaudy Night
1937 Busman's Honeymoon
1968 In the Teeth of the Evidence (SS) (1940)

0551
SCOTT, JACK S. 1922-
England
Real name: Jonathan Escott
1977 The Bastard's Name Was Bristow
1983 Corporal Smithers, Deceased

"Inspt. Pete Parsons"
1985 A Time of Fine Weather
1986 A Little Darling, Dead

"Det. Inspt. Alfred Stanley Rosher, C.I.D., Scotland Yard"
1976 The Poor Old Lady's Dead
1977 The Shallow Grave
1979 A Clutch of Vipers
1980 The Gospel Lamb
1981 The View from Deacon Hill
1982 An Uprush of Mayhem
1983 The Local Lads
1984 All the Pretty People
1985 A Death in Irish Town
1987 A Knife between the Ribs

0552
SELWYN, FRANCIS 1935-
"Sgt. Verity, Scotland Yard, Victorian Period"
1974 Cracksman on Velvet
1976 Sgt. Verity & the Imperial Diamond
1977 Sgt. Verity Presents His Compliments
1979 Sgt. Verity & the Blood Royal
1981 Sgt. Verity & the Swell Mob

0553
SHANNON, DELL 1921-
Real name: Elizabeth Linington; also writes as Lesley Egan, Elizabeth Linington, Egan O'Neill, & Anne Blaisdell
"Lt. Luis Mendoza, Los Angeles Police Dept."
1960 Case Pending
1961 The Ace of Spades
1962 Extra Kill
1962 Knave of Hearts
1963 Death of a Busybody
1963 Double Bluff
1964 The Death-Bringers
1964 Mark of Murder
1964 Root of All Evil
1965 Death by Inches
1966 Coffin Corner
1966 With a Vengeance
1967 Chance to Kill
1967 Rain with Violence
1968 Kill with Kindness
1969 Crime on Their Hands
1969 Schooled to Kill
1970 Unexpected Death
1971 Whim to Kill
1971 The Ringer
1972 Murder with Love
1972 With Intent to Kill
1973 No Holiday for Crime
1973 Spring of Violence
1974 Crime File
1975 Deuces Wild
1976 Streets of Death
1977 Appearances of Death
1978 Cold Trail
1979 Felony at Random
1980 Felony File
1981 Murder Most Strange
1982 The Motive on Record
1983 Exploit of Death
1984 Destiny of Death
1985 Chaos of Crime
1986 Blood Count
1987 Murder by the Tale (SS)

0554
SIMENON, GEORGES 1903-
France
"Maigret, Sûreté"
1931 Murder at the Crossroads
1939 The Patience of Maigret
1952 Maigret's Revolver
1953 No Vacation for Maigret
1954 Inspt. Maigret & the Killers

1954 Maigret & the Strangled Stripper
1955 Inspt. Maigret & the Dead Girl
1955 Maigret in New York's Underworld
1956 Inspt. Maigret & the Burglar's Wife
1957 The Methods of Maigret
1958 None of Maigret's Business
1959 Madame Maigret's Own Case
1961 Maigret Rents a Room
1963 Maigret's Memoirs
1964 Maigret's Dead Man
1965 Maigret Loses His Temper
1965 Maigret Sets a Trap (1955)
1966 Maigret Bides His Time
1967 Maigret & the Headless Corpse (1955)
1967 Maigret & the Nahour Case
1968 Maigret's Pickpocket
1969 Maigret & the Calame Report (1954)
1969 Maigret in Vichy
1970 Maigret Hesitates
1970 Maigret's Boyhood Friend (1968)
1971 Maigret & the Wine Merchant
1972 Maigret & the Madwoman (1970)
1972 Maigret & the Informer
1973 Maigret & the Bum (1963)
1974 Maigret & the Millionaires (1958)
1975 Maigret & the Loner (1971)
1975 Maigret & the Man on the Bench (1953)
1976 Maigret & the Black Sheep (1962)
1977 Maigret & the Hotel Majestic (1942)
1977 Maigret & the Spinster (1942)
1978 Maigret in Exile (1942)
1978 Maigret's Pipe (SS)
1979 Maigret & the Killer (1969)
1979 Maigret & the Toy Village (1944)
1979 Maigret's Rival (1944)
1982 Maigret & the Gangsters
1982 Maigret Has Doubts (1959)
1983 Maigret Afraid (1953)
1983 Maigret in Court (1960)
1984 Maigret's Revolver
1986 Maigret's War of Nerves
1976 Maigret & the Apparition
1987 Maigret on the Defensive (1966)
1980 Maigret at the Coroner's
1987 Maigret & the Yellow Dog (1936)
1988 Maigret on the Riviera
Simenon has written hundreds of titles since the 1930's using 17 pseudonyms. See also WORLD AUTHORS, 1444

0555
SIMON, ROGER L.
"Moses Wine, Private Investigator, California"
1973 The Big Fix
1975 Wild Turkey
1979 Peking Duck
1985 California Roll
1987 The Straight Man

0556
SJÖWALL, MAJ 1935- & WAHLÖÖ, PER 1926-1975
Sweden
"Martin Beck, Stockholm Police"
1967 Roseanna
1968 The Man on the Balcony
1969 The Man Who Went Up in Smoke
1970 The Laughing Policeman
1971 The Fire Engine That Disappeared
1971 Murder at the Savoy
1972 The Abominable Man
1973 The Locked Room
1975 Cop Killer
1977 The Terrorists

0557
SMITH, J. C. S. 1935-
"Quentin Jacoby, Retired Subway Police Officer, New York"
1980 Jacoby's First Case
1984 Nightcap

0558
SMITH, MARTIN CRUZ 1942-
1981 Gorky Park
See also HORROR, 0216 & HISTORICAL FICTION, 1099

0559
SNOW, C. P. 1905-1980
England
1932 Death under Sail
1979 A Coat of Varnish
See also BRITISH AUTHORS, 1388

0560
SPILLANE, MICKEY 1918-
Real name: Frank Morrison Spillane
1965 The Death Dealers
1972 The Erection Set

"Mike Hammer, Private Investigator"
1947 I, the Jury
1950 Vengeance Is Mine
1950 My Gun Is Quick
1951 The Big Kill

Section 5 - Mysteries

1951 The Long Wait
1951 One Lonely Night
1952 Kiss Me, Deadly
1961 The Deep
1962 The Girl Hunters
1963 Me, Hood
1963 The Tough Guys
1964 The Snake
1965 Bloody Sunrise
1966 The Twisted Thing
1967 The Body Lovers
1967 The Delta Factor
1970 Survival . . . Zero!
1973 The Last Cop Out

0561
STOUT, REX   1886-1975
1937 The Hand in the Glove
1939 Mountain Cat
1941 Alphabet Hicks
1977 Justice Ends at Home (SS)
1977 Red Threads

"Tecumseh Fox"
1939 Double for Death
1940 Bad for Business
1941 The Broken Vase

"Nero Wolfe, Private Investigator, New York"
1934 Fer-de-Lance
1935 The League of Frightened Men
1936 The Rubber Band
1937 The Red Box
1938 Too Many Cooks
1939 Some Buried Caesar
1940 Over My Dead Body
1940 Where There's a Will
1944 Not Quite Dead Enough
1946 The Silent Speaker
1947 Too Many Women
1948 And Be a Villain
1949 The Second Confession
1949 Trouble in Triplicate
1950 Curtains for Three
1950 In the Best Families
1950 Three Doors to Death
1951 Murder by the Book
1952 Prisoner's Base
1952 Triple Jeopardy
1953 The Golden Spiders
1954 The Black Mountain
1954 Three Men Out
1955 Before Midnight
1956 Might as Well Be Dead
1956 Three Witnesses
1957 If Death Ever Slept
1957 Three for the Chair
1958 And Four to Go
1958 Champagne for One
1959 Plot It Yourself
1960 Three at Wolfe's Door
1960 Too Many Clients
1961 The Final Deduction
1962 Gambit
1962 Homicide Trinity
1963 Black Orchids
1963 The Mother Hunt
1964 A Right to Die
1964 Trio for Blunt Instruments
1965 The Doorbell Rang
1966 Death of a Doxy
1968 The Father Hunt
1969 Death of a Dude
1973 Please Pass the Guilt
1975 A Family Affair

0562
SYMONS, JULIAN   1912-
England
1949 Bland Beginning
1950 The 31st of February
1953 The Broken Penny
1954 The Narrowing Circle
1957 Bogue's Fortune
1957 The Colour of Murder
1957 The Immaterial Murder Case (1945)
1960 The Progress of a Crime
1962 The Plain Man
1964 The End of Solomon Grundy
1965 The Belting Inheritance
1967 The Man Who Killed Himself
1969 The Man Whose Dreams Came True
1971 The Gigantic Shadow (The Pipe Dream, 1959)
1971 The Man Who Lost His Wife
1972 The Players & the Game
1973 The Plot against Roger Rider
1978 The Blackheath Poisonings
1980 Sweet Adalaide
1983 The Name of Annabel Lee
1983 The Tigers of Subtopia (SS)
1984 The Detling Secret
1986 A Criminal Comedy

"Sheridan Haynes, Actor, London"
1975 A Three-Pipe Problem
1988 The Kentish Manor Murders

0563
TEY, JOSEPHINE   1897-1952
England
Real name: Elizabeth MacKintosh

1931 The Expensive Halo
1948 Miss Pym Disposes (1946)
1949 The Franchise Affair
1950 Brat Farrar

"Inspt. Alan Grant, Scotland Yard"
1929 The Man in the Queue
1951 To Love & Be Wise
1952 The Daughter of Time
1953 The Singing Sands
1954 A Shilling for Candles (1936)

0564
THOMSON, JUNE
England
1971 Not One of Us

"Det. Inspt. Jack Rudd, Chelmsford, C.I.D., Scotland Yard"
1975 The Long Revenge
1977 Case Closed
1977 Death Cap
1977 A Question of Identity
1979 The Habit of Loving (Deadly Relations)
1980 Alibi in Time
1982 Shadow of a Doubt
1983 Portrait of Lilith
1985 Sound Evidence
1986 The Dark Stream
1986 A Dying Fall
1987 No Flowers, by Request
1988 Rosemary for Remembrance

0565
TIDYMAN, ERNEST 1928-
1974 Dummy
1974 Line of Duty

"John Shaft, Black Private Investigator"
1970 Shaft
1972 Shaft among the Jews
1972 Shaft's Big Score
1973 Goodbye, Mr. Shaft
1973 Shaft Has a Ball
1974 Shaft's Carnival of Killers
1975 The Last Shaft

0566
TRAVER, ROBERT
1958 Anatomy of a Murder
1981 People Versus Kirk

0567
TRUMAN, MARGARET 1924-
Daughter of President Harry Truman
1980 Murder in the White House
1981 Murder on Capitol Hill
1983 Murder in the Smithsonian
1983 Murder at the Supreme Court
1984 Murder on Embassy Row
1985 Murder at the FBI
1987 Murder in Georgetown
1987 Murder in the C.I.A.

0568
TRUSCOTT, LUCIAN 1947-
1979 Dress Gray

0569
UHNAK, DOROTHY 1933-
1973 Law & Order
1977 The Investigation
1981 False Witness
1985 The Victims

"Det. Christie Opara, New York Police Dept."
1968 The Bait
1969 The Witness
1970 The Ledger

0570
VALIN, JONATHAN 1948-
"Henry Stoner, Private Investigator, Cincinnati"
1980 Final Notice
1980 The Lime Pit
1981 Dead Letter
1982 Day of Wrath
1983 Natural Causes
1986 Life's Work
1987 Fire Lake

0571
VAN DE WETERING, JANWILLEM 1931-
The Netherlands
1982 The Butterfly Hunter
1985 Inspector Saito's Small Satori

"Adjutant Grijpstra & Sgt. de Gier, Amsterdam Police Dept."
1974 Tumbleweed
1974 Outsider in Amsterdam
1975 The Corpse on the Dike
1976 Death of a Hawker
1977 The Japanese Corpse
1978 The Blond Baboon
1979 The Maine Massacre

Section 5 - Mysteries

1981 The Mind-Murders
1983 The Streetbird
1985 The Rattle-Rat
1986 Hard Rain
1987 The Sergeant's Cat

0572
VAN DINE, S. S.   1888-1939
Real name: Willard Huntington Wright
"Philo Vance, Amateur Sleuth, New York"
1926 The Benson Murder Case
1927 The Canary Murder Case
1928 The Greene Murder Case
1929 The Bishop Murder Case
1930 The Scarab Murder Case
1933 The Dragon Pool Murder
1933 The Kennel Murder Case
1934 The Casino Murder Case
1936 The Kidnap Murder Case
1938 The Garden Murder Case
1938 The Gracie Allen Murder Case
1939 The Winter Murder Case

VAN GULIK, ROBERT
See GULIK, ROBERT HANS VAN, 0464

VIDAL, GORE
See as BOX, EDGAR, 0407

0573
VINE, BARBARA   1930-
1986 A Dark-Adapted Eye
1987 Fatal Inversion
See also as RENDELL, RUTH, 0542

0574
WAGER, WALTER   1924-
1970 Sledgehammer
1985 Otto's Boy

"Alison B. Gordon, Female Private Investigator & Sculptor, Los Angeles"
1979 Blue Leader
1980 Blue Moon
1981 Blue Murder
See also HEADLINES, 0315

0575
WAHLÖÖ, PER
See as Jt. author with SJÖWALL, MAJ, 0556

0576
WAMBAUGH, JOSEPH   1937-
"Los Angeles Police Dept."
1971 The New Centurions
1972 The Blue Knight
1975 The Choirboys
1978 The Black Marble
1981 The Glitter Dome
1983 The Delta Star
1985 The Secrets of Harry Bright
1987 Echoes in the Darkness
Also writes nonfiction, e.g., 1973, The Onionfield, & 1984, Lines & Shadows

0577
WARNER, MIGNON
England
"Mrs. Edwina Charles, Clairvoyante"
1976 A Medium for Murder
1978 The Tarot Murders
1982 Death in Time
1982 The Girl Who Was Clairvoyant
1983 Devil's Knell
1984 Illusion
1985 Speak No Evil

0578
WATSON, CLARISSA
"Persis Willum, Artist & Gallery Director"
1977 The Fourth Stage of Gainsborough Brown
1980 The Bishop in the Back Seat
1985 Runaway
1988 Last Plane from Nice

0579
WATSON, COLIN   1920-
England
"Inspt. Purbright, Flaxborough Village"
1962 Bump in the Night
1963 Hopjoy Was Here
1967 Coffin, Scarcely Used
1967 Lonelyhearts 4122
1968 Charity Ends at Home
1969 Just What the Doctor Ordered
1972 Kissing Covens
1975 Six Nuns & a Shotgun
1977 It Shouldn't Happen to a Dog
1981 Plaster Sinners
1983 Whatever's Been Going on at Mumblesby?

0580
WENTWORTH, PATRICIA   1878-1961
England

1910 A Marriage under the Terror
1911 More Than Kin

"Inspt. Lamb, Scotland Yard"
1923 The Astonishing Adventure of Jane Smith
1925 The Red Lacquer Case
1925 The Annam Jewel
1926 The Black Cabinet
1926 The Dower House Mystery
1927 The Amazing Chance
1927 Hue & Cry
1928 Anne Belinda
1928 Will-o'-the-Wisp
1929 Fool Errant
1930 The Coldstone
1931 Beggar's Choice
1931 Danger Calling
1931 Kingdom Lost
1932 Nothing Venture
1932 Red Shadow
1933 Outrageous Fortune
1933 Walk with Care
1934 Fear by Night
1934 Touch & Go
1935 Blindfold
1935 Hole & Corner
1935 Red Stefan
1936 Dead or Alive
1937 Down Under
1938 Mr. Zero
1938 Run!
1939 The Blind Side
1940 Rolling Stone
1941 Weekend with Death
1942 Pursuit of a Parcel
1945 Silence in Court

"Miss Maud Silver, Private Investigator, London"
1929 Grey Mask
1937 The Case Is Closed
1939 Lonesome Road
1940 Account Rendered
1941 In the Balance
1943 The Chinese Shawl
1943 Miss Silver Deals with Death
1944 The Clock Strikes Twelve
1944 The Key
1945 She Came Back
1946 Pilgrim's Rest (Dark Threat)
1947 Latter End
1947 Wicked Uncle
1948 The Case of William Smith
1948 Eternity Ring
1949 The Catherine Wheel
1949 Miss Silver Comes to Stay
1950 The Brading Collection
1950 Through the Wall
1951 Anna, Where Are You? (Death at Deep End)
1951 The Ivory Dagger
1951 The Watersplash
1952 Ladies' Bane
1953 Out of the Past
1953 Vanishing Point
1954 The Benevent Treasure
1954 The Silent Pool
1955 The Listening Eye
1955 Poison in the Pen
1956 The Fingerprint
1956 The Gazebo (The Summerhouse)
1958 The Alington Inheritance
1961 The Girl in the Cellar

0581
WESTLAKE, DONALD E.   1933-
Also writes as Curt Clark, Timothy J. Culver, & Richard Stark
Crime Novels:
1960 The Mercenaries
1961 Killing Time
1962 361
1963 Killy
1964 Pity Him Afterwards
1972 Cops & Robbers
1984 Levine (SS)
1988 Trust Me on This

Comic Crime Novels:
1965 The Fugitive Pigeon
1966 The Busy Body
1966 The Spy in the Ointment
1967 God Save the Mark
1969 Somebody Owes Me Money
1969 Who Stole Sassi Manoon?
1974 Help! I Am Being Held Prisoner
1975 Too Much
1976 Dancing Aztecs
1977 Enough
1980 Castle in the Air
1985 High Adventure

"John Archibald Dortmunder, Master Burglar"
1970 The Hot Rock
1972 Bank Shot
1974 Jimmy the Kid
1977 Nobody's Perfect
1983 Why Me
1985 Good Behavior
See also as COE, TUCKER, 0422

0582
WILCOX, COLLIN   1924-
Also writes as Carter Wick

Section 5 - Mysteries

1976 The Third Victim
1987 Spellbinder

"Stephen Drake, Crime Reporter"
1967 The Black Door
1968 The Third Figure

"Lt. Frank Hastings, San Francisco Police Dept."
1969 The Lonely Hunter
1970 The Disappearance
1971 Dead Aim
1973 Hiding Place
1974 Long Way Down
1975 Aftershock
1977 Doctor, Lawyer . . .
1978 The Watcher
1979 Night Games
1979 Power Plays
1980 Mankiller
1982 Stalking Horse
1984 Victims
1988 Bernhardt's Edge
1988 The Pariah

"Marshall McCloud"
1973 McCloud
1974 The New Mexico Connection

0583
WILLIAMS, DAVID
England
"Mark Treasure, Banker, London"
1977 Treasure by Degrees
1977 Unholy Writ
1978 Treasure Up in Smoke
1980 Murder for Treasure
1982 Copper, Gold & Treasure
1983 Treasure Preserved
1984 Advertise for Treasure
1985 Murder in Advent
1985 Wedding Treasure
1986 Treasure in Roubles
1988 Divided Treasure

0584
WILSON, COLIN   1931-
England
1960 Ritual in the Dark
1964 Necessary Doubt
1967 The Glass Cage
1970 Lingard
1974 Schoolgirl Murder Case
See also SCIENCE FICTION, 0735 & BRITISH AUTHORS, 1396

0585
WINSLOW, PAULINE GLEN
England
1984 Judgment Day

"Det. Supt. Merle Capricorn, C.I.D., Scotland Yard"
1975 Death of an Angel
1976 The Brandenburg Hotel
1977 The Witch Hill Murder
1978 Copper Gold
1978 Gallows Child
1980 The Counsellor Heart
1981 The Rockefeller Gift

0586
WOODS, SARA   1922-
England
Real name: Sara Bowen-Judd
"Anthony Maitland, Lawyer, London"
1962 Bloody Instructions
1963 The Third Encounter
1964 Trusted Like the Fox
1965 Though I Know She Lies
1965 The Windy Side of the Law
1966 Enter Certain Murderers
1966 Let's Choose Executors
1967 The Case Is Altered
1968 Knives Have Edges
1968 Past Praying For
1969 Tarry & Be Hanged
1971 An Improbable Fiction
1971 Serpent's Tooth
1972 And Shame the Devil
1972 They Love Not Poison
1972 Though I Know She Lies
1973 Enter the Corpse
1973 Yet She Must Die
1974 Done to Death
1975 A Show of Violence
1976 My Life Is Done
1977 The Law's Delay
1977 A Thief or Two
1978 Exit Murderer
1979 Proceed to Judgment
1979 This Fatal Writ
1980 They Stay for Death
1980 Weep for Her
1981 Cry Guilty
1981 Dearest Enemy
1982 Enter a Gentlewoman
1982 Most Grevious Murder
1982 Villains by Necessity
1983 Call Back Yesterday
1983 The Lie Direct
1983 Where Should He Die?
1984 The Bloody Book of Law
1984 Defy the Devil

1984 Murder's Out of Tune
1985 Away with Them to Prison
1985 An Obscure Grave
1985 Put Out the Light
1986 Most Deadly Hate
1986 Nor Live So Long
1987 Naked Villainy

0587
WRIGHT, ERIC
Canada
"Inspt. Charlie Salter, Toronto Police Dept."
1983 The Night the Gods Smiled
1984 Smoke Detector
1985 Death in the Old Country
1986 The Man Who Changed His Name
1987 A Body Surrounded by Water

0588
YORK, JEREMY   1908-1973
England
Real name: John Creasey
1958 Sight of Death (1956)
1961 The Girl with the Leopard-Skin Bag
1962 Two for the Money
1968 The Quiet Fear (1963)

"Supt. Folly, Scotland Yard"
1967 Find the Body (1945)
1969 Murder Came Late (1946)
1970 Run Away to Murder (1947)
1972 First a Murder
1973 Close the Door on Murder (1948)
1973 The Gallows are Waiting (1949)
1974 Mystery Motive (1947)
1976 Let's Kill Uncle Lionel (1947)
1976 Murder in the Family
See also as ASHE, GORDON, 0394; CREASEY, JOHN, 0428; HUNT, KYLE, 0477; MARRIC, J. J., 0514; MORTON, ANTHONY, 0522; SPY STORIES, 0358 & HISTORICAL FICTION, 1044 as CREASEY, JOHN

0589
YORKE, MARGARET   1924-
England
1975 The Small Hours of the Morning
1977 The Cost of Silence
1981 The Hand of Death
1981 The Scent of Fear
1982 Devil's Work
1983 Find Me a Villain

1984 The Smooth Face of Evil
1985 Intimate Kill
1986 Safely to the Grave
1987 Evidence to Destroy
1987 The Point of Murder (1978, The Come-On)
1988 Speak for the Dead

"Dr. Patrick Grant, Professor of Literature, Oxford University"
1970 Dead in the Morning
1973 Grave Matters
1973 Silent Witness
1974 Mortal Remains
1976 Cast for Death
1987 No Medals for the Major

SECTION SIX

SCIENCE FICTION AND FANTASY

OVERVIEW

"Science Fiction" is fiction which speculates about and examines options for the future and is often called "speculative" fiction. There has been an increase in the importance and popularity of women writers.

"Fantasy" is a story of the struggle between good and evil which incorporate elements of magic and the impossible. Fantasy is often based on myths and legends, especially those of the British Isles. There has been an increase in the popularity of sword and sorcery themes and of dungeon and dragon games.

The lines between science fiction and fantasy are often blurred. Science fiction usually contains elements of the future possible. Fantasy usually contains elements of the impossible.

For science fiction the two most prestigious awards are the Nebula, awarded annually by the Science Fiction Writers of America and the Hugo, determined annually by the votes of fans.

Some Representative Types of Science Fiction and Fantasy:
(Adapted from Rosenberg, Betty. *Genreflecting*, 2d ed. Littleton, CO: Libraries Unlimited, 1986.)

Science Fiction:

1. *Hard Science:*
   Emphasis on technology and scientific discovery: Arthur C. Clarke, *The Fountains of Paradise*; Isaac Asimov, *The Gods Themselves*.

2. *Alternate Worlds:*
   A world similar to yet different from Earth. Often used by author to provide a satiric look at the mores and culture of Earth: Ursula LeGuin, *The Left Hand of Darkness*.

3. *After Nuclear Disaster:*
   How the world survives after a nuclear disaster: Walter Miller, Jr., *A Canticle for Leibowitz*.

4. *Space Western:*
   Similar to the plots of westerns; knockout battles and chase: *Star Wars*.

5. *Utopia/Dystopia:*
   An ideal society/a destructive society. Utopia: Austin Tappan Wright, *Islandia*. Dystopia: Ray Bradbury, *Fahrenheit 451*.

6. *Alien Beings:*
   The creation by the author of nonhuman beings; some stories are of invasions, others are of creatures encountered: H. G. Wells, *The War of the Worlds*, Arthur C. Clarke, *Childhood's End*.

7. *The Quest for a Messiah:*
   A search for meaning and salvation: Frank Herbert, *Dune* series; a satire on this theme is Robert Heinlein, *Stranger in a Strange Land*.

Fantasy:

1. *Sword & Sorcery:*
   Adventure epics of good and evil: Ursula LeGuin, *The Earthsea Trilogy*. The games of "Dungeons and Dragons" are variations of this type of book.

2. *Sagas, Myths & Legends:*
   Like sword and sorcery, but based on Welsh and Celtic legends: Evangeline Walton, *The Mabinogion*. A subtheme is the Arthurian Legend: Marion Zimmer Bradley, *The Mists of Avalon*.

3. *Animal Fables:*
   Stories of animals with anthropomorphic characteristics: Richard Adams, *Watership Down*.

REFERENCE AND BIBLIOGRAPHIC SOURCES

Ash, Brian. *Who's Who in Science Fiction*. New York: Taplinger, 1976.

Ashley, Michael, ed. *Who's Who in Horror and Fantasy Fiction*. New York: Taplinger, 1978.

Barron, Neil. *Anatomy of Wonder: A Critical Guide to Science Fiction*, 3rd ed. New York: Bowker, 1987.

Bleiler, Everett F. *The Checklist of Science-Fiction and Supernatural Fiction*. Glen Rock, NJ: Fireball Books, 1978.

Cottrill, Tim and Others. *Science Fiction and Fantasy Series and Sequels; a Bibliography*. New York: Garland, 1986.

Currey, L. W. *Science Fiction and Fantasy Authors: A Bibliography of First Printings of Their Fiction and Selected Nonfiction*. Boston: G. K. Hall, 1980.

Fisher, Benjamin Franklin. *The Gothic's Gothic: Study Aids to the Tradition of the Tale of Terror*. New York: Garland, 1988.

Gallagher, Edward Joseph. *The Annotated Guide to Fantastic Adventures*. Mercer Island, WA: Starmont House, 1985

Section 6 - Science Fiction & Fantasy

Hall, H. W. *Science Fiction Book Review Index, 1923-1973.* Detroit: Gale, 1975. *Science Fiction Book Review Index, 1974-1979.* Detroit: Gale, 1981.

Heller, Terry. 1947-. *The Delights of Terror, An Aesthetics of the Tale of Terror.* Urbana: University of Illinois Press, 1987.

Joffery, Sheldon R. and Fred Cook. *The Collector's Index to Weird Tales.* Bowling Green, OH: Bowling Green State University Popular Press, 1985.

Naha, Ed. *The Science Fictionary: An A-Z Guide to the World of SF Authors, Films, and TV Shows.* New York: Wide View, 1980.

Reginald, R. *Science Fiction and Fantasy Literature: A Checklist, 1700-1974, with Contemporary Science Fiction Authors II.* Detroit: Gale, 1979.

Sargent, Lyman Tower. *British and American Utopian Literature 1516-1975: An Annotated Bibliography.* Boston: G. K. Hall, 1979.

Smith, Curtis C., ed. *Twentieth Century Science-Fiction Writers.* New York: St. Martin's Press, 1981.

Tymn, Marshall B. *Horror Literature: A Core Collection and Reference Guide.* New York: Bowker, 1981.

Tymn, Marshall B., ed. *The Science Fiction Reference Book: A Comprehensive Handbook and Guide to the History, Literature, Scholarship, and Related Activities of the Science Fiction and Fantasy Fields.* Mercer Island, WA: Starmont House, 1981.

AUTHORS AND TITLES

A. SCIENCE FICTION

0590
ABÉ, KOBO   1924-
Japan
1970 Inter Ice Age 4
See also WORLD AUTHORS, 1407

0591
ADAMS, DOUGLAS   1952-
England
1987 Dirk Gently's Holistic Detective Agency

"Hitchiker's Books":
1979 The Hitchhiker's Guide to the Universe
1980 The Restaurant at the End of the Universe
1982 Life, the Universe & Everything
1985 So Long, & Thanks for All the Fish

0592
ALDISS, BRIAN W.   1925-
England
1959 No Time Like Tomorrow (SS)
1959 Starship
1960 Bow Down to Nul
1960 Galaxies Like Grains of Sands (SS)
1961 The Primal Urge
1962 The Long Afternoon of Earth
1964 The Dark Light Years
1964 Greybeard
1964 Starswarm (SS)
1965 Earthworks
1966 Who Can Replace a Man? (SS)
1967 Cryptozoic!
1968 Report on Probability A
1969 Barefoot in the Head: A European Fantasy
1969 Neanderthal Planet (SS)
1971 A Soldier Erect
1972 Moment of Eclipse (SS)
1973 Frankenstein Unbound
1974 The Eighty Minute Hour: A Space Opera
1977 The Malacia Tapestry
1978 Enemies of the System
1978 A Rude Awakening
1979 New Arrivals, Old Encounters (SS)
1979 The Saliva Tree & Other Strange Growths
1981 An Island Called Moreau
1986 Seasons in Flight (SS)

"Helliconia":
1982 Helliconia Spring
1983 Helliconia Summer
1985 Helliconia Winter
Also edited Galactic Empires

0593
ANDERSON, POUL   1926-
Also writes as A. A. Craig, Michael Karageorge & Winston P. Sanders
1952 Vault of the Ages
1954 Brain Wave
1956 Star Ways
1958 The Enemy Stars
1958 The War of the Wing-Men
1960 The High Crusade
1964 Time & Stars
1965 The Corridors of Time
1965 The Star Fox
1966 Ensign Flandry
1969 Seven Conquests (SS)
1970 Tales of the Flying Mountains
1970 Tau Zero
1971 The Byworlder
1971 The Dancer from Atlantis
1971 Operation Chaos
1972 There Will Be Time
1973 Goat's Song
1974 Fire Time
1974 A Knight of Shadows & Ghosts
1975 Homeward & Beyond
1975 The Winter of the World
1978 The Avatar
1979 The Merman's Children

"Future History":
1963 Let the Spacemen Beware!
1973 The Day of Their Return
1973 The People of the Wind

"The History of the Polesotechnic League (Future History)":
1964 Trader to the Stars
1966 The Trouble Twisters (Trade Team)
1969 Satan's World
1977 Mirkheim
1978 The Earthbook of Stormgate (includes The Man Who Counts)

Section 6 - Science Fiction & Fantasy   113

"The Worlds of Poul Anderson":
1978 The Night Face (SS) (1963, Let
       the Spaceman Beware)
1978 The Byworlder (1971)
1978 The Horn of Time (1963)
1978 The Long Way Home (1955, No
       World of Their Own)
1978 Orbit Unlimited (1961)
1978 The Queen of Air & Darkness (SS)
1978 Two Worlds (1954, Question &
       Answer & Planet of No Return)
       (1966, World without Stars & The
       Ancient Gods)
See also FANTASY, 0741

0594
ANTHONY, PIERS   1934-
Real name: Piers Anthony Dillingham
Jacob
1967 Chthon
1969 Macroscope
1970 The E. S. P. Worm
1973 Prostho Plus
1973 Race against Time
1976 Steppe
1981 Mute
1982 Night Mare
1982 Ogre, Ogre
1983 Dragon on a Pedestal
1984 Crewel Lye: A Caustic Yarn
1985 Anthonology
1986 Ghost
1986 Hasan
1986 Shade of the Tree

"Apprentice Adept":
1980 Split Infinity
1981 Blue Adept
1982 Juxtaposition
1987 Out of Phaze
1988 Robot Adept

"Battle Circle":
1968 Sos the Rope
1973 Var the Stick
1975 Neq the Sword

"Bio of a Space Tyrant":
1983 Refuge (1)
1984 Mercenary (2)
1985 Executive (4)
1985 Politician (3)
1986 Statesman (5)

"Cluster":
1977 Vicinity Cluster
1978 Chaining the Lady
1978 Kirlian Quest

1980 Thousandstar
1982 Viscous Circle

"Incarnations of Immortality":
1983 On a Pale Horse
1984 Bearing an Hourglass
1985 With a Tangled Skein
1986 Wielding a Red Sword
1987 Being a Green Mother

"Of Man & Manta":
1970 Orn
1976 Ox
1978 Omnivore

"Tarot Sequence":
1977 God of Tarot
See also FANTASY, 0742

With HALL, FRANCES
1979 Pretender

With MARGROFF, ROBERT E.
1968 The Ring

0595
ASIMOV, ISAAC   1920-
1955 The End of Eternity
1955 The Martian Way (SS)
1957 Earth Is Room Enough
1959 Nine Tomorrows: Tales of the
       Near Future (SS)
1967 Through a Glass Clearly
1969 Nightfall (SS)
1972 The Gods Themselves
1974 Have You Seen These?
1975 Buy Jupiter (SS)
1975 The Heavenly Host
1976 The Bicentennial Man (SS)
1983 The Winds of Change (SS)
1986 Robot Dreams

"Fantastic Voyage":
1966 Fantastic Voyage
1987 Fantastic Voyage II: Destination
       Brain

"Foundation":
1951 Foundation
1952 Foundation & Empire
1953 Second Foundation
1982 Foundation's Edge
1985 Robots & Empire
1986 Foundation & Earth
1988 Prelude to Foundation

"Elijah Baley, Intersteller Police
Detective":

1954 The Caves of Steel
1957 The Naked Sun
1983 The Robots of Dawn
1985 Robots & Empire (Descendents of Baley)

"Robot":
1950 I, Robot
1964 The Rest of the Robots (SS) (contains The Caves of Steel & The Naked Sun)
1982 The Complete Robot (SS)
1983 The Robots of Dawn
1985 Robots & Empire

"Tratorian Empire":
1950 Pebble in the Sky
1951 The Stars, Like Dust
1952 The Currents of Space
1961 Triangle (Omnibus)
See also MYSTERIES, 0395

0596
AVALLONE, MICHAEL   1924-
1970 Beneath the Planet of the Apes

0597
BALLARD, J. G.   1930-
1964 The Terminal Beach (SS)
1968 The Overloaded Man (SS)
1971 Chronopolis (SS)
1971 The Day of Forever (SS)
1971 Vermilion Sands (SS)
1972 Love's Napalm: Export U.S.A. (SS)
1973 Concrete Island
1973 Crash
1977 High-Rise
1979 The Unlimited Dream Company
1988 Hello America
1988 Memories of the Space Age (SS)

"End of the World":
1962 The Wind from Nowhere (Air)
1962 The Drowned World (Water)
1964 The Burning World (Fire)
1966 The Crystal World (Ice)
Fictional autobiography: Empire of the Sun, 1985

0598
BARJAVEL, RENÉ   1911-
France
1967 Ashes, Ashes
1971 The Ice People
1974 The Immortals

0599
BASS, T. J.   1932-
Real name: Thomas Joseph Bassler
"Hive":
1971 Half Past Human
1974 The Godwhale

0600
BENFORD, GORDON
See as Jt. author with BENFORD, GREGORY, 0601

0601
BENFORD, GREGORY   1941-
1977 If the Stars Are Gods
1977 In the Ocean of Night
1978 The Stars in Shroud (1970, Deeper than Darkness)
1980 Timescape
1983 Against Infinity
1984 Across the Sea of Suns
1985 Artifact
1986 In Alien Flesh
1988 Great Sky River

With BENFORD, GORDON
1977 If the Stars Are Gods
1980 Find the Changeling

With BRIN, DAVID
1986 Heart of the Comet

0602
BERGER, THOMAS   1924-
1973 Regiment of Women
See also FANTASY, 0746 & AMERICAN AUTHORS, 1170

0603
BESTER, ALFRED   1913-
1953 The Demolished Man
1955 The Rat Race
1957 The Stars My Destination (Tiger! Tiger!)
1958 Starburst (SS)
1964 The Dark Side of Earth
1974 The Computer Connection
1976 The Light Fantastic (SS)
1976 Star Light, Star Bright (SS)
1977 Starlight (SS)
1980 Golem 100

0604
BIGGLE, LLOYD, JR.   1923-

Section 6 - Science Fiction & Fantasy   115

1961 The Angry Espers
1965 The Fury Out of Time
1967 The Rule of the Door (SS)
1968 The Still Small Voice of Trumpets
1971 The World Menders
1972 The Light That Never Was
1972 The Metallic Muse (SS)
1974 Monument
1977 Silence Is Deadly

"Detective Jan Darzek Adventures":
1963 All the Colors of Darkness
1966 Watchers of the Dark
1975 This Darkening Universe
1976 A Galaxy of Strangers
1979 The Whirligig of Time

0605
BLISH, JAMES   1921-1975
1957 The Seedling Stars
1967-77 Star Trek, Vols. 1-12
1970 Anywhen (SS)
1971 . . . And All the Stars a Stage
1972 Midsummer Century

"Cities in Flight":
1955 Earthman Come Home
1956 They Shall Have Stars
1958 The Triumph of Time
1962 A Life for the Stars

"After Such Knowledge":
1958 A Case of Conscience
1964 Doctor Mirabilis
1968 Black Easter
1971 The Day after Judgment

0606
BOULLE, PIERRE   1912-
France
1963 Planet of the Apes
1965 Garden on the Moon
See also HISTORICAL FICTION, 1037 &
WORLD AUTHORS, 1431

0607
BOVA, BEN   1932-
1959 The Star Conquerers
1964 Star Watchman
1967 The Weathermakers
1968 Out of the Sun
1969 The Dueling Machine
1970 Escape!
1972 As on a Darkling Plain
1973 Forward in Time (SS)
1973 When the Sky Burned

1973 The Winds of Altair
1975 End of Exile
1975 Starcrossed
1976 The Multiple Man
1976 Millennium
1976 City of Darkness
1979 Kinsman
1979 Quaker Astronaut Kills & Deals
     with Feelings
1984 Orion
1985 Privateers
1988 The Peacekeepers

"Exiles":
1971 Exiled from Earth
1972 Flight of Exiles

"Voyagers: Keith Stoner":
1981 Voyagers
1986 Voyagers II: The Alien Within

With DICKSON, GORDON R.
1974 Gremlins, Go Home!
See also DICKSON, GORDON R., 0631

With LUCAS, GEORGE
1971 THX 1138

0608
BOYD, JOHN   1919-
1968 The Last Starship from Earth
1969 The Pollinators of Eden
1970 Sex & the High Command
1979 The Girl with the Jade Green
     Eyes

0609
BRADBURY, RAY   1920-
1950 The Martian Chronicles
1951 The Illustrated Man (SS)
1953 Farenheit 451
1953 The Golden Apples of the Sun
1962 R Is for Rocket (SS)
1966 S Is for Space (SS)
1976 Long after Midnight (SS)
See also HORROR, 0158

0610
BRADLEY, MARION ZIMMER   1930-
1982 The Colors of Space

"Darkover":
1962 The Planet Savers (12)
1962 Sword of Aldones (11)
1964 The Bloody Sun (9)
1965 Star of Danger (7)

1970 The Winds of Darkover (8)
1971 The World Wreckers (13)
1972 Darkover Landfall (3)
1974 The Spell Sword (4)
1975 The Heritage of Hastur (10)
1976 The Shattered Chain (6)
1977 The Forbidden Tower (5)
1979 Stormqueen (1)
1987 Two to Conquer (2)
See also FANTASY, 0748

0611
BRIN, DAVID
See as Jt. author with BENFORD, GREGORY, 0601

0612
BRUNNER, JOHN   1934-
England
1964 No Future in It (SS)
1964 The Whole Man
1965 The Squares of the City
1967 Out of My Mind (SS)
1967 The Productions of Time
1968 Stand on Zanzibar
1969 The Jagged Orbit
1971 The Traveler in Black
1971 The Wrong End of Time
1972 The Sheep Look Up (Sequel to Stand)
1972 Entry to Elsewhen
1972 From This Day Forward (SS)
1972 The Stardroppers
1973 The Stone That Never Came Down
1974 Total Eclipse
1975 The Shockwave Rider
1980 Foreign Constellations (SS)
1980 Players at the Game of People
1983 The Crucible of Time

0613
BURGESS, ANTHONY   1917-
England
1962 A Clockwork Orange
1962 The Wanting Seed
1978 1985
See also BRITISH AUTHORS, 1354

0614
CAIDIN, MARTIN   1927-
1956 The Long Night
1964 Marooned
1966 Devil Take All
1967 The Last Fathom

1967 No Man's World
1968 Four Came Back
1968 The God Machine
1969 Anytime, Anywhere
1969 The Mendelov Conspiracy
1971 Almost Midnight
1971 The Cape
1972 Mary Jane Tonight at Angels Twelve

"Cyborg (Col. Steve Austin)":
1972 Cyborg
1973 Operation Nuke
1974 High Crystal
1975 Cyborg IV
See also HISTORICAL FICTION, 1039

0615
CALVINO, ITALO   1923-1985
Italy
1956 The Path to the Nest of Spiders (1947)
1974 Invisible Cities
1974 The Castle of Crossed Dreams
1985 Mr. Palomar

"QFWFQ":
1968 Cosmicomics
1969 T Zero
See also WORLD AUTHORS, 1457

0616
CHANDLER, A. BERTRAM   1912-
Australia
"Rim (ERIMES)":
1964 Into the Alternate Universe (9)
1967 Contraband from Outer Space (10)
1967 Nebula Alert (13)
1967 The Road to the Rim (1)
1968 False Fatherland (4)
1969 Catch the Star Winds (8)
1969 The Rim Gods (11)
1971 Alternate Orbits (12)
1971 The Dark Dimensions (15)
1971 To Prime the Pump (2)
1972 The Gateway to Never (14)
1972 The Hard Way Up (3)
1972 The Inheritors (5)
1975 The Big Black Mark (7)
1979 The Broken Cycle (6)

0617
CHARNAS, SUZY MCKEE   1939-
1974 Walk to the End of the World

Section 6 - Science Fiction & Fantasy

1979 Motherlines
See also HORROR, 0163

0618
CHRISTOPHER, JOHN 1922-
England
Real name: Chistopher Samuel Youd
1954 The Twenty-Second Century (SS)
1955 The Year of the Comet (Planet in Peril)
1957 No Blade of Grass (1956, The Death of Grass)
1958 The Caves of Night
1959 A Scent of White Poppies
1960 The White Voyage
1962 The Long Winter (The World in Winter)
1964 The Possessors
1964 Sweeney's Island (Cloud on Silver)
1965 The Ragged Edge (A Wrinkle in the Skin)
1966 The Little People
1968 Pendulum
1977 Empty World
Also writes for juveniles & young adults; e.g., "The Tripods" series & "The Prince" trilogy

0619
CLARKE, ARTHUR C. 1917-
1951 Prelude to Space
1952 Islands in the Sky
1953 Childhood's End
1955 Earthlight
1956 The City & the Stars (1953, Against the Fall of Night)
1956 Reach for Tomorrow (SS)
1957 The Deep Range
1961 A Fall of Moondust
1963 Dolphin Island
1963 Glide Path
1967 The Sands of Mars (1951)
1968 The Lion of Camarre (1946)
1972 The Wind from the Sun (SS)
1973 Rendezvous with Rama
1975 Imperial Earth
1979 The Fountains of Paradise
1983 The Sentinel (SS)
1986 The Songs of Distant Earth

"Odyssey":
1972 The Lost Worlds of 2001
1982 2010: Odyssey Two
1987 2061: Odyssey Three
There are many anthologies of Clarke's work; e.g., Across a Sea of Stars

With KUBRICK, STANLEY
1968 2001: A Space Odyssey

0620
CLEMENT, HAL 1922-
Real name: Henry Clement Stubbs
1950 Needle
1953 Iceworld
1957 Cycle of Fire
1969 Small Changes (SS)

"Meskin":
1954 Mission of Gravity
1964 Close to Critical
1971 Starlight

0621
COMPTON, DAVID G. 1930-
1968 Synthajoy
1970 The Steel Crocodile
1974 The Unsleeping Eye

0622
CRICHTON, MICHAEL 1942-
1969 The Andromeda Strain
1972 The Terminal Man
1987 Sphere
See also HEADLINES, 0269 & HISTORICAL FICTION, 0902

0623
CROSS, JOHN K. 1914-1967
"Stephen MacFarlane":
1945 The Angry Planet
1954 SOS from Mars

0624
CROWLEY, JOHN 1942-
1975 The Deep
1979 Engine Summer
See also FANTASY, 0760

0625
DAVIDSON, AVRAM 1923-
"Kar-Chee":
1965 Rogue Dragon
1966 Clash of the Star-Kings
1966 The Kar-Chee Reign
See also FANTASY, 0761

0626
DE CAMP, L. (Lyon) SPRAGUE 1907-

1948 Divide & Rule
1948 The Wheels of If (SS)
1949 Lest Darkness Fall (1941)
1960 The Glory That Was

"Viagens Interplanetarias, the Krishna Series":
1951 Rogue Queen
1953 The Continent Makers (SS)
1954 Cosmic Manhunt (The Queen of Zamba)
1958 The Tower of Zanid
1977 The Hostage of Zir
1962 The Search for Zei (The Floating Continent)
See also FANTASY, 0763 & HISTORICAL FICTION, 0963

With MILLER, PETER S. (Schuyler)
1950 Genus Homo

0627
DEFORD, MIRIAM ALLEN   1888-1975
1969 Xenogenesis (SS)
1971 Elsewhere, Elsewhen, Elsehow (SS)

0628
DELANY, SAMUEL R.   1942-
Black American
1965 The Ballad of Beta-2
1966 Empire Star
1967 The Einstein Intersection
1968 The Jewels of Aptor (1962)
1968 Nova
1971 Driftglass (SS)
1973 The Tides of Lust
1976 Triton
1977 Dhalgren (1975)
1978 Empire: A Visual Novel
1981 Distant Stars
1982 Babel-17 (1966)
1984 Stars in My Pocket Like Grains of Sand
1988 The Straits of Messina

"The Fall of the Towers" Trilogy:
1968 City of a Thousand Suns (1965)
1968 Out of the Dead City (1963, Captives of the Flame)
1968 The Towers of Toron, rev. (1964)
See also FANTASY, 0764

0629
DEL REY, LESTER   1915-
1948 And Some Were Human
1953 Attack from Atlantis

1962 The Eleventh Commandment
1966 The Infinite Worlds of Maybe
1971 Pstalemate

"Moon":
1954 Step to the Stars
1956 Mission to the Moon
1960 Moon of Mutiny

0630
DICK, PHILIP K.   1928-1982
1955 Solar Lottery
1956 The Man Who Japed
1956 The World Jones Made
1957 The Cosmic Puppets
1957 Eye in the Sky
1957 The Variable Man (SS)
1959 Time Out of Joint
1960 Dr. Futurity
1960 The Unteleported Man
1960 Vulcan's Hammer
1962 The Man in the High Castle
1963 The Game-Players of Titan
1964 Clans of the Alphane Moon
1964 Martian Time-Slip
1964 The Penultimate Truth
1964 The Simulacra
1964 The Three Stigmata of Palmer Eldritch
1965 Dr. Bloodmoney (Or How We Got Along after the Bomb)
1966 The Crack in Space
1966 Now Wait for Last Year
1967 Counter-Clock World
1967 The Zap Gun (1965)
1968 Do Androids Dream of Electric Sheep? (Blade Runner)
1969 Galactic Pot-Healer
1969 The Preserving Machine (SS)
1969 Ubik
1970 Our Friends from Frolix 8
1970 A Maze of Death
1972 Flow My Tears, the Policeman Said
1972 We Can Build You
1975 Confessions of a Crap Artist
1977 A Scanner Darkly
1978 A Handful of Darkness (SS)
1980 The Golden Man (SS)
1981 The Divine Invasion
1981 VALIS
1982 The Transmigration of Timothy Archer
1984 Robots, Androids & Mechanical Oddities (SS)
1985 I Hope I Shall Arrive Soon (SS)
1985 Puttering About in a Small Land
1985 Radio Free Albemuth

Section 6 - Science Fiction & Fantasy

Also wrote mainstream fiction, i.e. Mary & the Giant, 1987

With NELSON, RAY
1967 The Ganymede Takeover

With ZELAZNY, ROGER
1976 Deus Irae
See also ZELAZNY, ROGER, 0738 & FANTASY, 0821

0631
DICKSON, GORDON R.   1923-
1956 Alien from Arcturus
1956 Mankind on the Run
1960 Time to Teleport
1961 Delusion World
1961 Spacial Delivery
1965 The Alien Way
1965 Mission to Universe
1967 Planet Run
1967 The Space Swimmers
1969 None But Man
1969 Spacepaw
1969 Wolfling
1970 Danger--Human (SS)
1970 Hour of the Horde
1970 Mutants (SS)
1971 Sleepwalker's World
1972 The Outposter
1972 The Pritcher Mass
1973 The R-Master
1973 The Star Road (SS)
1974 Ancient My Memory (SS)
1977 Futurelove
1977 Time Storm
1978 The Far Call
1978 Home from the Shore
1979 Masters of Everon
1979 On the Run
1980 In Iron Years (SS)
1980 Naked to the Stars (1961)
1981 Love Not Human
1986 The Forever Man
1987 Way of the Pilgrim

"Childe Cycle--Dorsai":
1959 Dorsai! (The Genetic General)
1962 Necromancer (No Room for Man)
1967 Soldier, Ask Not
1971 Tactics of Mistake
1976 Three to Dorsai (Dorsai!; Necromancer; Tactics)
1979 The Spirit of Dorsai
1980 Lost Dorsai
1984 The Final Encyclopedia
1986 The Dorsai Companion

Also wrote for juveniles
See also FANTASY, 0765 & as Jt. author with BOVA, BEN, 0607

0632
DISCH, THOMAS M.   1940-
1965 The Genocides
1968 Camp Concentration
1971 Fun with Your New Head (SS)
1972 334
1978 Death In Florence
1978 Heroics
1979 On Wings of Song
1984 The Business Man

0633
ELLIOT, JOHN   1918-
See as Jt. author with HOYLE, FRED, 0655

0634
ELLISON, HARLAN   1934-
1967 Doomsman
1967 I Have No Mouth & I Must Scream (SS)
1969 The Beast That Shouted Love at the Heart of the World
1970 Over the Edge
1971 Alone against Tomorrow (SS)
1974 Approaching Oblivion (SS)
1975 Deathbird Stories
1978 Strange Wine (SS)
1980 Shatterday (SS)

Editor of:
1967 Dangerous Visions, Vols. I & II (SS)
1971 Partners in Wonder (SS)
1972 Again, Dangerous Visions, Vols. I & II (SS)
1985 Medea: Harlan's World (SS)

0635
ENGDAHL, SYLVIA LOUISE   1933-
"Elana Sequence":
1970 Enchantress from the Stars
1970 Journey between Worlds
1971 The Far Side of Evil

"Norren Sequence":
1972 This Star Shall Abide
1973 Beyond the Tomorrow Mountains
1981 The Doors of the Universe

0636
FARMER, PHILIP JOSE   1918-
1957 The Green Odyssey
1960 Strange Relations (SS)
1961 The Lovers
1962 The Alley Gods (SS)
1962 The Cashe from Outer Space
1962 The Celestial Blueprint (SS)
1964 Inside Outside
1964 Tongues of the Moon
1968 Flesh, rev. (1960)
1970 The Stone God Awakens
1971 Down in the Black Gang (SS)
1971 The Wind Whales of Ishmael
1979 Dark Is the Sun
1981 The Unreasoning Mask
1985 Two Hawks from Earth (1966, The Gate of Time)

"Daybreaker":
1985 Dayworld
1987 Dayworld Rebel

"Exorcism" Trilogy:
1968 The Image of the Beast
1969 Blown
1973 Traitor to the Living

"Lord Grandrith/Doc Caliban":
1969 A Feast Unknown
1970 Lord of the Trees
1970 The Mad Goblin

"The Lords, the World of Tiers":
1965 The Maker of Universes
1966 The Gates of Creation
1968 A Private Cosmos
1970 Behind the Walls of Terra
1977 The Lavalite World

"Riverworld":
1971 The Fabulous Riverboat (2)
1971 To Your Scattered Bodies Go (1)
1978 The Dark Design (3)
1979 The Magic Labyrinth (4)
1979 Riverworld (SS)
1983 Gods of Riverworld (5)
1983 River of Eternity (1952) (Origin of series)

"Wold Newton Family":
1972 Tarzan Alive
1973 The Other Log of Phileas Fogg
1974 The Adventure of the Peerless Peer
1975 Doc Savage: His Apocalyptic Life, rev. (1973)
1976 Ironcastle
See also as TROUT, KILGORE, JR., 0725

0637
FOSTER, ALAN DEAN   1946-
1974 Icerigger
1975 Midworld
1975 Star Trek, Log One
1975 Star Trek, Log Two
1978 Splinter of the Mind's Eye (Luke Skywalker)
1986 Into the Out Of
1988 To the Vanishing Point

0638
GALOUYE, DANIEL   1920-1976
1961 Dark Universe
1964 Counterfeit World (Simulacron-3)
1973 The Infinite Man

0639
GERROLD, DAVID   1944-
Real name: Jerrold David Friedman
1972 When Harlie Was One
1973 The Trouble with Tribbles
1973 The Man Who Folded Himself
1978 Deathbeast

With NIVEN, LARRY
1971 The Flying Sorcerers
See also NIVEN, LARRY, 0691

0640
GESTON, MARK   1946-
1976 The Seige of Wonder

"Havenyore":
1967 Lords of the Starship
1969 Out of the Mouth of the Dragon

0641
GREELEY, ANDREW M.   1928-
1986 God Game
1987 The Final Planet
See also MYSTERIES, 0461 & TRASH, 1128

0642
GUNN, JAMES E.   1923-
1961 The Joy Makers
1962 The Immortals
1972 The Burning
1972 The Listeners
1974 Some Dreams Are Nightmares
1975 The End of the Dreams (SS)
1976 The Magicians
1977 Kampus
1980 The Dreamers

Section 6 - Science Fiction & Fantasy

0643
GUTTERIDGE, LINDSAY 1923-
"Matthew Dilke":
1971 Cold War in a Country Garden
1973 Killer Pine

0644
HAIBLUM, ISIDORE 1935-
1971 The Tsaddik of the Seven Wonders
1973 The Return
1973 Transfer to Yesterday
1975 The Wilk Are among Us
1977 Interworld
1979 Nightmare Express
1980 Faster than a Speeding Bullet
1984 The Identity Plunderers
1984 The Mutants Are Coming
1985 The Hand of Ganz

0645
HALDEMAN, JOE 1943-
1974 The Forever War
1976 Mindbridge
1977 All My Sins Remembered
1977 The Thunderbridge
1978 Infinite Dreams (SS)
1981 Worlds
1983 Worlds Apart
1985 Dealing in Futures (SS)
1987 Tool of the Trade

"Star Trek":
1977 Planet of Judgment
1979 World without End

0646
HALL, FRANCES
See as Jt. author with ANTHONY, PIERS, 0594

0647
HARNESS, CHARLES 1915-
1953 Flight into Yesterday
1953 The Rose
1955 The Paradox

0648
HARRISON, HARRY 1925-
Real name: Henry Maxwell Dempsey
1962 Planet of the Damned
1965 Plague from Space
1967 The Technicolor Time Machine
1969 Captive Universe
1970 The Daleth Effect (In Our Hands, the Stars)
1970 One Step from Earth (SS)
1973 Make Room! Make Room! (1966)
1973 Star Smasher of the Galaxy Rangers
1974 The Man from P.I.G. & R.O.B.O.T.
1974 Queen Victoria's Revenge
1975 Montezuma's Revenge (1970)
1977 Skyfall
1982 Invasion: Earth

"Deathworld" Trilogy:
1960 Deathworld
1964 Deathworld 2
1968 Deathworld 3

"Eden":
1984 West of Eden
1986 Winter in Eden

"The Stainless Steel Rat":
1961 The Stainless Steel Rat
1970 The Stainless Steel Rat's Revenge
1980 The Stainless Steel Rat for President

0649
HARRISON, M. JOHN 1945-
England
1971 The Committed Men
1974 The Centauri Device

"Viriconium Sequence":
1972 The Pastel City
1980 A Storm of Wings

0650
HEINLEIN, ROBERT 1907-1988
1949 The Day after Tomorrow
1950 Magic, Inc.
1950 Waldo
1951 The Puppet Masters
1953 Assignment in Eternity
1955 Tunnel in the Sky
1956 Double Star
1956 Time for the Stars
1957 Citizen of the Galaxy
1957 The Door into Summer
1959 The Menace from Earth
1959 Starship Troopers
1961 Stranger in a Strange Land
1963 Glory Road
1964 Farnham's Freehold
1966 The Moon Is a Harsh Mistress
1970 I Will Fear No Evil
1980 The Number of the Beast

1982 Friday
1984 Job: A Comedy of Justice
1985 The Cat Who Walks through Walls
1987 To Sail beyond Sunset

"Future History":
1950 The Man Who Sold the Moon (2)
1951 The Green Hills of Earth (1)
1951 Universe (3)
1964 Orphans of the Sky (4)
1967 The Past through Tomorrow (Omnibus)

"Lazarus Long":
1958 Methuselah's Children
1973 Time Enough for Love
1978 The Note Books of Lazarus Long
Also wrote for juveniles

0651
HENDERSON, ZENNA   1917-1983
1965 The Anything Box
1971 Holding Wonder (SS)

"The People":
1961 Pilgrimage: The Book of the People
1966 The People: No Different Flesh

0652
HERBERT, FRANK   1920-1986
1956 The Dragon in the Sea
1966 Destination: Void
1966 The Eyes of Heisenberg
1966 The Green Brain
1966 The Heaven Makers
1967 The Santaroga Barrier
1970 Whipping Star
1972 The God Makers
1973 Project 40
1974 Hellstrom's Hive
1977 The Dolsadi Experiment (Sequel to Whipping)
1982 The White Plague

"Dune":
1965 Dune
1969 Dune Messiah
1976 Children of Dune
1981 God Emperor of Dune
1984 Heretics of Dune
1985 Chapterhouse: Dune

0653
HERSEY, JOHN   1914-
1960 The Child Buyer

1965 White Lotus
1974 My Petition for More Space
See also HISTORICAL FICTION, 0986

0654
HOSKINS, ROBERT   1933-
1975 The Shattered People
1978 To Escape the Stars

0655
HOYLE, FRED   1915-
1958 The Black Cloud
1959 Ossian's Ride
1966 October the First Is Too Late
1967 Element 79

With ELLIOT, JOHN
"Andromeda":
1962 A for Andromeda
1964 Andromeda Breakthrough

With HOYLE, GEOFFREY
1963 Fifth Planet
1970 Rockets in Ursa Major
1970 Seven Steps to the Sun
1971 The Molecule Men
1973 The Inferno
1974 Into Deepest Space
1978 The Westminster Disaster

0656
HOYLE, GEOFFREY   1941-
See as jt. author with HOYLE, FRED, 0655

0657
HUBBARD, L. RON (Lafayette Ronald) 1911-1986
1977 Buckskin Brigade (1937)
1983 Battlefield Earth

"Mission Earth, Dekalogy":
1985 The Invaders Plan (1)
1986 An Alien Affair (4)
1986 Black Genesis: A Fortress of Evil (2)
1986 Death Quest (6)
1986 The Enemy Within (3)
1986 Fortune of Fear (5)
1987 Disaster (8)
1987 The Doom Planet (10)
1987 Villany Victorious (9)
1987 Voyage of Vengeance (7)
Best known as a writer of scientology; also wrote Doc Methuselah series

Section 6 - Science Fiction & Fantasy   123

0658
HUXLEY, ALDOUS   1984-1963
England
1932 Brave New World
1939 After Many a Summer Dies the Swan
1948 Ape & Essence
1962 Island

0659
JOHNSON, GEORGE CLAYTON
See as Jt. author with NOLAN, WILLIAM, 0692

0660
JONES, DENNIS F.   1917-1981
1971 Denver Is Missing (Don't Pick the Flowers)
1979 Earth Has Been Found (Xeno)

"Colossus":
1966 Colossus
1974 The Fall of Colossus

0661
JOSEPH, FRANZ   1914-
1975 Star Fleet Technical Manual

0662
KEYES, DANIEL   1927-
1966 Flowers for Algernon
1968 The Touch
1980 The Fifth Sally

0663
KNIGHT, DAMON   1922-
1955 Hell's Pavement
Editor of "Orbit" anthologies, vols. 1-19, 1966-1979

0664
KORNBLUTH, CYRIL M.   1923-1958
1953 The Syndic

With POHL, FREDERIK
1985 Wolfbane (1959)
See also POHL, FREDERIK, 0701

0665
KOTZWINKLE, WILLIAM   1938-
"E.T.":
1982 E.T., the Extra-Terrestrial
1985 E.T.: The Book of the Green Planet

0666
KUBRICK, STANLEY
See as Jt. author with CLARKE, ARTHUR C., 0619

0667
KURTZ, KATHERINE   1944-
1983 Lammas Night
1986 The Legacy of Lehr
See also FANTASY, 0784

0668
LAUMER, KEITH   1925-
1965 Plague of Demons
1966 The Monitors
1969 The Long Twilight
1970 The House in November
1971 Dinosaur Beach
1971 The Star Treasure
1973 The Glory Game
1976 Bolo: Annals of the Dinochrome Brigade
1978 The Ultimax Man
1980 Star Colony

"Retief":
1963 Envoy to New Worlds (SS)
1965 Galatic Diplomat
1966 Retief's War
1968 Retief & the Warlords
1969 Retief: Ambassador to Space
1971 Retief's Ransom
1971 Retief of the CDT
1983 Retief to the Rescue

0669
LE GUIN, URSULA K.   1929-
1978 The Eye of the Heron
1985 Always Coming Home

"Future History (Hainish)":
1966 Planet of Exile (6)
1966 Rocannon's World (5)
1967 City of Illusions (7)
1969 The Left Hand of Darkness (8)
1971 The Lathe of Heaven (1)
1974 The Dispossessed (2)
1976 The Word for World Is Forest (4)
Also writes short stories & novels for young adults
See also FANTASY, 0788

0670
LEIBER, FRITZ   1910-
1950 Gather, Darkness!
1953 Conjure Wife
1953 The Green Millennium
1961 The Big Time
1965 The Wanderer
1969 A Specter Is Haunting Texas
1972 You're All Alone (The Sinful Ones)
Autobiography: The Ghost Light, 1984
See also FANTASY, 0789

0671
LEINSTER, MURRAY   1896-1975
Real name: William Fitzgerald Jenkins
1954 The Forgotten Planet
1957 Colonial Survey
1959 The Pirates of Zan
1964 The Greeks Bring Gifts

0672
LEM, STANISLAW   1921-
Poland
1970 Solaris
1973 The Invincible
1973 Memoirs Found in a Bath Tub
1974 The Cyberiad: Fables for the
       Cybernetic Age
1974 The Futurological Congress
1974 The Investigation
1976 The Star Diaries
1978 The Chain of Chance
1980 Return from the Stars
1986 One Human Minute
1987 Fiasco

0673
LESSING, DORIS   1919-
England
1969 The Four-Gated City
1972 Briefing for a Descent into Hell
1974 Memoirs of a Survivor

"Canopos in Argos":
1979 Shikasta
1980 The Marriage between Zones
       Three, Four, & Five
1981 The Sirian Experiments
1982 The Making of the Representative
       for Planet 8
1983 Documents Relating to the
       Sentimental Agents in the Volyen
       Empire
See also BRITISH AUTHORS, 1369

0674
LEVIN, IRA   1929-
1970 This Perfect Day
See also HORROR, 0196 & HEADLINES, 0342

0675
LEWIS, C. S.   1898-1963
England
"Outer Space" or "Ransom":
1938 Out of the Silent Planet
1943 Perelandra
1945 That Hideous Strength: A Modern
       Fairy Tale for Grownups
See also FANTASY, 0790

0676
LIGHTNER, A. M. (Alice Martha)   1904-
1969 The Day of the Drones

0677
LUCAS, GEORGE
See as Jt. author with BOVA, BEN, 0607

0678
MCCAFFREY, ANNE   1926-
1967 Restoree
1969 Decision at Doona
1969 The Ship Who Sang
1971 The Mark of Merlin
1971 Ring of Fear
1973 To Ride Pegasus
1975 The Kilternan Legacy
1977 Get Off the Unicorn

"Dragonriders of Pern":
1968 Dragonflight
1971 Dragonquest
1976 Dragonsong (Juvenile)
1977 Dragonsinger (Juvenile)
1978 The White Dragon
1979 Dragondrums (Juvenile)
1984 Moreta: Dragonlady of Pern
1986 Nerilka's Story: A Pern Adventure
1988 Dragonsdawn (Juvenile)

"Dinosaur Planet":
1978 Dinosaur Planet
1984 Dinosaur Planet Survivors

0679
MCINTYRE, VONDA K.   1948-
1975 The Exile Waiting

Section 6 - Science Fiction & Fantasy

1978 Dreamsnake
1979 Fire Flood (SS)

"Star Trek":
1981 The Entropy Effect
1984 III: The Search for Spock
1984 II: The Wrath of Khan
1986 Enterprise: The First Adventure
1986 IV: The Voyage Home

0680
MACLEAN, KATHERINE 1925-
1962 The Diploids
1975 Missing Man

0681
MALZBERG, BARRY N. 1939-
1972 Beyond Apollo
1973 Herovit's World
1974 Guernica Night
1974 The Destruction of the Temple
1975 Conversations
1976 Down Here in the Dream Quarter
1978 Dark Sins, Dark Dreams
1985 The Remaking of Sigmund Freud
1986 Underlay
See also MYSTERIES as Jt. author with PRONZINI, B., 0512

0682
MANO, D. KEITH 1942-
1969 Horn
1973 The Bridge

0683
MARGROFF, ROBERT E.
See as Jt. author with ANTHONY, PIERS, 0594

0684
MERLE, ROBERT 1908-
France
1969 The Day of the Dolphin
1974 Malevil
1977 The Virility Factor

0685
MERRIL, JUDITH 1923-
Real name: Josephine Juliet Grossman
1950 Shadow on the Hearth
1960 The Tomorrow People
1969 Daughters of Earth

0686
MILLER, PETER S. (Schuyler)
See as Jt. author with DE CAMP, L. SPRAGUE, 0626

0687
MILLER, WALTER, JR. 1922-
1960 A Canticle for Leibowitz
1962 Conditionally Human (SS)

0688
MITCHISON, NAOMI 1897-
1962 Memoirs of a Spacewoman

0689
MOORCOCK, MICHAEL 1939-
England
1969 The Black Corridor
1969 The Ice Schooner
"Oswald Bastable":
1971 The Warlord of the Air
1974 The Land Leviathan
"Cornelius Chronicles":
1968 The Final Programme
1971 A Cure for Cancer
1972 The English Assassin
1978 The Condition of Muzak
1979 The Lives & Times of Jerry Cornelius
1980 The Adventures of Una Persson & Catherine Cornelius in the 20th Century
"Dancers at the End of Time":
1973 An Alien Heat
1974 The Hollow Lands
1976 The End of All Songs
1976 Legends from the End of Time
1978 Messiah at the End of Time
"Karl Glogaver":
1969 Behold the Man
1974 Breakfast in the Ruins
Also writes nonscience fiction & fantasy
See also FANTASY, 0797

0690
NELSON, RAY
See as Jt. author with DICK, PHILIP K., 0630

0691
NIVEN, LARRY   1938-
1966 World of Ptaavs
1968 Neutron Star (SS)
1973 Protector
1976 The Lifeship
1976 A World Out of Time
1984 The Integral Trees
1987 The Smoke Ring (Sequel to Integral)

"Ringworld":
1970 Ringworld
1980 The Ringworld Engineers
See also as Jt. author with GERROLD, DAVID, 0639

With POURNELLE, JERRY
1974 The Mote in God's Eye
1976 Inferno
1977 Lucifer's Hammer
1981 Oath of Fealty
1985 Footfall
See also POURNELLE, JERRY, 0702

0692
NOLAN, WILLIAM   1928-
1965 The Pseudo People

With JOHNSON, GEORGE CLAYTON
1967 Logan's Run

0693
NORMAN, JOHN   1931-
"Gor":
1966 Tarnsman of Gor
1967 Outlaw of Gor
1968 Priest-Kings of Gor
1969 Nomads of Gor
1970 Assassin of Gor
1971 Raiders of Gor
1972 Captive of Gor
1974 Hunters of Gor

0694
NORTON, ANDRE   1912-
Real name: Alice Mary Norton
1952 Daybreak . . . 2250 A.D. (1952, Star Man's Son)
1954 At Sword's Point
1958 Star Gate
1959 The Beast Master
1959 Secret of the Lost Race
1961 Catseye
1962 Lord of Thunder
1964 Night of Masks

1965 The X Factor
1967 Operation Time Search
1968 Dark Piper
1970 Dread Companion
1970 High Sorcery
1970 Ice Crown
1971 Android at Arms
1972 Breed to Come
1975 No Night without Stars
1976 Wraiths of Time
1986 Flight in Yiktor

"Astra Sequence":
1954 The Stars Are Ours!
1957 Star Born

"Blackwalke":
1956 The Crossroads of Time
1965 Quest Crosstime

"Lydis Sequence":
1966 Moon of the Three Rings
1971 Exiles of the Stars

"Naill Rerfro":
1963 Judgment on Janus
1966 Victory on Janus

"Time Agents":
1958 The Time Traders
1959 Galatic Derelict
1962 The Defiant Agents
1963 Key Out of Time
Also writes for juveniles
See also FANTASY, 0800

0695
NOURSE, ALAN   1928-
1965 The Universe Between
1967 PSI High & Others
1968 The Mercy Man
1974 The Bladerunner

0696
OLIVER, CHAD   1928-
1954 Shadows in the Sun
1971 The Edge of Forever (SS)
1971 The Shores of Another Sea

0697
ORWELL, GEORGE   1903-1950
England
Real name: Eric Arthur Blair
1949 1984

Section 6 - Science Fiction & Fantasy

0698
PANGBORN, EDGAR   1909-1976
1953 West of the Sun
1954 A Mirror for Observers
1958 Wilderness of Spring
1961 The Trial of Callista Blake
1964 Davy
1966 The Judgment of Eve
1972 Good Neighbors & Other Strangers (SS)
1975 The Company of Glory

0699
PANSHIN, ALEXEI   1940-
1968 Rite of Passage

"Anthony Villiers":
1968 Star Well
1968 The Thurb Revolution
1969 Masque World

0700
PIPER, H. BEAM   1904-1964
"Fuzzy":
1962 Little Fuzzy
1964 The Other Human Race
1984 Fuzzies & Other People

0701
POHL, FREDERIK   1919-
1957 Slave Ship
1957 The Case against Tomorrow (SS)
1960 Dunkard's Walk
1960 The Man Who Ate the World (SS)
1961 Turn Life at Thursday (SS)
1969 The Age of the Pussyfoot
1970 Day Million (SS)
1976 Man Plus
1979 JEM
1981 The Cool War
1984 The Merchant's War (Sequel to Space Merchants)
1984 The Years of the City (SS)
1987 Chernobyl
1988 The Day the Martians Came
1988 Narabedla Ltd.

"Heechee Saga":
1979 Gateway
1980 Beyond the Blue Event Horizon
1984 Heechee Rendezvous
1987 The Annals of the Heechee

With KORNBLUTH, CYRIL M.
1953 The Space Merchants
1954 Search the Sky
1962 The Wonder Effect
1985 Gladiator-at-Law (1955)
See also as Jt. author with KORNBLUTH, CYRIL, M., 0664

With WILLIAMSON, JACK
1954 Undersea Quest
1956 Undersea Fleet
1958 Undersea City
See also WILLIAMSON, JACK, 0734

0702
POURNELLE, JERRY   1933-
1981 King David's Spaceship (Prequel to The Mote in God's Eye)
See also as Jt. author with NIVEN, LARRY, 0691

0703
PRATCHETT, TERRY
1981 Strata (Parody of Niven's Ringworld)
1983 The Colour of Magic
1987 The Light Fantastic (Sequel to Colour)

0704
PRIEST, CHRISTOPHER   1943-
England
1972 Darkening Island
1974 The Inverted World
1977 The Perfect Lover
1979 An Infinite Summer
1981 The Affirmation

0705
RAND, AYN   1905-1982
Born in Russia
Real Name: Alice Rosenbaum
1938 Anthem
See also AMERICAN AUTHORS, 1293

0706
REYNOLDS, MACK   1917-1983
1969 Armed Camps
1969 The Space Barbarians (1967)
1973 Looking Backward from the Year 2000
1977 Perchance to Dream

0707
ROBERTS, KEITH   1935-
England

1968 Pavane
1970 The Inner Wheel
1980 Molly's Zero
1987 Grainne

0708
ROBINETT, STEPHEN   1941-
1976 Stargate
1978 The Man Responsible
1979 Projections (SS)

0709
RUSS, JOANNA   1937-
1968 Picnic on Paradise
1970 And Chaos Died
1975 The Female Man
1976 Alyx
1977 We Who Are about to . . .
1978 The Two of Them
1984 Extra (Ordinary) People (SS)

0710
SHAW, BOB   1931-
Ireland
1968 The Two-Timers
1969 The Palace of Eternity
1972 Other Days, Other Eyes
1978 Vertigo
1985 The Peace Machine (1971, Ground Zero Man)

0711
SHECKLEY, ROBERT   1928-
1959 Immortality, Inc.
1962 Journey beyond Tomorrow
1966 Mindswap
1968 Dimension of Miracles
1978 Crompton Divided
1983 Dramocles

0712
SILVERBERG, ROBERT   1935-
1955 Revolt on Alpha C
1962 Recalled to Life
1966 Needle in a Timestack
1967 Planet of Death
1967 Thorns
1967 Those Who Watch
1967 The Time-Hoppers
1968 Hawksbill Station
1969 Across a Billion Years
1969 Nightwings
1969 To Live Again
1969 Up the Line

1970 The Cube Root of Uncertainty
1970 Downward to the Earth
1970 Tower of Glass
1970 Worlds of Maybe (SS)
1971 Moonferns & Starsongs
1971 Son of Man
1971 A Time of Changes
1971 The World Inside
1972 The Book of Skulls
1972 Dying Inside
1972 The Realm of Prester John
1972 The Second Trip
1973 Valley beyond Time
1974 Born with the Dead
1975 The Stochastic Man
1976 Shadrach in the Furnace
1978 Journey to the Sky
1979 The Androids Are Coming
1980 Lord Valentine's Castle
1981 Majipoor Chronicles
1983 Valentine Pontifex (Sequel to Lord)
1984 The Conglomeroid Cocktail Party
1985 Tom O'Bedlam
1986 Beyond the Safe Zone (SS)
1986 Star of Gypsies
1988 At Winter's End
1988 The Secret Sharer

0713
SIMAK, CLIFFORD D.   1904-
1951 Time & Again
1952 City (SS)
1953 Ring around the Sun
1961 Time Is the Simplest Thing
1962 They Walked Like Men
1963 Way Station
1965 All Flesh Is Grass
1967 The Werewolf Principle
1967 Why Call Them Back from Heaven?
1968 The Goblin Reservation
1970 Out of Their Minds
1971 Destiny Doll
1972 A Choice of Gods
1973 Cemetery World
1974 Our Children's Children
1975 Enchanted Pilgrimage
1976 Shakespeare's Planet
1977 A Heritage of Stars
1978 The Fellowship of the Talisman
1978 Mastodonia
1981 Project Pope
1982 Special Deliverance
1982 Where the Evil Dwells
1986 Highway to Eternity

Section 6 - Science Fiction & Fantasy   129

0714
SMITH, CORDWAINER   1913-1966
Real name: Paul M. A. Linebarger
1975 Norstrilia (1953)

"The Instrumentality of Mankind":
1963 You Will Never Be the Same (SS)
1964 The Planet Buyer
1965 Space Lords
1966 Quest of the Three Worlds
1968 The Underpeople
1970 Under Old World & Other
     Explorations
1971 Stardreamer

0715
SMITH, E. E. "Doc"   1890-1965
"Lensmen":
1948 Triplanetary
1950 First Lensman
1950 Galactic Patrol
1951 Gray Lensman
1953 Second Stage Lensman
1954 Children of the Lens
1960 The Vortex Blaster

0716
SPINRAD, NORMAN   1940-
1966 The Solarians
1967 Agent of Chaos
1969 Bug Jack Barron
1972 The Iron Dream
1975 No Direction Home (SS)
1975 Passing through the Flame
1983 The Void Captain's Tale
1985 Child of Fortune
1987 Little Heroes

0717
STABLEFORD, BRIAN M.   1948-
England
1969 Cradle of the Sun
1977 Realms of Tartarus

"Dies Irae":
1971 Day of Wrath
1971 The Days of Glory
1971 In the Kingdom of the Beasts

"Star Pilot Grainger":
1972 The Halcyon Drift (1)
1973 Rhapsody in Black (2)
1974 The Fenris Device (5)
1974 The Paradise Game (4)
1974 Promised Land (3)
1975 The Swan Song

0718
STAPLEDON, OLAF   1886-1950
England
1930 Last & First Men
1935 Odd John: A Story between Jest
     & Ernest
1944 Sirius: A Fantasy of Love &
     Discord
1976 Nebula Maker & Four Encounters
1987 Star Maker (1937)

0719
STEWART, GEORGE R.   1895-1980
1949 Earth Abides
1955 The Years of the City

0720
STRUGATSKY, ARKADY 1925- &
STRUGATSKY, BORIS 1933-
U.S.S.R.
1967 Far Rainbow
1968 The Snail on the Slope (1966)
1973 Hard to Be a God
1982 Escape Attempt
1987 The Time Wanderers

"Noon: Twenty Second Century":
1971 An Inhabited Island (The Prisoners
     of Power)
1973 The Kid (The Space Mowgli)
1974 The Guy from Hell
1978 Noon: Twenty Second Century
     (1962)
1980 A Beetle in the Anthill
1986 Waves Dampen Wind

0721
STRUGATSKY, BORIS   1933-
See as Jt. author with STRUGATSKY,
ARKADY, 0720

0722
STURGEON, THEODORE   1918-1985
Real name: Edward Hamilton Waldo
1953 More Than Human
1957 The Synthetic Man (1950, The
     Dreaming Jewels)
1958 The Cosmic Rape
1960 Venus Plus X
1975 Case & the Dreamer (SS)
1978 Visions & Venturers
1979 The Stars Are the Styx (SS)
1980 The Golden Helix (SS)
1984 Alien Cargo
1986 Godbody

0723
TEVIS, WALTER   1928-1984
1963   The Man Who Fell to Earth
1980   Mockingbird
1984   The Steps of the Sun

0724
TIPTREE, JAMES, JR.   1915-1987
Real name: Alice B. Sheldon
1978   Up the Walls of the World
1985   Brightness Falls from the Air
1986   The Starry Rift (SS)
1986   Tales of the Quintana Roo (SS)
1988   Crown of Stars (SS)

0725
TROUT, KILGORE, JR.   1918-
Real name: Philip Jose Farmer
1974   Venus on the Half Shell (Satire of books of Kurt Vonnegut, Jr.)
See also as FARMER, PHILIP JOSE, 0636

0726
VAN VOGT, A. E.   1912-
1950   The Voyage of the Space Beagle
1951   Slan (1940)
1952   Mission to the Stars (The Mixed Men)
1959   The War against the Rull
1969   The Silkie
1974   The Secret Galactics

"Isher":
1951   The Weapon Shops of Isher (1941)
1952   The Weapon Makers (1943)

"Null-A":
1948   World of Null-A
1956   The Pawns of Null-A

0727
VANCE, JACK   1916-
1950   The Dying Earth (SS)
1957   Big Planet (1952)
1963   The Dragon Masters
1966   The Blue World
1966   The Eyes of the Overworld
1967   The Last Castle
1969   Emphyrio
1973   Trullion: Alastor 2262
1976   Maske: Thaery
1978   A False Utopia
1978   The Killing Machine

1978   Star King
See also FANTASY, 0810

0728
VERNE, JULES   1828-1905
France
1872   A Journey to the Center of the Earth

"Captain Nemo":
1873   20,000 Leagues Under the Sea
1875   The Mysterious Island

"Gun Club":
1873   From the Earth to the Moon
1879   Around the Moon
1890   The Purchase of the North Pole

0729
VIDAL, GORE   1925-
1950   A Search for the King: A Twelfth Century Legend
1954   Messiah
1956   Visit to a Small Planet
1978   Kalki
See also HISTORICAL FICTION, 0941 & AMERICAN AUTHORS, 1331; MYSTERIES, 0407 as BOX, EDGAR

0730
VONNEGUT, KURT, JR.   1922-
1952   Player Piano
1959   The Sirens of Titan
1962   Mother Night
1963   Cat's Cradle
1965   God Bless You, Mr. Rosewater
1968   Welcome to the Monkey House (SS)
1969   Slaughterhouse-5
1972   Between Time & Timbukto
See also HISTORICAL FICTION, 1103 & AMERICAN AUTHORS, 1332

0731
WELLS, H. G.   1866-1946
England
1895   The Time Machine: An Invention
1987   The Invisible Man: A Grotesque Romance

0732
WHITE, JAMES   1928-
Ireland
1962   Second Ending

Section 6 - Science Fiction & Fantasy

1965 Escape Orbit
1966 The Watch Below
1974 The Dream Millennium

"Sector Twelve General Hospital":
1962 Hospital Station (SS)
1962 Star Surgeon (SS)
1971 Major Operation
1979 Ambulance Ship (SS)
1983 Sector General (SS)
1985 Star Healer
1987 Code Blue--Emergency

0733
WILHELM, KATE   1928-
1963 The Mile-Long Spaceship (SS)
1966 The Nevermore Affair
1967 The Killer Thing
1968 The Downstairs Room (SS)
1969 Let the Fire Fall
1971 Abyss
1974 City of Cain
1975 The Infinity Box (SS)
1976 The Clewiston Test
1976 Where Late the Sweet Bird Sang
1977 Fault Lines
1978 Somerset Dreams (SS)
1979 Juniper Time
1981 A Sense of Shadow
1983 Welcome, Chaos
1986 Huysman's Pets
1988 Crazy Time

0734
WILLIAMSON, JACK   1908-
1948 Darker Than You Think
1949 The Humanoids
1951 Seetee Ship
1964 Golden Blood
1982 Man Seed
1984 Lifeburst
1986 Firechild
1988 Dead Fall (Sequel to Lifeburst)

"Legion of Space Trilogy":
1947 Legion of Space (1934)
1950 The Cometeers (1936)
1950 One against the Legion (1939)
Autobiography: Wonder's Child, 1984
See also as Jt. author with POHL, FREDERIK, 0701

0735
WILSON, COLIN   1931-
England
1967 The Mind Parasites

1971 The Philosopher's Stone (1969)
1985 Lifeforce (1976, The Space Vampires)
See also MYSTERIES, 0584 & BRITISH AUTHORS, 1396

0736
WYNDHAM, JOHN   1903-1969
Real name: John Wyndham Rarkes L. B. Harris
England
1951 The Day of the Triffids
1953 Out of the Deeps
1955 Re-Birth
1956 Tales of Gooseflesh & Laughter (SS)
1957 The Midwich Cuckoo (SS)
1960 Trouble with Lichen
1968 Chocky

0737
ZAMYATIN, YEVGENY   1884-1937
U.S.S.R.
1924 We (1920)

0738
ZELAZNY, ROGER   1937-
1966 And Call Me Conrad
1966 The Dream Master
1966 This Immortal
1967 Lord of Light
1969 Isle of the Dead
1971 The Doors of His Face, the Lamps of His Mouth (SS)
1973 To Die in Italber
1976 Doorways in the Sand
1979 Roadmarks
1982 Eye of Cat
See also as Jt. author with DICK, PHILIP K., 0630 & FANTASY, 0821

B. FANTASY

0739
ADAMS, HAZARD   1926-
1971 The Truth about Dragons: An Anti-Romance

0740
ADAMS, RICHARD   1921-
1972 Watership Down
1974 Shardik
1978 The Plague Dogs

1984 Maia
1988 Traveller
See also HORROR, 0150 & BRITISH AUTHORS, 1344

0741
ANDERSON, POUL 1926-
1954 The Broken Sword (Norse Epic)
1961 Three Hearts & Three Lions
1971 Operation Chaos
1974 A Midsummer Tempest
See also SCIENCE FICTION, 0593

0742
ANTHONY, PIERS 1934-
"The Magic of Xanth":
1977 A Spell for Chameleon (1)
1979 Castle Roogna (3)
1979 The Source of Magic (2)
1981 Centaur Aisle (4)
1986 Golem in the Gears (5)
1987 Vale of the Vole (6)
1988 Heaven Cent (7)
See also SCIENCE FICTION, 0594

0743
BACH, RICHARD 1936-
1970 Jonathan Livingston Seagull
1977 Illusions: The Adventures of a Reluctant Messiah
1979 There's No Such Place as Far Away
1988 One

0744
BAUER, STEVEN
1980 Satyrday

0745
BEAGLE, PETER 1939-
1960 A Fine & Private Place
1968 The Last Unicorn: A Fantastic Tale
1974 Lila & the Werewolf
1986 The Folk of the Air

0746
BERGER, THOMAS 1924-
1978 Arthur Rex: A Legendary Novel
See also SCIENCE FICTION, 0602 & AMERICAN AUTHORS, 1170

0747
BRACKETT, LEIGH 1953-
1953 The Sword of Rhiannon

0748
BRADLEY, MARION ZIMMER 1930-
1980 The House between the Worlds
1983 The Mists of Avalon
1987 The Firebrand
See also SCIENCE FICTION, 0610

0749
BRADSHAW, GILLIAN 1956-
"Arthurian Trilogy":
1980 Hawk of May
1981 Kingdom of Summer
1982 In Winter's Shadow
See also HISTORICAL FICTION, 0956

0750
BRAMAH, ERNEST
Real name: Ernest Bramah Smith
1922 Kai-Lung's Golden Hours
1974 Kai-Lung Unrolls His Mat

0751
BROOKS, TERRY 1944-
"Landover Trilogy":
1986 Magic Kingdom For Sale--Sold!
1987 The Black Unicorn
1988 Wizard at Large

"Shannara":
1977 Sword of Shannara
1982 The Elfstones of Shannara
1984 The Wishsong of Shannara

0752
CANNING, VICTOR 1911-1986
"Arthurian Trilogy":
1977 The Circle of the Gods
1978 The Crimson Chalice
1978 The Immortal Wound
See also HEADLINES, 0262 & 0323 & MYSTERIES, 0411

0753
CARROLL, LEWIS 1832-1898
England
Real name: Charles L. Dodgsen
1865 Alice's Adventures in Wonderland
1872 Through the Looking Glass

Section 6 - Science Fiction & Fantasy

0754
CARTER, ANGELA   1940-
1968 The Magic Toyshop
1968 Several Perceptions
1969 Heroes & Villains
1972 The Infernal Desire Machine of Doctor Hoffman
1974 Fireworks
1974 The War of Dreams
1977 The Passion of New Eve
1979 The Bloody Chamber (SS)
1984 Nights at the Circus
1986 Saints & Strangers

0755
CARTER, LIN   1930-
1976 Realms of Wizardry
1978 Renegade of Callisto
1978 The Wizard of Zao
1984 Kellory the Warlock

"Prince Zarkon, Lord of the Unknown":
1975 Invisible Death
1975 The Nemesis of Evil
1976 The Volcano Evil
1982 The Earth-Shaker

0756
CHANT, JOY   1945-
1970 Red Moon & Black Mountain: The End of the House of Kendreth
1977 The Grey Mane of Morning (Prequel to Red)

0757
CHAPMAN, VERA   1898-
"The Three Damosels":
1975 The Green Knight
1976 King Arthur's Daughter
1976 The King's Damosel

0758
COATSWORTH, ELIZABETH   1893-
1951 The Enchanted: An Incredible Tale
1953 Silky: An Incredible Tale
1954 Mountain Bride: An Incredible Tale
1958 The White Room
1975 The Werefox

0759
COLLIER, JOHN   1901-
1951 Fancies & Goodnights (SS)

0760
CROWLEY, JOHN   1942-
1976 Beasts
1979 Engine Summer
1981 Little, Big
1987 Aegypt
See also SCIENCE FICTION, 0624

0761
DAVIDSON, AVRAM   1923-
1969 The Phoenix & the Mirror
1971 Peregrine Primus
1973 Ursus of Ultima Thule
1978 The Redward Edward Papers (SS)
1987 Vergil in Averno (Sequel to Phoenix)
See also SCIENCE FICTION, 0625

0762
DE CAMP, CATHERINE CROOK
See as Jt. author with DE CAMP, L. SPRAGUE, 0763

0763
DE CAMP, L. (Lyon) SPRAGUE   1907-
1951 The Undesired Princess
1957 Solomon's Stone
1963 A Gun for Dinosaur (SS)
1970 The Reluctant Shaman (SS)
1978 The Great Fetish
1979 The Purple Pterodactyls
1982 The Prisoner of Zhamanak
1983 The Unbeheaded King

"The Novaria Trilogy":
1968 The Goblin Tower
1971 The Clocks of Iraz
1973 The Fallible Fiend (SS)

"Posadian" Stories:
1953 The Tritonian Ring
Also collaborated with several others on the "Conan" series of Robert E. Howard
See also SCIENCE FICTION, 0626 & HISTORICAL FICTION, 0963

With DE CAMP, CATHERINE CROOK
1983 The Bones of Zora
1986 The Incorporated Knight

With PRATT, FLETCHER   1897-1956
1960 Wall of Serpents
1962 The Castle of Iron (1950) (Sequel to Incomplete)
1967 The Carnelian Cube (1948)

1970 The Land of Unreason (1941)
1975 The Compleat Enchanter: The Magical Misadventures of Harold Shea
1978 Tales from Gavagan's Bar, Expanded ed. (1953)
1979 The Incomplete Enchanter (1942)
1980 The Enchanter Completed
See also PRATT, FLETCHER, 0802

0764
DELANY, SAMUEL R.
"Return to Nevèrÿon":
1979 Tales of Nevèrÿon
1983 Neveryóna; or The Tale of Signs & Cities (SS)
1985 Flight from Nevèrÿon
1987 The Bridge of Lost Desire
See also SCIENCE FICTION, 0628

0765
DICKSON, GORDON R. 1923-
1976 The Dragon & the George
See also SCIENCE FICTION, 0631

0766
DONALDSON, STEPHEN R. 1947-
1984 Daughter of Regals (SS)

"The Chronicle of Thomas Covenant, the Unbeliever":
1977 Lord Foul's Bane
1977 The Illearth War
1977 The Power that Preserves

"The Second Chronicles of Thomas Covenant":
1980 The Wounded Land
1982 The One Tree
1983 White Gold Wielder

"Mordant's Need":
1986 The Mirror of Her Dreams
1988 A Man Rides Through

0767
EDDISON, ERIC 1882-1945
1972 The Warm Ouroboros

"Zimiavian Trilogy":
1935 Mistress of Mistresses
1941 A Fish Dinner in Memison
1958 The Mezentian Gate

0768
ENDE, MICHAEL 1930?-
Germany
1983 The Neverending Story
1985 Momo

0769
FARMER, PENELOPE 1939-
1972 A Castle of Bone
1974 William & Mary: A Story
1988 Eve: Her Story

"Emma":
1963 The Summer Birds
1966 Emma in Winter
1969 Charlotte Some Times

0770
FINNEY, JACK 1911-
1955 The Body Snatchers
1970 Time & Again
1973 Marion's Wall
1977 The Night People
1986 About Time (SS)
See also MYSTERIES, 0445

0771
GARDNER, JOHN C. (Champlin Jr.) 1933-1982
1971 Grendel
1974 The King's Indian (SS)
1981 The Art of Living (SS)
Also wrote fantasy for juveniles
See also HISTORICAL FICTION, 0975 & AMERICAN AUTHORS, 1212

0772
GARRETT, RANDALL 1927-1987
"Lord Darcy":
1967 Too Many Magicians
1979 Murder & Magic
1981 Lord Darcy Investigates

0773
GASKELL, JANE 1941-
1963 The Serpent
1965 Atlan
1966 The City
1977 Some Summer Lands

0774
GOLDMAN, WILLIAM 1931-
1973 The Princess Bride

Section 6 - Science Fiction & Fantasy   135

1983 The Silent Gondoliers: A Fable
See also HORROR, 0180; SPY STORIES, 0365; TRASH, 1127

0775
GRAHAM, KENNETH   1936-
England
1895 The Reluctant Dragon
1908 The Wind in the Willows

0776
GREGORIAN, JOYCE   1946-
1975 The Broken Citadel

0777
GUEST, LADY CHARLOTTE   1812-1895
England
Real name: Charlotte Guest Schreiber
1978 The Mabinogion (1906, 1838-42)

0778
HANCOCK, NEIL   1941-
"Circle of Light":
1977 Calix Stay (3)
1977 Faragon Fairingay (2)
1977 Grey Fax Grim Wald (1)
1977 Squaring the Circle (4)

0779
HILTON, JAMES   1900-1954
1933 Lost Horizon

0780
HOUSEHOLD, GEOFFREY   1900-
1986 Arrows of Desire
See also HORROR, 0187 & SPY STORIES, 0372

0781
JONES, GWYN   1907- &
JONES, THOMAS   1916?-
England
1974 Mabinogion (1948)

0782
JONES, THOMAS   1916?-
See as Jt. author with JONES, GWYN, 0781

0783
KING, STEPHEN   1947-
1987 The Eyes of the Dragon

"The Dark Tower":
1987 The Drawing of the Three
1988 The Gunslinger (1982)
See also HORROR, 0191 & as BACHMAN, RICHARD, 0153

0784
KURTZ, KATHERINE   1944-
"The Deryni":
1970 Deryni Rising
1972 Deryni Checkmate
1973 High Deryne

"The Histories of King Kelson":
1984 The Bishop's Heir
1985 The King's Justice
1986 The Quest for Saint Camber

"The Legends of Camber of Culdi":
1976 Camber of Culdi
1978 Saint Camber
1981 Camber the Heretic
1986 The Deryni Archives (collection for 3 series)
See also SCIENCE FICTION, 0667

0785
LAFFERTY, R. A. (Raphael Aloysius) 1914-
1968 Past Master
1968 The Reefs of Earth
1968 Space Chantey
1969 Fourth Mansions
1970 Nine Hundred Grandmothers (SS)
1971 Arrive at Easterwine: The Autobiography of a Ktistec Machine
1972 Okla Hannali
1972 Strange Doings
1976 Not to Mention Camels
1982 Aurelia
1983 The Annals of Klepsis

"The Devil Is Dead" Trilogy:
1971 The Devil Is Dead (2)
1979 Archipelago (1)
1983 More Than Melchisedech (3)

0786
LAUBENTHAL, AUDREY
1973 Excalibur

0787
LEE, TANITH   1947-
England
1971 Dragon Hoard
1976 The Winter Players
1977 Companions on the Road
1977 Volkhavar
1980 Kill the Dead
1980 Sabella
1981 Lycanthia
1981 The Silver Metal Lover
1983 Red as Blood (SS)
1984 Tamastara (SS)
1985 The Gorgon (SS)
1986 Dreams of Dark & Light (SS)

"Birthgrave":
1975 Birthgrave
1978 Quest For the White Witch
1978 Vazkor, Son of Vazkor

"Demon Lord":
1978 Night's Master
1979 Death's Master
1981 Delusion's Master

0788
LE GUIN, URSULA K.   1929-
1975 The Wind's Twelve Quarters (SS)
1976 Orsinian Tales (SS)
1979 Malafrena

"Earthsea Trilogy":
1968 A Wizard of Earthsea
1971 The Tombs of Atuan
1972 The Farthest Shore
Also writes fiction for young adults
See also SCIENCE FICTION, 0669

0789
LEIBER, FRITZ   1910-
1977 Our Lady of Darkness

"Fafhrds & the Gray Mouser Saga":
1968 Swords in the Mist
1968 Swords against Wizardry
1968 The Swords of Lankhmar
1970 Swords against Death
1970 Swords & Deviltry
1977 Swords & Ice Magic
1988 The Knight & Knave of Swords (SS)
Autobiography: The Ghost Light, 1984
See also SCIENCE FICTION, 0670

0790
LEWIS, C. S.   1898-1963
England
"Chronicles of Narnia":
1950 The Lion, the Witch & the Wardrobe
1951 Prince Caspian
1952 The Voyage of the Dawn Treader
1953 The Silver Chair
1954 The Horse & His Boy
1955 The Magician's Nephew
1956 The Last Battle
See also SCIENCE FICTION, 0675

0791
LINDROP, AUDREY
1976 The Self-Appointed Saint

0792
LUKEMAN, TIM
1979 Rajan
1981 Koren

0793
LYNN, ELIZABETH   1946-
"Chronicles of Tonor":
1979 Watchtower
1979 The Dancers of Arun
1980 The Northern Girl

0794
MERRITT, A. (Abraham)   1884-1943
1926 The Ship of Ishtar

0795
MIRRLESS, HOPE
1926 Lud-in-the-Midst

0796
MONACO, RICHARD   1940-
1977 Parsival
1979 The Grail War
1980 The Final Quest

0797
MOORCOCK, MICHAEL   1939-
1967 The Stealer of Souls (SS)
1973 The Silver Warriors
1974 The Singing Citadel (SS)
1981 The War Hound & the World's Pain

Section 6 - Science Fiction & Fantasy   137

1986 The City in the Autumn Stars
     (Sequel to War)

"Chronicles of Corum":
1971 The King of the Swords (3)
1971 The Knight of the Swords (1)
1971 The Queen of the Swords (2)
1973 The Bull & the Spear (4)
1973 The Oak & the Ram (5)
1974 The Sword & the Stallion (6)

"The Dorian Hawkmoon":
1967 The Jewel in the Skull
1968 The Sword of Dawn
1969 The Mad God's Amulet
1969 The Runestaff
1973 The Champion of Garathorn
1973 Count Brass
1976 The Quest for Tanelorn

"The Elric Saga":
1972 Elric of Melnibonbe
1972 The Sleeping Sorceress
1976 The Sailor on the Seas of Fate
1977 The Bane of the Black Sword
1977 Stormbringer
1977 The Vanishing Tower
1977 The Weird of the White Wolf
1984 Elric at the End of Time

"The History of John Daker, the Eternal Champion, the Erekose":
1970 The Eternal Champion
1970 Phoenix in Obsidian
1986 The Dragon in the Sword
Also writes nonscience fiction/fantasy titles
See also SCIENCE FICTION, 0689

0798
MORRIS, KENNETH   1941-
1913 The Fates of the Princes of Dyfed
1930 Book of the Three Dragons

0799
NATHAN, ROBERT   1894-1985
1925 Jonah
1935 Road of Ages
1936 The Enchanted Voyage
1940 Portrait of Jennie
1949 The River Journey
1950 The Adventures of Tapiola
1951 The Innocent Eve
1953 The Train in the Meadow
1955 Sir Henry
1963 The Devil with Love
1964 The Fair

1965 The Mallot Diaries
1967 Stonecliff
1970 Mia
1971 The Elixir
1973 The Summer Meadows
1975 Heaven & Hell & the Megas Factor

0800
NORTON, ANDRE   1912-
Real name: Alice Mary Norton
1968 Fur Magic
1977 Wraiths of Time
1985 Forerunner: The Second Venture

"Witch World":
1980 Lore of Witch World

First: "Estcarp Cycle":
1963 Witch World
1964 Web of Witch World
1965 Three against Witch World
1967 Warlock of Witch World
1968 Sorceress of Witch World
1977 Trey of Swords
1983 'Ware Hawk
1987 The Gate of the Cat

Second: "High Hallack":
1965 Year of the Unicorn
1972 The Crystal Gryphon
1972 Spell of Witch World (SS)
1974 The Jargoon Pard
1981 Gryphon in Glory
1984 Gryphon's Eyrie
Also writes for juveniles
See also SCIENCE FICTION, 0694

0801
PEAKE, MERVYN   1911-1968
England
1953 Mr. Pye

"Gormenghast Trilogy":
1946 Titus Groan (1)
1959 Titus Alone (3)
1968 Gormenghast (1950) (2)

0802
PRATT, FLETCHER   1897-1956
1948 The Well of the Unicorn
1969 The Blue Star
See also as Jt. author with DE CAMP, L. SPRAGUE, 0763

0803
SAINT-EXUPÉRY, ANTOINE DE   1900-
1943 The Little Prince

0804
SAXTON, MARK   1914-
"Islandia":
1969 The Islar (A Sequel to Austin Wright's Islandia)
1979 The Two Kingdoms

0805
STEWART, MARY   1916-
England
1980 A Walk in Wolf Wood: A Tale of Fantasy & Magic
1988 Thornyhold

"King Arthur":
1970 The Crystal Cave
1973 The Hollow Hills
1979 The Last Enchantment
1983 The Wicked Day
See also ROMANCES, 0136 & HEADLINES, 0309

0806
SWANN, THOMAS B.
1966 Day of the Minotaur
1971 The Forest of Forever
1976 Lady of the Bees

0807
THURBER, JAMES   1894-1961
1944 The Great Quillow
1945 The White Deer
1950 The 13 Clocks
1957 The Wonderful O

0808
TOLKIEN, J. R. R.   1892-1973
England
"The Lord of the Rings":
1954 The Fellowship of the Ring
1955 The Two Towers
1955 The Return of the King
1980 Unfinished Tales of Numenor & Middle Earth

"Middle Earth":
1937 The Hobbit (Prequel to The Lord)
1949 Farmer Giles of Ham
1964 Tree & Leaf
1967 Smith of Wootton Major

1977 The Silmarillion (Prequel to Hobbit)
See also BRITISH AUTHORS, 1392

0809
VAN LUSTBADER, ERIC   1946-
1977 The Sun Set Warrior
1980 Beneath an Opal Moon
See also TRASH, 1154

0810
VANCE, JACK   1916-
1983 Lyonesse: Book 1, Suldrun's Garden

"Dying Earth":
1983 Cugel's Saga
1984 Rhialto the Marvellous
See also SCIENCE FICTION, 0727

0811
VINGE, JOAN   1948-
1980 The Snow Queen
1984 World's End (Sequel to Snow)
Also writes for juveniles

0812
WALTON, EVANGELINE   1907-
1983 The Sword Is Forged

"The Four Branches of the Mabinogion":
1970 The Island of the Mighty (4)
1971 The Children of Llyr (2)
1972 The Song of Rhiannon (3)
1974 Prince of Annwn (1)

0813
WANGERIN, WALTER, JR.   1944-
1979 The Book of the Dun Cow

0814
WATSON, SALLY   1924-
1970 Magic at Wychwood

0815
WELLMAN, MANLEY WADE   1903-1986
"Minstrel John":
1963 Who Fears the Devil? (SS)
1979 The Old Gods Waken
1980 After Dark
1981 The Lost & the Lurking

Section 6 - Science Fiction & Fantasy

1982 The Hanging Stones
1984 The Voice From the Mountain

0816
WHITE, T. H.   1915-
1946 Mistress Masham's Repose
1981 The Maharajah (SS)

"King Arthur":
1938 The Sword in the Stone
1939 The Witch in the Wood
1940 The Ill-Made Knight
1958 The Candle in the Wind
1958 The Once & Future King
1978 The Book of Merlyn

0817
WIBBERLEY, LEONARD   1915-1983
1956 McGillicuddy McGotham

"Mouse":
1955 The Mouse That Roared
1958 Beware of the Mouse
1962 The Mouse on the Moon
1969 The Mouse on Wall Street
1981 The Mouse That Saved the West

0818
WILLIAMS, CHARLES   1886-1945
1930 War in Heaven
1931 Many Dimensions
1931 The Place of the Lion
1932 The Greater Trumps
1933 Shadows of Ecstasy
1937 Descent into Hell
1945 All Hallows Eve

0819
WRIGHT, AUSTIN TAPPIN   1883-1931
1943 Islandia

0820
YARBRO, CHELSEA QUINN   1942-
"Count de Saint-Germain":
1978 Hotel Transylvania: A Novel of
     Forbidden Love
1979 The Palace
1980 Blood Games: A Novel of
     Historical Horror
1981 Path of the Eclipse
1982 Tempting Fate
1983 The Saint-Germain Chronicles (SS)
1987 A Flame in Byzantium
1988 Crusader's Torch

0821
ZELAZNY, ROGER   1937-
"Amber, Part 1":
1970 Nine Princes in Amber
1972 The Guns of Avalon
1975 The Sign of the Unicorn
1976 The Hand of Oberon
1978 The Courts of Chaos
1981 The Changing Land
1981 Dilvish, the Damned

"Amber, Part 2":
1981 A Rhapsody of Amber
1985 Trumps of Doom
1986 Blood of Amber
1987 Sign of Chaos
See also SCIENCE FICTION, 0738 & as
Jt. author with DICK, PHILIP K., 0630

SECTION SEVEN

WESTERNS

OVERVIEW

Westerns, sometimes known as "horse operas" or "oaters," are stories of adventure set in the American West, usually during the nineteenth century. The struggle between the forces of good and evil is a general theme that allows for great variety. Characters are often stereotypical, and the roles of men and women are traditional. Often there is a fine line between westerns and historical fiction; many of the writers research background on events, social mores, and the daily life of the Old West.

The majority of writers of Westerns are men, but a woman author who has gained great popularity is Dana Fuller Ross with her novels about individual states. One of the best known authors of Westerns is Zane Grey, whose 80 titles, originally written earlier this century, continue to be published today. Louis Lamour, who has published more than 60 titles, is the best selling author of Westerns.

During the 1980s several publishers have produced "adult westerns," stories that include a great deal of sex in addition to traditional cowboy activities. Some of the popular series from the early 1980s include Jove's "Jake Logan" series and the "Longarm" series. These series have been designed to appeal to both men and women. Another trend is the expansion of time periods to include the contemporary Southwest. Although some bibliographies include novels about the contemporary Southwest as Westerns, this Handbook does not.

The Western Writers Association is the professional association of writers, and each year it issues its "Golden Spurs" award for westerns.

REFERENCE AND BIBLIOGRAPHIC SOURCES

Erisman, Fred and Richard W. Etulain, eds. *Fifty Western Writers, A Bio-Bibliographical Sourcebook.* Westport, CT: Greenwood Press, 1982.

Fairbanks, Carol. *Prairie Women: Images in American and Canadian Fiction.* New Haven, CT: Yale University Press, 1986.

Gale, Robert M. *Louis Lamour.* Boston: Twayne, 1985.

Morris, Mary Lee. *Southwestern Fiction, 1960-1980: A Classified Bibliography.* Albuquerque: University of New Mexico Press, 1986.

Nolan, William F., comp. *Max Brand, Western Giant: The Life and Times of Frederick Schiller Faust.* Bowling Green, OH: Bowling Green State University Popular Press, 1985.

Section 7 - Westerns 141

Taylor, J. Golden & Others, eds. *A Literary History of the American West.* Fort Worth: Texas Christian University Press, 1987.

Vincent, James, ed. *Twentieth Century Western Writers.* Detroit: Gale, 1982.

AUTHORS AND TITLES

0822
ABBEY, EDWARD 1927-
1956 The Brave Cowboy: An Old Tale in a New Time
1962 Fire on the Mountain
1971 Black Sun
1975 The Monkey Wrench Gang
1980 Good News

0823
ADAMS, ANDY 1859-1935
1903 The Log of a Cowboy: A Narrative of the Old Trail Days

0824
BAKER, BETTY 1916-
1963 Killer-of-Death
1970 And One Was a Wooden Indian

0825
BEAN, AMELIA
1958 The Fancher Train
1960 The Feud: The Story of the Graham-Tewksbury Feud
1967 Time for Outrage

0826
BENEDICT, REX 1920-
1972 Good Luck Arizona Man
1974 Last Stand at Goodbye Gulch

0827
BORLAND, HAL 1900-
1957 The Amulet
1960 The Seventh Winter
1963 When the Legends Die

0828
BRAND, MAX 1892-1944
Real name: Frederick Schiller Faust
Also wrote as George Owen Baxter, David Manning & Evan Evans
1919 The Untamed
1920 The Night Horseman
1920 Trailin'
1921 The Seventh Man
1923 Alcatraz
1925 The Black Signal
1926 Fire-Brain
1926 The White Wolf
1927 The Blue Jay
1927 The Fastest Draw
1927 The Garden of Eden
1928 Border Guns
1931 Ambush at Torture Canyon
1932 Drifter's Vengence
1934 One Man Posse
1935 Cheyenne Gold
1942 The Man from Mustang
1945 The Stolen Stallion
1948 Clung (1924)
1949 Bull Hunter (1921)
1949 Gunman's Reckoning (1921)
1951 The Outlaw (1933)
1952 The Gentle Gunman
1953 Smiling Desperado
1954 The Gambler
1956 The Big Trail (1934)
1958 The Outlaw of Buffalo Flat
1958 Rippon Rides Double
1959 Dan Barry's Daughter (1924)
1962 War Party
1963 Frontier Feud (1934)
1964 The Gentle Gunman
1967 Steve Train's Ordeal (1926)
1970 Black Jack (1922)
1970 Trouble Kid (1931)
1971 Harrigan (1926)
1972 The Last Chance
1974 The Californios
1975 Dead Man's Treasure
1975 The Last Showdown
1975 Thunder Moon
1976 Bandit of the Black Hills (1949)
1976 Destry Rides Again (1930)
1976 Rawhide Justice
1976 Shotgun Law
1978 Storm on the Range (1931)
1978 Way of the Lawless
1979 Galloping Danger (1923)
1979 Torture Trail
1979 The Untamed
1980 Gunfighter's Return (1922)
1980 The Man from the Wilderness
1980 Six-Gun Country
1981 The Stingaree (1930)
1981 Wild Freedom (1922)
1982 Thunder Moon Strikes
1982 Thunder Moon's Challenge (1927)
1983 Lawless Land (1932)
1984 Rogue Mustang
1984 Three on the Trail (The Killers)
1984 Trouble in Timberline
1985 The Gentle Desperado (SS)

Section 7 - Westerns   143

1985 Mountain Guns (1930)
1985 Rider of the High Hills (1933)
1986 Fightin' Fool
1986 Riders of the Silences
1986 Singing Guns (1938)
1988 Outlaw Tamer (1925)

"Silvertip":
1942 Silvertip
1942 Silvertip's Strike
1943 Silvertip's Roundup
1943 Silvertip's Trap
1944 Silvertip's Chase
1945 Silvertip's Search
See also as EVANS, EVAN, 0840

0829
BROWN, J. P. S.   1923-
1970 Jim Kane

0830
BRYANT, WILL   1923-
1971 The Big Lonesome
1973 Escape from Sonora
1976 Blue Russell
1987 A Time for Heroes

0831
CAPPS, BENJAMIN   1922-
1962 Hanging at Comanche Wells
1965 Sam Chance
1964 The Trail to Ogallala
1966 A Woman of the People
1969 The White Man's Road
1974 The Warren Wagontrain Raid
1979 Woman Chief

0832
CARTER, FORREST   1927?-1979
1975 Gone to Texas (The Rebel Outlaw Josey Wales)
1976 The Vengence Trail of Josey Wales

0833
CHARYN, JEROME   1937-
1980 Darlin' Bill: A Love Story of the Wild West
See also HISTORICAL FICTION, 1040 & AMERICAN AUTHORS, 1186

0834
CLARK, WALTER VAN TILBURG   1909-

1940 The Ox-Bow Incident
1949 The Track of the Cat

0835
DAY, ROBERT   1924-
1977 The Last Cattle Drive

0836
DECKER, WILLIAM   1926-
1967 To Be a Man
1979 The Holdouts

0837
DOCTOROW, E. L.   1931-
1960 Welcome to Hard Times
See also AMERICAN FICTION, 1197

0838
DURHAM, MARILYN   1930-
1972 The Man Who Loved Cat Dancing
1973 Dutch Uncle

0839
ESTLEMAN, LOREN D.
1976 The Oklahoma Punk
1978 The Hider
1981 Aces & Eights
1981 The Wolfer
1983 Mister St. John
1984 This Old Bill
1988 Bloody Season

"Deputy Page Murdock":
1979 The High Rocks
1980 Stamping Ground
1982 Murdock's Law
1984 The Stranglers
See also MYSTERIES, 0442

0840
EVANS, EVAN   1892-1944
Real name: Frederick Schiller Faust
1933 Montana Rides!
1934 Montana Rides Again
1936 The Song of the Whip
1947 The Border Bandit
1948 The Rescue of Broken Arrow
1949 Gunman's Legacy
1951 Lone Hand (1949, Smuggler's Trail)
1951 Sawdust & Sixguns
1952 Strange Courage

1953 Outlaw Valley
1953 Outlaw's Code
See also as BRAND, MAX, 0828

0841
FIELD, PETER   1901-
"Pocketbook" Paperbacks:
1959 Outlaw Express
1960 Powder Valley Plunder
1961 Rattlesnake Range
1961 Wolf Pack Trail
1963 Outlaw Deputy
1974 Double Cross Canyon
1974 Midnight & Roundup
1976 Coyote Gulch
1977 Powder Valley Getaway

0842
FISHER, VARDIS   1895-
1928 Toilers of the Hills
1931 Dark Bridwell
1941 City of Illusion
1943 The Mothers: An American Saga of Courage
1956 Pemmican: A Novel of the Hudson's Bay Company
1958 Tale of Valor: A Novel of the Lewis & Clark Expedition
1965 Mountain Man

"Vridar Hunter":
1932 In Tragic Life
1934 Passions Spin the Plot
1935 We Are Betrayed
1936 No Villain Need Be
Also wrote religious & psychological novels

0843
FORMAN, JAMES   1932-
1972 People of the Dream
1973 The Life & Death of Yellow Bird
Also writes for juveniles & young adults

0844
GARFIELD, BRIAN   1939-
Writes as Frank O'Brian & Frank Wynne
1961 The Arizonans
1962 Arizona Rider
1962 The Lawbringers
1962 Trail Drive
1962 The Vanquished
1963 Apache Canyon
1963 Vultures in the Sun
1969 Arizona

1970 Valley of the Shadow
1973 Tripwire
1978 Wild Times
See also HEADLINES, 0332 & MYSTERIES, 0452

0845
GREY, ZANE   1872-1939
1908 The Last of the Plainsmen
1910 The Heritage of the Desert
1912 Riders of the Purple Sage
1914 The Light of Western Stars
1915 The Lone Star Ranger
1915 The Rainbow Trail
1916 The Border Legion
1917 Wildfire
1918 The U. P. Trail
1919 The Desert of Wheat
1919 The Mysterious Rider
1920 The Man of the Forest
1921 To the Last Man
1923 Tappan's Burro (SS)
1923 The Wolf Tracker (SS)
1924 The Thundering Herd
1924 Wild Horse Mesa
1925 The Deer Stalker
1925 Under the Tonto Rim
1925 The Vanishing American
1926 Forlorn River
1926 The Ranger (SS)
1927 Lost Pueblo
1927 Valley of Wild Horses
1928 The Shepherd of Guadaloupe
1928 Stairs of Sand
1928 Sunset Pass
1929 The Drift Fence
1929 Fighting Caravans
1929 The Hash Knife Outfit
1929 Rogue River Feud
1930 The Dude Ranger
1930 Rustlers of Silver River
1931 Raiders of the Spanish Peaks
1931 The Trail Driver
1931 West of the Pecos
1932 The Lost Wagon Train
1932 Thunder Mountain
1936 Knights of the Range
1937 Majesty's Rancho
1937 Tex Thorne Comes Out of the West
1938 The Young Forester
1939 Western Union
1939 The Young Lion Hunter
1940 30,000 on the Hoof
1940 The Twin Sombreros
1941 The Last of the Duanes
1944 Wilderness Trek
1946 Shadow on the Trail

Section 7 - Westerns

1952 The Call of the Canyon (1892)
1956 Stranger from the Tonto
1957 Fugitive Trail
1958 Arizona Clan
1959 Horse Heaven Hill

"Trilogy":
1903 Betty Zane
1906 The Spirit of the Border
1909 The Last Trail

0846
GRUBER, FRANK 1904-1969
1941 Outlaw
1954 Bitter Sage
1957 Lonesome River
1959 The Bushwackers
1967 This Gun Is Still

0847
GULICK, BILL 1916-
1961 The Shaming of Broken Horn
1962 The Moon-Eyed Appaloosa
1963 Hallelujah Trail
1966 They Came to a Valley
1969 The Liveliest Town in the West
1979 Treasure in Hell's Canyon
See also HISTORICAL FICTION, 0913

0848
GUTHRIE, A. B. (Alfred Bertram) 1901-
1947 The Big Sky
1949 The Way West (Sequel to Big)
1956 These Thousand Hills
1960 The Big It (SS)
1982 Fair Land, Fair Land (Sequel to Big)

"Northwestern Chronicles":
1971 Arfive
1975 The Last Valley

"Sheriff Chick Charleston":
1973 The Wild Pitch
1977 The Genuine Article
1980 No Second Wind
1985 Playing Catch-Up
See also HISTORICAL FICTION, 0914

0849
HAYCOX, ERNEST 1899-1950
1939 The Border Trumpet
1944 Bugles in the Afternoon
1982 Sundown Jim (1938)

0850
HENRY, WILL 1912-
Real name: Henry Wilson Allen
1954 The Fourth Horseman
1960 Where the Sun Now Stands
1967 One More River to Cross

0851
HUFFAKER, CLAIR 1927-
1958 Cowboy
1958 Flaming Lance
1958 Guns of Rio Conchos
1963 Good Lord, You're Upside Down
1967 Nobody Loves a Drunken Indian
1973 The Cowboy & the Cossak
1975 Seven Ways from Sundown (1960)

"The War Wagon":
1957 Badge for a Gunfighter
1957 Rider from Thunder Mountain
1958 Posse from Hell
1975 Guns from Thunder Mountain
1975 The War Wagon (1958 Badman)

0852
JENNINGS, GARY 1928-
1975 The Terrible Teague Bunch
See also HISTORICAL FICTION, 0992

0853
JOHNSON, DOROTHY 1905-
1970 A Man Called Horse
1977 Buffalo Woman

0854
JONES, DOUGLAS C. 1924-
1979 Winding Stair
1987 Hickory Cured
See also HISTORICAL FICTION, 0920

0855
KELTON, ELMER 1926
1956 Hot Iron
1957 Buffalo Wagons
1959 Shadow of a Star
1960 The Texas Rifles
1961 Donovan
1962 Bitter Trail
1963 Horsehead Crossing
1965 Massacre at Goliad
1966 Llano River
1967 After the Bugles
1969 Captain's Rangers
1969 Hanging Judge

1971 The Day the Cowboys Quit
1973 The Time It Never Rained
1980 Barbed Wire (1957)
1980 The Wolf & the Buffalo
1984 Stand Proud
1985 Dark Thicket
1987 The Man Who Rode Midnight

0856
LA FARGE, OLIVER   1901-
1929 Laughing Boy
1937 The Enemy Gods

0857
L'AMOUR, LOUIS   1908-1988
1950 Westward the Tide
1953 Hondo
1953 Showdown at Yellow Butte
1954 Crossfire Trail
1954 Kilkenny
1954 Utah Blaine
1955 Guns of the Timberlands
1955 Heller with a Gun
1955 To Tame a Land
1956 The Burning Hills
1956 Silver Canyon
1957 Sitka
1958 Radigan
1959 The First Fast Draw
1959 Taggart
1960 The Daybreakers
1960 Flint
1962 High Lonesome
1962 Killoe
1962 Shalako
1963 Catlow
1963 Dark Canyon
1963 Fallon
1964 Hanging Woman Creek
1964 Kiowa Trail
1965 The High Graders
1965 The Key-Lock Man
1966 The Broken Gun
1966 Kid Rodelo
1966 Kilrone
1967 Matagorda
1968 Brionne
1968 Chancy
1968 Down the Long Hills
1969 Conagher
1969 The Empty Land
1970 The Man Called Noon
1970 Reilly's Luck
1971 North to the Rails
1971 Tucker
1971 Under the Sweetwater Rim
1972 Callaghen

1973 The Ferguson Rifle
1973 The Man from Skibbereen
1973 The Quick & the Dead
1974 The Californios
1975 Over on the Dry Side
1975 Rivers West
1975 War Party
1976 The Rider of Lost Creek
1976 Where the Long Grass Blows
1977 Borden Chantry
1978 Fair Blows the Wind
1978 The Mountain Valley War
1978 The Proving Trail
1979 Bendigo Shafter
1979 The Iron Marshal
1980 The Strong Shall Live
1980 Yondering
1981 Buckskin Run
1981 Comstock Lode
1981 Milo Talon
1982 Cherokee Trail
1982 How the West Was Won
1982 The Shadow Riders
1983 Bowdrie
1983 The Hills of Homocide
1983 Law of the Desert Born
1983 The Lonesome Gods
1983 Son of a Wanted Man
1984 Bowdrie's Law
1984 Frontier
1984 The Walking Drum (12th Cent. Asia)
1985 Passin' Through
1986 Last of the Breed
1987 The Haunted Mesa

"The Sacketts":
1960 The Daybreakers (4)
1961 Sackett (5)
1962 Lando (6)
1964 Mojave Crossing (7)
1965 The Sackett Brand (8)
1966 Mustang Man (11)
1967 The Sky-Liners (13)
1969 The Lonely Men (9)
1970 Galloway (12)
1972 Ride the Dark Trail (15)
1972 Treasure Mountain (10)
1975 The Man from the Broken Hills (14)
1975 Sackett's Land (1)
1976 To the Far Blue Mountains (2)
1980 Lonely on the Mountain (16)
1980 The Warrior's Path (3)
1983 Ride the River (17)
1985 Jubal Sackett (forerunner)

Section 7 - Westerns

0858
LEMAY, ALAN   1899-
1954 The Searchers
1957 The Unforgiven
1962 By Dim & Flaring Lamps

0859
LEONARD, ELMORE   1925-
1953 The Bounty Hunters
1955 The Law at Randado
1956 Escape from 5 Shadows
1957 Last Stand at Saber River
1961 Hombre
1970 Valdez Is Coming
1972 Forty Lashes Less One
See also MYSTERIES, 0495

0860
McCARTHY, GARY   1943-
1979 The First Sheriff
1985 The Last Buffalo Hunt
1987 The Mustangers

"The Derby Man":
1976 The Derby Man
1978 Showdown at Snakegrass Junction
1980 Mustang Fever
1980 The Pony Express War
1985 The Last Buffalo Hunt

0861
McMURTRY, LARRY   1936-
1961 Horseman, Pass By
1962 Leaving Cheyenne
1985 Lonesome Dove
1988 Anything for Billy
See also AMERICAN AUTHORS, 1262

0862
McNICKLE, D'ARCY   1904-1977
1936 The Surrounded
1954 Runner in the Sun
1978 Wind from an Enemy Sky

0863
MASTERS, ZEKE   1927-
"Faro Blake":
1980 The Big Gamble
1980 Luck of the Draw

0864
MITCHEM, HANK
"Stagecoach Station" Series

0865
MOMADAY, N. SCOTT   1934-
1968 House Made of Dawn
1976 The Names

0866
MORGAN, SPEER   1946-
1979 Belle Starr

0867
NICHOLS, JOHN T.   1940-
"New Mexico Trilogy":
1974 The Milagro Beanfield War
1978 The Magic Journey
1981 Nirvana Blues

0868
OVERHOLSER, STEPHEN   1944-
1975 A Hanging in Sweet Water
1975 Molly & the Confidence Man
1976 Search for the Fox
1977 Field of Death
1982 Track of a Killer

0869
OVERHOLSER, WAYNE D.   1906-
1947 Buckaroo's Code
1949 West of the Rimrock
1956 Gunlock
1967 Ride into Danger
1978 The Diablo Ghost
1980 Nightmare in Broken Bow

0870
PAINE, LAURAN
1984 Skye
1986 The Horseman
1987 The New Mexico Heritage
1987 The Peralta Country

0871
PATTEN, LEWIS B.   1915-1981
1963 Guns at Gray Butte
1964 Giant on Horseback
1964 Proudly They Die
1965 The Arrogant Guns
1965 The Gallows at Graneros
1966 Death Waited at Rialto Creek

1966 No God in Saguaro
1967 Bones of the Buffalo
1968 Death of a Gunfighter
1969 Posse from Poison Creek
1969 The Red Sabbath
1969 The Youngerman Guns
1970 Death in Indian Wells
1970 Red Runs the River
1971 Showdown at Mesilla
1972 The Cheyenne Pool
1972 The Trial of Judas Wiley
1973 The Ordeal of Jason Ord
1973 The Tired Gun
1974 The Angry Town of Pawnee Bluffs
1974 Bounty Man
1974 Lynching at Broken Butte
1975 The Gallows at Graneros
1976 Ambush at Soda Creek
1976 Man Outgunned
1977 Hunt the Man Down
1977 The Killings at Coyote Springs
1977 Villa's Rifles
1978 Cheyenne Captives
1978 Death Rides a Black Horse
1978 The Law in Cottonwood
1978 The Trail of the Apache Kid
1980 Ride a Tall Horse
1982 The Angry Horseman (1960)

0872
PORTER, DONALD C.   1939-
1979 White Indian
1980 The Renegade
1980 War Chief

0873
PORTIS, CHARLES   1933-
1966 Norwood
1968 True Grit
Also writes humor, e.g., The Dog of the South, 1979 & Masters of Atlantis, 1985

0874
PRONZINI, BILL   1943-
1983 The Gallows Land
1984 Starvation Camp
1985 Quincannon
1988 The Last Days of Horse-Sky Halloran
See also MYSTERIES, 0537

0875
ROSS, DANA FULLER   1912-
1982 Yankee
1984 Yankee Rogue

"Wagons West":
1978 Nebraska! (2)
1979 Wyoming! (3)
1980 Oregon! (4)
1980 Texas! (5)
1981 California! (6)
1981 Nevada! (8)
1982 Colorado! (7)
1982 Independence (1)
1982 Washington! (9)
1983 Dakota! (11)
1983 Montana! (10)
1984 Idaho! (13)
1984 Utah! (12)
1985 Louisiana! (16)
1985 Mississippi! (15)
1985 Missouri! (14)
1986 Illinois! (18)
1986 Tennessee! (17)
1987 Kentucky! (20)
1987 Wisconsin! (19)
1988 Arizona! (21)
1988 New Mexico! (22)

0876
RUSHING, JANE GILMORE   1925-
1964 Walnut Grove
1968 Against the Moon
1972 Tamzen
1974 Mary Dove
1974 The Raincrow
1983 Winds of Blame

0877
SCHAEFER, JACK
1949 Shane
1953 The Big Range (SS)
1953 The Canyon
1953 First Blood
1954 The Pioneers (SS)
1956 The Kean Land (SS)
1957 Company of Cowards
1960 Old Ramon
1963 Monte Walsh
1963 The Plainsmen
1963 The Great Endurance Horse Race
1967 Mavericks

0878
SHARPE, JON
"Trailsman Books":
1980 Seven Wagons West
1980 The Hanging Trail

Section 7 - Westerns

0879
SILKO, LESLIE MARMON   1948-
1981 The Storyteller

0880
STEGNER, WALLACE   1909-
1943 The Big Rock Candy Mountain
1971 Angel of Repose

0881
SWARTHOUT, GLENDON   1918-
1958 They Came to Cordura
1972 The Tin Lizzie Troop
1976 The Shootist
1985 The Old Colts
1988 The Homesman

0882
SWIFT, E. M.   1951-
1981 Each Thief Passing By

0883
THOM, JAMES ALEXANDER   1933-
1981 Follow the River

0884
WAGONER, DAVID   1926-
1970 Where Is My Wandering Boy
      Tonight?
1974 The Road to Many a Wonder
1975 Tracker

0885
WELCH, JAMES   1940-
1974 Winter in the Blood
1979 The Death of Jim Loney
1986 Fools Crow

0886
WISTER, OWEN   1860-1938
1925 The Virginian: A Horseman of the
      Plains

0887
ZOLLINGER, NORMAN   1921-
1978 Riders to Cinola
1981 Corey Lane

SECTION EIGHT

HISTORICAL FICTION

OVERVIEW

Historical fiction tells a story of an actual historical event or period, including historical figures or imaginary characters, and recreates the time and place of that event or period. Historical fiction is often judged first by how accurately the work recreates the details of the time and place, and how accurately the characters reflect the milieu of the time. More attention has been paid to the psychological accuracy of the portrayal of characters from the time. Some critics believe that a significant period of time must elapse before a novel can be written about an event or time period. This guideline has been disregarded for this handbook, and titles regarding the conflict in Viet Nam have been included because it is now studied as a historical event.

This section is divided into two parts: 1) historical fiction which takes place in the United States from the first explorers through the conflict in Viet Nam and 2) historical fiction which takes place elsewhere in the world. The first grouping of books includes a wide variety of times and locales; the second grouping focuses on fiction about the World War, 1939-1945.

Many bibliographers have edited bibliographies of historical fiction of various countries and time periods and countries. Historical fiction about the United States and the British Isles has been most popular with writers.

Some Representative Authors:

1. *John Jakes:*
   Popular family stories about the American Revolution ("The Kent Family Chronicles") and the Civil War (*North & South, Love & War, Heaven & Hell*).

2. *James Michener:*
   Massive novels about a particular place over a long period of time; *Centennial* (Colorado); *The Covenant* (South Africa).

3. *Jean Plaidy:*
   Novels of English kings and queens ("The Stuart Saga, "The Plantagenet Saga").

4. *Mary Renault:*
   Novels of ancient Greece ("Theseus" and "Alexander the Great" series).

5. *Paul Scott:*
   The end of British rule in India and Independence ("The Raj Quartet").

Section 8 - Historical Fiction　　　　　　　　　　　　　　　　151

6. *Irving Stone:*
   Fictionalized lives of famous people; *Lust for Life* (Vincent Van Gogh); *Love Is Eternal* (Mary Lincoln Todd).

REFERENCE AND BIBLIOGRAPHIC SOURCES

Baker, Ernest A. *A Guide to Historical Fiction.* New York: Burt Franklin, 1969.

Berger, Alan L. *Crisis and Covenant: The Holocaust in American Jewish Fiction.* Albany: State University of New York Press, 1985.

Cernyak-Spatz, Susan E. *German Holocaust Literature.* New York: P. Lang, 1985.

Ezrahi, Sidra DeKoven. *By Words Alone: The Holocaust in Literature.* Chicago: University of Chicago Press, 1980.

Gerhardstein, Virginia Brokaw. *Dickinson's American Historical Fiction, 4th ed.* Metuchen, NJ: Scarecrow, 1981.

Green, Martin Burgess. *The Great American Adventure.* Boston: Beacon Press, 1984.

Hager, Philip E., and Desmond Taylor. *The Novels of World War I: An Annotated Bibliography.* NY: Garland, 1981.

Irwin, Leonard Bertram. *A Guide to Historical Fiction, 10th ed. rev.* Brooklawn, NJ: McKinley, 1971.

Klein, Holger, John Flower and Eric Homberger, eds. *The Second World War in Fiction.* London: Macmillan, 1984.

Lomperis, Timothy J. and Pratt, John Clark. *Reading the Wind; The Literature of the Vietnam War.* Durham, NC: Asia Society, Duke University Press, 1987.

Menendez, Albert J. *Civil War Novels: An Annotated Bibliography.* New York: Garland, 1986.

Newman, John. *Vietnam War Literature: An Annotated Bibliography of Imaginative Works about Americans Fighting in Vietnam.* Metuchen, NJ: Scarecrow Press, 1982.

Newman, John and Michael Unsworth. *Future War Novels: An Annotated Bibliography of Works in English Published since 1946.* Phoenix, AZ: Oryx Press, 1984.

Skloot, Robert. *The Darkness We Carry: The Drama of the Holocaust.* Madison: University of Wisconsin Press, 1988.

Smith, Myron J. *War Story Guide: An Annotated Bibliography of Military Fiction.* Metuchen, NJ: Scarecrow Press, 1980.

Van Derhoof, Jack Warner. *A Bibliography of Novels Related to American Frontier and Colonial History.* Troy, NY: Whitston, 1971.

AUTHORS AND TITLES

A. AMERICAN HISTORICAL FICTION

0888
ARGO, ELLEN   1933-1983
Real Name: Ellen Argo Johnson
"Cape Cod Sailing Ships Trilogy":
1977 Jewel of the Seas
1978 The Crystal Star
1981 The Yankee Girl

0889
ARNOLD, ELLIOTT   1912-1980
1950 Blood Brother
1972 The Spirit of Cochise
See also WW II, 1031

0890
ARNOW, HARRIETTE   1908-1986
1949 Hunter's Horn
1974 The Kentucky Trace: A Novel of the American Revolution
See also AMERICAN FICTION, 1161

0891
BECKER, STEPHEN D.
1965 A Covenant with Death
1969 When the War Is Over
1973 Dog Tags
See also WORLD HISTORICAL FICTION, 0954

0892
BOWMAN, JOHN CLARKE
1973 Powhatan's Daughter

0893
BRICK, JOHN   1922-1973
1953 The Rifleman
1956 Jubilee
1963 The Richmond Raid

0894
BRISTOW, GWEN   1903-1980
1937 Deep Summer
1938 The Handsom Road
1940 This Side of Glory
1950 Jubilee Trail
1959 Celia Garth
1970 Calico Palace
See also ROMANCES, 0020

0895
BROWN, DEE   1908-
1980 Creek Mary's Blood
1983 Killdeer Mountain

0896
CALDWELL, TAYLOR   1900-1985
1946 This Side of Innocence
See also WORLD HISTORICAL FICTION, 0957; ROMANCES, 0025; ROMANCES, 0113 as REINER, MAX

0897
CAPUTO, PHILIP
1977 A Rumor of War
1987 Indian Country
See also AMERICAN AUTHORS, 1184

0898
CARLISLE, HENRY   1926-
1972 Voyage to the 1st of December
1975 The Land Where the Sun Dies
1984 The Jonah Man

0899
CASSEL, VIRGINIA
1981 Juniata Valley

0900
COLEMAN, TERRY   1931-
1981 Thanksgiving
See also WORLD HISTORICAL FICTION, 0960

0901
COONTS, STEPHEN 1946-
1986 Flight of the Intruder

0902
CRICHTON, MICHAEL   1942-
1975 The Great Train Robbery
See also HEADLINES, 0269 & SCIENCE FICTION, 0622

0903
DE HARTOG, JAN   1914-
1972 The Peaceable Kingdom
See also WORLD HISTORICAL FICTION, 0964 & WW II, 1046

0904
DEL VECCHIO, JOHN M. 1948-
1982 The 13th Valley

0905
ECKERT, ALLAN   1931-
1973 The Court Martial of Daniel Boone
1978 The Wilderness War: A Narrative

0906
FAST, HOWARD   1914-
1939 Conceived in Liberty: A Novel of Valley Forge
1941 Last Frontier
1942 The Unvanquished
1943 Citizen Tom Paine
1944 Freedom Road
1946 The American
1950 The Proud & the Free
1961 April Morning
1972 The Hessian
1988 The Pledge
See also WW II, 1054; WORLD HISTORICAL FICTION, 0971; ROMANCES, 0048; MYSTERIES, 0431 as CUNNINGHAM, E. V.

0907
FERBER, EDNA   1887-1968
1924 So Big
1926 Show Boat
1930 Cimarron
1941 Saratoga Trunk
1945 Great Son
1952 Giant
1958 Ice Palace

0908
FIELD, RACHEL   1894-1942
1935 Time Out of Mind
1938 All This & Heaven Too
1942 And Now Tomorrow
1962 Hitty, Her First Hundred Years (1929)

0909
FREEDMAN, BENEDICT   1919-
1947 Mrs. Mike

0910
GERSON, NOEL B.   1914-
Also writes as Ann Marie Burgess, Michael Burgess, Samuel Edwards, Paul Lewis, Leon Phillips, Carter A. Vaughan
1950 Savage Gentleman
1951 The Mohawk Ladder
1952 The Cumberland Rifles
1953 The Golden Eagle
1954 The Forest Land
1955 The Highwayman
1958 Daughter of Eve
1960 The Yankee from Tennessee
1961 The Land Is Bright
1964 Old Hickory
1965 Yankee Doodle Dandy
1965 The Slender Reed
1966 Give Me Liberty
1967 I'll Storm Hell
1967 Jefferson Square
1968 Sam Huston
1970 Clear For Action
1970 The Crusader
1970 TR
See also WORLD HISTORICAL FICTION, 0978 & HEADLINES, 0280

0911
GILES, JANICE   1909-1979
1953 The Kentuckians
1954 The Plum Thicket
1956 Hannah Fowler
1957 The Believers
1960 Johnny Osage
1961 Savanna
1962 Voyage to Santa Fe
1964 Run Me a River
1966 The Great Adventure
1966 Special Breed
1966 Time of Glory
1968 Shady Grove
1969 Six-Horse Hitch (Sequel to Hannah)
1974 The Land beyond the Mountains, rev. (1940)
1975 Wellspring
1977 Harbin's Ridge (1951)

"Piney Ridge Trilogy":
1971 The Enduring Hills (1950)
1971 Miss Willie (1951)
1972 Tara's Healing (1951)

Section 8 - Historical Fiction

0912
GRAVES, ROBERT   1895-1985
England
"Sergeant Lamb":
1940 Sergeant Lamb's America
1941 Proceed, Sergeant Lamb
See also WORLD HISTORICAL FICTION, 0982

0913
GULICK, BILL   1916-
1958 The Land Beyond
1963 The Hallelujah Trail
See also WESTERNS, 0847

0914
GUTHRIE, A. B.   1901-
1947 The Big Sky
1949 The Way West (Sequel to Big)
1956 These Thousand Hills

"Northwestern Chronicles":
1970 Arfive
1975 The Last Valley
1982 Fair Land, Fair Land (Sequel to Way)
1985 Playing Catch-Up
See also WESTERNS, 0848

HARTOG, JAN DE
See DE HARTOG, JAN, 0903

0915
HEIDISH, MARCY   1947-
1976 A Woman Called Moses
1980 Witnesses
1983 The Secret Annie Oakley
1984 Miracles: A Novel about Mother Seton, the First American Saint

0916
HILL, RUTH BEEBE   1913-
1979 Hanta Yo

0917
HOUSTON, JAMES   1921-
1971 A Native Son of the Golden West
1971 The White Dawn
1977 Ghost Fox
1978 Continental Drift
1983 Eagle Song

0918
HOWE, FANNY
1980 The White Slave

0919
JAKES, JOHN   1932-
"Civil War":
1982 North & South
1984 Love & War
1988 Heaven & Hell

"The Kent Family Chronicles":
1974 The Bastard
1974 The Rebels
1975 The Seekers
1976 The Furies
1976 The Titans
1977 The Warriors
1978 The Lawless
1980 The Americans

0920
JONES, DOUGLAS C.   1924-
1980 Elkhorn Tavern
1982 The Barefoot Brigade
1983 Season of Yellow Leaf
1984 Gone the Dreams & Dancing
1986 Roman
1988 Remember Santiago

"Trilogy":
1976 The Court Martial of George Armstrong Custer
1977 Arrest Sitting Bull
1978 A Creek Called Wounded Knee
See also WESTERNS, 0854

0921
KANTOR, MACKINLAY   1904-1977
1955 Andersonville
1961 If the South Had Won the Civil War
1961 Spirit Lake
1975 Valley Forge

0922
KENEALLY, THOMAS   1935-
Australia
1980 The Confederates
See also WORLD AUTHORS, 1420

0923
MASON, F. VAN WYCK   1901-1978
1946 Valley Forge; 24 December 1777

1951 Proud New Flags
1964 Rascals' Heaven
1966 Wild Horizon
1971 Brimstone Club
1973 Log Cabin Noble
1975 Trumpets Sound No More
1977 Guns for Rebellion
1980 Armored Giants: A Novel of the Civil War

"Maritime":
1938 Three Harbours
1940 Stars on the Sea
1942 Rivers of Glory
1948 Eagle in the Sky
1949 Cutlass Empire
1953 Golden Admiral
1954 Blue Hurricane
1959 The Young Titan
1969 Harpoons in Eden
1973 Log Cabin Noble
Also wrote mystery series, "Hugh North"
See also WORLD HISTORICAL FICTION, 0999

0924
MICHENER, JAMES   1907?-
1959 Hawaii
1974 Centennial
1978 Chesapeake
1984 Space
1985 Texas
1987 Legacy
1988 Alaska
See also WORLD HISTORICAL FICTION, 1001 & WW II, 1088

0925
MITCHELL, MARGARET   1900-1949
1936 Gone with the Wind

0926
MOORE, ROBIN
1965 The Green Berets
1967 The Country Team
1971 The Khaki Mafia

0927
NEVIN, DAVID
1984 Dream West

0928
O'BRIEN, TIM

1978 Going After Cacciato
1985 The Nuclear Age

0929
PAGE, ELIZABETH
1939 Tree of Liberty
1946 Wilderness Adventure

0930
PARK, GORDON
1981 Shannon

0931
PECK, ROBERT NEWTON   1928-
1972 A Day No Pigs Would Die
1975 Fawn
1976 Hang for Treason
1977 The King's Iron
1978 Eagle Fur
Also writes for juveniles

0932
PRICE, EUGENIA   1916-
1974 Don Juan McQueen--Margaret's Story
1977 Maria

"St. Simon's Island Trilogy":
1965 The Beloved Invader (3)
1969 New Moon Rising (2)
1971 Lighthouse (1)

"Savannah Quartet":
1983 Savannah
1985 To See Your Face Again
1987 Before the Darkness Falls

0933
ROBERTS, KENNETH (Lewis)   1885-1957
1930 Arundel
1931 The Lively Lady
1933 Rabble in Arms (Sequel to Arundel)
1934 Captain Caution
1937 Northwest Passage
1940 Oliver Wiswell
1956 Boon Island
See also WORLD HISTORICAL FICTION, 1011

0934
SANTMYER, HELEN HOOVEN
1895-1986

Section 8 - Historical Fiction

1983 ... And Ladies of the Club
1985 Herbs & Apples (1925)
1987 The Fierce Dispute
1988 Farewell, Summer

0935
SETON, ANYA
1941 My Theodosia
1948 The Hearth & the Eagle
1958 The Winthrop Woman
See also WORLD HISTORICAL FICTION, 1016; ROMANCES, 0122; HORROR, 0214

0936
SNOW, RICHARD   1947-
1981 The Burning

0937
SPEARE, ELIZABETH   1908-
1967 The Prospering

0938
STONE, IRVING   1903-
1944 Immortal Wife
1947 Adversary in the House
1951 The President's Lady
1954 Love Is Eternal
1959 The Passionate Journey
1965 Those Who Love
See also WORLD HISTORICAL FICTION, 1022

0939
STYRON, WILLIAM   1925-
1967 The Confessions of Nat Turner
See also AMERICAN AUTHORS, 1325

0940
TAYLOR, ROBERT LEWIS   1912-
1958 The Travels of Jamie McPheeters
1961 A Journey to Matecumbe
1964 Two Roads to Guadalupe
1978 A Roaring in the Wind
1980 Niagara

0941
VIDAL, GORE   1925-
"Burr":
1973 Burr
1976 1876
1984 Lincoln
1987 Empire

SCIENCE FICTION, 0729; AMERICAN AUTHORS, 1331; see also MYSTERIES, 0407 as BOX, EDGAR

0942
VINING, ELIZABETH   1902-
1955 The Virginia Exiles
1930 Meggy Macintosh
1972 The Taken Girl

0943
WALKER, MARGARET   1915-
Black American
1965 Jubilee

0944
WALKER, MILDRED   1905-
1944 Winter Wheat
1955 The Curlew's Cry

0945
WARREN, ROBERT PENN   1905-
1939 Night Rider
1946 All the King's Men
1950 World Enough & Time
1955 Band of Angels
1959 The Cave
1961 Wilderness

0946
WEBB, JAMES
1978 Fields of Fire
1981 A Sense of Honor
1983 A Country Such as This

0947
WEST, JESSAMYN   1902?-1984
1945 The Friendly Persuasion
1951 The Witch Diggers
1960 South of the Angels
1967 Leafy Rivers
1969 Except for Me & Thee
1975 The Massacre at Fall Creek

0948
WHEELER, GUY
1980 Cato's War

0949
WICKER, TOM   1926-
1984 Unto This Hour

B. WORLD HISTORICAL FICTION

1. GENERAL

0950
ANTHONY, EVELYN   1928-
England
Real name: Evelyn Bridget Patricia Ward Thomas
1953 Rebel Princess
1954 Royal Intrigue
1955 Far Fly the Eagles
1957 Anne Boleyn
1958 Victoria & Albert
1960 All the Queen's Men
1961 Charles the King
1963 Clandara
1964 The French Bride
1964 The Heiress
1966 Valentina
1968 The Cardinal & the Queen
1978 The Return
1988 The House of Vandekar
See also HEADLINES, 0259 & SPY STORIES, 0353

0951
AUCHINCLOSS, LOUIS   1917-
1981 The Cat & the King
See also AMERICAN AUTHORS, 1162

0952
AUEL, JEAN   1936-
Trilogy:
1980 The Clan of the Cave Bear
1982 The Valley of Horses
1985 The Mammoth Hunters

0953
BARNES, MARGARET CAMPBELL 1886-1967
1930 Years of Grace
1933 Within This Present
1935 Edna, His Wife
1945 The Passionate Brood
1946 My Lady of Cleves
1947 Within the Hollow Crown
1949 Brief Gaudy Hour
1953 The Tudor Rose
1957 Isabel the Fair
1959 King's Fool
1962 The King's Bed
1963 Lady on the Coin

0954
BECKER, STEPHEN D.
1951 The Season of the Stranger
1955 Shanghai Incident
1959 Juice
1967 The Outcasts
1987 A Rendezvous in Haiti

Trilogy:
1975 The Chinese Bandit
1979 The Last Mandarin
1982 The Blue-Eyed Shan
See also AMERICAN HISTORICAL FICTION, 0891

0955
BOLT, DAVID   1927-
1967 Gurkhas
1980 Samson

0956
BRADSHAW, GILLIAN   1956-
1986 The Beacon at Alexandria
1987 The Bearkeeper's Daughter
See also SCIENCE FICTION, 0749

0957
CALDWELL, TAYLOR   1900-1985
England
Real name: Janet Miriam Taylor Holland Caldwell
1959 Dear & Glorious Physician
1970 Great Lion of God
1974 Glory & the Lightning
1977 I, Judas
See also AMERICAN HISTORICAL FICTION, 0896; ROMANCES, 0025; ROMANCES, 0113 as REINER, MAX

0958
CARR, PHILIPPA   1906-
Real Name: Eleanor Hibbert; also writes as Eleanor Burford, Elbur Ford, Kathleen Kellow, Ellalice Tate
1951 Madame Serpent
1974 Madonna of the Seven Hills
See also as PLAIDY, JEAN, 1008; ROMANCES, 0026; ROMANCES, 0071 as HOLT, VICTORIA

0959
CLAVELL, JAMES   1924-
1975 Shogun
1983 Tai-Pan

Section 8 - Historical Fiction   159

See also WW II, 1041 & HEADLINES, 0265

0960
COLEMAN, TERRY   1931-
1979 Southern Cross
See also AMERICAN HISTORICAL FICTION, 0900

0961
CORNWELL, BERNARD   1944-
1988 Wildtrack

"Richard Sharpe":
1981 Sharpe's Eagle
1981 Sharpe's Gold
1982 Sharpe's Company
1983 Sharpe's Sword
1984 Sharpe's Enemy
1985 Sharpe's Honor
1987 Sharpe's Seige
1988 Sharpe's Rifles

0962
COSTAIN, THOMAS B.   1885-1965
1944 Ride with Me
1945 The Black Rose
1949 High Towers
1950 Son of a Hundred Kings
1952 The Silver Chalice
1955 The Tontine
1957 Below the Salt
1959 The Darkness & the Dawn
1963 The Last Love

0963
DE CAMP, L. SPRAGUE
1958 An Elephant for Aristotle
1960 The Bronze God of Rhodes
1961 The Dragon of Ishtar
1965 The Arrows of Hercules
1969 The Golden Wind
See also SCIENCE FICTION, 0626 & 0763

0964
DE HARTOG, JAN   1914-
1980 The Lamb's War
See also AMERICAN HISTORICAL FICTION, 0903 & WW II, 1046

0965
DEWHURST, KEITH   1931-
1981 Captain of the Sands

0966
DILLON, EILÍS   1920-
Ireland
1973 Across the Bitter Sea
1977 Blood Relations
1980 The Wild Geese
See also MYSTERIES, 0435

0967
DOUGLAS, LLOYD   1877-1951
1942 The Robe
1948 The Big Fisherman
1952 The Silver Chalice
Also wrote religious novels

0968
DRURY, ALLEN   1918-
1976 A God against the Gods
1977 Return to Thebes
See also HEADLINES, 0236

0969
DU MAURIER, DAPHNE   1907-1989
England
1936 Jamaica Inn
1942 Frenchman's Creek
1943 Hungry Hill
1946 The King's General
1963 The Glass Blowers
See also ROMANCES, 0041; HORROR, 0171; BRITISH AUTHORS, 1357

0970
ELEGANT, ROBERT   1928-
1979 Manchu
1983 Mandarin
1987 From a Far Land
See also ROMANCES, 0045

0971
FAST, HOWARD   1914-
1951 Spartacus
1958 Moses, Prince of Egypt
1964 Agrippa's Daughter
1966 Torquemada
See also AMERICAN HISTORICAL FICTION, 0906; WW II, 1054; ROMANCES, 0048; MYSTERIES, 0431 as CUNNINGHAM, E. V.

0972
FORBES, COLIN   1923-
1970 Tramp in Armor

See also WW II, 1056 & HEADLINES, 0276

0973
FORESTER, C. S.   1899-1966
England
1935   The African Queen

"The Hornblower Saga":
1937   Beat to Quarters
1938   Ship of the Line
1939   Flying Colours
1945   Commodore Hornblower
1946   Lord Hornblower
1950   Mr. Midshipman Hornblower
1952   Lieutenant Hornblower
1953   Hornblower & the Atropos
1958   Admiral Hornblower in the West Indies
1962   Hornblower & the Hotspur
See also WW II, 1057

0974
GANN, ERNEST K.   1910-
1954   Soldier of Fortune
1966   In the Company of Eagles
1971   The Antagonists
Also writes about aviation

0975
GARDNER, JOHN C. (Champlin Jr.) 1933-1982
1971   Wreckage of Agathon
See also SCIENCE FICTION, 0771 & AMERICAN AUTHORS, 1212

0976
GARRETT, GEORGE   1929-
1961   Which Ones Are the Enemy
1971   Death of the Fox
1984   The Succession

0977
GAVIN, CATHERINE   1907-
Scotland
1938   Clyde Valley
1940   The Hostile Shore
1941   The Black Mile Stone
1944   The Mountain of Light
1968   The Devil in Harbour
1970   The House of War
1972   Give Me the Daggers
1973   The Snow Mountain

"Second Empire Quartet":
1957   Madeleine
1962   The Cactus & the Crown
1964   The Fortress
1966   The Moon into Blood
See also WW II, 1062

0978
GERSON, NOEL B.   1914-
Also writes as Ann Marie Burgess, Michael Burgess, Samuel Edwards, Paul Lewis, Leon Phillips, Carter A. Vaughan
1954   The Imposter
1957   The Conqueror's Wife
1959   The Emperor's Ladies
1961   The Hittite
1962   The Trojan
1963   The Golden Lyre
1969   Golden Ghetto
See also AMERICAN HISTORICAL FICTION, 0910 & HEADLINES, 0280

0979
GOLDMAN, JAMES   1927-
1966   The Lion in Winter
1980   Myself as Witness

0980
GOUDGE, ELIZABETH   1900-1984
1970   The Child from the Sea
See also ROMANCES, 0057

0981
GRAHAM, WINSTON   1910-
England
1963   The Grove of Eagles
1974   The Black Moon

"Poldark, the Novels of Cornwall":
1951   The Renegade: 1783-1787 (1945)
1953   Demelza: 1788-1790
1954   Venture Once More: 1790-1791 (1950)
1955   The Last Gamble: 1972-1793 (1953)
1977   The Four Swans: 1795-1797
1978   The Angry Tide: 1798-1799
1982   The Stranger from the Sea: 1810 -1811

0982
GRAVES, ROBERT   1895-1985
England
1933   The Real David Copperfield

Section 8 - Historical Fiction

1938 Count Belisarius
1943 Wife to Mr. Milton
1945 Hercules, My Shipmate
1946 King Jesus
1949 The Isles of Unwisdom
1955 Homer's Daughter

"Claudius":
1934 I, Claudius
1935 Claudius the God
See also AMERICAN HISTORICAL FICTION, 0912

0983
GREENBERG, JOANNE   1932-
1963 The King's Person
See also AMERICAN AUTHORS, 1220

HARTOG, JAN DE
See DE HARTOG, JAN

0984
HAYDEN, STERLING   1916-
1976 Voyage: A Novel of 1856

0985
HENNESSY, MAX   1916-
England
Real name: John Harris; also writes as Mark Hebden
"Cavalry" Trilogy:
1980 Soldier of the Queen
1981 Blunted Lance
1982 The Iron Stallions

"Lion at Sea" Trilogy:
1978 The Lion at Sea
1979 The Dangerous Years
1980 Back to Battle

"Marquis" Trilogy:
1985 The Crimson Wind

"Quinney" Trilogy:
1983 The Bright Blue Sky
1983 The Challenging Heights
1984 Once More the Hawks

0986
HERSEY, JOHN   1914-
1956 A Single Pebble
1972 The Conspiracy
1985 The Call

See also WW II, 1068 & SCIENCE FICTION, 0653

0987
HEYER, GEORGETTE   1902-1974
Also wrote as Stella Martin
1975 My Lord John
1978 Simon the Coldheart
See also ROMANCES, 0064 & MYSTERIES, 0471

0988
HIGHWATER, JAMAKE   1942-
1978 Journey to the Sky
1980 The Sun, He Dies

0989
HOLLAND, CECELIA   1943-
1966 The Firedrake
1967 Rakossy
1968 The Kings in Winter
1969 Until the Sun Falls
1970 Antichrist
1971 The Earl
1973 The Death of Attila
1974 Great Maria
1977 Two Ravens
1979 City of God: A Novel of the Borgias
1982 The Sea Beggers
1984 The Belt of Gold
1985 Pillar of the Sky
1988 The Lords of Vaumartin

0990
HOUGH, RICHARD   1922-
1981 Buller's Guns
1982 Buller's Dreadnought
See also WW II, 1070

0991
JARMAN, ROSEMARY   1935-
1971 We Speak No Treason
1973 The King's Grey Mare
1978 Crown in Candlelight
1983 The Courts of Illusion

0992
JENNINGS, GARY   1928-
1980 Aztec
1984 The Journeyer
1987 Spangle
See also WESTERNS, 0852

0993
LLYWELYN, MORGAN
1980 Lion of Ireland
1984 Bard, the Odyssey of the Irish
1978 The Wind from Hastings
1986 Grania: She-King of the Irish Seas

0994
LOFTS, NORAH   1904-1983
England
1951 The Lute Player
1955 Eleanor, the Queen
1955 Winter Harvest
1957 Scent of Cloves
1963 The Concubine
1965 How Far to Bethlehem?
1968 Madselin
1969 The King's Pleasure
1969 The Lost Queen
1971 A Rose for Virtue
1974 Crown of Aloes
1979 Anne Boleyn
1984 Pargeters

Trilogy:
1975 Knight's Acre
1976 The Homecoming
1977 The Lonely Furrow
See also ROMANCES, 0084 & HORROR, 0198

0995
LONG, WILLIAM STUART   1914-
England
"The Australians":
1980 The Exiles
1980 The Settlers
1981 The Traitors
1982 The Explorers
1983 The Adventurers
1984 The Colonists
1985 The Gold Seekers
1986 The Gallant
1987 The Empire Builders
1988 The Nationalists
1988 The Seafarers

0996
MACINNES, COLIN   1914-1976
England
1969 Westward to Laughter
1970 Three Years to Play
See also BRITISH AUTHORS, 1372

0997
MAIER, PAUL   1930-
1981 The Flames of Rome

0998
MARTIN, MALACHI
1978 The Final Conclave
1981 King of Kings
1986 Vatican

0999
MASON, F. VAN WYCK   1901-1978
1949 Cutlass Empire
1953 Golden Admiral: A Novel of Sir Francis Drake & the Armada
1955 Silver Leopard
1961 The Sea Venture
See also AMERICAN HISTORICAL FICTION, 0923

1000
MASTERS, JOHN   1914-1983
1951 Nightrunners of Bengal
1954 Bhowani Junction
1955 Coromandel
1970 The Rock
1972 The Ravi Lancers

Trilogy:
1979 Now God Be Thanked
1980 Heart of War
1981 By the Green of the Spring

1001
MICHENER, JAMES   1907?-
1953 The Bridges at Toko-Ri
1954 Sayonara
1965 The Source
1980 The Covenant
1983 Poland
See also AMERICAN HISTORICAL FICTION, 0924 & WW II, 1088

1002
MYDANS, SHELLEY   1915-
1945 The Open City
1965 Thomas
1980 The Vermilion Bridge

1003
MYRER, ANTON   1922-
1968 Once an Eagle

Section 8 - Historical Fiction

1004
O'FAOLAIN, JULIA   1932-
Ireland
1975 Women in the Wall
See also BRITISH AUTHORS, 1379

1005
OLDENBOURG, ZOE   1916-
1948 The World Is Not Enough
1955 The Cornerstone
1961 Destiny of Fire
1963 Cities of the Flesh
1971 The Heirs of the Kingdom

1006
PEARSON, DIANE   1931-
1969 The Marigold Field
1971 Sarah Whitman (Sequel to Marigold)
See also ROMANCES, 0108

1007
PETRIE, GLEN
1977 Marianne
1980 Hand of Glory
1986 The Fourth King

1008
PLAIDY, JEAN   1906-
Real name: Eleanor Burford Hibbert; also writes as Eleanor Burford, Elbur Ford, Kathleen Kellow & Ellalice Tate
"The Georgian Saga":
1969 The Third George
1985 The Princess of Celle
1985 Queen in Waiting
1986 Victoria in the Wings
1987 Perdita's Prince
1988 Caroline the Queen
1988 Indiscretions of the Queen
1988 Sweet Lass of Richmond Hill

"The Lucrezia Borgia Series":
1974 Madonna of the Seven Hills
1976 Light on Lucrezia

"The Mary Queen of Scots Series":
1968 Royal Road to Fotheringay
1970 The Captive Queen of Scots

"The Medici Trilogy":
1975 The Italian Woman (2)
1975 Madame Serpent (1)
1976 Queen Jezebel (3)

"The Norman Trilogy":
1979 The Bastard King
1979 The Lion of Justice
1979 The Passionate Enemies

"The Stuart Saga":
1971 The Wandering Prince
1972 A Health unto His Majesty
1973 Here Lies Our Soverign Lord
1974 The Murder in the Tower
1976 The Three Crowns
1977 The Haunted Sisters
1978 The Queen's Favourites

"The Plantagenet Saga":
1980 The Heart of the Lion
1980 Plantagenet Prelude
1980 The Revolt of the Eaglets
1981 The Battle of the Queens
1981 Hammer of the Scots
1981 Passage to Pontefract
1981 The Prince of Darkness
1981 The Queen from Provence
1982 The Follies of the King
1982 The Star of Lancaster
1982 The Sun in Splendour
1982 The Vow on the Heron
1983 Epitaph for Three Women
1983 Red Rose of Anjou

"The Queen Victoria Series"
1976 The Captive of Kensington Palace
1977 The Queen & Lord M
1978 The Queen's Husband
1978 The Widow of Windsor

"The Tudor Novels":
1956 The Spanish Bridegroom
1969 The Sixth Wife
1970 St. Thomas's Eve
1971 Gay Lord Robert
1972 Murder Most Royal
1973 The Thistle & the Rose
1982 Uneasy Lies the Head
See also as CARR, PHILIPPA, 0958; ROMANCES 0026 as CARR, PHILIPPA & 0071 as HOLT, VICTORIA

1009
PLUNKETT, JAMES   1920-
1969 Strumpet City

1010
RENAULT, MARY   1905-1983
1956 The Last of the Wine
1962 The Bull from the Sea

"Theseus":
1958 The King Must Die
1962 The Bull from the Sea
1966 The Mask of Apollo

"Alexander the Great":
1969 Fire from Heaven
1972 The Persian Boy
1978 The Praise Singer
1981 Funeral Games
See also BRITISH AUTHORS, 1383

1011
ROBERTS, KENNETH   1885-1957
1947 Lydia Bailey
See also AMERICAN HISTORICAL
FICTION, 0933

1012
ROSS, ROBERT
See as Jt. author with WOODHOUSE, MARTIN, 1029

1013
SAID, KURBAN
1970 Ali & Nino

1014
SCOTT, PAUL   1920-1978
England
"The Raj Quartet":
1966 Jewel in the Crown
1968 The Day of the Scorpion
1972 Towers of Silence
1975 A Division of the Spoils
See also BRITISH AUTHORS, 1386

1015
SELINKO, ANNEMARIE
1953 Desiree

1016
SETON, ANYA
1954 Katherine
1955 The Mistletoe & Sword
1962 Devil Water
1965 Avalon
See also AMERICAN HISTORICAL
FICTION, 0935; ROMANCES, 0122;
HORROR, 0214

1017
SHELLABARGER, SAMUEL   1888-1954
Also wrote mysteries as John Esteven
& Peter Loring
1945 Captain from Castile
1947 Prince of Foxes
1950 The King's Cavalier
1953 Lord Vanity
1955 The Token

1018
SHORRIS, EARL   1936-
1980 Under the Fifth Sun

1019
SIMPSON, ROSEMARY
1980 The Seven Hills of Paradise

1020
SLAUGHTER, FRANK
1957 The Mapmaker
1959 The Crown & the Cross
1961 The Curse of Jezebel
1963 Upon This Rock
1965 Constantine
1965 The Purple Quest
1968 The Sins of Herod
See also ROMANCES, 0125

1021
SMITH, GENE   1929-
1980 Where Are My Legions

1022
STONE, IRVING   1903-
1934 Lust for Life
1961 The Agony & the Ecstasy
1971 The Passions of the Mind
1975 The Greek Treasure
1980 The Origin
1985 Depths of Glory
See also AMERICAN HISTORICAL
FICTION, 0938

1023
SUTCLIFF, ROSEMARY   1920-
1958 The Silver Branch
1960 The Rider of the White Horse
1963 Sword at Sunset
1970 The Flowers of Adonis
Also writes for juveniles

Section 8 - Historical Fiction

1024
THOMPSON, E. V.
1977 Chase the Wind
1981 Ben Retallick

1025
TURTON, GODFREY 1901-
1967 My Lord of Canterbury
1967 The Emperor Arthur

1026
URIS, LEON 1924-
1958 Exodus
1976 Trinity
1988 Mitla Pass
See also WW II, 1102 & HEADLINES, 0313

1027
WALTARI, MIKA
1949 The Egyptian
1950 The Adventurer
1951 The Wanderer
1953 The Dark Angel
1957 The Etruscan
1961 The Secret of the Kingdom
1966 The Roman

1028
WEISS, DAVID 1909-
1959 The Spirit & the Flesh
1963 Naked Came I
1968 Sacred & Profane
1971 The Assassination of Mozart
1974 Myself Christopher Wren
1975 Physican Extraordinary
1976 The Venetian
1979 I, Rembrandt

1029
WOODHOUSE, MARTIN 1952- &
ROSS, ROBERT
1974 The Medici Guns

2. WORLD WAR, 1939-1945

1030
ANATOLII, A. 1929-1979
U.S.S.R.
Real name: Anatolii Kuznetsov
1967 Babi Yar
See also WORLD AUTHORS, 1412

1031
ARNOLD, ELLIOTT 1912-1980
1942 The Commandos
1945 Tomorrow Will Sing
1950 Walk with the Devil
1967 A Night of Watching
1973 Proving Ground
See also AMERICAN HISTORICAL FICTION, 0889

1032
ASCH, SHOLEM 1880-1957
Poland
1948 Tales of My People

1033
BASSANI, GIORGIO 1916-
Italy
1965 The Garden of the Finzi Continis
1971 Five Stories of Ferrara
See also WORLD AUTHORS, 1456

1034
BEACH, EDWARD L. 1918-
1955 Run Silent, Run Deep
1972 Dust on the Sea
1978 Cold Is the Sea

1035
BECKER, JUREK
1975 Jacob the Liar

1036
BÖLL, HEINRICH 1917-1985
Germany
1965 Absent without Leave (1962)
1973 Group Portrait with Lady
1976 The Bread of Those Early Years (1957)

"Adam":
1970 Adam & the Train
1974 And Where Were You, Adam? (1951)
See also WORLD AUTHORS, 1449

1037
BOULLE, PIERRE 1912-
France
1954 The Bridge over the River Kwai
1965 Garden on the Moon
See also SCIENCE FICTION, 0606 & WORLD AUTHORS, 1431

1038
BRINKLEY, WILLIAM 1917-
1956 Don't Go Near the Water
1966 The Ninety & Nine

1039
CAIDIN, MARTIN 1927-
1974 The Last Dogfight
1976 Whip
See also SCIENCE FICTION, 0614

1040
CHARYN, JEROME 1937-
1969 American Scrapbook
See also WESTERNS, 0833 & AMERICAN AUTHORS, 1186

1041
CLAVELL, JAMES 1924-
1962 King Rat
See also WORLD HISTORICAL FICTION, 0959 & HEADLINES, 0265

1042
CLEARY, JON 1917-
Australia
1980 A Very Private War
1986 The City of Fading Light
See also MYSTERIES, 0421 & WORLD AUTHORS, 1418

1043
COLLINS, LARRY 1929-
1985 Fall from Grace
See also HEADLINES, 0266 & 0327

1044
CREASEY, JOHN 1908-1973
England
Published more than 600 books
"Bruce Murdock, Mary Dell & the Withered Man Saga":
1972 Unknown Mission (1940)
1972 Where Is the Withered Man? (1940)
1973 I Am the Withered Man (1971)
1974 Dangerous Journey (1971)
1974 Secret Errand (1968)
1974 The Withered Man (1972)
See also SPY STORIES, 0358 & MYSTERIES, 0428; MYSTERIES as ASHE, GORDON, 0394; HUNT, KYLE, 0477; MARRIC, J. J., 0514; MORTON, ANTHONY, 0522; YORK, JEREMY, 0588

1045
CRICHTON, ROBERT 1925-
1966 The Secret of Santa Vittoria

1046
DE HARTOG, JAN 1914-
1983 Star of Peace
1983 The Trail of the Serpent
See also AMERICAN HISTORICAL FICTION, 0903 & WORLD HISTORICAL FICTION, 0964

1047
DEIGHTON, LEN 1929-
1970 Bomber
1987 Winter
See also HEADLINES, 0328 & SPY STORIES, 0359

1048
DEMETZ, HANA
1980 The House on Prague Street

1049
DODSON, KENNETH 1907-
1954 Away All Boats

1050
ELMAN, RICHARD M. 1934-
"Trilogy":
1967 The Twenty-Eighth Day of Elul
1968 Lilo's Diary
1969 The Reckoning

1051
ELON, AMOS
1980 Timetable

1052
EPSTEIN, LESLIE 1938-
1979 King of the Jews
See also AMERICAN AUTHORS, 1204

1053
FARRELL, J. G. 1935-1979
1979 The Singapore Grip

Section 8 - Historical Fiction

1054
FAST, HOWARD   1914-
1959 The Winston Affair
See also AMERICAN HISTORICAL FICTION, 0906; WORLD HISTORICAL FICTION, 0971; ROMANCES, 0048; & MYSTERIES, 0431 as CUNNINGHAM, E. V.

1055
FITZGIBBON, C.   1919-1983
1973 In the Bunker

1056
FORBES, COLIN   1923-
1970 The Heights of Zervos
1984 The Leader & the Damned
See also WORLD HISTORICAL FICTION, 0972 & HEADLINES, 0276

1057
FORESTER, C. S.   1899-1966
England
1943 The Ship
1955 The Good Shepherd
See also WORLD HISTORICAL FICTION, 0973

1058
FRANK, ANNE   1929-1945
Germany
1952 The Diary of a Young Girl
1966 Tales from the House Behind
1982 Anne Frank's Tales from the Secret Annex

1059
FUKS, LADISLAV
Czechoslovakia
1968 Mr. Theodore Mundstock
1985 The Cremator

1060
GAINHAM, SARAH   1922-
Real name: Rachel Ames
1958 Appointment in Vienna
1974 Maculan's Daughter
1975 To the Opera Ball

"Julia Homburg Trilogy":
1967 Night Falls on the City
1969 A Place in the Country
1971 Private Worlds

1061
GALLICO, PAUL   1987-1967
1941 The Snow Goose
Also wrote for juveniles
See also HORROR, 0178

1062
GAVIN, CATHERINE   1907-
Scotland
Trilogy:
1976 Traitor's Gate
1978 None Dare Call It Treason
1980 How Sleep the Brave
See also WORLD HISTORICAL FICTION, 0977

1063
GREEN, GERALD
1967 The Artists of Terezin
1978 Holocaust

1064
GRIFFIN, GWYN   1922?-1967
1967 An Operational Necessity
1968 Occupying Power

HARTOG, JAN DE
See DE HARTOG, JAN, 1046

1065
HAVIARAS, STRATIS   1935-
1979 When the Tree Sings

1066
HEGGEN, THOMAS
1946 Mister Roberts

1067
HELLER, JOSEPH   1923-
1961 Catch-22
See also AMERICAN AUTHORS, 1226

1068
HERSEY, JOHN   1914-
1944 A Bell for Adano
1950 The Wall
1959 The War Lover
Also writes nonfiction, e.g., Hiroshima, 1946 & 1985
See also WORLD HISTORICAL FICTION, 0986 & SCIENCE FICTION, 0653

1069
HOCHHUTH, ROLF   1931-
Germany
1980 A German Love Story

1070
HOUGH, RICHARD   1922-
"RAF Battle of Britain" Trilogy:
1979 Wings against the Sky
1979 The Flight of the Few
1981 Wings of Victory
See also WORLD HISTORICAL FICTION, 0990

1071
HUNTER, JACK D.
1964 The Blue Max
1979 The Blood Order
1981 The Tin Cravat

1072
JACOT, MICHAEL
France
1973 The Last Butterfly

1073
JAHN, MIKE   1943-
1978 Black Sheep Squadron: Devil in the Slot

1074
JOFFO, JOSEPH
1974 A Bag of Marbles

1075
JONES, JAMES   1921-1977
Trilogy:
1951 From Here to Eternity
1962 The Thin Red Line
1978 Whistle
See also AMERICAN AUTHORS, 1240

1076
KA-TZETNIK 135633 (YEHILE DE NUR)
1963 Atrocity
1969 House of Dolls
1971 Star Eternal
1977 Sunrise over Hell

1077
KILLENS, JOHN O.   1916-
1958 Pistol
1963 And Then We Heard the Thunder

1078
KIRST, HANS HELLMUT   1914-
Germany
1963 The Night of the Generals
1963 The Officer Factory
1966 Soldiers' Revolt
1968 The Wolves
1969 Last Stop Camp 7
1971 The Adventures of Private Faust
1976 The Nights of the Long Knives
1979 The Affairs of the Generals

"Gunner Asch":
1956 Forward, Gunner Asch!
1956 The Revolt of Gunner Asch
1957 The Return of Gunner Asch
1964 What Became of Gunner Asch?
See also WORLD AUTHORS, 1454

1079
KOSINSKI, JERZY   1933-
Born in Poland, U.S. citizen
1965 The Painted Bird
See also AMERICAN AUTHORS, 1251

1080
KUPER, JACK
1967 A Child of the Holocaust

1081
LANGFUS, ANNA
France
"Trilogy":
1962 The Whole Land Brimstone
1963 The Lost Shore
1965 Saute Barbara

1082
LEVIN, MEYER   1905-1978
1959 Eva
1965 The Stronghold

1083
LLEWELLYN, RICHARD   1906-1983
Wales
1969 None But the Lonely Hearts (1943)
See also BRITISH AUTHORS, 1370

Section 8 - Historical Fiction

1084
LUSTIG, ARNOST
Czechoslovakia
1962 Night & Hope
1962 Diamonds of the Night
1973 A Prayer for Katerina Horovitzova
1978 Darkness Casts No Shadows
1985 The Unloved
1988 Indecent Dreams
See also WORLD AUTHORS, 1427

1085
MACLEAN, ALISTAIR 1922-1987
Scotland
1955 H.M.S. Ulysses
1957 The Guns of Navarone
1967 Where Eagles Dare
1968 Force 10 from Navarone
1982 Partisans
See also HEADLINES, 0293

1086
MAILER, NORMAN 1923-
1948 The Naked & the Dead
See also AMERICAN AUTHORS, 1263

1087
MANNING, OLIVIA 1915-1980
"The Balkan Trilogy":
1961 The Great Fortune
1962 The Spoilt City
1966 Friends & Heroes

"The Levant Trilogy":
(Sequel to "The Balkan Trilogy")
1977 The Danger Tree
1979 The Battle Lost & Won
1981 The Sum of the Thing
See also BRITISH AUTHORS, 1373

1088
MICHENER, JAMES 1907?-
1947 Tales from the South Pacific
See also AMERICAN HISTORICAL FICTION, 0924 & WORLD HISTORICAL FICTION, 1001

1089
MONSARRAT, NICHOLAS 1910-1979
1951 The Cruel Sea
1974 The Kappillan of Malta

1090
MOSKIN, MARIETTA
1972 I Am Rosemarie

1091
NATHANSON, E. M.
1965 The Dirty Dozen

1092
NOSTLINGER, CHRISTINE
1975 Fly Away Home

1093
REEMAN, DOUGLAS 1924-
1958 A Prayer for the Ship
1964 With Blood & Iron
1969 The Pride & the Anguish
1970 The Greatest Enemy
1970 To Risks Unknown
1972 Rendezvous--South Atlantic
1973 His Majesty's U-Boat
1974 The Destroyers
1975 Winged Escort
1977 Surface with Daring
1978 Strike from the Sea
1979 A Ship Must Die
1981 Torpedo Run
1986 The Iron Pirate

1094
REMARQUE, ERICH M. 1898-1970
Germany
1941 Flotsam
1946 Arch of Triumph
1952 Spark of Life
1954 A Time to Love & a Time to Die
1957 The Black Obelisk
1964 The Night in Lisbon
1972 Shadows in Paradise

1095
RYBAKOV, ANATOLI
U.S.S.R.
1981 Heavy Sand
1988 Children of the Arbat

1096
SCHAEFFER, SUSAN FROMBERG 1941-
1974 Anya
See also AMERICAN AUTHORS, 1309

1097
SHAW, IRWIN   1913-1984
1948 The Young Lions
See also AMERICAN AUTHORS, 1315

1098
SILLIPHANT, STIRLING 1918-
1978 Pearl

1099
SMITH, MARTIN CRUZ   1942-
1986 Stallion Gate
See also HORROR, 0216 & MYSTERIES, 0558

1100
SUHL, YURI   1908-1986
Poland
1974 Uncle Misha's Partisans
1975 On the Other Side of the Gate

1101
TOLAND, JOHN
1985 Gods of War

1102
URIS, LEON   1924-
1953 Battle Cry
1955 Angry Hills
1958 Exodus
1961 Mila 18
1962 Warsaw Uprising
1964 Armageddon
1972 QBVII
See also WORLD HISTORICAL FICTION, 1026 & HEADLINES, 0313

1103
VONNEGUT, KURT, JR.   1922-
1969 Slaughter House 5
See also SCIENCE FICTION, 0730 & AMERICAN AUTHORS, 1332

1104
WESTHEIMER, DAVID   1917-
1964 Von Ryan's Express
1968 Song of the Young Sentry
1979 Rider on the Wind
1980 Von Ryan's Return (Sequel to Express)
See also HEADLINES, 0351

1105
WHITE, ALAN
England
1965 Death Finds the Day
1969 The Long Night's Walk
1970 The Long Drop
1971 The Long Watch
1974 The Long Fuse
1974 The Long Midnight
1975 The Long Summer
1977 The Long Silence

1106
WIESEL, ELIE
France
1960 Night
1961 Dawn
1962 The Accident
1964 The Town beyond the Wall
1966 The Gates of the Forest
1973 Ani ma amin
1973 The Oath
Also writes nonfiction, e.g., A Beggar in Jerusalem, 1970
See also WORLD AUTHORS, 1446

1107
WINWARD, WALTER   1938-
1979 Hammerstrike

1108
WOUK, HERMAN   1915-
1951 The Caine Mutiny
1971 The Winds of War
1978 War & Remembrance (Sequel to Winds)
See also AMERICAN AUTHORS, 1340

1109
WYLIE, JAMES
1978 The Homestead Grays

1110
YATES, RICHARD   1926-
1969 Special Providence
See also AMERICAN AUTHORS, 1342

SECTION NINE

THE TRASH MASTERS

OVERVIEW

The "Trash Masters" are a small but popular group of authors who write novels with several common characteristics: glamorous characters who are often entertainers or part of jet-set society; exotic settings (often New York, Los Angeles, London, Paris, the Riviera); and most importantly, lots of sex with lots of variety. These novels often are *romans a clef*, with thinly disguised characters based on famous individuals, especially entertainers. Jacqueline Susann in her 1966 book *Valley of the Dolls* created a prototype both for the modern scandalous *roman a clef* and for merchandising such books through television appearances. These books ususally achieve their greatest popularity in paperback format and often are made into films.

Some Popular Authors and Their Specialities:

1. *Jackie Collins:*
   Inside views of sex, drugs, and making it in Hollywood.

2. *Dominick Dunne:*
   Scandalous meetings of old money and *nouveau riche* society.

3. *Judith Krantz:*
   The lives of the super rich and famous; name-brand fantasy from a woman's perspective.

4. *Mario Puzo:*
   Inside the Mafia.

5. *Harold Robbins:*
   Long, involved stories of the rise and fall of glamorous men and women usually because of drugs and/or sex.

6. *Sidney Sheldon:*
   Intriguing stories, often of revenge, with a variety of international settings; the women tend to be brave but in peril.

7. *Jacqueline Susann:*
   Glittery, ambitious characters who come to realize that the price of fame and fortune can be too high.

REFERENCE AND BIBLIOGRAPHIC SOURCES

No works were identified that specifically cover these types of books. There are articles about individual authors in standard biographical sources and in *Reader's Guide to Periodic Literature*.

AUTHORS AND TITLES

1111
ASHE, PENELOPE   1936-
Real name: Billie Young
1969 Naked Came the Stranger
1975 Viva la Difference

1112
BLYTH, MYRNA   1939-
1976 Cousin Suzanne
1979 For Better & for Worse

1113
BOGNER, NORMAN   1935-
1967 Seventh Avenue
1968 The Madonna Complex
1973 The Hunting Animal
1975 Making Love
1978 Snowman
1979 Arena
1981 California Dreamers

1114
BRADY, JAMES   1928-
1976 Paris One
1978 Neilsen's Children

1115
BRISKIN, JACQUELINE   1927-
1970 California Generation
1983 Everything & More
1985 Too Much, Too Soon
1987 Dreams Are Not Enough
See also ROMANCES, 0019

1116
CASSILL, R. V. (Ronald Verlin)   1919-
1961 Clem Anderson
1970 Doctor Cobb's Game
1974 The Goss Woman
Also writes short stories

1117
COLLINS, JACKIE
1979 The Bitch
1981 Chances
1983 Hollywood Wives
1985 Lucky (Sequel to Chances)
1986 Hollywood Husbands
1988 Rock Star

1118
COLLINS, JOAN
England
1988 Prime Time

1119
CONRAN, SHIRLEY   1932-
1982 Lace
1985 Lace II
1987 Savages

1120
COOPER, MORTON
1967 The King
1969 Black Star
1974 The Queen
1977 Rich People

1121
DAVIS, GWEN   1936-
1960 Naked in Babylon
1961 Someone's in the Kitchen with Dinah
1966 The War Babies
1967 Sweet William
1969 The Pretenders
1971 Touching
1973 Kingdom Come
1974 The Motherland
1978 The Aristocrats
1979 Ladies in Waiting

1122
DUNNE, DOMINICK
1982 The Winners
1986 The Two Mrs. Grenvilles
1988 People Like Us

1123
ELBERT, JOYCE
1972 Drunk in Madrid
1973 The Three of Us
1979 The Crazy Ladies
1979 The Crazy Lovers
1980 A Very Cagey Lady

1124
FRENCH, MICHAEL   1944-
1979 Abingdons

Section 9 - The Trash Masters

1125
GEASLAND, JACK
See as Jt. author with WOOD, BARI, 1158

1126
GENT, PETER   1942-
1974 North Dallas Forty
1983 The Franchise

1127
GOLDMAN, WILLIAM   1931-
1979 Tinsel
1984 The Color of Light
See also HORROR, 0180; SPY STORIES, 0365; SCIENCE FICTION, 0774

1128
GREELEY, ANDREW M.   1928-
1980 Death in April
1981 The Cardinal Sins
1982 Thy Brother's Wife
1988 Angel Fire

"Passover Trilogy":
1983 Ascent Into Hell
1984 Lord of the Dance
1985 Virgin & Martyr
See also MYSTERIES, 0461 & SCIENCE FICTION, 0641

1129
GREENE, GAEL
1976 Blue Skies, No Candy
1982 Dr. Feelgood

1130
HABER, JOYCE   1932-
1976 The Users

1131
HAILEY, ARTHUR   1920-
1959 The Final Diagnosis
1962 In High Places
1965 Hotel
1968 Airport
1971 Wheels
1975 The Moneychangers
1979 Overload
1984 Strong Medicine

1132
HIRSCHFELD, BURT   1923-
1968 Behold Zion
1970 Fire Island
1971 Acapulco
1971 Cindy on Fire
1971 The Masters Affair
1971 Moment of Power
1972 Father Pig
1972 Fire in the Embers
1973 Generation of Victors
1975 Aspen
1975 Secrets
1977 Provincetown
1978 Why Not Everything
1979 Key West
1982 The Men of Dallas
1983 King of Heaven
1984 Flawless
1988 King Pin

1133
JAFFE, RONA   1932-
1958 The Best of Everything
1965 Mr. Right Is Dead
1966 The Cherry in the Martini
1969 The Fame Game
1972 The Other Woman
1976 The Last Chance
1979 Class Reunion
1985 After the Reunion (Sequel to Class)
See also MYSTERIES, 0481

1134
JENKINS, DAN   1929-
1972 Semi-Tough
1974 Dead Solid Perfect
1976 Limo
1981 Baja Oklahoma
1984 Life Its Ownself

1135
KANIN, GARSON   1912-
1959 Blow Up a Storm
1960 The Rat Race
1969 Cast of Characters (SS)
1969 Where It's At
1973 A Thousand Summers
1977 One Hell of an Actor
1979 Moviola
1980 Smash
1982 Cordelia?

1136
KORDA, MICHAEL   1933-
1979 Charmed Lives
1982 Worldly Goods
1985 Queenie

1137
KRANTZ, JUDITH   1927-
1978 Scruples
1980 Princess Daisy
1982 Mistral's Daughter
1986 I'll Take Manhattan
1988 Till We Meet Again

1138
METALIOUS, GRACE   1924-1964
1956 Peyton Place
1959 Return to Peyton Place

1139
PALMER, LINDA
1981 Starstruck

1140
PAYNE, CHARLOTTE
1980 Glitterati

1141
PUZO, MARIO   1920-
1955 The Dark Arena
1969 The Godfather
1978 Fools Die
1984 The Sicilian

1142
QUINN, SALLY
1986 Regrets Only

1143
RAINER, IRIS
1980 The Boys In The Mailroom

1144
RIMMER, ROBERT   1917-
1966 The Harrad Experiment
1968 Proposition Thirty-One
1972 Thursday, My Love
1974 The Premar Experiment
1985 The Immoral Reverend

1145
ROBBINS, HAROLD   1916-
1949 The Dream Merchants
1949 Never Love a Stranger
1952 A Stone for Danny Fisher
1961 The Carpetbaggers
1962 Where Love Has Gone
1966 The Adventurers
1969 The Inheritors
1971 The Betsy
1974 The Pirate
1976 The Lonely Lady
1977 Dreams Die First
1977 Seventy-Nine Park Avenue
1978 Never Leave Me
1979 Stiletto
1979 Memories of Another Day
1981 Goodbye Janette
1982 Spellbinder
1984 Descent from Xanadu
1985 The Storyteller

1146
ROGERS, ROSEMARY   1932-
1978 The Crowd Pleasers
1979 The Insiders
1980 Lost Love, Last Love
1981 Love Play
See also ROMANCES, 0115

1147
SHELDON, SIDNEY   1917-
1970 The Naked Face
1974 The Other Side of Midnight
1976 A Stranger in the Mirror
1977 Bloodline
1980 Rage of Angels
1983 Master of the Game
1985 If Tomorrow Comes
1987 Windmills of the Gods
1988 Sands of Time
See also HEADLINES, 0305

1148
SLAVITT, DAVID   1935-
Also writes as Henry Sutton
1968 The Exhibitionist
1968 The Voyeur
1975 The Killing of the King
1977 King of Hearts
1978 Jo Stern
1979 The Sacrifice
1980 The Outer Mongolian
1980 The Proposal

Section 9 - The Trash Masters

1149
STEWART, EDWARD
1979 Ballerina
See also ROMANCES, 0134 & HORROR, 0220

1150
SUSANN, JACQUELINE   1921-1974
1963 Every Night Josephine
1966 Valley of the Dolls
1969 The Love Machine
1973 Once Is Not Enough
1976 Dolores
1979 Yargo

1151
THOMPSON, EARL   1931?-1978
1970 A Garden of Sand
1974 Tattoo
1976 Caldo Largo
1981 The Devil to Pay

1152
THOMPSON, THOMAS   1933-1982
1982 Celebrity
Also wrote nonfiction; e.g., Blood & Money, 1976.

1153
TRYON, TOM   1926-
1974 Lady
1976 Crowned Heads
1987 All That Glitters
See also HORROR, 0226

1154
VAN LUSTBADER, ERIC   1946-
1978 Dai-San
1978 Shallows of Night
1980 The Ninja
1981 The Sirens
1983 Black Heart
1984 The Miko (Sequel to Ninja)
1985 Jian
1988 Zero
See also SCIENCE FICTION, 0809

1155
WALLACE, IRVING   1916-
1960 The Chapman Report
1962 The Prize
1963 The Three Sirens
1967 The Plot
1969 The Seven Minutes
1972 The Word
1973 The Fan Club
1979 The Pigeon Project
1984 The Miracle
1987 The Celestial Bed
See also HEADLINES, 0254 & 0350

1156
WALLACE, SYLVIA
1976 The Fountains
1980 Empress

1157
WALLACH, ANNE TOLSTOI
1981 Women's Work

1158
WOOD, BARI   1936-   &
GEASLAND, JACK   1944-
1977 Twins
See also HORROR, 0228

SECTION TEN

AMERICAN AUTHORS

OVERVIEW

The authors in this section are linked together only by two characteristics: they were born in or lived in the United States and they have achieved some level of acclaim from reviewers and literary critics. Other than these characteristics shared in common, the authors are not easily categorized. Individual works by an author may also vary greatly so that it becomes difficult to characterize an author's works.

Occasionally an individual title by an author will appear in one of the genre sections. Such a work may contain many of the elements of the genre, but may transcend the genre in literary quality, freshness of approach, and insight into character. For example, E. L. Doctorow's novel *Welcome to Hard Times* can be classified as a western; its literary qualities make it appealing to a more literate reader, and those very appealing qualities may make it much less appealing to a reader who enjoys traditional westerns.

Among the most prestigious prizes awarded to American authors are the Pulitzer Prize and the National Book Awards. Several contemporary American authors have won the Nobel Prize: Saul Bellow and Isaac Bashevis Singer.

Some Representative Groupings:

1. *Absurdists:*
   Authors who view the absurdities of life with a very dark or "black humor" perspective: John Barth, Donald Barthelme, Thomas Berger, Bruce Jay Friedman, Joseph Heller, John Irving, Kurt Vonnegut, Jr.

2. *Black Americans:*
   James Baldwin, Toni Cade Bambera, David Bradley, Ralph Ellison, Ernest J. Gaines, Chester Himes, Gayl Jones, Toni Morrison, Gloria Naylor, Ishmael Reed, Ntozake Shange, Alice Walker, John Edgar Wideman, Richard Wright.

3. *Brat Pack Writers:*
   A group of very young authors who write about the angst of life among bored young people who are often involved with drugs: Jill Eisenstadt, Bret Easton Ellis, Tama Janowitz, Jay McInerney.

4. *Chroniclers of Ethnic Experiences:*
   Authors who write about the experiences of specific ethnic and religious groups: Saul Bellow (Jewish Americans), Bernard Malamud (Jewish Americans), Edwin O'Connor (Irish Americans), Harry Mark Petrakis (Greek Americans), Chaim Potok (Jewish Americans), Philip

Section 10 - American Authors

Roth (Jewish Americans), Thomas Sanchez (Mexican Americans), Hyemeyohsts Storm (Native Americans).

5. *Humorists:*
   Authors whose works contain humor, although approaches to humor vary greatly: Richard Brautigan, Peter DeVries, J. P. Donleavy, Bruce Jay Friedman, Tom Robbins, Terry Southern.

6. *Authors of the Novel of Manners:*
   Authors who examine the social, moral, and psychological milieu of the middle and upper classes: Louis Auchincloss, Anne Bernays, John Cheever, John O'Hara, John Updike.

7. *Southern Writers:*
   Authors who live or grew up south of the Mason Dixon line and who write about life in the South: Truman Capote, Pat Conroy, James Dickey, Shirley Ann Grau, Carson McCullers, Bobbie Ann Mason, Flannery O'Connor, Walker Percy, William Styron, John Kennedy Toole, Eudora Welty.

8. *Women:*
   Women writers who explore the role of women in society, often in very nontraditional ways: Lisa Alther, Sheila Ballantyne, Ann Beattie, Rita Mae Brown, Paula Fox, Marilyn French, Mary Gordon, Lois Gould, Francine Du Plessix Gray, Doris Grumbach, Judith Guest, Elizabeth Hardwick, Sandra Hochman, Susan Isaacs, Erica Jong, Sue Kaufman, Norma Klein, Alison Lurie, Bobbie Ann Mason, Grace Paley, Marge Piercy, Sylvia Plath, Joyce Rebeta-Burditt, Anne Richardson Roiphe, Judith Rossner, Susan Fromberg Schaeffer, Alix Kates Shulman, Helen Ygelsias.

REFERENCE AND BIBLIOGRAPHIC SOURCES

Adelman, Irving and Rita Dworkin. *The Contemporary Novel: A Checklist of Critical Literature on the British and American Novel since 1945.* Metuchen, NJ: Scarecrow Press, 1972.

Kaplan, Fred, ed. *The Reader's Adviser: A Layman's Guide to Literature,* 13th ed. Volume I: The Best in American and British Fiction. . . . New York: Bowker, 1986.

Rosa, Alfred F. and Paul A. Eschholz. *Contemporary Fiction in America and England, 1950-1970: A Guide to Information Sources.* Detroit: Gale, 1976.

Somer, John and Barbara Eck Cooper. *American and British Literature, 1945-1975: An Annotated Bibliography of Contemporary Scholarship.* Lawrence: Regents Press of Kansas, 1980.

Woodress, James Leslie. *American Fiction, 1900-1950: A Guide to Information Sources.* Detroit: Gale, 1974.

AUTHORS AND TITLES

1159
ADAMS, ALICE   1926-
1966   Careless Love
1967   The Fall of Daisy Duke
1975   Families & Survivors
1978   Listening to Billie
1979   Beautiful Girl (SS)
1980   Rich Rewards
1982   To See You Again (SS)
1984   Superior Women
1985   Return Trips (SS)
1988   Second Chances

1160
ALTHER, LISA   1944-
1976   Kinflicks
1981   Original Sins
1984   Other Women

1161
ARNOW, HARRIETTE   1908-1986
1936   Mountain Path
1949   Hunter's Horn
1954   The Dollmaker
1969   The Weedkiller's Daughter
1974   The Kentucky Trace: A Novel of the American Revolution
See also HISTORICAL FICTION, 0890

1162
AUCHINCLOSS, LOUIS   1917-
Also wrote as Andrew Lee
1950   The Injustice Collectors
1952   Sybil
1953   A Law for the Lion
1954   The Romantic Egoists
1956   The Great World & Timothy Colt
1958   Venus in Sparta
1959   Pursuit of the Prodigal
1960   The House of Five Talents
1962   Portrait in Brownstone
1963   Powers of Attorney
1964   The House of Mirth
1964   The Rector of Justin
1965   Counterpoint
1966   The Embezzler
1967   Tales of Manhattan
1968   A World of Profit
1970   Second Chance
1972   I Come as a Thief
1974   The Partners
1976   The Winthrop Covenant
1977   The Dark Lady
1978   The Country Cousin
1980   The House of the Prophet
1981   The Cat & the King
1982   Narcissa & Other Fables
1982   Watchfires
1983   Exit Lady Masham
1984   The Book Class
1985   Honorable Men
1985   The Next-to-Last Puritan
1986   Diary of a Yuppie
1987   Skinny Island: More Tales of Manhattan
1988   The Golden Calves
See also HISTORICAL FICTION, 0951

1163
BALDWIN, JAMES   1924-1987
Black American
1953   Go Tell It on the Mountain
1956   Giovanni's Room
1962   Another Country
1966   Going to Meet the Man
1968   Tell Me How Long the Train's Been Gone
1974   If Beale Street Could Talk
1979   Just above My Head
Also writes nonfiction, e.g., The Fire Next Time, & drama, e.g., The Amen Corner

1164
BALLANTYNE, SHEILA   1936-
1975   Norma Jean, the Termite Queen
1982   Imaginary Crimes
1988   Life on Earth (SS)

1165
BAMBARA, TONI CADE   1939-
Black American
1971   Tales & Stories for Black Folks
1972   Gorilla My Love (SS)
1977   The Sea Birds Are Still Alive (SS)
1980   The Salt Eaters

1166
BARTH, JOHN   1930-
1956   The Floating Opera
1958   The End of the Road
1960   The Sot-Weed Factor
1966   Giles Goat Boy

Section 10 - American Authors					179

1968	Lost in the Funhouse
1972	Chimera
1979	Letters
1982	Sabbatical

1167
BARTHELME, DONALD	1931-
1964	Come Back, Dr. Caligari (SS)
1967	Snow White
1968	Unspeakable Practices, Unnatural Acts (SS)
1970	City Life (SS)
1972	Sadness (SS)
1975	The Dead Father
1976	Amateurs
1979	Great Days (SS)
1981	Sixty Stories
1983	Overnight to Many Distant Cities
1987	The Tidewater Tales
1988	Two against One

1168
BEATTIE, ANN	1947-
1976	Chilly Scenes of Winter
1976	Distortions (SS)
1979	Secrets & Surprises (SS)
1980	Falling in Place
1985	Love Always
1986	Where You'll Find Me (SS)

1169
BELLOW, SAUL	1915-
Nobel Prize, 1976
1944	Dangling Man
1947	The Victim
1953	The Adventures of Augie March
1956	Seize the Day
1959	Henderson the Rain King
1964	Herzog
1968	Mosby's Memoirs (SS)
1970	Mr. Sammler's Planet
1975	Humboldt's Gift
1982	The Dean's December
1984	Him with His Foot in Mouth (SS)
1987	More Die of Heartbreak

1170
BERGER, THOMAS	1924-
1964	Little Big Man
1967	Killing Time
1973	Regiment of Women
1975	Sneaky People
1978	Arthur Rex
1980	Neighbors
1983	The Feud

1987	Being Invisible
1988	The Houseguest

"Carl Reinhart":
1958	Crazy in Berlin
1962	Reinhart in Love
1970	Vital Parts
1981	Reinhart's Women

"Russel Wren, Private Investigator":
1977	Who Is Teddy Villanova?
1985	Nowhere
See also SCIENCE FICTION, 0602

1171
BERNAYS, ANNE	1930-
Real name: Anne Bernays Kaplan
1962	Short Pleasures
1965	The New York Ride
1966	Prudence, Indeed
1975	The First to Know
1975	Growing Up Rich
1980	The School Book
1983	The Address Book

1172
BIRSTEIN, ANN	1927-
1950	Star of Glass
1955	The Troublemaker
1966	The Sweet Birds of Gorham
1972	Summer Situation
1973	Dickie's List
1980	American Children
1982	The Rabbi of 47th Street
1988	The Last of the Believers

1173
BOURJAILY, VANCE	1922-
1947	The End of My Life
1952	Confessions of a Spent Youth
1953	The Hound of Earth
1958	The Violated
1962	The Unnatural Enemy
1967	The Man Who Knew Kennedy
1970	Brill among the Ruins
1976	Now Playing at Canterbury
1980	A Game Men Play
1986	The Great Fake Book

1174
BOYLE, KAY	1903-
1930	Wedding Day (SS)
1931	Plagued by the Nightingale
1932	Year before Last
1933	The First Lover (SS)

1933 Gentlemen, I Address You Privately
1934 My Next Bride
1936 Death of a Man
1936 The White Horses of Vienna (SS)
1936 365 Days (SS)
1938 Monday Night
1940 The Crazy Hunter
1942 Primer for Combat
1944 Avalanche
1946 A Frenchman Must Die
1946 Thirty Stories
1948 1939
1949 His Human Majesty
1951 The Smoking Mountain (SS)
1955 The Seagull on the Steps
1960 Generation without Farewell
1966 Nothing Ever Breaks Except the Heart (SS)
1974 The Underground Woman
1980 Fifty Stories

1175
BRADLEY, DAVID   1950-
Black American
1975 South Street
1981 The Chaneysville Incident

1176
BRAUTIGAN, RICHARD   1935-1984
1965 A Confederate General from Big Sur
1967 In Watermelon Sugar
1967 Trout Fishing in America
1971 The Abortion: An Historical Romance, 1966
1971 Revenge of the Lawn (SS)
1974 The Hawkline Monster
1975 Willard & His Bowling Trophies
1976 Sombrero Fallout: A Japanese Novel
1977 Dreaming of Babylon: A Private Eye Novel, 1942
1978 June 30th, June 30th
1980 The Tokyo-Montana Express
1982 So the Wind Won't Blow It All Away

1177
BROWN, RITA MAE   1944-
1973 Rubyfruit Jungle
1976 In Her Day
1976 A Plain Brown Rapper
1978 Six of One
1982 Southern Discomfort
1983 Sudden Death

1986 High Hearts
Also a poet

1178
BROWN, ROSELLEN   1939-
1974 Street Games (SS)
1976 The Autobiography of My Mother
1978 Tender Mercies
1984 Civil Wars
Also a poet

1179
BRYANT, DOROTHY   1930-
1972 Ella Price's Journal
1976 Kin of Ata Are Waiting for You
1978 Miss Giardino
1979 The Garden of Eros
1980 Prisoners
1981 Killing Wonder
1986 Confessions of Madame Psyche

1180
BURROUGHS, WILLIAM   1914-
Also writes as William Lee & Willy Lee
1953 Junkie: Confessions of an Unredeemed Drug Addict
1959 Naked Lunch
1960 The Exterminator
1961 The Soft Machine
1963 The Ticket That Exploded
1963 The Yage Letters
1964 Nova Express
1965 Darazt
1965 Time
1969 The Dead Star
1970 Third Mind
1971 The Wild Boys
1980 Port of Saints
1984 The Burroughs File
1985 Queer

"Trilogy":
1981 Cities of the Red Night: A Boy's Book
1984 The Place of Dead Roads
1987 The Western Lands

1181
BUTLER, OCTAVIA E.   1947-
1978 Survivor
1984 Clay's Ark

"Patternist":
1976 Patternmaster
1977 Mind of My Mind (Prequel)

Section 10 - American Authors   181

1980 Wild Seed (Prequel)

1182
CALISHER, HORTENSE   1911-
1951 In the Absence of Angels (SS)
1961 False Entry
1962 Tale for the Mirror (SS)
1963 Textures of Life
1964 Extreme Magic (SS)
1965 Journal from Ellipsia
1966 The Railway Police (and) The Last Trolley Ride
1969 The New Yorkers
1971 Queenie
1972 Standard Dreaming
1973 Eagle Eye
1977 On Keeping Women
1983 Mysteries of Motion
1985 Saratoga, Hot (SS)
1986 The Bobby-Soxer
1987 Age
Autobiography: Herself, 1972

1183
CAPOTE, TRUMAN   1924-1984
1948 Other Voices, Other Rooms
1949 A Tree of Night (SS)
1951 The Grass Harp
1958 Breakfast at Tiffany's
1966 In Cold Blood (NF Novel)
1980 Music for Chameleons
1983 One Christmas
1986 Answered Prayers: The Unfinished Novel

1184
CAPUTO, PHILIP   1941-
1977 A Rumor of War
1980 Horn of Africa
1983 Delcorso's Gallery
1987 Indian Country
See also HISTORICAL FICTION, 0897

1185
CARROLL, JAMES   1943-
1976 Madonna Red
1979 Mortal Friends
1980 Fault Lines
1982 Family Trade
1984 Prince of Peace
1986 Supply of Heroes
See also HEADLINES, 0263

1186
CHARYN, JEROME   1937-
1964 Once Upon a Droshky
1965 On the Darkening Green
1967 Going to Jerusalem
1967 The Man Who Grew Younger (SS)
1969 American Scrapbook
1969 The Single Voice
1970 The Troubled Vision
1971 Eisenhower, My Eisenhower
1973 The Tar Baby
1977 The Franklin Scare
1979 The Seventh Babe
1980 The Catfish Man
1980 Darlin' Bill: A Love Story of the Wild West
1982 Panna Maria
1983 Pinocchio's Nose
1985 War Cries over Avenue C
1987 Paradise Man

"Isaac Sidel Quartet":
1975 Blue Eyes (1)
1976 The Education of Patrick Silver (3)
1976 Marilyn the Wild (2)
1978 Secret Isaac (4)
See also WESTERNS, 0833 & HISTORICAL FICTION, 1040

1187
CHEEVER, JOHN   1912-1982
1943 The Way Some People Live (SS)
1953 The Enormous Radio (SS)
1958 The Housebreaker of Shady Hill (SS)
1964 The Brigadier & the Golf Widow
1969 Bullet Park
1973 The World of Apples
1977 Falconer
1978 Stories
1982 Oh, What a Paradise It Seems

"The Wapshot Books"
1957 The Wapshot Chronicle
1964 The Wapshot Scandal

1188
CONDON, RICHARD   1915-
1958 The Oldest Confession
1959 The Manchurian Candidate
1960 Some Angry Angel
1961 A Talent for Loving
1964 An Infinity of Mirrors
1966 Any God Will Do

1967 The Ecstasy Business
1969 Mile High
1971 The Vertical Smile
1972 Arigato
1974 The Star Spangled Crunch
1974 Winter Kills
1975 Money Is Love
1976 The Whisper of the Axe
1977 The Abandoned Woman
1978 Bandicoot
1979 Death of a Politician
1980 The Entwining
1983 A Trembling upon Rome

"Prizzi":
1982 Prizzi's Honor
1986 Prizzi's Family (Prequel)
1988 Prizzi's Glory
See also HEADLINES, 0234

1189
CONROY, PAT   1945-
1970 The Boo
1972 The Water Is Wide
1976 The Great Santini
1980 Lords of Discipline
1986 Prince of Tides

1190
COOVER, ROBERT   1932-
1966 The Origin of the Brunists
1968 The Universal Baseball Association, Henry Waugh, Prop.
1977 The Public Burning
1980 A Political Fable
1982 Spanking the Maid
1986 Gerald's Party
1986 A Night at the Movies, or You Must Remember This
1987 Whatever Happened to Gloomy Gus of the Chicago Bears?

1191
CREWS, HARRY   1935-
1968 The Gospel Singer
1969 Naked in Garden Hills
1970 This Thing Don't Lead to Heaven
1972 Karate Is a Thing of the Spirit
1972 Car
1973 The Hawk Is Dying
1974 The Gypsy's Curse
1976 A Feast of Snakes
1981 The Enthusiast
1987 All We Need of Hell
1988 The Knockout Artist
Autobiography: A Childhood, 1978

1192
CUNNINGHAM, LAURA   1947-
1977 Sweet Nothings
1980 Third Parties

1193
DELILLO, DON   1936-
1971 Americana
1972 End Zone
1973 Great Jones Street
1976 Ratner's Star
1977 Players
1978 Running Dog
1982 The Names
1986 White Noise
1988 Libra

1194
DE VRIES, PETER   1910-
1940 But Who Wakes the Burglar?
1943 The Handsome Heart
1944 Angels Can't Do Better
1952 No But I Saw the Movie (SS)
1954 The Tunnel of Love
1956 Comfort Me With Apples
1958 The Mackerel Plaza
1959 The Tents of Wickedness
1961 Through the Fields of Clover
1962 The Blood of the Lamb
1964 Reuben, Reuben
1965 Let Me Count the Ways
1967 The Vale of Laughter
1968 The Cat's Pajamas & Witch's Milk
1970 Mrs. Wallop
1971 Into Your Tent I'll Creep
1972 Without a Stitch in Time (SS)
1973 Forever Panting
1974 The Glory of the Hummingbird
1976 I Hear America Swinging
1977 Madder Music
1980 Consenting Adults, or the Dutchess Will Be Furious
1981 Sauce for the Goose
1983 Slouching toward Kalamazoo
1985 The Prick of Noon
1986 Peckham's Marbles

1195
DICKEY, JAMES   1923-
1970 Deliverance
1987 Alnilam
Best known as a poet

1196
DIDION, JOAN   1934-

Section 10 - American Authors

1963 Run River
1970 Play It as It Lays
1977 A Book of Common Prayer
1984 Democracy
Also writes nonfiction; e.g., Slouching toward Bethlehem, 1968; The White Album, 1979

1197
DOCTOROW, E. L. (Edgar Lawrence) 1931-
1960 Welcome to Hard Times
1966 Big as Life
1971 The Book of Daniel
1975 Ragtime
1980 Loon Lake
1984 Lives of the Poets (SS)
1985 World's Fair
See also WESTERNS, 0837

1198
DONLEAVY, J. P. (James Patrick) 1926-
1955 The Ginger Man
1963 A Singular Man
1964 Meet My Maker the Mad Molecule
1966 The Saddest Summer of Samuel S.
1968 The Beastly Beatitudes of Balthazar B.
1971 The Onion Eaters
1973 A Fairy Tale of New York
1977 The Destinies of Darcy Dancer
1979 Schultz
1983 Leila: Further in the Destinies of Darcy Dancer, Gentleman
1988 Are You Listening Rabbi Low? (Sequel to Schultz)

1199
DUNNE, JOHN GREGORY 1932-
1967 Delano
1976 A Star Is Born
1977 True Confessions
1978 Quintana & Friends
1983 Dutch Shea, Jr.
1987 The Red, White & Blue

1200
EISENSTADT, JILL 1963-
1987 From Rockaway

1201
ELKIN, STANLEY 1930-
1964 Boswell
1967 A Bad Man
1970 The Dick Gibson Show
1976 The Franchiser
1978 The Living End
1982 George Mills
1985 The Magic Kingdom
1987 The Rabbi of Lud

1202
ELLIS, BRET EASTON 1964-
1986 Less Than Zero
1987 The Rules of Attraction

1203
ELLISON, RALPH 1914-
Black American
1952 Invisible Man
Also published many short stories

1204
EPSTEIN, LESLIE 1938-
1975 P. D. Kimerakov
1976 The Steinway Quintet (SS)
1979 King of the Jews
1982 Regina
1985 Goldkorn Tales (SS)
See also HISTORICAL FICTION, 1052

1205
ERDRICH, LOUISE 1954-
"Tetralogy":
1984 Love Medicine
1986 The Beet Queen
1988 Tracks

1206
FLOREY, KITTY BURNS
1979 Family Matters
1980 Chez Cordelia
1983 The Garden Path
1986 Real Life
1987 Duet

1207
FOX, PAULA 1923-
1967 A Likely Place
1967 Poor George
1970 Desperate Characters
1972 The Western Coast
1976 The Widow's Children
1984 A Servant's Tale
Also writes fiction for juveniles

1208
FRENCH, MARILYN   1929-
1977 The Women's Room
1980 The Bleeding Heart
1987 Her Mother's Daughter

1209
FRIEDMAN, BRUCE JAY   1930-
1962 Stern
1963 Far from the City of Class
1964 A Mother's Kisses
1966 Black Angels (SS)
1970 The Dick
1974 About Harry Towns
1985 Tokyo Woes

1210
GADDIS, WILLIAM   1922-
National Book Award for JR
1955 The Recognitions
1975 JR
1985 Carpenter's Gothic

1211
GAINES, ERNEST J.   1933-
Black American
1964 Catherine Carmier
1967 Of Love & Dust
1970 Bloodline (SS)
1971 The Autobiography of Miss Jane Pittman
1971 A Long Day in November
1978 In My Father's House
1983 A Gathering of Old Men

1212
GARDNER, JOHN C. (Champlin, Jr.)
1933-1982
1966 The Resurrection
1970 The Wreckage of Agathon
1971 Grendel
1972 The Sunlight Dialogues
1973 Nickel Mountain: A Pastoral Novel
1974 The King's Indian (SS)
1976 October Light
1980 Freddy's Book
1981 The Art of Living (SS)
1982 Mickelsson's Ghosts
1986 Stillness; &, Shadows
Also wrote fantasy for juveniles
See also SCIENCE FICTION, 0771 & HISTORICAL FICTION, 0975

1213
GODWIN, GAIL   1937-
1970 The Perfectionists
1972 Glass People
1974 The Odd Woman
1976 Dream Children (SS)
1978 Violet Clay
1982 A Mother & Two Daughters
1983 Mr. Bedford & the Muses (SS)
1985 The Finishing School
1987 A Southern Family

1214
GOLD, HERBERT   1924-
1951 Birth of a Hero
1954 The Prospect before Us
1956 The Man Who Was Not with It
1956 Room Clerk
1959 The Optimist
1960 Therefore Be Bold
1963 Salt
1967 Fathers
1969 The Great American Jackpot
1970 Biafra Goodbye
1971 The Magic Will (SS)
1972 My Last Two Thousand Years
1974 Swiftie the Magician
1978 Waiting for Cordelia
1979 Slave Trade
1980 He/She
1981 Family
1982 True Love
1984 Mister White Eyes
1985 Stories of Misbegotten Love (SS)
1986 A Girl of Forty
1986 Lovers & Cohorts (SS)
1988 Dreaming

1215
GORDON, MARY   1949-
1978 Final Payments
1981 The Company of Women
1985 Men & Angels
1987 Temporary Shelter (SS)

1216
GOULD, LOIS   1938?-
1970 Such Good Friends
1972 Necessary Objects
1974 Final Analysis
1977 A Sea Change
1978 X: A Fabulous Child's Story
1981 La Presidenta
1988 Subject to Change

Section 10 - American Authors

1217
GRAU, SHIRLEY ANN   1929-
1955 The Black Prince (SS)
1958 The Hard Blue Sky
1961 The House on Coliseum Street
1964 The Keepers of the House
1971 The Condor Passes
1973 The Wind Shifting West (SS)
1977 Evidence of Love
1985 Nine Women (SS)

1218
GRAY, FRANCINE DU PLESSIX   1930-
1976 Lovers & Tyrants
1981 World without End
1985 October Blood

1219
GREEN, HANNAH   1932-
Real name: Joanne Greenberg
1964 I Never Promised You a Rose Garden
1972 The Dead of the House
See also as GREENBERG, JOANNE, 1220

1220
GREENBERG, JOANNE   1932-
Also writes as Hannah Green
1963 The King's Persons
1965 The Monday Voices
1965 Summering (SS)
1968 In This Sign
1971 Rites of Passage (SS)
1976 Founder's Praise
1979 High Crimes & Misdemeanors (SS)
1981 A Season of Delight
1983 The Far Side of Victory
1986 Simple Gifts
1987 Age of Consent
1988 Of Such Small Differences
See also HISTORICAL FICTION, 0983;
as HANNAH GREEN, 1219

1221
GRUMBACH, DORIS   1918-
1962 The Spoil of the Flowers
1964 The Short Throat, the Tender Mouth
1967 The Magician's Girl
1979 Chamber Music
1981 The Missing Person
1984 The Ladies

1222
GUEST, JUDITH   1936-
1976 Ordinary People
1982 Second Heaven

1223
HARDWICK, ELIZABETH   1916-
1945 The Ghostly Lover
1955 The Simple Truth
1974 Seduction & Betrayal
1979 Sleepless Nights

1224
HAWKES, JOHN   1925-
1949 The Cannibal
1951 The Beetle Leg
1951 The Goose on the Grave
1951 The Owl
1961 The Lime Twig
1964 Second Skin
1971 The Blood Oranges
1974 Death, Sleep & the Traveler
1976 Travesty
1979 The Passion Artist
1982 Virginie, Her Two Lives
1985 Adventures in the Alaskan Skin Trade

1225
HAZZARD, SHIRLEY   1931-
Born in Australia
1963 Cliffs of Fall (SS)
1966 The Evening of the Holiday
1967 People in Glass Houses (SS)
1970 The Bay of Noon
1980 The Transit of Venus

1226
HELLER, JOSEPH   1932-
1961 Catch-22
1974 Something Happened
1979 Good as Gold
1984 God Knows
1988 Picture This
Known also for drama, e.g., We Bombed in New Haven
See also HISTORICAL FICTION, 1067

1227
HERLIHY, JAMES LEO   1927-
1959 The Sleep of Baby Filbertson (SS)
1960 All Fall Down

1965 Midnight Cowboy
1971 The Season of the Witch

1228
HIGGINS, GEORGE V.
1972 The Friends of Eddie Coyle
1973 The Digger's Game
1974 Cogan's Trade
1975 A City on a Hill
1979 A Year or So with Edgar
1982 The Patriot Game
1984 A Choice of Enemies
1987 Outlaws
See also HEADLINES, 0239 & MYSTERIES, 0472

1229
HILL, CAROL   1942-
1970 Jeremiah 8:20
1975 Let's Fall in Love
1978 An Unmarried Woman
1985 The Eleven Million Mile High Dancer

1230
HIMES, CHESTER   1909-1984
Black American
1945 If He Hollers, Let Him Go
1947 Lonely Crusade
1952 Cast the First Stone
1954 The Third Generation
1955 The Primitive
1965 Pinktoes (1962)
1973 Baby Sister (SS)

"Harlem Stories":
1959 The Real Cool Killers (1958)
1960 All Shot Up
1960 The Big Gold Dream
1960 The Crazy Kill (1958)
1965 Cotton Comes to Harlem (1964)
1965 A Rage in Harlem (1957, For Love of Imabelle)
1966 The Heat's On (1960)
1966 Run Man Run (1959)
1969 Blind Man with a Pistol
1970 Hot Day Hot Night

1231
HOCHMAN, SANDRA   1936-
1971 Walking Papers
1976 Happiness is Too Much Trouble
1977 Endangered Species
1979 Jogging: A Love Story

1981 Playing Tahoe

1232
HOFFMAN, ALICE   1952-
1977 Property of
1979 The Drowning Season
1980 Angel Landing
1982 White Horses
1985 Fortune's Daughter
1987 Illumination Night
1988 At Risk

1233
IRVING, JOHN   1942-
1969 Setting Free the Bears
1972 The Water Method Man
1974 The One Hundred & Fifty Eight Pound Marriage
1978 The World According to Garp
1981 The Hotel New Hampshire
1985 The Cider House Rules

1234
ISAACS, SUSAN   1943-
1978 Compromising Positions
1980 Close Relations
1984 Almost Paradise
1988 Shining Through

1235
JACKSON, SHIRLEY   1919-1965
1948 The Road through the Wall
1949 The Lottery (SS)
1951 Hangsman
1953 Life among the Savages
1954 The Bird's Nest
1956 The Other Side of the Street
1957 Lizzie
1957 Raising Demons
1958 The Bad Children
1958 The Sundial
1959 The Haunting of Hill House
1960 And Baby Makes Three
1962 We Have Always Lived in the Castle
1966 Famous Sally
1968 Come Along with Me
See also HORROR, 0188

1236
JANOWITZ, TAMA
1981 American Dad
1986 Slaves of New York (SS)
1987 A Cannibal in Manhattan

Section 10 - American Authors

1237
JHABVALA, RUTH PRAWER   1927-
Born in Cologne, lived in India, lives in U.S.
1955 Amrita
1956 The Nature of Passion
1958 Esmond in India
1962 Get Ready for Battle
1963 Like Birds, Like Fishes
1965 A Backward Place
1968 A Stronger Climate
1970 The Householder (1960)
1972 An Experience of India
1975 Heat & Dust
1976 How I Became a Holy Mother (SS)
1983 In Search of Love & Beauty
1987 Three Continents

1238
JOHNSON, DIANE   1934-
1965 Fair Game
1968 Loving Hands at Home
1971 Burning
1973 Lesser Lives
1974 The Shadow Knows
1978 Lying Low
1987 Persian Nights

1239
JONES, GAYL   1949-
Black American
1975 Corregidora
1976 Eva's Man
1977 White Rat (SS)

1240
JONES, JAMES   1921-1977
1951 From Here to Eternity
1958 Some Came Running
1959 The Pistol
1962 The Thin Red Line
1967 Go to the Widow-Maker
1968 The Ice-Cream Headache (SS)
1971 The Merry Month of May
1973 A Touch of Danger
1978 Whistle
See also HISTORICAL FICTION, 1075

1241
JONG, ERICA   1942-
1973 Fear of Flying
1977 How to Save Your Own Life
1980 Fanny
1984 Parachutes & Kisses

1987 Serenissma
Also a poet

1242
KAUFMAN, BEL
1965 Up the Down Staircase
1979 Love, Etc.

1243
KAUFMAN, SUE   1926-1977
Real name: Sue Kaufman Barondess
1959 The Happy Summer Days
1962 Green Holly
1967 Diary of a Mad Housewife
1969 The Headshrinker's Test
1970 Life with Prudence: A Chilling Tale
1974 Falling Bodies
1976 The Master (SS)

1244
KAZAN, ELIA   1909-
1962 America, America
1967 The Arrangement
1972 The Assassins
1975 The Understudy
1978 Acts of Love
1982 The Anatolian

1245
KELLOGG, MARJORIE   1922-
1968 Tell Me That You Love Me, Junie Moon
1972 Like the Lion's Tooth

1246
KENNEDY, WILLIAM   1928-
1984 The Ink Truck
1986 The Masakado Lesson
1988 Quinn's Book
1988 Toy Soldiers

"The Albany Cycle":
1979 Billy Phelan's Greatest Game
1975 Legs
1983 Ironweed

1247
KEROUAC, JACK   1922-1969
Real name: Jean-Louis Lebridde Kerouac; also wrote as Jean-Louis, Jean-Louis Incognito, John Kerouac
1950 The Town & the City

1957 On the Road
1958 The Dharma Bums
1958 The Subterraneans
1959 Doctor Sax
1959 Maggie Cassidy
1960 Tristessa
1960 Visions of Cody
1962 Big Sur
1963 Visions of Gerard
1965 Desolation Angels
1966 Satori in Paris
1968 Vanity of Duluoz
1971 Pic

1248
KESEY, KEN   1935-
1962 One Flew Over the Cuckoo's Nest
1964 Sometimes a Great Notion
1973 Kesey's Garage Sale
1986 Demon Box

1249
KLEIN, NORMA   1938-1989
1972 Love & Other Euphemisms
1974 Coming to Life
1975 Sunshine
1976 Girls Turn Wives
1979 French Postcards
1981 Domestic Arrangement
1982 Wives & Other Women
1983 Sextet in a Minor (SS)
1987 American Dreams
1988 That's My Baby
Also writes novels for juveniles & for young adults

1250
KNOWLES, JOHN   1926-
1960 A Separate Peace
1962 Morning in Antibes
1966 Indian Summer
1968 Phineas (SS) (Related to Separate)
1971 The Paragon
1974 Spreading Fires
1978 A Vein of Riches
1981 Peace Breaks Out (Sequel to Separate)
1986 The Private Life of Avie Reed

1251
KOSINSKI, JERZY   1933-
Born in Poland; U.S. citizen
National Book Award: Steps

1968 Steps
1970 Being There
1970 The Painted Bird (1965)
1973 The Devil Tree
1975 Cockpit
1977 Blind Date
1979 Passion Play
1982 Pinball
1988 The Hermit of 69th Street
See also HISTORICAL FICTION, 1079

1252
LAHR, JOHN   1941-
1973 The Autograph Hound
1974 Hot to Trot

1253
LEFFLAND, ELLA   1931-
1970 Mrs. Munck
1974 Love Out of Season
1979 Rumors of Peace
1980 Last Courtesies (SS)

1254
LOWRY, BEVERLY   1938-
1977 Come Back, Lolly Ray
1978 Emma Blue
1981 Daddy's Girl
1987 The Perfect Sonya
1988 Breaking Gentle

1255
LURIE, ALISON   1926-
1962 Love & Friendship
1965 The Nowhere City
1967 Imaginary Friends
1969 Real People
1974 The War Between the Tates
1979 Only Children
1984 Foreign Affairs
1988 The Truth about Lorin Jones

1256
MCCARTHY, MARY   1912-
1942 The Company She Keeps
1949 The Oasis
1950 Cast a Cold Eye (SS)
1952 The Groves of Academe
1955 A Charmed Life
1963 The Group
1964 The Humanist in the Bathtub
1965 Birds of America
Published autobiography, Memoirs of a Catholic Girlhood, 1957; also known

Section 10 - American Authors   189

for nonfiction writing, e.g., Cannibals & Missionaries, 1979

1257
MCCULLERS, CARSON   1917-1967
1940 The Heart Is a Lonely Hunter
1941 Reflections in a Golden Eye
1946 The Member of the Wedding
1951 The Ballad of the Sad Cafe
1961 Clock without Hands

1258
MACDOUGALL, RUTH D.   1939-
1965 The Lilting House
1971 The Cost of Living
1971 One Minus One
1973 The Cheerleader
1976 Wife & Mother
1978 Aunt Pleasantine
1981 The Flowers of the Forest
1982 A Lovely Time Was Had by All

1259
MCGUANE, THOMAS   1939-
1969 The Sporting Club
1971 The Bushwacked Piano
1973 Ninety Two in the Shade
1978 Panama
1982 Nobody's Angel
1984 Something to Be Desired
1986 To Skin a Cat (SS)

1260
MCINERNEY, JAY   1955-
1984 Bright Lights, Big City
1985 Ransom
1988 The Story of My Life

1261
MACKENZIE, RACHEL   1909-1980
1970 Risk
1974 The Wine of Astonishment

1262
MCMURTRY, LARRY   1936-
1961 Horseman, Pass By
1962 Leaving Cheyenne
1966 The Last Picture Show
1970 Moving On
1972 All My Friends Are Going to Be Strangers
1978 Somebody's Darling
1982 Cadillac Jack
1983 The Desert Rose
1983 Terms of Endearment
1985 Lonesome Dove
1987 Texasville (Sequel to Last)
1988 Anything for Billy
See also WESTERNS, 0861

1263
MAILER, NORMAN   1923-
1948 The Naked & the Dead
1951 Barbary Shore
1955 The Deer Park
1965 An American Dream
1967 Why Are We in Viet Nam?
1971 Maidstone: A Mystery
1979 The Executioner's Song
1983 Ancient Evenings
1984 Tough Guys Don't Dance
Equally well known for nonfiction; e.g., The Armies of the Night, 1968
See also HISTORICAL FICTION, 1086

1264
MALAMUD, BERNARD   1914-1986
1952 The Natural
1957 The Assistant
1958 The Magic Barrel (SS)
1961 A New Life
1963 Idiots First (SS)
1966 The Fixer
1969 Pictures of Fidelman
1971 The Tenants
1973 Rembrandt's Hat
1979 Dubin's Lives
1982 God's Grace
1983 The Stories of Bernard Malamud (1950)

1265
MASON, BOBBIE ANN   1940-
1982 Shiloh (SS)
1985 In Country
1988 Spence + Lila

1266
MATTHIESSEN, PETER   1927-
1954 Race Rock
1955 Partisans
1965 At Play in the Fields of the Lord
1975 Far Tortuga
1986 On The River Styx (SS)
1987 Raditzer (1961)
Also writes nonfiction; e.g., The Snow Leopard, 1978

1267
MICHAELS, LEONARD   1933-
1969 Going Places (SS)
1975 I Would Have Saved Them If I Could (SS)
1981 The Men's Club

1268
MILLER, HENRY   1891-1980
1935 Tropic of Cancer
1936 Black Spring
1939 Tropic of Capricorn
1941 The Colossus of Maroussi

"The Rosy Crucifixion":
1949 Sexus (Book 1)
1950 Plexus (Book 2)
1950 Nexus (Book 3)

1269
MOJTABAI, A. G. (Ann Grace)   1938-
1974 Mundome
1976 The 400 Eels of Sigmund Freud
1979 A Stopping Place
1982 Autumn

1270
MORRISON, TONI   1931-
Black American
1969 The Bluest Eye
1973 Sula
1974 The Black Book
1977 Song of Solomon
1981 Tar Baby
1987 Beloved

1271
NABOKOV, VLADIMIR   1899-1977
Emigrated from Russia & began to write in English, then translated earlier works into English
1938 Laughter in the Dark (1936, Camera Obscura)
1941 The Real Life of Sebastian Knight
1947 Bend Sinister
1955 Lolita
1957 Pnin
1959 Invitation to a Beheading
1962 Pale Fire
1963 The Gift
1964 The Defense
1965 The Eye
1968 Despair (1937)
1968 King, Queen, Knave

1969 Ada, or Ardor: A Family Chronicle
1970 Mary
1971 Glory
1972 Transparent Things
1973 A Russian Beauty (SS)
1974 Look at the Harlequins!
1975 Tyrants Destroyed (SS)
1976 Details of a Sunset (SS)
1986 The Enchanter

1272
NAYLOR, GLORIA   1950-
Black American
1982 The Women of Brewster Place
1985 Linden Hills
1988 Mama Day

1273
NIN, ANAIS   1903-1977
Born in France
1945 This Hunger
1946 Ladders to Fire
1947 Children of the Albatross
1948 Under a Glass Bell (SS)
1950 The Four-Chambered Heart
1954 A Spy in the House of Love
1958 House of Incest (1936)
1961 Seduction of the Minotaur
1961 Winter of Artifice (1939)
1964 Collages
1970 Nuances
1972 Paris Revisited
1977 Delta of Venus
1977 Waste of Timelessness (SS)
1979 Little Birds: Erotica

1274
OATES, JOYCE CAROL   1938-
1963 By the North Gate (SS)
1964 With Shuddering Fall
1965 Them
1966 Upon the Sweeping Flood (SS)
1967 A Garden of Earthly Delights
1968 Expensive People
1971 Wonderland
1972 The Wheel of Love (SS)
1973 Marriage & Infidelities (SS)
1973 Scenes from American Life
1974 Do with Me What You Will
1974 The Goddess & Other Women (SS)
1974 The Hungry Ghosts (SS)
1975 The Assassins
1975 The Poisoned Kiss (SS)

1975 The Seduction (SS)
1976 Childwold
1976 Crossing the Border (SS)
1977 Night-Side
1977 The Triumph of the Spider Monkey
1978 All the Good People I've Left Behind
1978 Son of the Morning
1979 Cybele
1979 Unholy Loves
1980 Bellefleur
1981 Angel of Light
1981 A Sentimental Education (SS)
1982 A Bloodsmoor Romance
1984 Last Days (SS)
1984 Mysteries of Winterthurn
1985 Solstice
1986 Marya: A Life
1988 The Assignation (SS)

1275
O'CONNOR, EDWIN   1918-1968
1951 The Oracle
1956 The Last Hurrah
1957 Benjy
1961 The Edge of Sadness
1964 I Was Dancing
1966 All in the Family

1276
O'CONNOR, FLANNERY   1925-1965
1952 Wise Blood
1960 The Violent Bear It Away
1965 Everything That Rises Must Converge (SS)
1968 A Good Man Is Hard to Find (SS)
1971 The Complete Stories

1277
O'HARA, JOHN   1905-1970
1934 Appointment in Samarra
1935 Butterfield-8
1935 The Doctor's Son (SS)
1938 Hope of Heaven (SS)
1939 Files on Parade
1940 Pal Joey
1945 Pipe Night (SS)
1947 Hellbox (SS)
1949 A Rage to Live
1951 The Farmers Hotel
1955 Ten North Frederick
1956 A Family Party
1958 From the Terrace
1960 Ourselves to Know
1960 Sermons & Soda Water (SS)

1962 The Big Laugh
1962 The Cape Cod Lighter (SS)
1963 Elizabeth Appleton
1963 The Hat on the Bed (SS)
1964 The Horse Knows the Way
1965 The Lockwood Concern
1967 The Instrument
1967 Waiting for Winter (SS)
1969 Lovey Childs
1972 The Ewings
1972 The Time Element (SS)
1974 The Good Samaritan

1278
OZICK, CYNTHIA   1928-
1966 Trust
1971 The Pagan Rabbi (SS)
1976 Bloodshed (SS)
1981 Levitation: Five Fictions
1983 The Cannibal Galaxy
1987 The Messiah of Stockholm

1279
PALEY, GRACE   1922-
1959 The Little Disturbances of Man (SS)
1974 Enormous Changes at the Last Minute (SS)
1985 Later the Same Day (SS)

1280
PARENT, GAIL   1940-
1972 Sheila Levine Is Dead & Living in New York
1976 David Meyer Is a Mother
1980 The Best Laid Plans
1984 A Little Bit Married
1987 A Sign of the Eighties

1281
PERCY, WALKER   1916-
1961 The Moviegoer
1966 The Last Gentleman
1971 Love in the Ruins
1977 Lancelot
1980 The Second Coming
1987 The Thanatos Syndrome (Sequel to Love)

1282
PERRIN, URSULA   1935-
1967 Ghosts
1978 Heart Failures

1981 Unheard Music
1983 Old Devotions

1283
PETRAKIS, HARRY MARK   1923-
1959 Lion at My Heart
1963 The Odyssey of Kastas Volakis
1965 Pericles on Thirty-First Street (SS)
1966 A Dream of Kings
1969 The Waves of Night (SS)
1973 In the Land of Morning
1976 The Hour of the Bell
1978 A Petrakis Reader (SS)
1979 Nick the Greek
1983 Days of Vengence
Autobiography: Stelmark, 1970

1284
PHILLIPS, JAYNE ANNE   1952-
1976 Sweethearts
1978 Counting
1979 Black Tickets
1984 Machine Dreams
1987 Fast Lanes

1285
PIERCY, MARGE   1936-
1969 Going Down Fast
1971 Dance the Eagle to Sleep
1973 Small Changes
1976 Woman on the Edge of Time
1978 The High Cost of Living
1980 Vida
1982 Braided Lives
1984 Fly Away Home
1987 Gone to Soldiers

1286
PLANTE, DAVID   1940-
1970 The Ghost of Henry James
1971 Slides
1972 Relatives
1974 The Darkness of the Body
1976 Figures in Bright Air
1983 Difficult Women

"Francouer Family":
1978 The Family
1981 The Country
1982 The Woods
1984 The Foreigner
1985 The Catholic
1988 The Native

1287
PLATH, SYLVIA   1932-1963
1962 Johnny Panic & the Bible of Dreams (SS)
1963 The Bell Jar
Best known as a poet

1288
PORTER, KATHERINE ANNE   1890-1980
1921 My Chinese Marriage
1927 What Price Marriage
1930 Flowering Judas
1937 Noon Wine
1939 Pale Horse, Pale Rider
1944 The Leaning Tower (SS)
1952 The Days Before
1962 Ship of Fools
1967 A Christmas Story
1977 The Never Ending Wrong

1289
POTOK, CHAIM   1929-
1967 The Chosen
1969 The Promise
1972 My Name Is Asher Lev
1975 In the Beginning
1981 The Book of Lights
1985 Davita's Harp

1290
PRICE, RICHARD   1949-
1974 The Wanderers
1976 Bloodbrothers
1978 Ladies' Man
1983 The Breaks

1291
PURDY, JAMES   1923-
1956 Don't Call Me by My Right Name
1957 The Color of Darkness (SS)
1959 Malcolm
1960 The Nephew
1964 Cabot Wright Begins
1967 Eustace Chisholm & the Works
1967 An Oyster Is a Wealthy Beast
1972 I Am Elijah Thrush
1973 Sunshine Is an Only Child
1977 A Day after the Fair
1977 In a Shallow Grave
1979 Narrow Rooms
1981 Mourners Below
1984 On Glory's Course
1986 The Candles of Your Eyes (SS)
1986 In the Hollow of His Hand

Section 10 - American Authors

"Sleepers in Moon-Crowned Valleys":
1970 Jeremy's Version
1974 The House of Solitary Maggot

1292
PYNCHON, THOMAS   1937-
1963 V
1966 The Crying of Lot 49
1973 Gravity's Rainbow
1984 Slow Learner (SS)

1293
RAND, AYN   1905-1982
Born in Russia
Real name: Alice Rosenbaum
1936 We the Living
1941 Night of January 16th
1943 The Fountainhead
1946 Anthem
1957 Atlas Shrugged
1984 The Early Ayn Rand (SS)
See also SCIENCE FICTION, 0705

1294
REBETA-BURDITT, JOYCE
1977 The Cracker Factory
1981 Triplets

1295
REED, ISHMAEL   1938-
Black American
1967 The Free-Lance Pallbearers
1969 Yellow Black Radio Broke-Down
1972 Mumbo Jumbo
1974 The Last Days of Louisiana Red
1976 Flight to Canada
1978 Shrovetide in Old New Orleans
1982 The Terrible Twos
1986 Reckless Eyeballing

1296
REED, KIT
1961 Mother Isn't Dead, She's Only Sleeping
1964 At War as Children
1967 The Better Part
1970 Armed Camps
1971 Cry of the Daughter
1973 Mister Da V. (SS)
1973 Tiger Rag
1976 Captain Grownup
1979 The Ballad of T. Rantula
1980 Magic Time

1981 Other Stories & The Attack of the Giant Baby
1985 Fort Privilege
1986 The Revenge of the Senior Citizens (SS)
1987 Catholic Girls

1297
REVELEY, EDITH
1976 The Etruscan Couple (SS)
1979 A Pause for Breath
1980 Skin Deep (SS)
1983 In Good Faith

1298
RICE, ANNE   1941-
Also writes as Anne Rampling
1976 Interview with the Vampire
1980 The Feast of All Saints
1982 Cry to Heaven
1985 The Vampire Lestat
1988 The Queen of the Damned
See also HORROR, 0208

1299
ROBBINS, TOM   1936-
1971 Another Roadside Attraction
1976 Even Cowgirls Get the Blues
1980 Still Life with Woodpecker
1984 Jitterbug Perfume

1300
ROIPHE, ANNE RICHARDSON   1935-
1967 Digging Out
1970 Up the Sandbox!
1974 Long Division
1977 Torch Song
1987 Loving Kindness

1301
ROSSNER, JUDITH   1935-
1966 To the Precipice
1969 Nine Months in the Life of an Old Maid
1972 Any Minute I Can Split
1975 Looking for Mr. Goodbar
1977 Attachments
1980 Emmeline
1983 August

1302
ROTH, PHILIP   1933-
1959 Goodbye, Columbus (SS)

1962 Letting Go
1967 When She Was Good
1969 On the Air
1969 Portnoy's Complaint
1971 Our Gang
1972 The Breast
1973 The Great American Novel
1974 My Life as a Man
1977 The Professor of Desire

"The Zukerman Books":
1979 The Ghost Writer
1981 Zukerman Unbound
1983 The Anatomy Lesson
1985 Zukerman Bound
1986 The Counterlife

1303
RULE, JANE   1931-
1964 Desert of the Heart
1970 This Is Not for You
1971 Against the Season
1975 Theme for Diverse Instruments
1977 The Young in One Another's Arms
1980 Contract with the World
1981 Outlander (SS)
1985 A Hot-Eyed Moderate
1985 Inland Passage (SS)
1987 Memory Board

1304
SALINGER, J. D.   1919-
1951 The Catcher in the Rye
1953 Nine Stories
1961 Franny & Zooey
1963 Raise High the Roof Beam, Carpenter & Seymour, An Introduction

1305
SANCHEZ, THOMAS   1944-
1973 Rabbit Boss
1978 Zoot-Suit Murders

1306
SARTON, MAY   1912-
1938 The Single Hound
1946 The Bridge of Years
1950 Shadow of a Man
1952 A Shower of Summer Days
1957 The Birth of a Grandfather
1957 The Fur Person
1961 The Small Room
1963 Joanna & Ulysses

1965 Mrs. Stevens Hears the Mermaids Singing
1966 Miss Pickthorn & Mr. Hair
1969 The Poet & the Donkey
1970 Kinds of Love
1972 Faithful Are the Wounds (1955)
1973 As We Are Now
1975 Crucial Conversations
1978 A Reckoning
1982 Anger
1985 The Magnificent Spinster

1307
SAVAGE, THOMAS   1926-
1944 The Pass
1948 Lona Hanson
1953 A Bargain with God
1961 Trust in Chariots
1967 The Power of the Dog
1969 The Liar
1970 Daddy's Girl
1972 And Now a Word from Our Creator
1974 A Strange God
1976 Midnight Line
1977 I Heard My Sister Speak My Name
1981 Her Side of It
1983 For Mary, with Love
1988 The Corner of Rife & Pacific

1308
SAYLES, JOHN   1950
1956 Bang the Drum Slowly
1975 Pride of the Bimbos
1977 Union Dues
1979 The Anarchists' Convention

1309
SCHAEFFER, SUSAN FROMBERG   1941-
1973 Falling
1974 Anya
1978 Time in Its Flight
1979 The Blue Man
1980 Love
1980 The Queen of Egypt (SS)
1983 The Madness of a Seduced Woman
1985 Mainland
1986 The Injured Party
Also a poet
See also HISTORICAL FICTION, 1096

1310
SCHWAMM, ELLEN

Section 10 - American Authors

1978 Adjacent Lives
1983 How He Saved Her

1311
SCHWARTZ, LYNNE SHARON 1939-
1980 Rough Strife
1981 Balancing Acts
1983 The Accounting
1983 Disturbances in the Field
1984 Acquainted with the Night (SS)
1987 The Melting Pot (SS)

1312
SELBY, HUBERT, JR. 1928-
1964 Last Exit to Brooklyn
1971 The Room
1977 The Demon
1978 Requiem for a Dream
1986 Song of the Silent Snow

1313
SETTLE, MARY LEE 1918-
1954 The Love Eaters
1955 The Kiss of Kin
1966 All the Brave Promises
1971 The Clam Shell
1977 Blood Tie
1986 Celebration

"Beulah Quintet":
1956 O Beulah Land (2)
1960 Know Nothing (3)
1964 Fight Night on a Sweet Saturday (5)
1973 Prisons (1)
1980 The Scapegoat (4)
1982 The Killing Ground (5) (Revision of Fight)

1314
SHANGE, NTOZAKE 1948-
Black American
1976 Sassafrass, Cypress & Indigo
1985 Betsey Brown
Best known as a playwright & a poet

1315
SHAW, IRWIN 1913-1984
1936 Bury the Dead
1939 The Gentle People
1939 Sailor Off the Bremen (SS)
1942 Welcome to the City (SS)
1946 Act of Faith (SS)
1946 The Assassins
1948 The Young Lions
1950 Mixed Company
1951 The Troubled Air
1956 Lucy Crown
1957 Tip on a Dead Jockey (SS)
1960 Two Weeks in Another Town
1964 In the Company of Dolphins
1965 Voices of a Summer Day
1965 Love on a Dark Street (SS)
1969 Rich Man, Poor Man
1972 God Was Here, But He Left Early (SS)
1973 Evening in Byzantium
1975 Nightwork
1977 Beggarman, Thief (Sequel to Rich)
1979 The Top of the Hill
1981 Bread upon the Waters
1982 Acceptable Losses
See also HISTORICAL FICTION, 1097

1316
SHEED, WILFRID 1930-
1960 A Middle-Class Education
1963 The Hack
1965 Square's Progress
1966 Office Politics
1968 The Blacking Factory Pennsylvania Gothic
1970 Max Jamison
1973 People Will Always Be Kind
1977 Transatlantic Blues
1987 The Boys of Winter

1317
SHEEHY, GAIL 1937-
1970 Lovesounds
1971 Speed Is of the Essence
Best known for nonfiction; e.g., Passages, 1976

1318
SHULMAN, ALIX KATES 1932-
1972 Memoirs of an Ex-Prom Queen
1978 Burning Question
1981 On the Stroll
1987 In Every Woman's Life . . .

1319
SINGER, ISAAC BASHEVIS 1904-
Born in Poland; writes in Yiddish
Nobel Prize, 1978
1950 The Family Moskat
1955 Satan in Goray (SS) (1935)
1957 Gimpel the Fool (SS)

1960 The Magician of Lublin
1961 The Spinoza of Market Street (SS)
1962 The Slave
1964 Short Friday (SS)
1966 In My Father's Court
1967 The Manor
1968 The Seance (SS)
1969 The Estate
1970 A Friend of Kafka (SS)
1972 Enemies: A Love Story
1973 A Crown of Feathers (SS)
1975 Passions (SS)
1978 Shosha
1979 Old Love (SS)
1980 Reaches of Heaven
1983 The Penitent
1983 Yentl, the Yeshiva Boy
1985 The Image (SS)
1988 The Death of Methuselah (SS)
1988 The King of the Fields

1320
SONTAG, SUSAN   1933-
1963 The Benefactor
1967 Death Kit
1978 I, Etcetera (SS)
Best known as a critic.

1321
SORRENTINO, GILBERT   1929-
1966 The Sky Changes
1970 Steelwork
1971 Imaginative Qualities of Actual Things
1973 Splendide Hotel
1979 Mulligan Stew
1980 Aberration of Starlight
1981 Crystal Vision
1983 Blue Pastoral

1322
SOUTHERN, TERRY   1926-
1958 Flash & Filigree
1959 Candy
1959 The Magic Christian
1967 Red-Dirt Marijuana
1970 Blue Movie

1323
STONE, ROBERT   1937-
1967 A Hall of Mirrors
1974 Dog Soldiers
1981 A Flag for Sunrise
1986 Children of Light

1324
STORM, HYEMEYOHSTS   1935-
Native American
1971 The Magnifying Glass
1972 Seven Arrows
1981 Song of Heyoehkah

1325
STYRON, WILLIAM   1925-
The Pulitzer Prize for The Confessions of Nat Turner and Sophie's Choice
1951 Lie Down in Darkness
1957 The Long March
1960 Set This House on Fire
1967 The Confessions of Nat Turner
1979 Sophie's Choice
See also HISTORICAL FICTION, 0939

1326
TALLENT, ELIZABETH   1908-
1983 In Constant Flight (SS)
1985 Museum Pieces
1987 Time with Children (SS)

1327
THEROUX, PAUL   1941-
Lives in London
1967 Waldo
1968 Fong & the Indians
1969 Girls at Play
1969 Murder in Mount Holly
1971 Jungle Lovers
1972 Sinning with Annie (SS)
1973 Saint Jack
1974 The Black House
1976 The Family Arsenal
1977 The Consul's File (SS)
1978 Picture Palace
1980 World's End (SS)
1982 The Mosquito Coast
1983 The London Embassy (SS)
1984 Doctor Slaughter
1984 Half Moon Street
1986 O-Zone
Also writes nonfiction; e, g., The Great Railway Bazaar, 1975, & The Old Patagonian Express, 1979

1328
TOOLE, JOHN KENNEDY   1937-1969
1980 A Confederacy of Dunces

1329
TYLER, ANNE   1941-

Section 10 - American Authors

1964 If Morning Ever Comes
1965 The Tin Can Tree
1970 A Slipping-Down Life
1972 The Clock Winder
1974 Celestial Navigation
1976 Searching for Caleb
1977 Earthly Possessions
1980 Morgan's Passing
1982 Dinner at the Homesick Restaurant
1985 The Accidental Tourist
1988 Breathing Lessons

1330
UPDIKE, JOHN   1932-
1959 The Poorhouse Fair
1959 The Same Door (SS)
1962 Pigeon Feathers (SS)
1963 The Centaur
1964 Olinger Stories: A Selection
1965 Of the Farm
1966 The Music School (SS)
1968 Couples
1972 Museums & Women (SS)
1973 Warm Wine: An Idyll
1975 A Month of Sundays
1976 Marry Me
1978 The Coup
1979 Problems (SS)
1979 Too Far to Go: The Maple Stories
1984 The Witches of Eastwick
1986 Roger's Version
1987 Trust Me (SS)
1988 S.

"Rabbit Angstrom":
1960 Rabbit, Run
1971 Rabbit Redux
1981 Rabbit Is Rich

"Bech":
1970 Bech: A Book
1982 Bech Is Back (SS)

1331
VIDAL, GORE   1925-
Also writes as Edgar Box
1946 Williwaw
1947 In a Yellow Wood
1948 The City & the Pillar
1949 The Season of Comfort
1950 A Search for the King
1950 Dark Green, Bright Red
1952 The Judgment of Paris
1954 Messiah
1956 A Thirsty Evil (SS)
1964 Julian

1967 Washington, D.C.
1968 Myra Breckenridge
1970 Two Sisters: A Memoir in the Form of a Novel
1973 Burr
1974 Myron (Sequel to Myra)
1976 1876 (Sequel to Burr)
1978 Kalki
1981 Creation
1983 Duluth
1984 Lincoln
See also SCIENCE FICTION, 0729; HISTORICAL FICTION, 0941; MYSTERIES, 0407 as BOX, EDGAR

1332
VONNEGUT, KURT, JR.   1922-
1952 Player Piano
1959 The Sirens of Titan
1961 Canary in a Cathouse (SS)
1962 Mother Night
1963 Cat's Cradle
1965 God Bless You, Mr. Rosewater
1968 Welcome to the Monkey House (SS)
1969 Slaughterhouse-5
1971 Happy Birthday, Wanda June
1973 Breakfast of Champions
1976 Slapstick
1979 Jailbird
1982 Deadeye Dick
1985 Galapagos
1987 Bluebeard
Also writes nonfiction; e.g., Palm Sunday, 1981
See also SCIENCE FICTION, 0730 & HISTORICAL FICTION, 1103

1333
WALKER, ALICE   1944-
Black American
1970 The Third Life of Grange Copeland
1973 In Love & Trouble: Stories of Black Women (SS)
1976 Meridian
1981 You Can't Keep a Good Woman Down (SS)
1982 The Color Purple
Also writes poetry; e.g., Horses Make a Landscape Look More Beautiful, 1985

1334
WEINGARTEN, VIOLET   1915-1976
1968 Mrs. Beneker
1969 A Loving Wife

1975 A Woman of Feeling
1976 Half a Marriage
1978 Intimations of Mortality

1335
WELTY, EUDORA   1909-
1941 A Curtain of Green (SS)
1942 The Robber Bridegroom
1943 The Wide Net (SS)
1946 Delta Wedding
1948 Music from Spain
1949 The Golden Apples (SS)
1954 The Ponder Heart
1955 The Bride of Inisfallen (SS)
1964 The Shoe Bird
1970 Losing Battles
1971 One Time, One Place
1972 The Optimist's Daughter
1980 Collected Stories

1336
WHARTON, WILLIAM   1925-
1978 Birdy
1981 Dad
1982 A Midnight Clear
1983 Scumbler
1985 Pride
1987 Tidings

1337
WIDEMAN, JOHN EDGAR   1941-
Black American
1967 A Glance Away
1970 Hurry Home
1981 Damballah
1981 Hiding Place
1983 Sent for You Yesterday
1986 The Lynchers
1987 Reuben
Also writes nonfiction; e.g., Brothers & Keepers, 1985

1338
WILLIS, MEREDITH SUE   1946-
1979 A Space Apart
1981 Higher Ground
1985 Only Great Changes

1339
WOIWODE, LARRY   1941-
1969 What I'm Going to Do I Think
1975 Beyond the Bedroom Wall
1981 Poppa John
1988 Born Brother (Sequel to Beyond)

1340
WOUK, HERMAN   1915-
1947 Aurora Dawn
1948 The City Boy
1955 Marjorie Morningstar
1962 Youngblood Hawke
1965 Don't Stop the Carnival
1966 The Caine Mutiny
1971 The Winds of War
1978 War & Remembrance (Sequel to Winds)
1985 Inside, Outside
See also HISTORICAL FICTION, 1108

1341
WRIGHT, RICHARD   1908-1960
Black American
1938 Uncle Tom's Children (SS)
1940 Native Son
1945 Black Boy
1953 The Outsider
1954 Savage Holiday
1958 The Long Dream
1961 Eight Men (SS)
1963 Lawd Today
1971 The Man Who Lived Underground

1342
YATES, RICHARD   1926-
1961 Revolutionary Road
1962 Eleven Kinds of Loneliness (SS)
1969 A Special Providence
1975 Disturbing the Peace
1976 The Easter Parade
1978 A Good School
1981 Liars in Love (SS)
1984 Young Hearts Crying
1986 Cold Spring Harbor
See also HISTORICAL FICTION, 1110

1343
YGELSIAS, HELEN   1915-
1972 How She Died
1976 Family Feeling
1981 Sweetsir
1987 Saviors

SECTION ELEVEN

AUTHORS OF THE BRITISH ISLES

OVERVIEW

Authors included in this section were born or have lived in the British Isles and their works have received some measure of critical acclaim from reviewers and literary critics. In addition, these authors have been published in American editions and become known to American readers.

In a tradition begun with the Brontes, George Eliot, and Jane Austen, women authors play a role of first importance in British fiction. The British Isles are particularly well represented by women who write in a variety of styles with a range of themes: Beryl Bainbridge, Lynne Reid Banks, Nina Bawden, Caroline Blackwood, Elizabeth Bowen, Brigid Brophy, Ivy Compton-Burnett, Margaret Drabble, Daphne Du Maurier, Nell Dunn, Penelope Gilliatt, Rummer Godden, Margaret Lane, Olivia Manning, Penelope Mortimer, Iris Murdoch, Mary Renault, Bernice Rubens, Muriel Spark, Elizabeth Taylor and Fay Weldon.

Doris Lessing has had a particularly large following among American women. Among the newer women authors are Anita Brookner, who won the Booker Prize, and Alice Thomas Ellis. Barbara Pym, who wrote in the 1940s, 50s, and 60s, began to be published in this country in the 1980s, and she has developed a very devoted following. Jean Rhys, an older author, also achieved success in the late 1970s.

The Irish authors, again well represented by women, include Benedict Kiely, Edna O'Brien, Frank O'Connor, Julia O'Faolain, Sean O'Faolain, and Tracy Honor; short stories are an important part of their work. Immigrants to Britain have achieved great critical success, especially V.S. Naipaul, who was born in Trinidad. It should be noted that Salman Rushdie, who is an Indian writer currently living in London, became instantly known for his work *The Satanic Verses* after it was condemned by the Muslims.

A group of writers and playwrights in the late 1950s became known as "the angry young men" because they focused on the plight of the working classes and presented it in stark realism: among them were Kingsley Amis, John Braine, and Alan Sillitoe. Several British writers are well known for groups of related books: Anthony Burgess for "Enderby" and "The Long Day Wanes," Laurence Durrell for "The Alexandria Quartet" and "The Avignon Quintet," Anthony Powell for "A Dance to the Music of Time," and Paul Scott for "The Raj Quartet." Two immensely popular authors in the United States are Graham Greene and John Fowles.

The most prestigious literary prize awarded to a novel published in Great Britain is the Booker Prize for Fiction; it is given by the Book Trust. William Golding won the Nobel Prize in 1983.

REFERENCE AND BIBLIOGRAPHIC SOURCES

Adelman, Irving and Rita Dworkin. *The Contemporary Novel; A Checklist of Critical Literature on the British and American Novel since 1945.* Metuchen, NJ: Scarecrow Press, 1972.

Burgess, Anthony. *99 Novels: The Best in English since 1939, a Personal Choice.* New York: Summit Books, 1984.

Kaplan, Fred, ed. *The Reader's Adviser: A Layman's Guide to Literature,* 13th ed. Volume I: The Best in American and British Fiction. . . . New York: Bowker, 1986

Rosa, Alfred F. and Paul A. Eschholz. *Contemporary Fiction in America and England, 1950-1970: A Guide to Information Sources.* Detroit: Gale, 1976.

Somer, John and Barbara Eck Cooper. *American and British Literature, 1945-1975: An Annotated Bibliography of Contemporary Scholarship.* Lawrence, Regents Press of Kansas, 1980.

Stanton, Robert J. *A Bibliography of Modern British Novelists.* Troy, NY: Whitston, 1978.

AUTHORS AND TITLES

1344
ADAMS, RICHARD   1920-
1972 Watership Down
1974 Shardik
1978 The Plague Dogs
1970 The Girl in a Swing
1984 Maia
1988 Traveller
See also HORROR, 0150 & SCIENCE FICTION, 0740

1345
AMIS, KINGSLEY,   1922-
Also writes as Robert Markham
1954 Lucky Jim
1955 That Uncertain Feeling
1958 I Like It Here
1960 Take a Girl Like You
1962 My Enemy's Enemy (SS)
1963 One Fat Englishman
1966 The Anti-Death League
1969 I Want It Now
1969 The Green Man
1971 Girl, 20
1972 Dear Illusion (SS)
1973 The Riverside Villas Murder
1974 Ending Up
1977 The Alteration
1978 Jake's Things
1984 Stanley & the Women
1987 The Old Devils

1346
BAINBRIDGE, BERYL   1933-
1968 Another Part of the Wood
1973 Harriet Said . . .
1973 The Secret Glass
1974 The Bottle Factory Outing
1975 Sweet William
1977 A Quiet Life
1978 Injury Time
1979 Young Adolph
1981 Winter Garden
1982 A Weekend with Claud
1984 Watson's Apology
1987 Mum & Mr. Armitage (SS)
See also HORROR, 0154

1347
BANKS, LYNNE REID   1929-
1961 The L-Shaped Room
1962 House of Hope

1969 Children at the Gate
1971 The Backward Shadow (Sequel to L)
1973 One More River
1974 Two Is Lonely (Sequel to Backward)
1977 Dark Quartet
1978 Path to the Silent Country
1981 Defy the Wilderness
1987 Casualities
Also writes for juveniles

1348
BAWDEN, NINA   1925-
Real name: Nina Mary Kark
1953 Eyes of Green
1955 The Odd Flamingo
1956 The Solitary Child
1957 Change Here for Babylon
1957 Devil by the Sea
1960 Glass Slippers Always Pinch
1961 In Honour Bound
1963 Tortoise by Candlelight
1964 Under the Skin
1966 A Little Love, A Little Learning
1967 A Woman of My Age
1968 The Grain of Truth
1970 The Birds on the Trees
1972 Anna Apparent
1974 George Beneath a Paper Moon
1977 Afternoon of a Good Woman
1979 Familiar Passions
1981 Walking Naked
1983 The Ice House
1987 Circles of Deceit
Also writes for juveniles

1349
BLACKWOOD, CAROLINE   1931-
1973 For All That I Found There (SS)
1976 The Stepdaughter
1977 Great Granny Webster
1981 The Fate of Mary Rose
1985 Corrigan

1350
BOWEN, ELIZABETH   1899-1973
1923 Encounters (SS)
1927 The Hotel
1928 Ann Lee's (SS)
1929 The Last September
1931 Friends & Relations

1932 To the North
1933 The Cat Jumps (SS)
1935 The House in Paris
1939 The Death of the Heart
1941 Look at All Those Roses (SS)
1946 Ivy Gripped the Steps (SS)
1948 The Heat of the Day
1955 A World of Love
1963 The Little Girls
1965 A Day in the Dark (SS)
1968 Eva Trout or Changing Scenes
1972 Joining Charles (SS) (1929)
1975 Pictures & Conversations

1351
BRAINE, JOHN   1922-
1957 Room at the Top
1960 From the Hand of the Hunter
1962 Life at the Top
1965 The Jealous God
1968 The Crying Game
1970 The View from Tower Hill
1972 The Queen of a Distant Country
1975 The Pious Agent
1977 Finger of Five
1980 Waiting for Sheila

1352
BROOKNER, ANITA   1938-
1981 The Debut
1982 Providence
1983 Look at Me
1984 Hotel du Lac
1985 Family & Friends
1987 A Misalliance
1988 A Friend from England

1353
BROPHY, BRIGID   1929-
Ireland
1953 The Crown Princess (SS)
1953 Hackenfeller's Ape
1957 The King of a Rainy Country
1963 Flesh
1963 The Finishing Touch
1964 The Snow Ball
1970 In Transit
1974 The Adventures of God in His Search for the Black Girl
1978 Palace without Chairs: A Baroque Novel

1354
BURGESS, ANTHONY   1917-
1960 The Right to an Answer
1960 The Doctor Is Sick
1961 Devil of a State
1961 One Hand Clapping
1961 The Worm & the Ring
1962 The Wanting Seed
1962 A Clockwork Orange
1963 Honey for the Bears
1964 The Eve of Saint Venus
1964 Nothing Like the Sun
1965 A Vision of Battlements
1966 Tremor of Intent
1971 MF
1974 Napoleon Symphony
1976 Beard's Roman Women
1977 Abba, Abba
1978 1985
1979 Man of Nazareth
1980 Earthly Powers
1983 The End of the World News
1985 The Kingdom of the Wicked
1986 The Pianoplayers

"Enderby":
1963 Inside Mr. Enderby
1968 Enderby Outside
1974 The Clockwork Testament, or Enderby End
1984 Enderby's Dark Lady, or No End to Enderby

"The Long Day Wanes":
1956 Time for a Tiger
1958 The Enemy in the Blanket
1959 Beds in the East
Also writes for juveniles
See also SCIENCE FICTION, 0613

1355
COMPTON-BURNETT, IVY   1892-1969
1911 Dolores
1925 Pastors & Masters
1930 Brothers & Sisters
1931 Men & Wives
1933 More Women than Men
1935 A House & Its Head
1937 Daughters & Sons
1939 A Family & a Fortune
1941 Parents & Children
1944 Elders & Better
1947 Manservant & Maidservant
1949 Two Worlds & Their Ways
1951 Darkness & Day
1954 The Present & the Past
1956 Mother & Son
1958 A Father & His Fate
1960 A Heritage & Its History
1962 The Mighty & Their Fall
1963 A God & His Gifts

Section 11 - Authors Of The British Isles

1971 The Last & the First

1356
DRABBLE, MARGARET   1939-
1964 A Summer Bird-Cage
1965 The Garrick Year
1966 The Millstone
1967 Jerusalem the Golden
1969 The Waterfall
1972 The Needle's Eye
1975 The Realms of Gold
1977 The Ice Age
1980 The Middle Ground
1987 The Radiant Way

1357
DU MAURIER, DAPHNE   1907-1989
1931 The Loving Spirit
1932 I'll Never Be Young Again
1933 The Progress of Julius
1936 Jamaica Inn
1938 Rebecca
1940 Come Wind, Come Weather (SS)
1941 Frenchman's Creek
1943 Hungry Hill
1946 The King's General
1950 The Parasites
1952 The Apple Tree (SS)
1952 My Cousin Rachel
1954 Mary Anne
1957 The Scapegoat
1959 The Breaking Point (SS)
1962 Castle d'Or
1963 The Glassblowers
1965 The Flight of the Falcon
1969 The House on the Strand
1971 Don't Look Now (SS)
1972 Rule Britannia
1976 Echoes from the Macabre (SS)
1976 The Winding Stair
1980 The Rebecca Notebook (SS)
1980 The Rendez-vous (SS)
See also ROMANCES, 0041; HORROR, 0171; HISTORICAL FICTION, 0969

1358
DUNN, NELL   1936-
Real name: Nell Mary Sanford
1963 Up the Junction (SS)
1967 Poor Cow
1971 The Incurable
1972 I Want
1975 Tear His Head Off His Shoulder
1976 Living Like I Do

1359
DURRELL, LAURENCE   1912-
1935 Pied Piper of Lovers
1958 The Dark Labyrinth (1947, Cefalû)
1960 The Black Book

"The Alexandria Quartet":
1957 Justine
1958 Balthazar
1958 Mountolive
1960 Clea

"The Avignon Quintet":
1974 Monsieur (2)
1979 Livia, or, Buried Alive (1)
1982 Constance, or, Solitary Practices (3)
1983 Sebastian, or, Ruling Passions (4)
1985 Quinx, or, the Ripper's Tale (5)

"The Revolt of Aphrodite":
1968 Tunc
1970 Nunquam

1360
ELLIS, ALICE THOMAS   1932-
1977 The Sin Eater
1981 The Birds of the Air
1983 Mrs. Donald
1983 The Other Side of the Fire
1987 Unexplained Laughter

1361
FOWLES, JOHN   1926-
1963 The Collector
1969 The French Lieutenant's Woman
1974 The Ebony Tower
1977 Daniel Martin
1978 The Magus, rev. (1966)
1985 A Maggot

1362
GILLIATT, PENELOPE   1932-
1965 One By One
1968 A State of Change
1969 Come Back If It Doesn't Get Better (SS)
1972 Nobody's Business (SS)
1977 Splendid Lives (SS)
1979 The Cutting Edge
1983 Mortal Matters
1986 22 Stories

1363
GODDER, RUMER 1907-
1936 Chinese Puzzle
1938 The Lady & the Unicorn
1939 Black Narcissus
1940 Gypsy, Gypsy
1942 Breakfast with the Nikolides
1945 Bengal Journey
1945 Take Three Tenses: A Fugue in Time
1946 The River
1947 The Doll's House
1948 A Candle for St. Jude
1950 A Breath of Air
1951 The Mousewife
1953 Kingfishers Catch Fire
1955 An Episode of Sparrows
1956 The Fairy Doll
1957 Mouse House
1958 The Greengage Summer
1958 The Story of Holly & Ivy
1960 Candy Floss
1961 China Court: The Hours of a Country House
1963 The Battle of the Villa Fiorita
1964 Home Is the Sailor
1967 The Kitchen Madonna
1968 Gone: A Thread of Stories (SS)
1969 In This House of Brede
1972 The Diddakoi
1975 The Peacock Spring
1979 Five for Sorrow, Five for Joy

1364
GOLDING, WILLIAM 1911-
Nobel Prize, 1983
1954 Lord of the Flies
1955 The Inheritors
1960 Free Fall
1964 The Spire
1965 The Hot Gates
1966 Pincher Martin (The Two Deaths of Christopher Martin)
1967 The Pyramid
1971 The Scorpion God (SS)
1979 Darkness Visible
1980 Rites of Passage
1984 The Paper Men

1365
GREENE, GRAHAM 1904-
1929 The Man Within
1930 The Name of Action
1931 Rumour of Nightfall
1932 The Orient Express
1934 It's A Battlefield
1935 Basement Room (SS)

1935 England Made Me
1935 The Bear Fell Free
1936 This Gun for Hire
1938 Brighton Rock
1939 Another Mexico
1939 The Confidential Agent
1943 The Ministry of Fear
1946 The Power & the Glory
1947 Nineteen Stories
1948 The Heart of the Matter
1950 The Third Man
1951 The End of the Affair
1953 The Shipwrecked
1955 Loser Take All
1955 The Quiet American
1958 Our Man in Havanna
1959 A Visit to Moran (SS)
1961 A Burnt-Out Case
1962 The Destructors (SS)
1963 A Sense of Reality (SS)
1966 The Comedians
1967 May We Borrow Your Husband & Other Comedies of the Sexual Life (SS)
1969 Papa Doc
1969 Travels with My Aunt
1973 The Honorary Consul
1977 The Human Factor
1980 Doctor Fischer of Geneva
1982 Monsignor Quixote
1988 The Captain & the Enemy
See also SPY STORIES, 0367

1366
HUGHES, RICHARD 1900-1976
1926 A Moment of Time (SS)
1929 The Innocent Voyage (A High Wind in Jamaica)
1930 Burial & the Dark Child
1938 In Hazard
1961 The Fox in the Attic
1979 In the Lap of Atlas: Stories of Morocco

1367
KIELY, BENEDICT 1919-
Ireland
1946 Land without Stars
1949 In a Harbour Green
1950 Call for a Miracle
1952 Honey Seems Bitter
1953 The Cards of the Gambler
1955 There Was an Ancient House
1960 The Captain with the Whiskers
1963 A Journey to the Seven Streams (SS)
1968 Dogs Enjoy the Morning

Section 11 - Authors Of The British Isles

1973 A Ball of Malt & Madame Butterfly (SS)
1978 A Cow in the House (SS)
1980 Proxopera
1980 The State of Ireland (SS)
1985 Nothing Ever Happens in Carmincross
1988 A Letter to Peachtree (SS)

1368
LANE, MARGARET   1907-
1935 Faith, Hope, No Charity
1937 At Last the Island
1941 Walk into My Parlor
1944 Where Helen Lies
1963 Life with Ionides
1965 A Night at Sea
1966 A Smell of Burning
1968 The Day of the Feast

1369
LESSING, DORIS   1919-
Born in Rhodesia
Also writes as Jane Somers
1950 The Grass Is Singing
1952 This Was the Old Chief's Country (SS)
1956 Retreat to Innocence
1957 Going Home
1962 The Golden Notebook
1963 A Man & Two Women (SS)
1964 African Stories (SS)
1971 Briefing for a Descent into Hell
1972 The Temptation of Jack Orkney (SS)
1973 The Summer before the Dark
1974 The Habit of Loving (SS)
1975 Memoirs of a Survivor
1985 The Good Terrorist

"The Children of Violence":
1952 Martha Quest
1954 A Proper Marriage
1958 A Ripple from the Storm
1966 Landlocked
1969 The Four-Gated City

"Canopus in Argos":
1979 Shikasta: Canopus in Argos Archives
1980 The Marriages between Zones Three, Four & Five
1981 The Sirian Experiments
1982 The Making of the Representative for Planet 8

1983 Documents Relating to the Sentimental Agents in the Volyen Empire
See also SCIENCE FICTION, 0673

1370
LLEWELLYN, RICHARD   1906-1983
Wales
"Valley":
1945 How Green Was My Valley
1960 Up into the Swinging Mountains
1966 Down Where the Moon Is Small
1975 Green, Green My Valley Now
See also HISTORICAL FICTION, 1083

1371
LOWRY, MALCOLM   1909-1957
1933 Ultramarine
1947 Under the Volcano
1961 Hear Us O Lord from Heaven Thy Dwelling Place (SS)
1963 Lunar Caustic
1968 Dark as the Grave Wherein My Friend Is Laid
1970 October Ferry to Gabriola

1372
MACINNES, COLIN   1914-1976
1950 To the Victor the Spoils
1952 June in Her Spring
1966 All Day Saturday
1969 Westward to Laughter
1970 Three Years to Play
1974 Out of the Garden

"The London Novels":
1957 City of Spades
1959 Absolute Beginners
1960 Mr. Love & Justice
See also HISTORICAL FICTION, 0996

1373
MANNING, OLIVIA   1915-1980
1938 The Wind Changes
1947 The Reluctant Rescue
1948 Growing Up (SS)
1949 Artist Among the Missing
1951 School for Love
1953 A Different Face
1955 The Doves of Venus
1956 My Husband Cartwright (SS)
1967 Extraordinary Cats
1967 A Romantic Hero (SS)

1969 The Play Room
1974 The Rain Forest

"The Balkan Trilogy":
1961 The Great Fortune
1962 The Spoilt City
1966 Friends & Heroes

"The Levant Trilogy":
(Sequel to "The Balkan Trilogy")
1977 The Danger Tree
1979 The Battle Lost & Won
1981 The Sum of the Thing
See also HISTORICAL FICTION, 1087

1374
MORTIMER, PENELOPE 1918-
Wales
Also writes as Penelope Dimont & Ann Temple
1947 Johanna
1954 A Villa in Summer
1956 The Bright Prison
1959 A Cave of Ice
1960 Saturday Lunch with the Brownings (SS)
1963 The Pumpkin Eater
1967 My Friends Say It's Bullet-Proof
1971 The Home
1974 Long Distance
1985 The Handyman

1375
MURDOCH, IRIS 1919-
Born in Ireland
1954 Under the Net
1956 The Flight from the Enchanter
1957 The Sandcastle
1958 The Bell
1961 A Severed Head
1962 An Unofficial Rose
1963 The Unicorn
1964 The Italian Girl
1965 The Red & the Green
1966 The Time of the Angels
1968 The Nice & the Good
1969 Bruno's Dream
1970 A Fairly Honorable Defeat
1971 An Accidental Man
1973 The Black Prince
1974 The Sacred & Profane Love Machine
1975 A Word Child
1977 Henry & Cato
1978 The Sea, the Sea
1980 Nuns & Soldiers
1983 The Philosopher's Pupil

1985 The Good Apprentice
1988 The Book & the Brotherhood

1376
NAIPAUL, V. S. (Vidiadhar Surajprasad)
1932-
Born in Trinidad
1957 The Mystic Masseur
1958 The Suffrage of Elvira
1959 Miguel Street
1963 Mr. Stone & the Knight's Companion
1967 The Mimic Men
1968 A Flag on the Island (SS)
1969 A House for Mr. Biswas
1971 In a Free State
1979 A Bend in the River
1987 The Enigma of Arrival
Also writes nonfiction; e.g., Among the Believers: An Islamic Journey, 1981

1377
O'BRIEN, EDNA 1936-
Ireland
1960 The Country Girls
1962 The Lonely Girl
1964 Girls in Their Married Bliss
1965 August Is A Wicked Month (SS)
1966 Casualties of Peace
1968 The Love Object (SS)
1970 The Girl with Green Eyes
1970 A Pagan Place
1970 Zee & Company
1972 Night
1974 A Scandalous Woman (SS)
1976 Mother Ireland
1978 I Hardly Knew You
1979 A Rose in the Heart (SS)

1378
O'CONNOR, FRANK 1903-1966
Ireland
Real name: Michael John O'Donovan
1931 Guests of the Nation (SS)
1932 The Saint & Mary Kate
1936 Bones of Contention (SS)
1940 Dutch Interior
1941 Three Tales
1942 The Tailor & Ansty (2d ed., 1970)
1944 Crab Apple Jelly (SS)
1946 Selected Stories
1947 The Common Chord (SS)
1951 Traveller's Samples (SS)
1952 The Stories
1957 Domestic Relations (SS)
1963 My Oedipus Complex (SS)

1964 Collection Two (SS)
1969 Collection Three (SS)
1969 A Life of Your Own (SS)
1969 Masculine Protest (SS)
1969 A Set of Variations (SS)
1981 Collected Stories

1379
O'FAOLAIN, JULIA   1932-
Ireland
1975 Women in the Wall
1982 The Obedient Wife
1985 The Irish Signorina
1986 No Country for Young Men
See also HISTORICAL FICTION, 1004

1380
O'FAOLAIN, SEAN   1900-
Ireland
1932 Midsummer Night Madness (SS)
1933 A Nest of Simple Folk (SS)
1935 There's a Birdie in the Cage (SS)
1936 Bird Alone
1936 A Short Story
1937 A Purse of Coppers (SS)
1940 Come Back to Erin (SS)
1948 The Man Who Invented Sin (SS)
1957 The Finest Stories
1962 I Remember! I Remember! (SS)
1966 The Heat of the Sun (SS)
1970 The Talking Trees (SS)
1972 And Again?
1976 Foreign Affairs (SS)
1977 One True Friend (SS)
1978 Selected Stories
1980 Collected Stories

1381
POWELL, ANTHONY   1905-
1963 What's Become of Waring
1968 From a View to a Death
1983 O, How the Wheel Becomes It!
1986 The Fisher King

"A Dance to the Music of Time":
Spring:
1951 A Question of Upbringing
1952 A Buyer's Market
1955 The Acceptance World
Summer:
1957 At Lady Molly's
1960 Cassanova's Chinese Restaurant
1962 The Kindly Ones

Autumn:
1964 The Valley of Bones
1966 The Soldier's Art
1968 The Military Philosophers
Winter:
1971 Books Do Furnish a Room
1973 Temporary Kings
1975 Hearing Secret Harmonies

1382
PYM, BARBARA   1913-1980
Real name: Mary Crampton
1950 Some Tame Gazelle
1952 Excellent Women
1955 Less than Angels
1958 A Glass of Blessings
1961 No Fond Return of Love
1978 Quartet in Autumn
1978 The Sweet Dove Died
1980 A Few Green Leaves
1981 Jane & Prudence
1982 An Unsuitable Attachment
1981 Crampton Hodnot (1939-40)
1986 An Academic Question
1987 Civil to Strangers (SS)
Autobiography: A Very Private Eye, 1984

1383
RENAULT, MARY   1905-
Born in South Africa
1939 Promise of Love
1940 Kind Are Her Answers
1945 The Middle Mist
1947 Return to Night
1948 North Face
1953 The Charioteer
1956 The Last of the Wine
1958 The King Must Die
1962 The Bull from the Sea
1966 The Mask of Apollo

"Alexander the Great":
1969 Fire from Heaven
1972 The Persian Boy
1978 The Praise Singer
1981 Funeral Games
See also HISTORICAL FICTION, 1010

1384
RHYS, JEAN   1894-1979
1927 The Left Bank (SS)
1929 Quartet
1930 After Leaving Mr. Mackenzie
1934 Voyage in the Dark

1939 Good Morning, Midnight
1966 Wide Sargasso Sea
1967 Tigers Are Better Looking (SS)
1975 My Day
1976 Sleep It Off, Lady
Autobiography: Smile Please, 1980

1385
RUBENS, BERNICE   1923-
1960 Set on Edge
1966 Mate in Three
1969 Chosen People
1971 Sunday Best
1973 Go Tell the Lemming
1977 I Sent a Letter to My Love
1977 The Ponsonby Post
1979 Favours
1982 Birds of Passage
1983 Brothers
1985 Madame Sousatzka (1962)
1985 Mr. Wakefield's Crusade

1386
SCOTT, PAUL   1920-1978
1952 Johnnie Sahib
1953 Six Days in Marapore
1956 A Male Child
1958 The Mark of the Warrior
1960 The Love Pavilion
1962 The Birds of Paradise
1963 The Bender
1964 The Corrida at San Feliu
1977 Staying on (Related to Raj)

"The Raj Quartet":
1966 The Jewel in the Crown
1968 The Day of the Scorpion
1972 The Towers of Silence
1975 A Division of Spoils
See also HISTORICAL FICTION, 1014

1387
SILLITOE, ALAN   1928-
1958 Saturday Night & Sunday Morning
1959 The Loneliness of the Long Distance Runner (SS)
1961 The General
1961 Key to the Door
1961 The Ragman's Daughter (SS)
1965 The Death of William Posters
1967 A Tree on Fire
1968 Guzman Go Home (SS)
1970 A Start in Life
1971 Travels in Nihilon

1972 Raw Material
1973 Men, Women & Children (SS)
1974 The Flame of Life
1976 The Widower's Son
1980 The Storyteller
1981 The Second Chance (SS)
1982 Her Victory
1983 The Lost Flying Boat
1984 Down from the Hill
1985 Life Goes On
1988 Out of the Whirlpool

1388
SNOW, C. P.   1905-1980
1932 Death under Sail
1958 The Search
1963 In Their Wisdom
1972 The Malcontents
1979 A Coat of Varnish

"Strangers & Brothers":
1947 The Light & the Dark (4)
1949 Time of Hope (1)
1951 The Masters (5)
1954 The New Men (6)
1956 Homecoming (7)
1958 The Conscience of the Rich (3)
1960 The Affair (8)
1964 Corridors of Power (9)
1968 The Sleep of Reason (10)
1970 Last Things (11)
1973 George Passant (2) (Strangers & Brothers)
See also MYSTERIES, 0559

1389
SPARK, MURIEL   1918-
Scotland
1957 The Comforters
1958 Robinson
1959 Memento Mori
1960 The Bachelors
1960 The Ballad of Peckham Rye
1961 Voices at Play (SS)
1962 The Prime of Miss Jean Brodie
1963 The Girls of Slender Means
1965 The Mandelbaum Gate
1967 Collected Stories I (SS)
1968 The Public Image
1970 The Driver's Seat
1972 Not to Disturb
1973 The Hothouse by the East River
1974 The Abbess of Crewe
1976 The Takeover
1979 Territorial Rights
1981 Loitering with Intent

Section 11 - Authors Of The British Isles

1983 Bang-Bang You're Dead (SS)
1984 The Only Problem
1988 A Far Cry from Kensington

1390
TAYLOR, ELIZABETH   1912-1975
1953 The Sleeping Beauty
1954 Hester Lilly (SS)
1955 Now I Lay Me Down to Die
1957 Angel
1964 The Soul of Kindness
1965 A Dedicated Man (SS)
1968 The Wedding Group
1971 Mrs. Palfrey at the Claremont
1972 The Devastating Boys (SS)
1976 Blaming
1978 Tarifa

1391
THOMAS, D. M.   1935-
Wales
1979 The Flute-Player
1981 The White Hotel
1982 Birthstone
1983 Ararat
1984 Swallow

1392
TOLKIEN, J. R. R.   1892-1973
1937 The Hobbit
1949 Farmer Giles of Ham
1977 The Silmarillion
1980 Unfinished Tales of Numenor & Middle Earth
1984 The Book of Lost Tales

"Lord of the Rings" Trilogy:
1954 The Fellowship of the Ring
1954 The Two Towers
1955 The Return of the King
See also SCIENCE FICTION, 0808

1393
TRACY, HONOR   1913-
Ireland
1954 The Deserters
1956 The Straight & Narrow Path
1958 The Prospects Are Pleasing
1960 A Number of Things
1961 A Season of Mists
1963 The First Day of Friday
1966 Men at Work
1968 Settled in Chambers
1970 The Butterflies of the Province
1972 The Quiet End of Evening

1975 In a Year of Grace
1977 The Man from Next Door
1980 The Ballad of Castle Reef

1394
WELDON, FAY   1933-
1968 And the Wife Ran Away
1971 Down among the Women
1975 Female Friends
1976 Remember Me
1977 Words of Advice
1978 Praxis
1980 Puffball
1983 The President's Child
1984 The Life & Loves of a She-Devil
1987 The Rules of Life
1987 The Shrapnel Academy
1988 The Hearts & Lives of Men
1988 The Heart of the Country

1395
WILSON, ANGUS   1913-
1949 The Wrong Set (SS)
1950 Such Darling Dodos (SS)
1952 Hemlock & After
1956 Anglo-Saxon Attitudes
1957 A Bit off the Map (SS)
1959 The Middle Age of Mrs. Elliott
1961 Old Men at the Zoo
1964 Late Call
1967 No Laughing Matter
1970 The God of the Labyrinth
1970 The Killer
1970 Strindberg: Playscript 31
1971 The Blue Room
1973 As If by Magic
1974 Return of the Lloigor
1980 Setting the World on Fire

1396
WILSON, COLIN   1931-
1960 Ritual in the Dark
1961 Adrift in Soho
1963 The Sex Diary of Gerard Sorme
1963 The Violent World of Hugh Greene
1963 Man without a Shadow
1964 Necessary Doubt
1967 The Glass Cage
1967 The Mind Parasites
1974 The School Girl Murder
1976 The Space Vampires
See also MYSTERIES, 0584 & SCIENCE FICTION, 0735

SECTION TWELVE

WORLD AUTHORS

OVERVIEW

These authors represent world literature as it is known to reading audiences in the United States. With the exception of some Canadian, South African, Australian, and Indian authors writing in English, the works are published first in the language of the country and then at some time translated into English and published in the United States. Authors who may be greatly respected in their own countries may not be known at all or not known until years later in the United States. Sometimes an author's works are translated by a new translator who is able to capture the sense of the original much better, and thus provides a new access to that author. The works of Hermann Hesse began to be retranslated in the 1960s, and a new generation of young people were captivated by Hesse's ideas that seemed very contemporary to them.

Traditionally the authors of Western Europe, especially Germany and France, have been best known in the United States. Günter Grass and Heinrich Böll, who won the Nobel Prize in 1972, are widely read and studied. As world events and social and economic awareness develop, American readers expand their reading interests. During the 1960s the Russian authors gained great popularity, beginning with Boris Pasternak and his novel *Doctor Zhivago*. All of the novels of Alexander Solzenhitsyn were publishing events, and he ultimately came to live in the United States.

During the 1970s the Japanese authors became popular, especially Kobo Abé and Yukio Mishima. Nadine Gordimer of South Africa helped to explicate apartheid; Chinua Achebe of Nigeria began to be included on college and high school reading lists. In the 1980s Americans have become fascinated with the literature of South and Central America because of authors such as Gabriel García Márquez of Colombia and Carlos Fuentes of Mexico.

There often is a considerable time lag between the original publication in the country and the publication in the United States. If more than a year elapses, the year of publication in the original country is placed in parentheses after the title.

REFERENCE AND BIBLIOGRAPHIC SOURCES

Anderson, G.L. *Asian Literature in English: A Guide to Information Sources*. Detroit: Gale, 1981.

Anderson-Imbert, E. *Spanish American Literature: A History*, 2d ed., rev. Detroit: Wayne State University Press, 1969.

Section 12 - World Authors

Bede, Jean-Albert, and William B. Edgerton, general eds., *Columbia Dictionary of Modern European Literature*, 2d ed., fully rev. and enl. New York: Columbia University Press, 1980.

Bonadella, Peter, and Julia Conway Bonadella, eds. *Dictionary of Italian Literature*. Westport CT: Greenwood, 1979.

Charney, Maurice, ed. *The Reader's Advisor: A Layman's Guide to Literature*, 13th ed., Volume 2: *The Best in American and British Drama and World Literature in English Translation*. New York: Bowker, 1986.

Foster, David William. *Mexican Literature: A Bibliography of Secondary Sources*. Metuchen, NJ: Scarecrow Press, 1981.

Garland, Henry, and Mary Garland. *The Oxford Companion to German Literature*. New York: Oxford University Press, 1976.

Herdeck, Donald E., ed. *Caribbean Writers: A Bio-Bibliographical-Critical Encyclopedia*. Washington: Three Continents Press, 1979.

Lecker, Robert, and Jack David, eds. *The Annotated Bibliography of Canada's Major Authors*. Boston: G.K. Hall, 1980.

Lindos. *Black African Literature in English: A Guide to Information Sources*. Detroit: Gale, 1979.

Lock, Frederick, and Alan Lawson. *Australian Literature: A Reference Guide*, 2d ed. New York: Oxford University Press, 1980.

Popkin, Debra, and Michael Popkin, comps. *Modern French Literature*. New York: Unger, 1977.

Ward, Philip, ed. *The Oxford Companion to Spanish Literature*. New York: Oxford University Press, 1978.

Zell, Hans, and Helene Silver. *A Reader's Guide to African Literature*. New York: Africana, 1972.

AUTHORS AND TITLES

A. AFRICA

1. NIGERIA

1397
ACHEBE, CHINUA   1930-
1958 Things Fall Apart
1962 No Longer at Ease
1962 The Sacrificial Egg (SS)
1964 Arrow of God
1965 Chike & the River
1966 A Man of the People
1971 The Insiders: Stories of War & Peace from Nigeria
1973 Girls at War (SS)
1987 Anthills of the Savannah

2. SOUTH AFRICA

1398
COETZEE, J. M.   1940-
1974 Dusklands
1983 Life & Times of Michael K.
1986 Foe

1399
FUGARD, ATHOL   1932-
1980 Tsotsi
Best known as a playwright; e.g., Master Harold & the Boys

1400
GORDIMER, NADINE   1923-
1952 The Soft Voice of the Serpent (SS)
1953 The Lying Days
1956 Six Feet of the Country (SS)
1958 A World of Strangers
1960 Friday's Footprint (SS)
1963 Occasion for Loving
1965 Not for Publication (SS)
1966 The Late Bourgeois World
1970 A Guest of Honor
1971 Livingstone's Companions (SS)
1975 The Conservationist
1979 Burger's Daughter
1980 A Soldier's Embrace
1981 July's People
1984 Something Out There (SS)
1986 Lifetimes: Under Apartheid
1987 A Sport of Nature

1401
PATON, ALAN   1903-1988
1948 Cry, the Beloved Country
1953 Too Late the Phalarope
1961 Debbie Go Home (SS)
1961 Tales from a Troubled Land (SS)
1968 Instrument of Thy Peace
1969 For You Departed
1981 Ah, But Your Land Is Beautiful

B. ASIA

1. INDIA

JHABVALA, RUTH PRAWER
See AMERICAN AUTHORS, 1237

1402
MARKANDAYA, KAMALA   1924-
Real name: Kamala Taylor
1954 Nectar in a Sieve
1955 Some Inner Fury
1960 A Silence of Desire
1963 Possession
1966 A Handful of Rice
1969 The Coffer Dams
1972 The Nowhere Man
1973 Two Virgins
1977 The Golden Honeycomb
1982 Shalimar

1403
NARAYAN, R. K.   1906-
1935 Swami & Friends
1937 The Bachelor of Arts
1938 The Dark Room
1941 Malgudi Days (SS)
1943 Dodu (SS)
1944 Cyclone (SS)
1947 An Astrologer's Day (SS)
1952 The Financial Expert
1953 Grateful to Life & Death
1955 Waiting for the Mahatma

Section 12 - World Authors

1956 Lawley Road (SS)
1957 Mr. Sampath, the Printer of Malgudi
1958 The Guide
1961 The Man-Eater of Malgudi
1965 Gods, Demons & Others (SS)
1967 The Vendor of Sweets
1970 A Horse & Two Goats (SS)
1976 The Painter of Signs
1980 The English Teacher (1945)
1983 A Tiger for Malgudi
1985 Under the Banyan Tree
1986 Talkative Man

1404
RUSHDIE, SALMAN   1947-
1981 Midnight's Children
1982 Grimus (1975)
1983 Shame
1988 Satanic Verses

2. ISRAEL

1405
BARAK, MICHAEL   1938-
Real name: Michael Bar-Zohar
1976 The Secret List of Heinrich Roehm
1978 The Enigma
1980 The Phantom Conspiracy
See also HEADLINES, 0319

1406
TAMMUZ, BENJAMIN   1919-
1958 A Boat Sails to Sea
1973 Castle in Spain (1966)
1975 Bottle Parallels
1979 Requiem for Na'aman
1979 The Scent of Geranium (SS)
1980 Alexander Abrmov
1981 Minotaur

3. JAPAN

1407
ABE, KOBO   1924-
1964 The Woman in the Dunes
1966 The Face of Another
1969 The Ruined Map
1970 Inter Ice Age Four
1975 The Box Man
1976 The Man Who Turned into a Stick

1979 Secret Rendezvous
1988 The Ark Sakura
See also SCIENCE FICTION, 0590

1408
KAWABATA, YASUNARI   1899-1972
Nobel prize, 1968
1957 Snow Country (1937)
1959 Thousand Cranes (1952)
1964 The Izu Dancer (1925)
1969 House of the Sleeping Beauties (SS) (1933)
1970 The Sound of the Mountains (1952)
1972 The Master of Go (1954)
1974 The Lake (1961)
1975 Beauty & Sadness (1965)

1409
MISHIMA, YUKIO   1925-1970
Real name: Kimitake Hiraoka
Nobel Prize, 1969
1956 The Sound of Waves (1954)
1958 Confessions of a Mask (1958)
1959 The Temple of the Golden Pavilion (1956)
1963 After the Banquet (1960)
1965 The Sailor Who Fell from Grace with the Sea (1963)
1966 Death in Midsummer (SS) (1952)
1968 Forbidden Colors (1954)
1968 Madame de Sade
1968 Young Samurai (1967)
1969 Thirst for Love (1950)
1970 Sun & Steel (1968)

"The Sea of Fertility: A Cycle of Four Novels":
1972 Spring Snow
1973 Runaway Horses
1973 The Temple of Dawn
1974 The Decay of the Angel

1410
TANIZAKI, JUN'ICHIRO   1886-1965
1927 A Spring-Time Case
1955 Some Prefer Nettles (1936)
1957 The Makioka Sisters (1949)
1960 The Key
1963 Seven Japanese Tales
1965 Diary of an Old Man
1965 A Portrait of Shunkin (1933)
1970 Ashikari (1936) (&) The Story of Shunkin: Two Japanese Novels
1977 In Praise of Shadows

1982 The Secret History of the Lord of Mushahi; & Arrowroot
1985 Naomi

1411
YOSHIKAWA, EIJI   1892-1962
1981 Musashi (A Samurai epic)

4. U.S.S.R. (UNION OF SOVIET SOCIALIST REPUBLICS)

1412
ANATOLII, A.   1929-1979
Real name: Anatolii Kuznetsov
1967 Babi Yar
1984 The Journey
See also HISTORICAL FICTION, 1030

1413
BULGAKOV, MIKHAIL   1891-1940
1967 The Master & Margarita
1967 Black Snow
1968 The Heart of a Dog
1971 The White Guard
1972 Diaboliad (SS)

1414
PASTERNAK, BORIS   1890-1960
Nobel Prize, 1958
1958 Doctor Zhivago
1958 Safe Conduct

1415
SHALAMOV, VARLAM   1907-1982
1980 Kolyma Tales (1975)
1981 Graphite

1416
SHOLOKOV, MIKHAIL   1905-1984
Nobel Prize, 1965
1934 And Quiet Flows the Don
1935 Seeds of Tomorrow
1940 The Don Flows Home to the Sea
1960 Harvest on the Don
1961 Tales from the Don
1962 Tales of the Don
1967 Fierce & Gentle Warriors (SS)

1417
SOLZENHITSYN, ALEXANDER   1918-
Nobel Prize, 1970

Lives in Vermont
1963 One Day in the Life of Ivan Denisovich
1963 We Never Make Mistakes
1964 For the Good of the Cause
1968 The First Circle
1968 Cancer Ward
1972 August 1914
1974 The GULAG Archipelago, Vol. 1
1975 The Calf & the Oak (Memoirs)
1976 The GULAG Archipelago, Vol. 2
1976 Lenin in Zurich

C. AUSTRALIA

1418
CLEARY, JON   1917-
1947 You Can't See around Corners
1952 The Sundowners
1956 Justin Bayard
1958 The Green Helmet
1959 Back of Sunset
1961 North from Thursday
1962 The Country of Marriage
1963 A Flight of Chariots
1963 Forests of the Night
1964 The Fall of an Eagle
1966 The Pulse of Danger
1967 The Long Pursuit
1968 Season of Doubt
1969 Remember Jack Hoxie
1971 The Liberators
1972 The Ninth Marquess
1974 Peter's Pence
1975 The Safe House
1976 A Sound of Lightening
1977 High Road to China
1978 Vortex
1979 The Beufort Sisters
1981 The Golden Sabre
1982 Spearfield's Daughter
See also MYSTERIES, 0421 &
HISTORICAL FICTION, 1042

1419
HALL, RODNEY   1935-
1972 The Ship on the Coin: A Fable of the Bourgeoisie
1983 Just Relations
1988 Captivity Captive

1420
KENEALLY, THOMAS   1935-
1972 The Chant of Jimmie Blacksmith
1974 Blood Red, Sister Rose

Section 12 - World Authors   215

1978 A Victim of the Aurora
1979 The Playmaker
1980 The Confederates
1982 Schindler's List
1986 A Family Madness
See also HISTORICAL FICTION, 0922

1421
MCCULLOUGH, COLLEEN   1938?-
1974 Tim
1977 The Thorn Birds
1981 An Indecent Obsession
1985 A Creed for the Third
      Millennium
1987 The Ladies of Missalonghi
See also ROMANCES, 0090

1422
STEAD, CHRISTINA   1902-1983
1934 The Salzburg Tales
1935 Seven Poor Men of Sidney
1938 House of All Nations
1940 The Man Who Loved Children
1944 For Love Alone (SS)
1946 Letty Fox: Her Luck
1948 A Little Tea, A Little Chat
1952 The People with the Dogs
1966 Dark Places of the Heart
1967 The Puzzleheaded Girl (SS)
1974 House of All Nations
1975 The Little Hotel
1976 Blaming
1976 Miss Herbert (The Suburban
      Wife)
1986 Ocean of Story (SS)
1987 I'm Dying Laughing

1423
WHITE, PATRICK   1912-
Real Name: Victor Martindale
Nobel Prize, 1973
1940 Happy Valley
1941 The Living & the Dead
1948 The Aunt's Story
1955 The Tree of Man
1957 Voss
1961 Riders in the Chariot
1964 The Burnt Ones (SS)
1966 The Solid Mandala
1970 The Vivisector
1973 The Eye of the Storm
1974 The Cockatoos (SS)
1977 A Fringe of Leaves
1980 The Twyborn Affair

D. EUROPE

1. CZECHOSLOVAKIA

1424
KLIMA, IVAN   1931-
1970 A Ship Named Hope (1969)
1985 My Merry Mornings: Stories from
      Prague

1425
KOHOUT, PAVEL   1928-
1972 From the Diary of a
      Counter-Revolutionary
1973 Whitebook in Case of Adam
      Juracek
1980 The Hangwoman
Also a playwright

1426
KUNDERA, MILAN   1929-
1969 The Joke
1974 Laughable Loves (SS) (1969)
1974 Life Is Elsewhere
1976 The Farewell Party
1980 The Book of Laughter &
      Forgetting
1984 The Unbearable Lightness of
      Being

1427
LUSTIG, ARNOST   1926-
1962 Night & Hope
1962 Diamonds of the Night
1973 A Prayer for Katerina
      Horovitzova
1978 Darkness Casts No Shadows
1979 Dita Sayova
1985 The Unloved
1988 Indecent Dreams
See also HISTORICAL FICTION, 1084

2. DENMARK

1428
DINESEN, ISAK   1885-1962
Born in Denmark/Lived in Kenya
Real name: Karen Blixen
1934 Seven Gothic Tales
1937 Out of Africa
1942 Winter's Tales
1946 The Angelic Avengers

1957 Last Tales
1961 Shadows on the Grass
1962 Ehrengard
1977 Carnival (SS)
1985 Anecdotes of Destiny; &, Ehrengard

3. FRANCE

1429
BEAUVOIR, SIMONE DE   1908-1986
1948 The Blood of Others (1945)
1949 She Came to Stay (1943)
1955 All Men Are Mortal (1946)
1956 The Mandarins (1954)
1968 Les Belles Images (1966)
1969 The Woman Destroyed (1968)
Best known for nonfiction work, The Second Sex, 1952, & autobiography, Memoirs of a Dutiful Daughter, 1958

1430
BECKETT, SAMUEL   1906-
Born in Ireland
1934 More Pricks Than Kicks (SS)
1938 Murphy
1945 Mercier & Camier
1953 Watt
1955 Molloy (1951)
1956 Malone Dies (1951)
1958 The Unnameable (1953)
1964 How It Is (1961)
1972 The Lost Ones
1974 First Love (SS)
1980 Company
Best known as a playwright; e.g., Waiting for Godot, 1956

1431
BOULLE, PIERRE   1912-
1950 William Conrad
1954 The Bridge over the River Kwai (1952)
1955 Not the Glory
1956 Face of a Hero (1953)
1959 S.O.P.H.I.A.
1961 The Executioner (1954)
1963 Planet of the Apes
1964 Garden on the Moon
1966 Time Out of Mind (SS)
1968 The Other Side of the Coin
1968 The Photographer
1971 Because It Is Absurd (On Earth as in Heaven)
1972 Ears of the Jungle

1973 Desperate Games
1974 The Virtues of Hell
1977 The Marvelous Palace (SS)
1978 The Good Leviathan
1983 The Whale of Victoria Cross
1986 Mirrors of the Sun
See also SCIENCE FICTION, 0606 & HISTORICAL FICTION, 1037

1432
CAMUS, ALBERT   1913-1960
Nobel Prize, 1957
1946 The Stranger (1942)
1948 The Plague
1957 The Fall
1960 Exile & the Kingdom
1972 A Happy Death

1433
CÉLINE, LOUIS-FERDINAND   1894-1961
Real name: Louis Ferdinand Destouches
1936 Death on the Installment Plan
1969 Guignol's Band (1944)
1983 Journey to the End of Night (1932)

"Trilogy":
1968 Castle to Castle (1957)
1972 North (1960)
1974 Rigadoon (1969)

DE BEAUVOIR, SIMONE
See BEAUVOIR, SIMONE DE, 1429

1434
DURAS, MARGUERITE   1914-
Real name: Marguerite Donnadieu
1952 The Sea Wall
1959 The Square
1960 The Little Horses of Tarquinias
1960 Moderato Cantabile
1961 Hiroshima, Mon Amour
1963 Ten-Thirty on a Summer Night
1965 The Afternoon of Mr. Andesmas
1965 The Rivers & the Forests
1966 The Ravishing of Lol Stein
1966 The Sailor from Gibraltar
1968 The Vice-Consul
1970 Destroy, She Said
1976 India Song
1984 The Malady of Death
1985 The Lover
1986 The War: A Memoir

Section 12 - World Authors

1987 L'Amante Anglaise (1968)
1988 Blue Eyes, Black Hair

1435
GARY, ROMAIN   1914-1980
Real name: Romain Kacew. Also wrote as Roman Kacew, Emile Ajar, Shatan Bogat, Rene Deville & Fosco Sinibaldi
1944 Forest of Anger
1950 The Company of Men (1949)
1953 The Colors of the Day (1952)
1958 The Roots of Heaven (1956)
1959 Lady L.
1960 Nothing Important Ever Dies (1945)
1961 Promise at Dawn
1961 The Talent Scout
1964 Hissing Tales (1962)
1965 The Ski Bum
1968 The Dance of Gengis Cohn
1969 The Guilty Head
1970 White Dog
1973 The Gasp
1975 Direct Flight to Allah
1975 The Enchanters (1973)
1977 Your Ticket Is No Longer Valid
1977 The Way Out
1978 Momo
1978 Europa (1972)
1983 King Solomon

1436
GENET, JEAN   1910-1986
1954 The Thief's Journal (1949)
1963 Our Lady of the Flowers (1942)
1966 Querelle of Brest (1947)
1969 Funeral Rites (1947)
Also known as a playwright; e.g., The Balcony, 1958; The Miracle of the Rose, 1966.

1437
GIDE, ANDRÉ   1869-1951
1927 The Counterfeiters
1930 The Immoralist
1949 Fruits of the Earth (1897)
1950 Corydon (1924)
1959 So Be It, or The Chips Are Down
1964 Urien's Voyage

1438
LEDUC, VIOLETTE   1907-1971
1961 The Golden Buttons
1965 La Bâtarde

1966 Ravages
1966 The Woman with the Little Fox (SS)
1967 Thérèse & Isabelle
1970 In the Prison of Her Skin (1946)
1971 Mad In Pursuit (Sequel to Bâtarde)
1972 The Taxi

1439
QUENEAU, RAYMOND   1903-1976
1948 The Skin of Dreams (1944)
1958 Exercises in Style (1947)
1960 Zazie (1959)
1967 The Blue Flowers (1965)
1971 The Bark Tree (1933)
1973 The Flight of Icarus (1968)
1977 The Sunday of Life (1951)
1981 We Always Treat Women Too Well (1949)

1440
ROBBE-GRILLET, ALAIN   1922-
1958 The Voyeur
1959 Jealousy (1957)
1960 In the Labyrinth (1959)
1962 Last Year at Marienbad (1961)
1966 La Maison de Rendez-vous
1968 Snapshots (SS) (1962)
1971 Dreams of a Young Girl
1972 Project for a Revolution in New York
1982 Djinn

1441
SAGAN, FRANÇOISE   1935-
Real name: Françoise Quoirez
1955 Bonjour, Tristesse
1956 A Certain Smile
1957 Those without Shadows
1960 Aimez-Vous Brahms?
1961 The Wonderful Clouds
1966 La Chamade
1968 The Heart Keeper
1971 A Few Hours of Sunlight
1974 Scars on the Soul
1976 Lost Profile
1977 Silken Eyes (SS)
1978 The Unmade Bed
1983 Incidental Music (SS)
1983 The Painted Lady
1984 Salad Days
1986 The Still Storm
1987 A Reluctant Hero
Autobiography: With Fondest Regards, 1985

1442
SARRAUTE, NATHALIE   1902-
1958 Portrait of a Man Unknown
1959 Martereau
1960 Planetarium
1964 The Golden Fruits
1967 Tropisms
1969 Between Life & Death
1969 Silence & the Lie
1973 Do You Hear Them?
1976 Fools Say

1443
SARTRE, JEAN-PAUL   1905-1980
Refused Nobel Prize, 1964
1947 The Age of Reason
1947 The Reprieve
1948 The Wall (SS)
1949 Nausea (1938)

"The Roads to Freedom":
1951 Troubled Sleep
1956 Intimacy (SS)
Best known for writings on existentialism; e.g., Being & Nothingness

1444
SIMENON, GEORGES   1903-
Born in Belgium
Has written hundreds of novels under Simenon & pseudonyms. A selection of his novels of crisis include:
1937 The Murderer
1955 The Fugitive
1955 The Watchmaker
1962 The Lodger
1963 The Bells of Bicêtre
1963 The Iron Staircase
1964 The Accomplices
1964 The Blue Room
1964 The Premier
1964 The Train
1965 The Little Saint
1967 The Cat
1967 The Confessional
1967 Monsieur Morde Vanishes
1967 The Old Man Dies
1969 The Prison
1970 The Man on the Bench in the Barn
1970 November
1971 The Rich Man
1971 Teddy Bear
1973 The Glass Cage
1973 The Innocents
1974 The Venice Train (1963)

1975 A House on Quai Notre Dame (1962)
1976 The Hatter's Phantoms (1949)
1976 Sunday (1960)
1978 The Family Lie
1978 The Girl with a Squint
1978 The Little Doctor
1979 African Trio
1980 The White Horse Inn
1981 Big Bob
1982 The Disappearance of Odile
1982 The Widower
1983 The Long Exile
1984 The Reckoning
1985 The Couple from Poitiers
1985 Justice (1941)
1986 The Murderer (1937)
1986 The Outlaw (1941)
See also MYSTERIES, 0554

1445
TOURNIER, MICHEL   1924-
1969 Friday
1972 The Ogre
1981 Gemini
1982 The Four Wise Men
1984 The Fetishist (SS)
1987 Gilles & Jeanne
1987 The Golden Droplet

1446
WIESEL, ELIE   1928-
Born in Hungary
1960 Night
1961 Dawn
1962 The Accident
1964 The Town beyond the Wall
1966 The Gates of the Forest
1973 Ani ma amin
1973 The Oath
1983 The Golem
1985 The Fifth Son
Also writes nonfiction, e.g., A Beggar in Jerusalem, 1970
See also HISTORICAL FICTION, 1106

1447
WITTIG, MONIQUE   1935?-
1966 The Opoponax
1969 Les Guerilleres
1975 The Lesbian Body

1448
YOURCENAR, MARGUERITE
1903-1987

Real name: Marguerite de Crayencour
- 1954 The Memoirs of Hadrian
- 1957 Coup de Grace (1939)
- 1976 The Abyss
- 1981 Fires (1935)
- 1984 Alexis, or, the Treatise of Vain Struggle
- 1987 Two Lives & a Dream

4. GERMANY

1449
BÖLL, HEINRICH   1917-1985
Nobel Prize, 1972
- 1954 Acquainted with the Night
- 1956 The Train Was on Time (1949)
- 1956 Traveller, If You Come to the Spa (1950)
- 1957 Tomorrow & Yesterday
- 1963 Billiards at Half-Past Nine (1959)
- 1965 Absent without Leave (1962)
- 1965 The Clown
- 1967 End of a Mission
- 1970 Children Are Civilians Too
- 1973 Group Portrait with Lady
- 1975 The Lost Honor of Katherina Blum
- 1976 The Bread of Those Early Years (1957)
- 1978 And Never Said a Word
- 1982 The Safety Net
- 1986 A Soldier's Legacy
- 1987 The Casualty
- 1988 Woman in a River Landscape

"Adam":
- 1970 Adam & the Train
- 1974 And Where Were You, Adam? (1951)
- See also HISTORICAL FICTION, 1036

1450
BUCHHEIM, LOTHAR-GUENTHER   1918-
- 1975 The Boat
- 1978 The U-Boat War
- See also HEADLINES, 0321

1451
GRASS, GÜNTER   1927-
- 1962 The Tin Drum
- 1963 Cat & Mouse
- 1965 Dog Years
- 1970 Local Anaesthetic
- 1973 From the Diary of a Snail
- 1978 The Flounder
- 1981 The Meeting of Telgte
- 1987 The Rat
- 1982 Headbirths, or, the Germans Are Dying Out

1452
HESSE, HERMANN   1877-1962
Nobel Prize, 1946
- 1951 Siddhartha (1922)
- 1956 The Journey to the East (1932)
- 1963 Steppenwolf (1929)
- 1965 Demian (1919, 1923)
- 1968 Narcissus & Goldmund (1930)
- 1969 Beneath the Wheel (1906)
- 1969 Gertrude (1910)
- 1969 Magister Ludi (The Glass Bead Game) (1949)
- 1969 Peter Camenzind (1904)
- 1970 Klingsor's Last Summer (1920)
- 1970 Rosshalde
- 1971 Knulp (1915)
- 1972 Stories of Five Decades
- 1972 Strange News from Another Star (SS) (1918)
- 1976 Tales of Student Life

1453
KAFKA, FRANZ   1883-1924
Born in Czechoslovakia
- 1915 The Metamorphosis
- 1925 The Trial
- 1927 Amerika
- 1930 The Castle

1454
KIRST, HANS HELLMUT   1914-
- 1951 The Lieutenant Must Be Mad
- 1959 The Seventh Day
- 1963 The Night of the Generals
- 1963 The Officer Factory
- 1966 Soldiers' Revolt
- 1967 Brothers in Arms
- 1967 The Last Card
- 1968 The Wolves
- 1969 Last Stop Camp 7
- 1970 No Fatherland
- 1971 The Adventures of Private Faust
- 1972 Hero in the Tower
- 1973 Damned to Success
- 1974 A Time for Truth
- 1976 Everything Has Its Price
- 1976 The Nights of the Long Knives
- 1979 The Affairs of the Generals
- 1980 Party Games

"Gunner Asch":
1956 Forward, Gunner Asch
1956 The Revolt of Gunner Asch
1957 The Return of Gunner Asch
1964 What Became of Gunner Asch?
See also HISTORICAL FICTION, 1078

5. GREECE

1455
KAZANTZAKIS, NIKOS   1883-1957
1953 The Greek Passion
1956 Freedom or Death
1956 Zorba the Greek
1960 The Last Temptation of Christ
1962 Saint Francis
1963 Rock Garden
1964 The Fratricides
1965 Report to Greco (1961)
1971 Symposium
1980 Serpent & Lily (1906)

6. ITALY

1456
BASSANI, GIORGIO   1916-
1960 The Gold-Rimmed Spectacles
1965 The Garden of the Finzi-Continis
1970 The Heron
1971 Five Stories of Ferrara (1965)
1972 Behind the Door
1975 The Smell of Hay (SS)
See also HISTORICAL FICTION, 1033

1457
CALVINO, ITALO   1923-1985
1956 The Path to the Nest of Spiders (1947)
1957 Adam, One Afternoon (SS) (1952)
1959 The Baron in the Trees
1959 The Non-Existent Knight & the Cloven Viscount (1952)
1968 Cosmicomics (SS)
1969 T Zero (SS)
1971 The Watcher (SS)
1974 Invisible Cities
1975 Tarot, the Visconti Pack in Bergamo & New York
1977 The Castle of Crossed Dreams
1981 If on a Winter's Night a Traveler
1983 Marcavaldo; or the Seasons in the City
1984 Difficult Loves

1985 Mr. Palomar
1988 Under the Jaguar Sun (SS)
See also SCIENCE FICTION, 0615

1458
FUSCO, LUIGI
1977 The Piazza of the Decameron

1459
GUARESCHI, GIOVANNI   1908-1968
1967 A Husband in Boarding School (1944)
1968 Duncan & Clotilda: An Extravaganza with a Long Digression (1942)

"Don Camillo":
1950 The Little World of Don Camillo
1952 Don Camillo & His Flock
1953 The House That Nino Built
1954 Don Camillo's Dilemma (1953)
1957 Don Camillo Takes the Devil by the Tail (1956)
1964 Comrade Don Camillo
1969 Don Camillo Meets the Flower Children
1974 The Don Camillo Omnibus

1460
LAMPEDUSA, GIUSEPPE   1896-1957
1960 The Leopard
1962 Two Stories & a Memory (SS) (1961)

1461
MORANTE, ELSA   1918-1985
1951 House of Liars
1959 Arturo's Island
1977 History: A Novel
1984 Aracoeli

1462
MORAVIA, ALBERTO   1907-
Real name: Alberto Pincherle
1947 The Fancy Dress Party (1941)
1949 The Women of Rome (1947)
1950 Two Adolescents
1951 The Conformist
1951 Conjugal Love (1949)
1953 Time of Indifference (1929)
1955 A Ghost at Noon
1955 Mistaken Ambitions
1956 Bitter Honeymoon (SS) (1952)
1956 Roman Tales (1954)

Section 12 - World Authors

1958 Two Women
1960 The Wayward Wife (SS)
1961 The Empty Canvas
1963 More Roman Tales (SS) (1959)
1964 The Fetish (SS) (1963)
1966 The Lie (1965)
1969 Command & I Will Obey You (1967)
1971 Bought & Sold (SS)
1971 Paradise (SS)
1972 Two: A Phallic Novel
1975 Lady Godiva
1980 Time of Desecration
1983 1934
1986 Erotic Tales
1987 The Voyeur

1463
PAVESE, CESARE   1908-1950
1953 Among Women Only
1953 The Moon & the Bonfires
1959 The Devil in the Hills
1961 The House on the Hill
1965 Dialogues with Leuco

1464
SILONE, IGNAZIO   1900-1978
Real name: Secundo Tranquilli
1934 Fontamara (Rev. 1960)
1935 Mr. Aristotle (SS)
1937 Bread & Wine
1942 The Seed beneath the Snow
1953 A Handful of Blackberries (1952)
1961 The Fox & the Camellias
1971 The Story of a Humble Christian

7. SPAIN

1465
GOYTISOLO, JUAN   1931-
1958 Children of Chaos
1959 The Young Assassins
1960 Fiestas
1962 Island of Women
1966 The Party's Over: Four Attempts to Define a Love Story (SS) (1962)
1969 Marks of Identity
1974 Count Julian
1977 Juan the Landless
1981 Makbara
1987 Landscapes after the Battle

E. NORTH AMERICA--CANADA

1466
ATWOOD, MARGARET   1939-
1969 The Edible Woman
1972 Surfacing
1976 Lady Oracle
1977 Dancing Girls (SS)
1980 Life before Man
1982 Bodily Harm
1986 Bluebeard's Egg (SS)
1986 The Handmaid's Tale

1467
BLAIS, MARIE-CLAIRE   1939-
French Canada
1961 Mad Shadows (1959)
1961 Tete Blanche (1960)
1966 A Season in the Life of Emmanuel (1965)
1967 The Day Is Dark (and) Three Travellers
1970 The Manuscripts of Pauline Archange
1971 The Wolf
1973 David Sterne (1967)
1974 St. Lawrence Blues
1981 Deaf to the City

1468
GALLANT, MAVIS   1922-
1956 The Other Paris
1959 Green Water, Green Sky
1964 My Heart Is Broken (SS)
1970 A Fairly Good Time
1971 The Affair of Gabrielle Russier
1973 The Pegnitz Junction (SS)
1974 The End of the World (SS)
1979 From the Fifteenth District (SS)
1985 Home Truths (SS)
1987 Overhead in a Balloon

1469
HERBERT, ANNE
1963 The Torrent (SS)
1970 Kamouraska

1470
HOSPITAL, JANETTE TURNER   1942-
1982 The Ivory Swing
1983 The Tiger in the Tiger Pit
1985 Borderline
1988 Dislocations (SS)

1471
LAURENCE, MARGARET   1926-1987
1960 This Side Jordan
1964 The Stone Angel
1964 The Tomorrow-Tamer (SS)
1964 New Wind in a Dry Land
1966 A Jest of God
1969 The Fire Dwellers
1970 A Bird in the House (SS)
1974 The Diviners

1472
MOORE, BRIAN   1921-
Born in Ireland
1956 The Lonely Passion of Judith Hearne
1957 The Feast of Lupercal
1960 The Luck of Ginger Coffey
1962 An Answer from Limbo
1965 The Emperor of Ice Cream
1968 I Am Mary Dunne
1970 Fergus
1972 Catholics
1975 The Great Victorian Collection
1976 The Doctor's Wife
1979 The Mangan Inheritance
1981 The Temptations of Eileen Hughes
1983 Cold Heaven
1985 Black Robe
1987 The Color of Blood

1473
MUNRO, ALICE   1931-
1968 Dance of the Happy Shades (SS)
1971 Lives of Girls & Women (SS)
1974 Something I've Been Meaning to Tell You (SS)
1982 The Moons of Jupiter (SS)
1979 The Begger Maid (SS)

1474
RICHLER, MORDECAI   1931-
1954 The Acrobats
1955 Son of a Smaller Hero
1957 A Choice of Enemies
1959 The Apprenticeship of Duddy Kravitz
1963 Stick Your Neck Out (The Incomparable Atuk)
1968 Cocksure
1969 The Street (SS)
1971 Saint Urbain's Horseman
1980 Joshua Then & Now

1475
ROY, GABRIELLE   1909-1983
French Canada
1947 The Tin Flute
1951 Where Nests the Water Hen
1955 The Cashier
1957 Street of Riches
1962 The Hidden Mountain
1966 The Road Past Altamont
1970 Windflower
1976 Enchanted Summer
1977 Children of My Heart
1977 Garden in the Wind

F. SOUTH & CENTRAL AMERICA

1. ANTIGUA

1476
KINCAID, JAMAICA   1949-
1984 At the Bottom of the River (SS)
1985 Annie John

2. ARGENTINA

1477
BORGES, JORGE LUIS   1899-1986
1962 Ficciones
1964 Labyrinths (SS)
1970 The Aleph (SS) (1949)
1972 Doctor Brodie's Report (1970)
1972 A Universal History of Infamy (1935)
1974 The Congress (1970)
1974 In Praise of Darkness
1977 The Book of Sand (SS)
1981 Six Problems for Don Isidro Parodi (SS) (1945)
Also wrote poetry

1478
CORTÁZAR, JULIO   1914-1984
1965 The Winners (1960)
1966 Hopscotch
1967 End of the Game (SS)
1968 Blow Up (SS) (1966)
1969 Cronopios & Famas
1972 62: A Model Kit
1973 All Fires the Fire (SS) (1966)
1978 A Manual for Manuel
1980 A Change of Light (SS)
1982 We Love Glenda So Much (SS)
1984 A Certain Lucas

1479
PUIG, MANUEL   1932-
1971 Betrayed by Rita Hayworth
1973 Heartbreak Tango
1976 The Buenos Aires Affair
1980 Kiss of the Spider Woman
1982 External Curse on the Reader of These Pages
1984 Blood of Requited Love

1480
SÁBATO, ERNESTO   1911-
1950 The Outsider (The Tunnel)
1974 Abbadon, the Exterminator
1981 On Heroes & Tombs

3. BRAZIL

1481
AMADO, JORGE   1912-
1962 Gabriela, Clove & Cinnamon (1958)
1964 Home Is the Sailor (1961)
1965 The Two Deaths of Quincas Wateryell (1962)
1965 The Violent Land, rev. (1945)
1966 Shepherds of the Night (1964)
1969 Dona Flor & Her Two Husbands (1966)
1971 Jubiaba (1935)
1971 Tent of Miracles (1969)
1975 Tereza Batista: Home from the Wars (1972)
1979 Tieta, the Goat Girl
1982 The Swallow & the Tom Cat
1984 The Sea of Death
1985 Pen, Sword, Camisole

1482
LISPECTOR, CLARICE   1925-1977
1967 The Apple in the Dark (1961)
1972 Family Ties (SS)
1986 An Apprenticeship, or, the Book of Delights
1986 The Foreign Legion (SS)

4. CHILE

1483
ALLENDE, ISABEL   1942-
1985 The House of Spirits
1987 Of Love & Shadows
1988 Eva Luna

5. COLOMBIA

1484
GARCÍA MÁRQUEZ, GABRIEL   1928-
Nobel Prize, 1982
1968 No One Writes to the Colonel (SS)
1970 One Hundred Years of Solitude (1967)
1972 Leaf Storm (SS)
1972 Innocent Erendira (SS)
1976 The Autumn of the Patriarch
1979 In Evil Hour
1982 Chronicle of a Death Foretold
1988 Love in the Time of Cholera

6. MEXICO

1485
FUENTES, CARLOS   1929-
1960 Where the Air Is Cleaner (1958)
1961 The Good Conscience (1959)
1964 The Death of Artemio Cruz (1962)
1965 Aura (1962)
1968 A Change of Skin (1967)
1972 Holy Place (1967)
1976 Terra Nostra
1978 The Hydra Head
1980 Burnt Water (SS)
1982 Distant Relations
1985 The Old Gringo

7. PERU

LLOSA, MARIO VARGAS
See VARGAS LLOSA, MARIO, 1486

1486
VARGAS LLOSA, MARIO   1936-
1966 The Time of the Hero
1968 The Green House
1975 Conversation in the Cathedral
1982 Aunt Julia & the Scriptwriter
1984 The War of the End of the World
1986 The Real Life of Alejandro Mayta
1987 Who Killed Palomino Molero?

AUTHOR INDEX

AUTHOR	LOCATION(S)
A:	
ABBEY, EDWARD	0822
ABÉ, KOBO	0590; 1407
ACHEBE, CHINUA	1397
ADAMS, ALICE	1159
ADAMS, ANDY	0823
ADAMS, DORIS	0001
ADAMS, DOUGLAS	0591
ADAMS, HAZARD	0739
ADAMS, RICHARD	0150; 0740; 1344
AIKEN, JOAN	0002; 0389
AIRD, CATHERINE	0390
ALBERT, MARVIN	0257; 0318
ALDISS, BRIAN W.	0592
ALDRIDGE, JAMES	0258
ALLAN, STELLA	0391
ALLARDYCE, PAULA	0003
ALLENDE, ISABEL	1483
ALLINGHAM, MARGERY	0392
ALTHER, LISA	1160
AMADO, JORGE	1481
AMBLER, ERIC	0352
AMIS, KINGSLEY	1345
ANATOLII, A.	1030; 1412
ANDERSON, PATRICK	0229
ANDERSON, POUL	0593; 0741
ANDREWS, V. C.	0151
ANSON, JAY	0152
ANTHONY, EVELYN	0259; 0353; 0950
ANTHONY, PIERS	0594; 0742
ARCHER, JEFFREY	0004; 0230; 0260
ARGO, ELLEN	0888
ARMSTRONG, CHARLOTTE	0393
ARNOLD, ELLIOTT	0889; 1031
ARNOW, HARRIETTE	0890; 1161
ASCH, SHOLEM	1032
ASHE, GORDON	0394
ASHE, PENELOPE	1111
ASIMOV, ISAAC	0395; 0595
ATWOOD, MARGARET	1466
AUCHINCLOSS, LOUIS	0951; 1162
AUEL, JEAN	0952
AVALLONE, MICHAEL	0596
B:	
BACH, RICHARD	0743
BACHMAN, RICHARD	0153
BAILEY, C.	0231
BAINBRIDGE, BERYL	0154; 1346
BAKER, BETTY	0824
BALDWIN, FAITH	0005
BALDWIN, JAMES	1163

BALL, JOHN	0396
BALLANTYNE, SHEILA	1164
BALLARD, J. G.	0597
BAMBARA, TONI CADE	1165
BANIS, V. J.	0006
BANKS, LYNNE REID	1347
BARAK, MICHAEL	0319; 1405
BARBER, NOEL	0007
BARJAVEL, RENÉ	0598
BARKER, CLIVE	0155
BARLAY, STEPHEN	0354
BARNARD, ROBERT	0397
BARNES, LINDA	0398
BARNES, MARGARET	0953
BARRON, ANN FORMAN	0008
BARTH, JOHN	1166
BARTH, RICHARD	0399
BARTHELME, DONALD	1167
BARWICK, JAMES	0320
BASS, T. J.	0599
BASSANI, GIORGIO	1033; 1456
BAUER, STEVEN	0744
BAWDEN, NINA	1348
BEACH, EDWARD L.	1034
BEAGLE, PETER	0745
BEAN, AMELIA	0825
BEATTIE, ANN	1168
BEAUMAN, SALLY	0009
BEAUVOIR, SIMONE DE	1429
BECKER, JUREK	1035
BECKER, STEPHEN D.	0891; 0954
BECKETT, SAMUEL	1430
BELLAIRS, GEORGE	0400
BELLOW, SAUL	1169
BENCHLEY, PETER	0156
BENEDICT, REX	0826
BENFORD, GORDON	0600
BENFORD, GREGORY	0601
BENTLEY, E. C.	0401
BERCOVICI, ERIC	0402
BERGER, THOMAS	0602; 0746; 1170
BERKELEY, ANTHONY	0403
BERMANT, CHAIM	0010
BERNAYS, ANNE	1171
BESTER, ALFRED	0603
BIGGERS, EARL DERR	0404
BIGGLE, LLOYD, JR.	0604
BINCHY, MAEVE	0011
BIRSTEIN, ANN	1172
BLACK, LAURA	0012
BLACKWOOD, CAROLINE	1349
BLAIS, MARIE-CLAIRE	1467
BLAKE, JENNIFER	0013
BLAKE, NICHOLAS	0405
BLATTY, WILLIAM P.	0157
BLISH, JAMES	0605
BLOOM, URSULA	0014
BLYTH, MYRNA	1112

BOGNER, NORMAN	1113
BÖLL, HEINRICH	1036; 1449
BOLT, DAVID	0955
BORGES, JORGE LUIS	1477
BORLAND, HAL	0827
BOUCHER, ANTHONY	0406
BOULLE, PIERRE	0606; 1037; 1431
BOURJAILY, VANCE	1173
BOVA, BEN	0607
BOWEN, ELIZABETH	1350
BOWMAN, JOHN CLARKE	0892
BOX, EDGAR	0407
BOYD, JOHN	0608
BOYLE, KAY	1174
BRACKETT, LEIGH	0747
BRADBURY, RAY	0158; 0609
BRADFORD, BARBARA TAYLOR	0015
BRADLEY, DAVID	1175
BRADLEY, MARION ZIMMER	0610; 0748
BRADSHAW, GILLIAN	0749; 0956
BRADY, JAMES	1114
BRAINE, JOHN	1351
BRAMAH, ERNEST	0750
BRAMBLE, FORBES	0016
BRAND, MAX	0828
BRAUTIGAN, RICHARD	1176
BRENT, MADELEINE	0017
BRETT, SIMON	0408
BRICK, JOHN	0893
BRIN, DAVID	0611
BRINKLEY, WILLIAM	1038
BRISCO, PATTY	0018
BRISKIN, JACQUELINE	0019; 1115
BRISTOW, GWEN	0020; 0894
BROMIGE, IRIS	0021
BROOKNER, ANITA	1352
BROOKS, TERRY	0751
BROPHY, BRIGID	1353
BROWN, DEE	0895
BROWN, J. P. S.	0829
BROWN, RITA MAE	1177
BROWN, ROSELLEN	1178
BRUNNER, JOHN	0612
BRYANT, DOROTHY	1179
BRYANT, WILL	0830
BUCHANAN, MARIE	0159
BUCHHEIM, LOTHAR-GUENTHER	0321; 1450
BUCK, PEARL	0022
BUCKLEY, WILLIAM F.	0355
BULGAKOV, MIKHAIL	1413
BULLIET, RICHARD	0261
BURDICK, EUGENE	0232
BURGER, NEAL	0322
BURGESS, ANTHONY	0613; 1354
BURROUGHS, WILLIAM	1180
BUTLER, GWENDOLINE	0023; 0409
BUTLER, OCTAVIA E.	1181

Author Index

C:

CADELL, ELIZABETH	0024
CAIDIN, MARTIN	0614; 1039
CAIN, JAMES M.	0410
CALDWELL, TAYLOR	0025; 0957
CALISHER, HORTENSE	1182
CALVINO, ITALO	0615; 1457
CAMERON, JOHN	0160
CAMPBELL, RAMSEY	0161
CAMUS, ALBERT	1432
CANNING, VICTOR	0262; 0323; 0411; 0752
CAPOTE, TRUMAN	1183
CAPPS, BENJAMIN	0831
CAPUTO, PHILIP	0897; 1184
CARLISLE, HENRY	0898
CARR, JOHN DICKSON	0412
CARR, PHILIPPA	0026; 0958
CARROLL, JAMES	0263; 1185
CARROLL, LEWIS	0753
CARTER, ANGELA	0754
CARTER, FORREST	0832
CARTER, LIN	0755
CARTER, YOUNGMAN	0413
CARTLAND, BARBARA	0027
CASPARY, VERA	0414
CASSEL, VIRGINIA	0899
CASSILL, R. V.	1116
CAVE, EMMA	0162
CÉLINE, LOUIS-FERDINAND	1433
CHALKER, JACK L.	0324
CHANDLER, A. BERTRAM	0616
CHANDLER, RAYMOND	0415
CHANT, JOY	0756
CHAPMAN, VERA	0757
CHARNAS, SUZY MCKEE	0163; 0617
CHARTERIS, LESLIE	0416
CHARYN, JEROME	0833; 1040; 1186
CHASTAIN, THOMAS	0417
CHEEVER, JOHN	1187
CHESTER, DEBORAH	0028
CHESTERTON, G. K.	0418
CHEVALIER, PAUL	0325
CHRISTIE, AGATHA	0419
CHRISTOPHER, JOHN	0618
CLANCY, TOM	0264
CLARK, MARY HIGGINS	0420
CLARK, NORMA LEE	0029
CLARK, WALTER VAN TILBURG	0834
CLARKE, ARTHUR C.	0619
CLAVELL, JAMES	0265; 0959; 1041
CLEARY, JON	0421; 1042; 1418
CLEMENT, HAL	0620
CLINE, C. TERRY, JR.	0164
CLIVE, JOHN	0326
COATSWORTH, ELIZABETH	0758
COE, TUCKER	0422
COETZEE, J. M.	1398
COFFMAN, VIRGINIA	0030

COHEN, WILLIAM S.	0233
COLEMAN, LONNIE	0031
COLEMAN, TERRY	0900; 0960
COLES, MANNING	0356
COLLIER, JOHN	0759
COLLINS, JACKIE	1117
COLLINS, JOAN	1118
COLLINS, LARRY	0266; 0327; 1043
COLLINS, MAX ALLAN	0423
COLLINS, MICHAEL	0424
COLLINS, WILKIE	0425
COMPTON, DAVID G.	0621
COMPTON-BURNETT, IVY	1355
CONDON, RICHARD	0234; 1188
CONRAN, SHIRLEY	1119
CONROY, PAT	1189
CONSTANTINE, K. C.	0426
COOK, ROBIN	0165
COOKSON, CATHERINE	0032
COONTS, STEPHEN	0901
COOPER, MORTON	1120
COOVER, ROBERT	1190
COPPEL, ALFRED	0267
CORLEY, EDWIN	0268
CORNWELL, BERNARD	0961
CORTÁZAR, JULIO	1478
COSTAIN, THOMAS B.	0962
COURTER, GAY	0033
COX, RICHARD	0357
COYNE, JOHN	0166
CRAIG, ALISA	0427
CREASEY, JOHN	0358; 0428; 1044
CREWS, HARRY	1191
CRICHTON, MICHAEL	0269; 0622; 0902
CRICHTON, ROBERT	1045
CRISPIN, EDMUND	0429
CROMWELL, ELSIE	0034
CROSS, AMANDA	0430
CROSS, JOHN K.	0623
CROWLEY, JOHN	0624; 0760
CUNNINGHAM, E. V.	0431
CUNNINGHAM, LAURA	1192
CUSSLER, CLIVE	0270

D:

DAHL, ROALD	0167
DAILEY, JANET	0035
DALEY, ROBERT	0432
DANIELS, DOROTHY	0036
DARCY, CLARE	0037
DAVIDSON, AVRAM	0625; 0761
DAVIDSON, LIONEL	0271
DAVIES, L. P.	0168
DAVIS, GWEN	1121
DAY, ROBERT	0835
DE BEAUVOIR, SIMONE	
see BEAUVOIR, SIMONE DE	

DE BORCHGRAVE, ARNAUD	0235
DE CAMP, CATHERINE CROOK	0762
DE CAMP, L. SPRAGUE	0626; 0763; 0963
DECKER, WILLIAM	0836
DE FELITTA, FRANK	0169
DEFORD, MIRIAM ALLEN	0627
DE HARTOG, JAN	0903; 0964; 1046
DEIGHTON, LEN	0328; 0359; 1047
DELANY, SAMUEL R.	0628; 0764
DELDERFIELD, R. F.	0038
DELILLO, DON	1193
DEL REY, LESTER	0629
DEL VECCHIO, JOHN M.	0904
DEMETZ, HANA	1048
DEMILLE, NELSON	0272
DENYS, THERESA	0039
DERLUTH, AUGUST	0170
DEVERAUX, JUDE	0040
DE VRIES, PETER	1194
DEWHURST, KEITH	0965
DICK, PHILIP K.	0630
DICKEY, JAMES	1195
DICKINSON, PETER	0433
DICKSON, CARTER	0434
DICKSON, GORDON R.	0631; 0765
DIDION, JOAN	1196
DILLON, EILÍS	0435; 0966
DINESEN, ISAK	1428
DISCH, THOMAS M.	0632
DISNEY, DORIS MILES	0436
DOCTOROW, E. L.	0837; 1197
DODSON, KENNETH	1049
DOLINER, ROY	0360
DOMINIC, R. B.	0437
DONALDSON, STEPHEN R.	0766
DONLEAVY, J. P.	1198
DOUGLAS, LLOYD	0967
DOYLE, SIR ARTHUR CONAN	0438
DRABBLE, MARGARET	1356
DRURY, ALLEN	0236; 0968
DU MAURIER, DAPHNE	0041; 0171; 0969; 1357
DUNN, NELL	1358
DUNNE, DOMINICK	1122
DUNNE, JOHN GREGORY	1199
DURAS, MARGUERITE	1434
DURHAM, MARILYN	0838
DURRELL, LAURENCE	1359
DUVAUL, VIRGINIA	0042

E:

EBERHART, MIGNON GOOD	0439
EBERSOHN, WESSEL	0440
ECKERT, ALLAN	0905
EDDISON, ERIC	0767
EDEN, DOROTHY	0043
EDGAR, JOSEPHINE	0044

EGLETON, CLIVE	0273; 0329
EHRLICH, MAX	0172
EHRLICHMAN, JOHN	0237
EISENSTADT, JILL	1200
ELBERT, JOYCE	1123
ELEGANT, ROBERT	0045; 0970
ELKIN, STANLEY	1201
ELLIOT, JOHN	0633
ELLIS, ALICE THOMAS	1360
ELLIS, BRET EASTON	1202
ELLISON, HARLAN	0634
ELLISON, RALPH	1203
ELMAN, RICHARD M.	1050
ELON, AMOS	1051
ELWARD, JAMES	0046
ENDE, MICHAEL	0768
ENGDAHL, SYLVIA LOUISE	0635
EPSTEIN, LESLIE	1052; 1204
ERDMAN, PAUL E.	0274
ERDRICH, LOUISE	1205
ERICSON, ERIC	0173
ERSKINE, MARGARET	0441
ERWIN, ANNABEL	0047
ESTLEMAN, LOREN D.	0442; 0839
EVANS, EVAN	0840

F:

FAIR, A. A.	0443
FARMER, PENELOPE	0769
FARMER, PHILIP JOSE	0636
FARRELL, J. G.	1053
FARRIS, JOHN	0174
FAST, HOWARD	0048; 0906; 0971; 1054
FEELEY, PAT	0175
FERBER, EDNA	0907
FERRARS, E. X.	0444
FIELD, PETER	0841
FIELD, RACHEL	0908
FINNEY, JACK	0445; 0770
FISHER, VARDIS	0842
FITZGIBBON, C.	1055
FLEETWOOD, HUGH	0176
FLEMING, IAN	0361
FLEMING, THOMAS	0049
FLETCHER, DAVID	0177
FLOREY, KITTY BURNS	1206
FOLLETT, KEN	0275; 0330
FORBES, COLIN	0276; 0972; 1056
FORESTER, C. S.	0973; 1057
FORMAN, JAMES	0843
FORSYTH, FREDERICK	0277; 0331
FOSTER, ALAN D.	0637
FOWLES, JOHN	1361
FOX, PAULA	1207
FRANCIS, DICK	0446
FRANK, ANNE	1058

Author Index

FRANK, PAT	0278
FRASER, ANTONIA	0447
FRASER, JAMES	0448
FREEDMAN, BENEDICT	0909
FREELING, NICHOLAS	0449
FREEMAN, CYNTHIA	0050
FREEMANTLE, BRIAN	0279; 0362
FREMLIN, CELIA	0450
FRENCH, MARILYN	1208
FRENCH, MICHAEL	1124
FRIEDMAN, BRUCE JAY	1209
FUENTES, CARLOS	1485
FUGARD, ATHOL	1399
FUKS, LADISLAV	1059
FUSCO, LUIGI	1458

G:

GADDIS, WILLIAM	1210
GAINES, ERNEST J.	1211
GAINHAM, SARAH	1060
GALLAGHER, PATRICIA	0051
GALLANT, MAVIS	1468
GALLICO, PAUL	0178; 1061
GALOUYE, DANIEL	0638
GANN, ERNEST K.	0974
GARCÍA MÁRQUEZ, GABRIEL	1484
GARDNER, ERLE STANLEY	0451
GARDNER, JOHN C.	0771; 0975; 1212
GARDNER, JOHN (EDMUND)	0363
GARFIELD, BRIAN	0332; 0452; 0844
GARRETT, GEORGE	0976
GARRETT, RANDALL	0772
GARVE, ANDREW	0453
GARY, ROMAIN	1435
GASH, JONATHAN	0454
GASKELL, JANE	0773
GASKIN, CATHERINE	0052
GAVIN, CATHERINE	0977; 1062
GEASLAND, JACK	1125
GEESLIN, CAMPBELL	0053
GELLIS, ROBERTA	0054
GENET, JEAN	1436
GENT, PETER	1126
GERROLD, DAVID	0639
GERSON, NOEL B.	0280; 0910; 0978
GESTON, MARK	0640
GIDE, ANDRÉ	1437
GIDLEY, CHARLES	0055
GIFFORD, THOMAS	0333
GILBERT, MICHAEL	0455
GILES, JANICE	0911
GILL, BARTHOLOMEW	0456
GILLIATT, PENELOPE	1362
GILMAN, DOROTHY	0364; 0457
GILMAN, J. D.	0334
GLOAG, JULIAN	0179
GODDEN, RUMER	1363

GODWIN, GAIL	1213
GOLD, HERBERT	1214
GOLDING, WILLIAM	1364
GOLDMAN, JAMES	0979
GOLDMAN, WILLIAM	0180; 0365; 0774; 1127
GOLDTHWAITE, EATON K.	0458
GOLON, SERGEANNE	0056
GORDIMER, NADINE	1400
GORDON, MARY	1215
GORDON, RICHARD	0181
GOUDGE, ELIZABETH	0057; 0980
GOULD, LOIS	1216
GOYTISOLO, JUAN	1465
GRAFTON, SUE	0459
GRAHAM, KENNETH	0775
GRAHAM, WINSTON	0981
GRANGER, BILL	0366
GRANT, MAXWELL	0058
GRASS, GÜNTER	1451
GRAU, SHIRLEY ANN	1217
GRAVES, ROBERT	0912; 0982
GRAY, FRANCINE DU PLESSIX	1218
GRAYSON, RICHARD	0460
GREELEY, ANDREW	0461; 0641; 1128
GREEN, GERALD	1063
GREEN, HANNAH	1219
GREENBERG, JOANNE	0983; 1220
GREENE, GAEL	1129
GREENE, GRAHAM	0367; 1365
GREER, BEN	0182
GREGORIAN, JOYCE	0776
GREY, ZANE	0845
GRIFFIN, GWYN	1064
GRIFFITHS, JOHN	0368
GRIMES, MARTHA	0462
GRINDAL, RICHARD	0463
GROSS, JOEL	0059
GRUBER, FRANK	0846
GRUMBACH, DORIS	1221
GUARESCHI, GIOVANNI	1459
GUEST, LADY CHARLOTTE	0777
GUEST, JUDITH	1222
GULICK, BILL	0847; 0913
GULIK, ROBERT HANS VAN	0464
GUNN, JAMES E.	0642
GUTCHEON, BETH	0465
GUTHRIE, A. B.	0848; 0914
GUTTERIDGE, LINDSAY	0643

H:

HABER, JOYCE	1130
HACKETT, JOHN	0281
HAGER, JEAN	0060
HAIBLUM, ISIDORE	0644
HAILEY, ARTHUR	1131
HAINES, PAMELA	0061

Author Index

HALDEMAN, JOE	0645
HALL, ADAM	0369
HALL, FRANCES	0646
HALL, RODNEY	1419
HAMMETT, DASHIELL	0466
HANCOCK, NEIL	0778
HANSEN, JOSEPH	0467
HARDWICK, ELIZABETH	1223
HARE, CYRIL	0468
HARNESS, CHARLES	0647
HARRIS, MARILYN	0062; 0183
HARRIS, THOMAS	0184; 0282
HARRISON, HARRY	0648
HARRISON, M. JOHN	0649
HART, GARY	0238
HARTOG, JAN DE see DE HARTOG, JAN	
HAVIARAS, STRATIS	1065
HAWKES, JOHN	1224
HAYCOX, ERNEST	0849
HAYDEN, STERLING	0984
HAYMON, S. T.	0469
HAZZARD, SHIRLEY	1225
HEALD, TIM	0470
HEAVEN, CONSTANCE	0063
HEGGEN, THOMAS	1066
HEIDISH, MARCY	0915
HEINLEIN, ROBERT	0650
HELLER, JOSEPH	1067; 1226
HENDERSON, ZENNA	0651
HENNESSY, MAX	0985
HENRY, WILL	0850
HERBERT, ANNE	1469
HERBERT, FRANK	0652
HERLIHY, JAMES LEO	1227
HERSEY, JOHN	0653; 0986; 1068
HERZOG, ARTHUR	0185
HESSE, HERMANN	1452
HEYER, GEORGETTE	0064; 0471; 0987
HIGGINS, GEORGE V.	0239; 0472; 1228
HIGGINS, JACK	0283; 0335
HIGH, MONIQUE	0065
HIGHSMITH, PATRICIA	0473
HIGHWATER, JAMAKE	0988
HILL, CAROL	1229
HILL, FIONA	0066
HILL, GRACE LIVINGSTON	0067
HILL, PAMELA	0068
HILL, REGINALD	0370; 0474
HILL, RUTH BEEBE	0916
HILLERMAN, TONY	0475
HILTON, JAMES	0779
HIMES, CHESTER	1230
HINTZE, NAOMI	0186
HIRSCHFIELD, BURT	1132
HITCHCOCK, RAYMOND	0336
HOCHHUTH, ROLF	1069
HOCHMAN, SANDRA	1231

HODGE, JOAN AIKEN	0069
HOFFMAN, ALICE	1232
HOLLAND, CECELIA	0989
HOLLAND, ISABELLE	0070; 0476
HOLLAND, WILLIAM	0916
HOLT, VICTORIA	0071
HONE, JOSEPH	0371
HOSKINS, ROBERT	0654
HOSPITAL, JANETTE TURNER	1470
HOUGH, RICHARD	0990; 1070
HOUSEHOLD, GEOFFREY	0187; 0372; 0780
HOUSTON, JAMES	0917
HOWAR, BARBARA	0240
HOWATCH, SUSAN	0072
HOWE, FANNY	0918
HOYLE, FRED	0655
HOYLE, GEOFFREY	0656
HUBBARD, L. RON	0657
HUFF, TOM	0073
HUFFAKER, CLAIR	0851
HUGHES, RICHARD	1366
HUNT, E. HOWARD	0373
HUNT, KYLE	0477
HUNTER, ALAN	0478
HUNTER, JACK D.	1071
HUNTER, STEPHEN	0284; 0337
HUXLEY, ALDOUS	0658
HYDE, ANTHONY	0285

I:

ILES, FRANCIS	0479
INNES, RALPH HAMMOND	0286
INNES, MICHAEL	0480
IRVING, JOHN	1233
ISAACS, SUSAN	1234

J:

JACKSON, SHIRLEY	0188; 1235
JACOT, MICHAEL	1072
JAFFE, RONA	0481; 1133
JAHN, MIKE	1073
JAKES, JOHN	0919
JAMES, HENRY	0189
JAMES, P. D.	0482
JANOWITZ, TAMA	1236
JARMAN, ROSEMARY	0991
JEFFREYS, J. G.	0483
JENKINS, DAN	1134
JENNINGS, GARY	0852; 0992
JHABVALA, RUTH PRAWER	1237
JOFFO, JOSEPH	1074
JOHNSON, BARBARA	0074
JOHNSON, DIANE	1238
JOHNSON, DOROTHY	0853
JOHNSON, GEORGE CLAYTON	0659
JOHNSON, MENDAL	0190

JOHNSTON, VELDA	0075
JONES, DENNIS F.	0660
JONES, DOUGLAS C.	0854; 0920
JONES, GAYL	1239
JONES, GWYN	0781
JONES, JAMES	1075; 1240
JONES, THOMAS	0782
JONG, ERICA	1241
JOSEPH, FRANZ	0661

K:

KAFKA, FRANZ	1453
KALB, BERNARD	0287
KALB, MARVIN	0241
KALLEN, LUCILLE	0484
KANFER, STEFAN	0338
KANIN, GARSON	1135
KANTOR, MACKINLAY	0921
KA-TZETNIK 135633	1076
KAUFMAN, BEL	1242
KAUFMAN, SUE	1243
KAWABATA, YASUNARI	1408
KAYE, M. M.	0076; 0485
KAZAN, ELIA	1244
KAZANTZAKIS, NIKOS	1455
KEATING, H. R. F.	0486
KELLERMAN, JONATHAN	0487
KELLEY, WILLIAM	0077
KELLOGG, MARJORIE	1245
KELLY, JOHN	0339
KELTON, ELMER	0855
KEMELMAN, HARRY	0488
KENEALLY, THOMAS	0922; 1420
KENNEDY, WILLIAM	1246
KEROUAC, JACK	1247
KESEY, KEN	1248
KEYES, DANIEL	0662
KEYES, FRANCIS PARKINSON	0078
KIELY, BENEDICT	1367
KIENZLE, WILLIAM X.	0489
KILLENS, JOHN O.	1077
KINCAID, JAMAICA	1476
KING, STEPHEN	0191; 0783
KING, TABITHA	0192
KIRST, HANS HELLMUT	1078; 1454
KLEIN, EDWARD	0340
KLEIN, NORMA	1249
KLIMA, IVAN	1424
KNEBEL, FLETCHER	0242; 0288
KNIGHT, DAMON	0663
KNOWLES, JOHN	1250
KNOX, BILL	0490
KOEN, KARLEEN	0079
KOHOUT, PAVEL	1425
KONVITZ, JEFFREY	0193
KOONTZ, DEAN R.	0194

KOPPEL, TED	0243
KORDA, MICHAEL	1136
KORNBLUTH, CYRIL M.	0664
KOSINSKI, JERZY	1079; 1251
KOTZWINKLE, WILLIAM	0665
KRANTZ, JUDITH	1137
KUBRICK, STANLEY	0666
KUNDERA, MILAN	1426
KUPER, JACK	1080
KURTZ, KATHERINE	0667; 0784
KYLE, DUNCAN	0195; 0341
KYLE, MARLAINE	0080

L:

LA FARGE, OLIVER	0856
LAFFERTY, R. A.	0785
LAHR, JOHN	1252
LAKER, ROSALIND	0081
L'AMOUR, LOUIS	0857
LAMPEDUSA, GIUSEPPE	1460
LANE, MARGARET	1368
LANGFUS, ANNA	1081
LAPIERRE, DOMINIQUE	0289
LATHEN, EMMA	0491
LATIMER, JONATHAN	0492
LA TOURETTE, JACQUELINE	0082
LAUBENTHAL, AUDREY	0786
LAUMER, KEITH	0668
LAURENCE, MARGARET	1471
LE CARRÉ, JOHN	0374; 0493
LE GUIN, URSULA K.	0669; 0788
LEDERER, WILLIAM	0244
LEDUC, VIOLETTE	1438
LEE, TANITH	0787
LEFFLAND, ELLA	1253
LEIBER, FRITZ	0670; 0789
LEINSTER, MURRAY	0671
LEM, STANISLAW	0672
LEMARCHAND, ELIZABETH	0494
LEMAY, ALAN	0858
LEONARD, ELMORE	0495; 0859
LESSING, DORIS	0673; 1369
LEVIN, IRA	0196; 0342; 0674
LEVIN, MEYER	1082
LEWIN, MICHAEL Z.	0496
LEWIS, C. S.	0675; 0790
LIDDY, G. GORDON	0375
LIEBERMAN, HERBERT	0197
LIGHTNER, A. M.	0676
LINDLEY, ERICA	0083
LINDROP, AUDREY	0791
LISPECTOR, CLARICE	1482
LITTELL, ROBERT	0376
LLOSA, MARIO VARGAS see VARGAS LLOSA, MARIO	
LLEWELLYN, RICHARD	1083; 1370
LLYWELYN, MORGAN	0993
LOCKRIDGE, FRANCES	0497

Author Index

LOCKRIDGE, RICHARD	0498
LOFTS, NORAH	0084; 0198; 0994
LONG, WILLIAM S.	0995
LORD, BETTE BAO	0085
LORING, EMILIE BAKER	0086
LOURIE, RICHARD	0290
LOVECRAFT, H. P.	0199
LOVESEY, PETER	0499
LOWRY, BEVERLY	1254
LOWRY, MALCOLM	1371
LUCAS, GEORGE	0677
LUDLUM, ROBERT	0245; 0291; 0343
LUSTIG, ARNOST	1084; 1427
LUKEMAN, TIM	0792
LURIE, ALISON	1255
LYLE, ELIZABETH	0087
LYNN, ELIZABETH	0793
LYONS, ARTHUR	0500

M:

MCALLISTER, AMANDA	0088
MCBAIN, ED	0501
MCBAIN, LAURIE	0089
MACBETH, GEORGE	0377
MCCAFFREY, ANNE	0678
MCCARRY, CHARLES	0246; 0378
MCCARTHY, GARY	0860
MCCARTHY, MARY	1256
MCCLURE, JAMES	0502
MCCULLERS, CARSON	1257
MCCULLOUGH, COLLEEN	0090; 1421
MCDONALD, GREGORY	0503
MACDONALD, JOHN D.	0504
MACDONALD, MALCOLM see ROSS-MACDONALD, MALCOLM	
MACDONALD, PHILIP	0505
MACDONALD, ROSS	0506
MACDOUGALL, RUTH D.	1258
MCEWAN, IAN	0200
MCGIVERN, WILLIAM	0201
MCGUANE, THOMAS	1259
MCINERNEY, JAY	1260
MCINERNY, RALPH M.	0507
MACINNES, COLIN	0996; 1372
MACINNES, HELEN	0292
MACINTYRE, LORN	0091
MCINTYRE, VONDA K.	0679
MACKAY, AMANDA	0508
MACKENZIE, DONALD	0509
MACKENZIE, RACHEL	1261
MACLEAN, ALISTAIR	0293; 1085
MACLEAN, KATHERINE	0680
MACLEOD, CHARLOTTE	0510
MCMURTRY, LARRY	0861; 1262
MCNICKLE, D'ARCY	0862
MAIER, PAUL	0997
MAILER, NORMAN	1086; 1263

MALAMUD, BERNARD	1264
MALING, ARTHUR	0294; 0511
MALPASS, ERIC	0092
MALZBERG, BARRY N.	0512; 0681
MANNING, OLIVIA	1087; 1373
MANO, D. KEITH	0682
MANTELL, LAURIE	0513
MARASCO, ROBERT	0202
MARCHANT, CATHERINE	0093
MARGROFF, ROBERT E.	0683
MARKANDAYA, KAMALA	1402
MARLOW, EDWINA	0094
MARLOWE, DEREK	0203; 0379
MARLOWE, STEPHEN	0204; 0295; 0344
MARQUAND, JOHN P.	0380
MÁRQUEZ, GABRIEL GARCÍA see GARCÍA MÁRQUEZ, GABRIEL	
MARRIC, J. J.	0514
MARSH, NGAIO	0515
MARSHALL, CATHERINE	0095
MARSHALL, WILLIAM	0516
MARTIN, MALACHI	0998
MARTIN, WILLIAM	0096
MASON, BOBBIE ANN	1265
MASON, F. VAN WYCK	0923; 0999
MASTERS, JOHN	1000
MASTERS, ZEKE	0863
MATHESON, RICHARD	0205
MATTHEWS, CLAYTON	0097
MATTHEWS, PATRICIA	0098
MATTHIESSEN, PETER	1266
MAUGHAM, SOMERSET	0381
MAYBURY, ANNE	0099
MELVILLE, JAMES	0517
MELVILLE, JENNIE	0100; 0518
MERCER, CHARLES	0101
MERLE, ROBERT	0684
MERRIL, JUDITH	0685
MERRITT, A.	0794
METALIOUS, GRACE	1138
MEYER, NICHOLAS	0519
MICHAELS, BARBARA	0102; 0206
MICHAELS, LEONARD	1267
MICHENER, JAMES	0924; 1001; 1088
MILLER, HENRY	1268
MILLER, PETER S.	0686
MILLER, WALTER, JR.	0687
MIRRLESS, HOPE	0795
MISHIMA, YUKIO	1409
MITCHELL, MARGARET	0925
MITCHEM, HANK	0864
MITCHISON, NAOMI	0688
MITGANG, HERBERT	0382
MOFFAT, GWEN	0520
MOJTABAI, A. G.	1269
MOMADAY, N. SCOTT	0865
MONACO, RICHARD	0796
MONSARRAT, NICHOLAS	1089

MOORCOCK, MICHAEL	0689; 0797
MOORE, BRIAN	1472
MOORE, ROBIN	0926
MORANTE, ELSA	1461
MORAVIA, ALBERTO	1462
MORGAN, SPEER	0866
MORGULAS, JERROLD	0345
MORICE, ANNE	0521
MORRELL, DAVID	0296
MORRIS, KENNETH	0798
MORRISON, TONI	1270
MORTIMER, PENELOPE	1374
MORTON, ANTHONY	0522
MOSKIN, MARIETTA	1090
MOSS, ROBERT	0247; 0297
MOYES, PATRICIA	0523
MULLER, MARCIA	0524
MUNRO, ALICE	1473
MURDOCH, IRIS	1375
MYDANS, SHELLEY	1002
MYRER, ANTON	1003

N:
NABOKOV, VLADIMIR	1271
NAIPAUL, V. S.	1376
NARAYAN, R. K.	1403
NATHAN, ROBERT	0799
NATHANSON, E. M.	1091
NAYLOR, GLORIA	1272
NELSON, RAY	0690
NESSEN, RON	0248
NEVIN, DAVID	0927
NICHOLS, JOHN T.	0867
NIN, ANAIS	1273
NIVEN, LARRY	0691
NOLAN, WILLIAM	0692
NORMAN, JOHN	0693
NORTH, JESSICA	0103
NORTH, SARA	0104
NORTON, ANDRE	0694; 0800
NOSTLINGER, CHRISTINE	1092
NOURSE, ALAN	0695

O:
OATES, JOYCE CAROL	1274
O'BRIEN, EDNA	1377
O'BRIEN, TIM	0928
O'CONNOR, EDWIN	1275
O'CONNOR, FLANNERY	1276
O'CONNOR, FRANK	1378
O'DONNELL, LILLIAN	0525
O'FAOLAIN, JULIA	1004; 1379
O'FAOLAIN, SEAN	1380
OGILVIE, ELISABETH	0105
O'HARA, JOHN	1277
OLDENBOURG, ZOE	1005

OLIVER, ANTHONY	0526
OLIVER, CHAD	0696
ORWELL, GEORGE	0697
OVERHOLSER, STEPHEN	0868
OVERHOLSER, WAYNE D.	0869
OZICK, CYNTHIA	1278

P:

PAGE, ELIZABETH	0929
PAINE, LAURAN	0870
PALEY, GRACE	1279
PALMER, LINDA	1139
PANGBORN, EDGAR	0698
PANSHIN, ALEXEI	0699
PARENT, GAIL	1280
PARETSKY, SARA	0527
PARK, GORDON	0930
PARKER, BEATRICE	0106
PARKER, ROBERT B.	0528
PASTERNAK, BORIS	1414
PATON, ALAN	1401
PATTEN, LEWIS B.	0871
PATTERSON, HARRY	0346
PATTERSON, JAMES	0298
PAVESE, CESARE	1463
PAYNE, CHARLOTTE	1140
PEAKE, MERVYN	0801
PEARCE, MARY EMILY	0107
PEARSON, DIANE	0108; 1006
PEARSON, DREW	0249
PECK, ROBERT NEWTON	0931
PENTECOST, HUGH	0529
PERCY, WALKER	1281
PERRIN, URSULA	1282
PERRY, ANNE	0530
PERRY, RITCHIE	0383
PETERS, ELIZABETH	0531
PETERS, ELLIS	0532
PETRAKIS, HARRY MARK	1283
PETRIE, GLEN	1007
PHILIPS, JUDSON	0533
PHILLIPS, JAYNE ANNE	1284
PIERCY, MARGE	1285
PILCHER, ROSAMUNDE	0109
PILHES, RENE VICTOR	0299
PIPER, H. BEAM	0700
PLAIDY, JEAN	1008
PLAIN, BELVA	0110
PLANTE, DAVID	1286
PLATH, SYLVIA	1287
PLUNKETT, JAMES	1009
POE, EDGAR ALLAN	0534
POHL, FREDERIK	0701
PORTER, DONALD C.	0872
PORTER, JOYCE	0384; 0535
PORTER, KATHERINE ANNE	1288
PORTIS, CHARLES	0873

Author Index

POTOK, CHAIM	1289
POURNELLE, JERRY	0702
POWELL, ANTHONY	1381
PRATCHETT, TERRY	0703
PRATHER, RICHARD SCOTT	0536
PRATT, FLETCHER	0802
PRICE, EUGENIA	0932
PRICE, REYNOLDS	0111
PRICE, RICHARD	1290
PRIEST, CHRISTOPHER	0704
PRONZINI, BILL	0537; 0874
PUIG, MANUEL	1479
PURDY, JAMES	1291
PUZO, MARIO	1141
PYM, BARBARA	1382
PYNCHON, THOMAS	1292

Q:

QUEEN, ELLERY	0538
QUENEAU, RAYMOND	1439
QUILL, MONICA	0539
QUINN, SALLY	1142

R:

RACINA, THOM	0207
RADLEY, SHEILA	0540
RAINER, IRIS	1143
RAND, AYN	0705; 1293
RANDALL, RONA	0112
RATHBONE, JULIAN	0300; 0541
REBETA-BURDITT, JOYCE	1294
REED, ISHMAEL	1295
REED, KIT	1296
REEMAN, DOUGLAS	1093
REINER, MAX	0113
REMARQUE, ERICH M.	1094
RENAULT, MARY	1010; 1383
RENDELL, RUTH	0542
REVELEY, EDITH	1297
REYNOLDS, MACK	0706
RHYS, JEAN	1384
RICE, ANNE	0208; 1298
RICE, JEFF	0209
RICH, VIRGINIA	0543
RICHLER, MORDECAI	1474
RIMMER, ROBERT	1144
RINEHART, MARY ROBERTS	0544
ROBBE-GRILLET, ALAIN	1440
ROBBINS, HAROLD	1145
ROBBINS, TOM	1299
ROBERTS, KEITH	0707
ROBERTS, KENNETH	0933; 1011
ROBINETT, STEPHEN	0708
ROCK, PHILLIP	0114
ROGERS, ROSEMARY	0115; 1146
ROHMER, RICHARD	0301

ROHMER, SAX	0545
ROIPHE, ANNE R.	1300
ROSS, DANA FULLER	0875
ROSS, MARILYN	0116
ROSS, ROBERT	1012
ROSS-MACDONALD, MALCOLM	0117
ROSSNER, JUDITH	1301
ROSTEN, LEO	0546
ROTH, PHILIP	1302
ROUECHE, BERTON	0210
ROWAN, HESTER	0118
ROY, GABRIELLE	1475
ROYCE, KENNETH	0302; 0347; 0547
RUBENS, BERNICE	1385
RULE, JANE	1303
RUSHDIE, SALMAN	1404
RUSHING, JANE GILMORE	0876
RUSS, JOANNA	0709
RUTHERFORD, DOUGLAS	0548
RYBAKOV, ANATOLI	1095

S:

SABATO, ERNESTO	1480
SAFIRE, WILLIAM	0250
SAGAN, FRANÇOISE	1441
SAID, KURBAN	1013
ST. CLAIR, KATHERINE	0119
SAINT-EXUPÉRY, ANTOINE DE	0803
SALINGER, J. D.	1304
SAMSON, JOAN	0211
SANCHEZ, THOMAS	1305
SANDERS, LAWRENCE	0251; 0303; 0549
SANTMYER, HELEN HOOVEN	0934
SARRAUTE, NATHALIE	1442
SARTON, MAY	1306
SARTRE, JEAN-PAUL	1443
SAUL, JOHN	0212
SAVAGE, THOMAS	1307
SAXTON, MARK	0804
SAYERS, DOROTHY	0550
SAYLES, JOHN	1308
SCHAEFFER, JACK	0877
SCHAEFFER, SUSAN F.	1096; 1309
SCHWAMM, ELLEN	1310
SCHWARTZ, LYNNE S.	1311
SCOTT, JACK S.	0551
SCOTT, PAUL	1014; 1386
SEGAL, ERICH	0120
SELBY, HUBERT, JR.	1312
SELINKO, ANNEMARIE	1015
SELLERS, CON	0121
SELTZER, DAVID	0213
SELWYN, FRANCIS	0552
SERLING, ROBERT	0252
SETON, ANYA	0122; 0214; 0935; 1016
SETTLE, MARY LEE	1313

SEYMOUR, GERALD	0304
SHAGAN, STEVE	0348
SHALAMOV, VARLAM	1415
SHANGE, NTOZAKE	1314
SHANNON, DELL	0553
SHARPE, JON	0878
SHAW, BOB	0710
SHAW, IRWIN	1097; 1315
SHECKLEY, ROBERT	0711
SHEED, WILFRID	1316
SHEEHY, GAIL	1317
SHELDON, SIDNEY	0305; 1147
SHELLABARGER, SAMUEL	1017
SHELLEY, MARY	0215
SHERIDAN, JANE	0123
SHOLOKOV, MIKHAIL	1416
SHORRIS, EARL	1018
SHULMAN, ALIX KATES	1318
SHUTE, NEVIL	0306
SILKO, LESLIE MARMON	0879
SILLIPHANT, STIRLING	1098
SILLITOE, ALAN	1387
SILONE, IGNAZIO	1464
SILVERBERG, ROBERT	0712
SIMAK, CLIFFORD D.	0713
SIMENON, GEORGES	0554; 1444
SIMMONS, MARY KAY	0124
SIMON, ROGER L.	0555
SIMPSON, GEORGE	0349
SIMPSON, ROSEMARY	1019
SINGER, ISAAC BASHEVIS	1319
SJÖWALL, MAJ	0556
SLAUGHTER, FRANK	0125; 1020
SLAVITT, DAVID	1148
SLOAN, JAMES P.	0307
SMALL, BERTRICE	0126
SMITH, CORDWAINER	0714
SMITH, E. E. "DOC"	0715
SMITH, GENE	1021
SMITH, J. C. S.	0557
SMITH, JOAN	0127
SMITH, MARTIN CRUZ	0216; 0558; 1099
SMITH, WILBUR A.	0128; 0308
SNOW, C. P.	0559; 1388
SNOW, RICHARD	0936
SOLOMON, RUTH FREEMAN	0129
SOLZENHITSYN, ALEXANDER	1417
SONDHEIM, VICTOR	0130
SONTAG, SUSAN	1320
SORRENTINO, GILBERT	1321
SOUTHERN, TERRY	1322
SPARK, MURIEL	1389
SPEARE, ELIZABETH	0937
SPILLANE, MICKEY	0560
SPINRAD, NORMAN	0716
STABLEFORD, BRIAN M.	0717
STANWOOD, BROOKS	0217
STAPLEDON, OLAF	0718

STATHAM, FRANCES PATTON	0131
STEAD, CHRISTINA	1422
STEEL, DANIELLE	0132
STEGNER, WALLACE	0880
STEIN, SOL	0218
STEPHENS, JEANNE	0133
STEVENSON, ROBERT LOUIS	0219
STEWART, EDWARD	0134; 0220; 1149
STEWART, FRED MUSTARD	0135; 0221
STEWART, GEORGE R.	0719
STEWART, MARY	0136; 0309; 0805
STEWART, RAMONA	0222
STOKER, BRAM	0223
STONE, GEORGE	0224
STONE, IRVING	0938; 1022
STONE, ROBERT	1323
STORM, HYEMEYOHSTS	1324
STOUT, REX	0561
STOVALL, WALTER	0253
STRAUB, PETER	0225
STRUGATSKY, ARKADY	0720
STRUGATSKY, BORIS	0721
STUBBS, JEAN	0137
STURGEON, THEODORE	0722
STYRON, WILLIAM	0939; 1325
SUHL, YURI	1100
SUSANN, JACQUELINE	1150
SUTCLIFF, ROSEMARY	1023
SWANN, THOMAS B.	0806
SWARTHOUT, GLENDON	0881
SWIFT, E. M.	0882
SYMONS, JULIAN	0562

T:

TALLENT, ELIZABETH	1326
TAMMUZ, BENJAMIN	1406
TANIZAKI, JUN'ICHIRO	1410
TATTERSALL, JILL	0138
TAYLOR, ELIZABETH	1390
TAYLOR, ROBERT LEWIS	0940
TENNENBAUM, SILVIA	0139
TEVIS, WALTER	0723
TEY, JOSEPHINE	0563
THEROUX, PAUL	1327
THOM, JAMES ALEXANDER	0883
THOMAS, CRAIG	0310; 0385
THOMAS, D. M.	1391
THOMAS, MICHAEL M.	0311
THOMAS, ROSS	0386
THOMPSON, ANNE A.	0312
THOMPSON, E. V.	1024
THOMPSON, EARL	1151
THOMPSON, THOMAS	1152
THOMSON, JUNE	0564
THORPE, SYLVIA	0140
THURBER, JAMES	0807
TIDYMAN, ERNEST	0565

Author Index

TIPTREE, JAMES, JR.	0724
TOLAND, JOHN	1101
TOLKIEN, J. R. R.	0808; 1392
TOOLE, JOHN KENNEDY	1328
TOURNIER, MICHEL	1445
TRACY, HONOR	1393
TRAVER, ROBERT	0566
TREVANIAN	0387
TROUT, KILGORE, JR.	0725
TRUMAN, MARGARET	0567
TRUSCOTT, LUCIAN	0568
TRYON, TOM	0226; 1153
TURNBULL, AGNES SLIGH	0141
TURTON, GODFREY	1025
TYLER, ANNE	1329

U:
UHNAK, DOROTHY	0569
UPDIKE, JOHN	1330
URIS, LEON	0313; 1026; 1102

V:
VALIN, JONATHAN	0570
VAN DE WETERING, JANWILLEN	0571
VAN DINE, S. S.	0572
VAN GREENAWAY, PETER	0314
VAN GULICK, ROBERT See GULIK, ROBERT VAN	
VAN LUSTBADER, ERIC	0809; 1154
VAN SLYKE, HELEN	0142
VAN VOGT, A. E.	0726
VANCE, JACK	0727; 0810
VARGAS LLOSA, MARIO	1486
VERNE, JULES	0728
VERRETTE, JOYCE	0143
VIDAL, GORE	0729; 0941; 1331
VINE, BARBARA	0573
VINGE, JOAN	0811
VINING, ELIZABETH	0942
VONNEGUT, KURT, JR.	0730; 1103; 1332

W:
WAGER, WALTER	0315; 0574
WAGONER, DAVID	0884
WAHLÖÖ, PER	0575
WALKER, ALICE	1333
WALKER, MARGARET	0943
WALKER, MILDRED	0944
WALLACE, IRVING	0254; 0350; 1155
WALLACE, SYLVIA	1156
WALLACH, ANNE TOLSTOI	1157
WALLER, LESLIE	0144
WALTARI, MIKA	1027
WALTON, EVANGELINE	0812
WAMBAUGH, JOSEPH	0576

WANGERIN, WALTER, JR.	0813
WARNER, MIGNON	0577
WARREN, ROBERT PENN	0945
WATSON, CLARISSA	0578
WATSON, COLIN	0579
WATSON, SALLY	0814
WEBB, JAMES	0946
WEINGARTEN, VIOLET	1334
WEISS, DAVID	1028
WELCH, JAMES	0885
WELDON, FAY	1394
WELLMAN, MANLEY WADE	0815
WELLS, H. G.	0731
WELTY, EUDORA	1335
WENTWORTH, PATRICIA	0580
WEST, JESSAMYN	0947
WEST, MORRIS	0316
WESTHEIMER, DAVID	0351; 1104
WESTLAKE, DONALD E.	0581
WHARTON, WILLIAM	1336
WHEELER, GUY	0948
WHEELER, HARVEY	0255
WHITE, ALAN	1105
WHITE, JAMES	0732
WHITE, PATRICK	1423
WHITE, T. H.	0816
WHITNEY, PHYLLIS	0145
WHITTEN, LES	0256
WIBBERLEY, LEONARD	0817
WICKER, TOM	0949
WIDEMAN, JOHN EDGAR	1337
WIESEL, ELIE	1106; 1446
WILCOX, COLLIN	0582
WILDE, JENNIFER	0146
WILDE, OSCAR	0227
WILHELM, KATE	0733
WILLIAMS, ALAN	0317
WILLIAMS, CHARLES	0818
WILLIAMS, DAVID	0583
WILLIAMSON, JACK	0734
WILLIS, MEREDITH SUE	1338
WILSON, ANGUS	1395
WILSON, COLIN	0584; 0735; 1396
WINSLOW, PAULINE GLEN	0585
WINWARD, WALTER	1107
WISEMAN, THOMAS	0388
WISTER, OWEN	0886
WITTIG, MONIQUE	1447
WOIWODE, LARRY	1339
WOOD, BARI	0228; 1158
WOODHOUSE, MARTIN	1029
WOODIWISS, KATHLEEN E.	0147
WOODS, SARA	0586
WOUK, HERMAN	1108; 1340
WRIGHT, AUSTIN TAPPIN	0819
WRIGHT, ERIC	0587
WRIGHT, PATRICIA	0148
WRIGHT, RICHARD	1341

WYLIE, JAMES	1109
WYNDHAM, JOHN	0736

Y:

YARBRO, CHELSEA QUINN	0820
YATES, RICHARD	1110; 1342
YERBY, FRANK	0149
YGELSIAS, HELEN	1343
YORK, JEREMY	0588
YORKE, MARGARET	0589
YOSHIKAWA, EIJI	1411
YOURCENAR, MARGUERITE	1448

Z:

ZAMYATIN, YEVGENY	0737
ZELAZNY, ROGER	0738; 0821
ZOLLINGER, NORMAN	0887